WASHINGTON DC

History & Mystery Walks

AA

Author: Carolyn Crouch
Series Editor: Donna Wood
Art Editor: Alison Fenton
Copy Editors: Polly Boyd and Helen Ridge
Proofreader: Fiona Wild
Picture Research: Luped Picture Research
Image retouching and internal repro: Sarah Montgomery
Cartography provided by the Mapping Services
Department of AA Publishing
Production: Stephanie Allen

Produced by AA Publishing

Published by AA Publishing (a trading name of Automobile Association Developments Limited, whose registered office is Fanum House, Basing View, Basingstoke, Hampshire RG21 4EA; registered number 1878835).

A03625

ISBN 978-0-7495-6000-3

A CIP catalogue record for this book is available from the British Library.

The contents of this book are believed correct at the time of printing. Nevertheless, the publishers cannot be held responsible for any errors or omissions or for changes in the details given in this book or for the consequences of any reliance on the information it provides. We have tried to ensure accuracy in this book, but things do change and we would be grateful if readers would advise us of any inaccuracies they may encounter. This does not affect your statutory rights.

We have taken all reasonable steps to ensure that the walks in this book are safe and achievable by people with a realistic level of fitness. However, all outdoor activities involve a degree of risk and the publishers accept no responsibility for any injuries caused to readers while following these walks.

Visit AA Publishing's website www.theAA.com/travel

Colour reproduction by Keene Group, Andover
Printed in China by Leo Paper Group

Front cover: United States Capitol

OPPOSITE: THOMAS JEFFERSON MEMORIAL

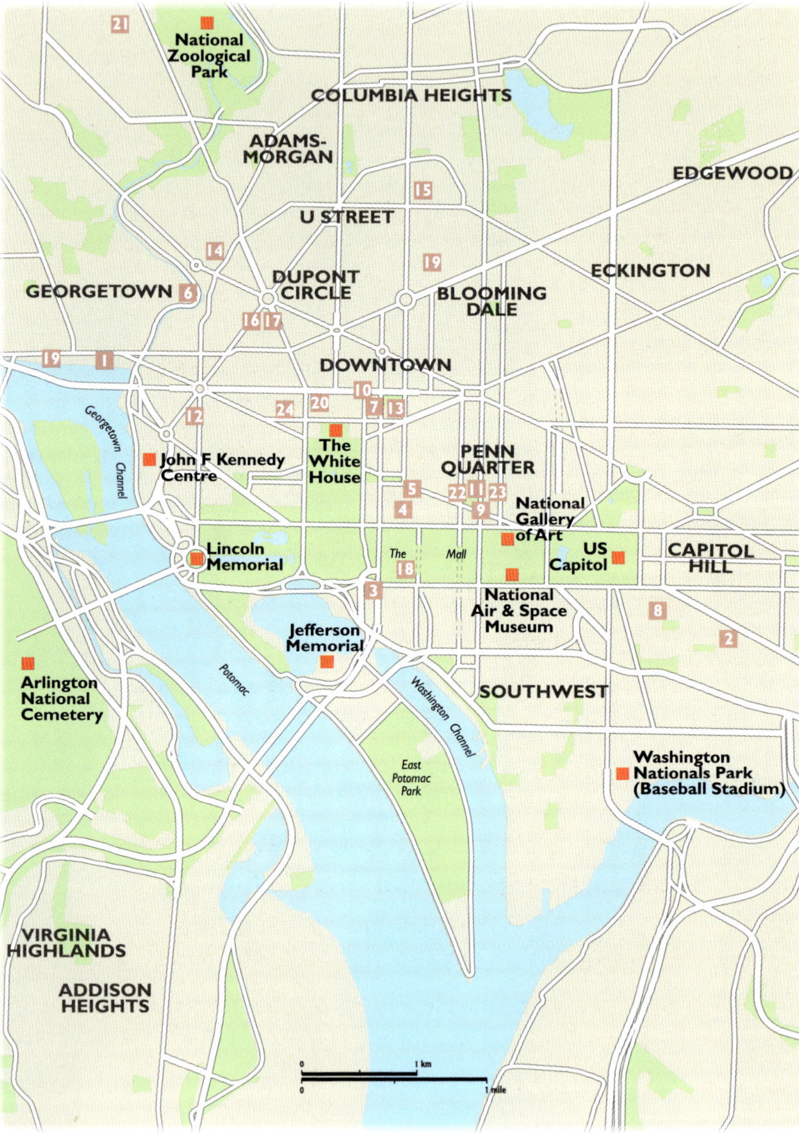

21
National Zoological Park
COLUMBIA HEIGHTS
ADAMS-MORGAN
EDGEWOOD
15
U STREET
14
19
ECKINGTON
DUPONT CIRCLE
GEORGETOWN
6
BLOOMING DALE
16
17
19
1
DOWNTOWN
10
24
20
7
13
12
Georgetown Channel
The White House
John F Kennedy Centre
PENN QUARTER
5
22
11
23
4
9
National Gallery of Art
Lincoln Memorial
The Mall
18
US Capitol
CAPITOL HILL
3
National Air & Space Museum
8
2
Jefferson Memorial
Arlington National Cemetery
Potomac
Washington Channel
SOUTHWEST
East Potomac Park
Washington Nationals Park (Baseball Stadium)
VIRGINIA HIGHLANDS
ADDISON HEIGHTS
0
1 km
0
1 mile

CONTENTS

Introduction 6

1 On the Georgetown Waterfront 8

2 At Home on Capitol Hill 14

3 Tidal Basin Memorials and Cherry Trees 22

4 A Visit to the Memorial Sites 30

5 A Walk along America's Grand Avenue 38

6 Great Estates of Georgetown 44

7 Scandals in the Presidents' Backyard 50

8 A Walk through the Corridors of Power 56

9 Washington during the Civil War 66

10 The Tragic Death of a Revered President 73

11 Urban Scavenger Hunt in Penn Quarter 78

12 History and Culture in Foggy Bottom 84

13 Elegant Circles and Squares 92

14 A Feast for the Senses at Kalorama 100

15 Duke Ellington's Washington 106

16 Gracious Homes and Vibrant Streets 112

17 Grandes Dames of Embassy Row 120

18 The Best-kept Smithsonian Secrets 128

19 The Kennedys in Georgetown 136

20 The Haunted Houses of Lafayette Square 140

21 An Oasis of Peace and Calm 148

22 Blazing the Sculpture Trail 154

23 Washington's Niche Museums 160

24 International Washington 166

Index 174

Acknowledgements 176

Introduction

Washington, DC, known as 'DC', is renowned for its memorials, museums and politics. Even those who have never visited the US can probably identify the Capitol building, the White House and the soaring obelisk known as the Washington Monument. For US citizens and international visitors alike, the lure of a trip to Washington is the chance to take the pulse of America's political process, seeing for themselves where and how the wheels of one of the world's largest democracies turn, as well as making the pilgrimage to commemorate figures from the past who dedicated their lives to advancing principles of freedom, justice and equality.

Yet consider another popular American saying: 'There's no place like home'. Washington is hometown to half a million people who revel in an urban life, complete with pedestrian-friendly streets, an extensive subway system, 19th-century townhouses, and shops, bars and restaurants galore. This is the Washington that can capture the imagination and win the heart of any visitor who is willing to take the time to explore beyond the sweeping National Mall. You'll be amazed by the estates and large gardens that remain intact as Washington has grown up around them, and when it comes to the buildings, hints of the past nestle intriguingly among sparkling new developments – two centuries of Washington life, past and present, co-existing happily side by side.

This is the Washington you'll discover in the walking tours found in this guide. Fear not – the majestic memorials and other famous sites are included, as are the lesser-known byways and buildings that surprise even Washington residents. Many of the walks in this book place you smack in the middle of the US capital at work, while others introduce you to the breathtaking areas beyond the city centre. Casual strolls among the city's hidden gems such as out-of-the-way museums, outdoor sculptures or alleyways lined with tiny houses complement grander walks along majestic Pennsylvania Avenue or through elegant Lafayette Square.

If you have only a day or two in Washington, make sure to choose a walk that includes sites along the National Mall. Then select one of the thematic excursions that convey an aspect of the city that is unfamiliar to you. It's vital to take a stroll through at least one residential area, because it is in these neighbourhoods that you'll find some of the best reasons to return to Washington again and again.

Eat whenever and wherever you can. Washington residents will tell you that the city's culinary scene offers an abundance of appealing options, from ethnic food served in humble surroundings to cosy cafés, hip bars and award-winning restaurants. In warm weather, stop by one of the numerous weekly farmers' markets. Nearly all the eateries recommended in this guide are owned and operated by Washingtonians, allowing you to experience local colour and local flavour simultaneously.

Keep your eyes open as you soak up Washington on foot. Although relatively young compared with other world capitals, Washington celebrates its two centuries of history almost everywhere you look – on plaques, heritage markers, statues or during the vibrant festivals that seem to occur almost every weekend. This guide can tell only some of the stories, so delight in the serendipity of discovering others as you walk. You'll quickly realize that all it requires is a step or two, and you're on the way to making Washington your own.

WHERE TO EAT

$	=	Inexpensive
$$	=	Moderate
$$$	=	Expensive

ABOVE: UNITED STATES CAPITOL

WALK 1

On the Georgetown Waterfront

Quaint houses, river walks and tiny alleyways tell the story of a once-thriving waterfront community on the banks of the Potomac River.

Named after King George II of England, 'George' was the original name of the small Maryland town founded in 1751. Thanks to its location, Georgetown became a bustling port and, throughout the 18th century, it was a busy, gritty place, with wharves and rowdy taverns. However, by the 1820s the Potomac River had become filled with silt, and the advent of steam navigation meant that cities with deeper natural ports captured much of the river trade. By the early 20th century, the Georgetown economy had reinvented itself in the form of mills built along the waterfront. On this walk, you'll see the façades of some of these buildings, formerly operating as a power plant, flour and paper mills and an incinerator. They are interspersed with terraced houses that continue to be family homes and small businesses. Today's Georgetown waterfront is a fascinating amalgamation of hidden alleyways, narrow streets, and commercial office buildings. It is also the site of the longest National Park in the US.

1 Exiting the Foggy Bottom Metro, turn left and proceed to Washington Circle. Turn left and walk around the circle, exiting onto Pennsylvania Avenue, NW by bearing left. Follow Pennsylvania Avenue to the intersection of 28th Street, NW. Follow M Street, NW for two blocks, crossing 28th and 29th Streets, NW. At 30th Street, NW turn left. About mid-block on your left, find a white house at No. 1068.

This house is typical of the Federal-style brick houses that were built throughout Georgetown between 1790 and 1820, although the residences found along the waterfront are usually substantially smaller than their cousins north of M Street. Like many in this area, this house was raised when the Chesapeake & Ohio (C & O) Canal was built in 1850; the original ground floor is now below street level. Look out for star emblems on the sides of buildings. Until the mid-19th century, structures were held together with a cast-iron pole running from wall to wall, and the ends were secured on the exterior using a cast-iron tie rod, usually in the form of a decorative star. This helped maintain the integrity of structures that were more than one storey tall.

2 Walk downhill on 30th Street until you come to the C & O Canal lock No. 3 on your right. Turn right onto the towpath.

A ceremony to celebrate the start of construction of the C & O Canal took place in Georgetown on 4 July 1828, amid much fanfare. It began as a speculative development to link the eastern seaports with the Ohio River and the plan was to extend all the way inland to Pittsburgh, Pennsylvania. However, funding for the project did not follow and the canal never got as far as the Ohio River.

When work ceased in 1852, the C & O Canal stretched 185 miles (300km) from Georgetown to Cumberland, Maryland (about half the distance originally planned). In its heyday, for over half a decade, the canal was a lifeline for communities and businesses along the Potomac River. Coal, lumber, grain and other agricultural products floated down the canal to market. However, by 1924 the canal was obsolete – floods had devastated the waterway, and it was no longer considered of economic use because railways provided cheaper transportation. The canal was abandoned until 1971, when it came under the jurisdiction of the National Historic Park Service and was subsequently restored. During the summer months, the canal relives its past and the public can enjoy mule-drawn barge rides. The C & O Canal Visitors Center also offers guided tours of Georgetown and lectures. The bust on the pedestal along the canal is of US Supreme Court Justice William O. Douglas, who successfully crusaded to save the Georgetown portion of the canal in the 1940s.

C & O NATIONAL HISTORIC PARK;
www.nps.gov/choh

OPPOSITE: BARGE RIDES ON THE C & O CANAL ARE AVAILABLE TO THE PUBLIC

DISTANCE 3 miles (4.8km)

ALLOW 2.5 hours

START Foggy Bottom Metro station

FINISH Foggy Bottom Metro station

3 Follow the towpath to the intersection of Thomas Jefferson Street, NW. Turn right and proceed to No. 1069 on your right.

This house is another classic example of Federal-style architecture. Notice how the house has two doorways, one leading to a former shop on the ground floor and the other to the residence on the upper two floors. The shop door, originally to the left of the existing door, was bricked up during renovations in 1941. Just up the way is the former Birch Funeral Home and Stable at 1083 Thomas Jefferson Street. The building with the garage was the stable for the funeral home, which was located just around the corner at M Street. The stable is considered to be the only late 19th-century structure of its kind left in the Georgetown waterfront area. By 1891, Joseph Birch had died, leaving the business to his sons, George and Isaac. It remained in the family until the property was sold in 1966.

4 Head away from M Street down Thomas Jefferson Street. You will pass over the C & O Canal and then under the elevated Whitehurst Freeway. Cross busy K Street, NW and proceed into Washington Harbor until you reach the Potomac River.

'Xanadu on the Potomac' was how one Washington arbiter of taste described Washington Harbor – a huge complex of shops, offices and condominiums created by US architect Arthur Cotton Moore (born 1935) in 1986. The merits of the development aside, it's the sweeping views that grab your attention. Looking from left to right you can pick out Thompson's Boat Center (which rents out kayaks and canoes), the curved façade of the Watergate Complex (a famous residential building), the gleaming white John F. Kennedy Center for the Performing Arts, Theodore Roosevelt Island directly across the way, and to the right the Francis Scott Key Memorial Bridge connecting Georgetown to Virginia.

WHERE TO EAT

1 AGRARIA,
3000 K Street, NW;
Tel: 1-202-298-0003.
This Washington Harbor restaurant provides not only a view to the Potomac River but also dishes made with ingredients procured from family farms across the US. $$$

2 DEAN & DELUCA,
3276 M Street, NW;
Tel: 1-202-342-2500.
From produce to pastries to prepared meals to take away, this high-end food emporium also offers light fare at its outdoor patio. $$

3 FILOMENA,
1063 Wisconsin Avenue, NW;
Tel: 1-202-337-2782.
A Georgetown institution for over 20 years, offering traditional Italian food near the C & O Canal. $$

5 Follow the path through the park. At K Street, NW (beneath the Whitehurst Freeway), cross the street and begin to walk up the hill of Wisconsin Avenue, NW. Stop to look at 1000 Wisconsin Avenue, immediately on your left.

Originally a warehouse, this building was constructed in 1800 by two merchant brothers, Ebenezer and Francis Dodge, whose family epitomized the successful merchant class of early Georgetown. With their own fleet of schooners, the Dodge brothers brought sugar and molasses into Georgetown, trading tobacco, flour and lime. After the death of Francis in 1851, the brothers' two sons continued the tradition of trade with the West Indies, but by 1857 they were bankrupt.

6 Walk a bit further up Wisconsin Avenue and then turn right onto South Street, NW. Follow it until you see the Ritz Carlton Hotel complex on the right at 3134–3136 South Street.

The house facing the street was the home of the first mayor of Georgetown, Robert Peter. Originally from Scotland, Peter arrived in what was then called 'George Town' and quickly became a wealthy tobacco merchant and landholder; he became mayor in 1790. This house and the building behind it were both moved in July 1999 so as not to be in the way of construction for the Ritz Carlton Hotel. After the restoration work, the historic buildings were returned to the site and now house the hotel's administrative offices. The hotel itself is built around what was once the DC incinerator plant – the smokestack is still in evidence.

7 Turn and cross South Street, climbing the small staircase to Grace Episcopal Church at 1041 Wisconsin Avenue.

A small wooden chapel was constructed on this site in 1855, but it was later razed and replaced with the stone church that you see today. It was founded to serve the labourers, craftsmen, shopkeepers and boatmen who lived in this tiny district known as Brickyard Hill because it was built on the site of the old brickworks. An 1895 edition of the *Washington Evening Star* reported, 'It is the only church here in a really poor district and whenever its pastor is not in the pulpit or fulfilling his own immediate wants he is out among his people dispensing aid to the unfortunate.' Outreach continues to be integral to the parish identity: the Georgetown Ministry Center for the Homeless is based here, as well as a Montessori nursery.

8 Exit the churchyard and cross Wisconsin Avenue. Notice the commemorative plaque for the C & O Canal outside the entrance to the Georgetown Park shopping mall. Cross the pedestrian bridge to the left of the mall entrance over onto Grace Street, NW. Follow it to the intersection of the Cecil Place alley. Walk into the alley to view the terraced houses at 1033–1043 Cecil Place.

These houses were part of Cherry Hill, a residential area that would have been entirely separate from Brickyard Hill across Wisconsin Avenue. Speculators built simple structures like these in the middle of the 19th century to accommodate a growing population of workers seeking low-cost housing. Such was the demand that this area was filled

ABOVE: GRACE EPISCOPAL CHURCH STILL REACHES OUT TO THE LOCAL COMMUNITY

in with terraces between 1870 and 1890. Each house is exactly 24ft (7.3m) long and 12ft (3.6m) wide, with a garden at the back. Today, given their Georgetown address, the houses are no longer inexpensive or lived in by labourers, but they are a poignant reminder of a bygone era of Washington's working waterfront.

9 Follow Grace Street until you reach an area that opens out to the C & O Canal. On your left is a large white building known as the Bomford Mill.

Colonel George Bomford operated a flour mill here from 1832 until 1844, when it was destroyed by fire. He then erected a cotton mill on the ruins. A number of mills were sited along the Georgetown waterfront in order to take advantage of the steep drop to the river. Notice the rod stars on the façade.

10 Turn around and cross the pedestrian bridge over the C & O Canal. Climb the stairs and walk along the plaza between the Georgetown Park shops and Dean & DeLuca market. The front entrance to the market is at 3276 M Street, NW.

Butcher's Market, the earliest Georgetown public market, was established before the American War of Independence (1775–83). Since then, this site has always accommodated a market of some sort. The current building, which dates from the early 1800s, also served as the site for meetings of Georgetown's early commissioners. In 1992 it became Dean & DeLuca, the gourmet grocer from New York City. In warm weather, there's nothing more enjoyable than sitting out on the adjoining patio and sampling the offerings while (on Sunday mornings) listening to live jazz.

11 The route back to the walk start point takes you along M Street, Georgetown's busy commercial thoroughfare. Nearly every building you pass is historic, but the one to stop at is 3051 M Street. The Old Stone House is a National Park site.

The Old Stone House was built in 1765, making it the oldest structure built in Washington. Christopher Layman, a cabinetmaker, used the charming granite building as both a residence and a shop. After his death, the house was sold to Cassandra Chew, who added the rear wing in 1767. Until it was purchased by the federal government in 1953, the building had been continuously used as a residence or a residence and shop. It is one of the few examples in Washington of American vernacular architecture that predates the American War of Independence.

12 To return to Foggy Bottom Metro, turn left into M Street as you exit the building grounds. Follow M Street to 28th Street, where it changes its name to Pennsylvania Avenue. Follow Pennsylvania Avenue to Washington Circle, bearing right to walk around the circle. Exit the circle by turning right into 23rd Street. The station is on the right, halfway down the block.

WALK 2

At Home on Capitol Hill

Nestled next to the US Capitol is Capitol Hill, where long-time residents and newcomers alike relish their unique place in the city's urban identity.

Although the outside world may associate Capitol Hill solely with the US Congress, those who make Washington their home conjure up a very different image: that of a vibrant area spread across one of the largest historic districts in the country and filled with quaint terraces, leafy parks, shops, cafes, churches and schools. Pride in the place is evident in the careful restoration and loving upkeep bestowed upon the 19th-century homes, adorned with flowerbeds and shrubs. Although many of the stately townhouses seen on this walk were not built until after the US Civil War (1861–65), Capitol Hill is nonetheless one of Washington's oldest areas, its first development occurring during the late 1790s, just as the federal government prepared to locate here permanently. It proved an attractive area for those who desired to live near to where they worked. Over the years, though, the allure of life on 'the Hill' has been such that Washingtonians with no connection to congressional matters have been eager to call it home.

1 From Eastern Market Metro station, cross 7th Street, SE at the public library and proceed along D Street, SE. Look for No. 619 on the right.

A social-service organization called Friendship House occupies this site today, but you can see the roof of the original house through the entry court. The Maples was an estate constructed between 1795 and 1806 for a wealthy trader named William Mayne Duncanson, who would have appreciated the peace and quiet provided by what was, at the time, a tranquil woodland environment. Capitol Hill was undergoing a development spurt when pioneering journalist Emily Edson Briggs (the first woman to receive White House press credentials) purchased The Maples in 1870. She added 21 rooms to the house and decorated it with artefacts and treasures obtained on her many travels abroad. In 1936, her heirs sold the house to an anonymous buyer, who in turn donated it to Friendship House.

2 Continue along D Street to 6th Street, SE. Turn right. Take note of Mr Henry's, a venerable Capitol Hill pub known for its live jazz, at the intersection of 6th Street and Pennsylvania Avenue, SE. Turn left. Follow Pennsylvania Avenue past Seward Square on the right. At the corner of Pennsylvania Avenue and 4th Street, SE look for 330 Pennsylvania Avenue.

The Naval Lodge Building was constructed in 1895 as a meeting place for Naval Lodge No. 4. The organization, which continues to meet twice-monthly in a stately space upstairs, is proud to reside in the oldest Masonic structure in the city. The Lodge makes its space available throughout the year for the popular Ruth Ann Overbeck Lecture Series, named after a beloved Hill resident and historian. Focusing on the history of Capitol Hill, the lectures draw residents from throughout the city.

3 From the Lodge, turn left onto 4th Street, SE and continue to Independence Avenue, SE. Turn right,

WHERE TO EAT

1 MARKET LUNCH,
Eastern Market,
7th Street, SE;
Tel: 1-202-547-8444.
Crab cakes, eggs and grits, and blueberry buckwheat pancakes are just a few of the favourites served at this popular lunch counter. $

2 MONTMARTRE,
327 7th Street, SE;
Tel: 1-202-544-1244.
A cheerful French bistro near Eastern Market. $$

3 SONOMA,
223 Pennsylvania Avenue, SE;
Tel: 1-202-544-8088.
The Sonoma Valley in Northern California is the inspiration for this romantic wine bar. $$

OPPOSITE: BEAUTIFULLY MAINTAINED BRICK TERRACE HOUSES, TYPICAL OF CAPITOL HILL

DISTANCE **1 mile (1.6km)**

ALLOW **1.5 hours (more with site visits)**

START **Eastern Market Metro station**

FINISH **Eastern Market Metro station**

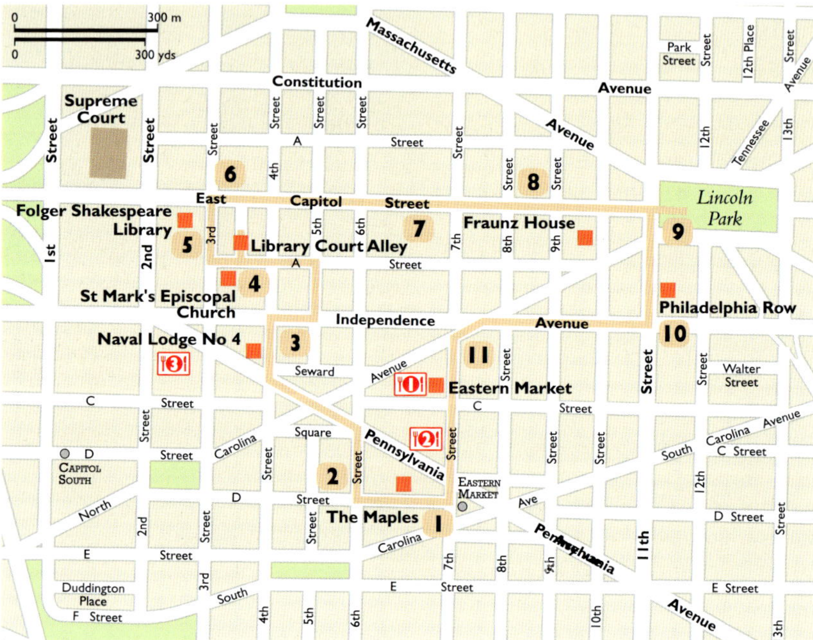

then one block later turn left onto 5th Street, SE. Next, turn left onto A Street, SE. Between 4th and 3rd Streets, look for the entrance to Library Court alley.

By the end of the 19th century, over 300 residential alleys such as Library Court existed. Many had been developed following the US Civil War, when the city swelled with new arrivals seeking low-cost housing. They often found it in these tiny two-up, two-down houses. By the 1920s, the alleys were notorious for their overcrowded, basic conditions: many lacked indoor plumbing and electricity. Large numbers were torn down and their sites redeveloped with more expensive houses. On Capitol Hill, however, alley houses can still be found and are considered a quiet, off-the-beaten-path alternative to the hurried pace of city life.

4 Double back to A Street. Across from the Library Court entrance is St Mark's Episcopal Church.

In the mid-1960s, as older couples moved out of Capitol Hill, middle-class families, attracted to the area's relatively cheap homes, Victorian architecture and community spirit, moved in with ideals and energy. St Mark's Church was a gathering place for this 'back to the city' movement of young, white families who became intensely involved with one another and their new-found community. The Romanesque Revival church building was constructed here in 1889. St Mark's continues to be an integral part of Capitol Hill life. The St Mark's Players are the church's resident theatre group, the St Mark's Dance Studio offers classes to the public, as does the St Mark's Yoga Center. The church Arts Council brings together visual artists, writers, architects and needleworkers.

5 From the church, turn right onto 3rd Street. At the intersection of 3rd and East Capitol Streets is the Folger Shakespeare Library on the left.

Henry Clay Folger (1857–1930), a millionaire Standard Oil executive, devoted a great deal of his life to the acquisition of what is now the largest collection of Shakespearean materials in the world. Perhaps the most famous work in his collection is the first edition of Shakespeare's works, printed in 1623 and known as the *First Folio*. Out of a world supply of 238 First Folios, Folger collected 79 copies, one of which is always on display in the Great Hall of the Shakespeare Library. A recreated Elizabethan theatre is still used for live

performances. Notice the nine bas-relief panels depicting scenes from Shakespeare's plays on the library's main façade.

FOLGER SHAKESPEARE LIBRARY;
MON–SAT 10–5; www.folger.edu

6 Stop to admire East Capitol Street, then follow the avenue to No. 506, which will be on the left.

Following the US Civil War, members of the large, stable government workforce found Capitol Hill a convenient area to live in. The resulting building boom accounts for the majestic terraces found on East Capitol Street. This broad avenue, stretching from the Capitol to the Potomac River, was conceived to be 160ft (48m) wide. When it was finally constructed in 1870, a 50ft (15m) road was paved down the middle, leaving

ABOVE: ONE OF THE NINE BAS-RELIEF PANELS ON THE MAIN FAÇADE OF THE FOLGER SHAKESPEARE LIBRARY

55ft (17m) garden strips on either side. These represent one of the chief benefits of owning a home on East Capitol Street. The house at No. 506 was built in 1873, but by 1887 it had been completely remodelled, lending it the Romanesque Revival style that is still evident today. The prominent bay window is referred to as a pressed-tin oriel. The ability to press and form materials, including brick, gave late 19th-century homeowners a myriad of choices in the appearance of their homes and made possible the projecting towers and bays seen on many of these homes.

7 Continue on East Capitol Street four blocks to No. 923 on the right.

The Fraunz house, built in 1892, is a classic Queen Anne-style terraced townhouse. Unlike the exuberant 'painted ladies' of San Francisco, the Queen Anne-style houses on Capitol Hill reflected the conservative tastes of their middle-class occupants. The style, which was popular in the US between 1860 and 1910, is distinguished by bays and towers or turrets topped by elaborate caps or, as in the case of this house, a pediment. This style of house is usually clad in timber and shingle, but on Capitol Hill pressed brick was the preferred architectural material.

8 Follow East Capitol Street across 10th and 11th Streets, SE then cross into Lincoln Park.

This is one of the best spots to observe day-to-day life of Capitol Hill residents, whether they are out walking dogs, attending their children at the playground or staying in shape by jogging around the park's perimeter. Look for the Emancipation monument, unveiled in 1876 and depicting President Abraham Lincoln bidding a slave to rise to freedom. Opposite this sculpture is another that honours Mary McLeod Bethune, founder of the National Council of Negro Women (see Walk 13). It is the first memorial in Washington dedicated to an African-American leader as well as the first to honour an American woman.

9 Return to 11th Street from the park and turn left. Cross East Capitol Street by the dry cleaning shop on the corner. Continue to 124–154 11th Street.

These 16 terraced houses are associated with one of Capitol Hill's most enduring urban legends. The story goes that developer Charles Gessford built them to resemble townhouses in Philadelphia in order to soothe his wife's homesickness for her native city. While the Philadelphia connection is accurate, the name of the developer is not. In fact, Philadelphia tugboat manufacturer Stephen Flanagan constructed the houses in 1862 on speculation. Flanagan may have been overly optimistic in selecting this location, because it was 30 years before this part of Capitol Hill became populated with residents and it took until 1897 for Flanagan to sell the last of his houses.

10 Follow 11th Street to Independence Avenue, SE. Turn right and proceed to where 7th Street and North Carolina Avenue, SE intersect with Independence Avenue. Turn left onto 7th Street. You will be by Eastern Market.

Many consider Eastern Market to be the heart and soul of Capitol Hill. This is where the local residents gather to shake off the working week and fill up their larders – and stomachs! Completed in 1873, it was designed by Adolph Cluss, a prominent local architect. It is one of the few public markets left in the city, and the only one retaining its original public market function. Indoor vendors continue to sell flowers, produce, meat and bread seven days a week. At the weekend, they are joined outdoors by a lively farmers' and arts-and-crafts market. A severe fire destroyed the interior of Eastern Market on 30 April 2007. During its restoration, the vendors have been located in a temporary structure across the street from their original home, continuing to welcome the citizenry of Capitol Hill.

11 To get back to the Metro, follow 7th Street to Pennsylvania Avenue. Cross Pennsylvania Avenue and then turn left and cross 7th Street. Eastern Market station will be directly in front of you.

ABOVE: A CAPITOL HILL STOREFRONT WITH WARES DISPLAYED OUTSIDE AT WEEKENDS

STATUE OF MARY McLEOD BETHUNE AND AFRICAN-AMERICAN CHILDREN, LINCOLN PARK

WALK 3

Tidal Basin Memorials and Cherry Trees

A man-made creation of the late 19th century, the Tidal Basin is the site of several memorials. Surrounding it are thousands of flowering cherries.

If you embark on this walk in late March or early April, be prepared to share the path with happy hordes on their way to bask in the transient beauty of Washington's flowering Japanese cherry trees. Otherwise, this route can be appreciated for passing through a portion of the National Mall that does not attract constant crowds. It's best done in the early morning or late afternoon, when daylight allows you to read the various inscriptions and plaques. America's third president, Thomas Jefferson, is honoured here, and the life and times of President Franklin Delano Roosevelt is chronicled in a memorial that combines landscape architecture and sculptural forms. Virginian statesman George Mason sits peacefully amidst a garden setting, while the spirit of civil-rights champion Martin Luther King whispers through a site that is being prepared as a memorial to the country's greatest African-American leader. Discover the two original Japanese cherry trees, and glimpse the White House on Pennsylvania Avenue.

1 **Upon exiting Smithsonian Metro station, turn left and proceed along Independence Avenue, SW past the Department of Agriculture buildings. Cross 14th Street, SW.**

Many a visitor has mistaken this red-brick Romanesque-style building for the Smithsonian Castle, which is located a few blocks east. However, it actually houses the US Forest Service, as the Smokey the Bear figure often placed outside the 14th Street entrance would indicate. Originally constructed in 1880 for the Bureau of Printing and Engraving, it is now the oldest of the buildings comprising the Department of Agriculture (of which the Forest Service is part).

2 **Continue along Independence Avenue, turning left at 15th Street, SW (Raoul Wallenberg Place). Walk about a quarter of a block on 15th Street.**

Close to the National Mall, the US Holocaust Memorial Museum provides a powerful lesson about the 'fragility of freedom'. Architect James Ingo Freed (1930–2005), who was born in Germany but lived most of his life in the US, visited Holocaust sites, including camps and ghettos, as he was designing the building (completed in 1993). Above the entrance on Raoul Wallenberg Place – named after the Swedish diplomat who rescued thousands of Hungarian Jews – is a solitary window containing 16 solid 'panes' made of smooth, soft stone, each framed by clear glass, thus reversing the normal configuration and obscuring one's ability to look in or out. Joel Shapiro's sculpture *Loss and Regeneration* evokes the disintegration of families and of shattered lives. The larger piece is a towering, tree-like form. Nearby, a smaller, house-like structure is tipped upside-down on its roof. Shapiro created the piece to commemorate children who perished during the Holocaust.

US HOLOCAUST MEMORIAL MUSEUM;
DAILY 10–5.30; TEL: 1-202-488-0400;
www.ushmm.org

3 **Proceed along 15th Street to the next building, the Bureau of Engraving and Printing.**

You are standing outside the largest producer of security documents in the US. Although the building is best known for printing paper money, it also produces portions of US passports, military ID cards

OPPOSITE: CHERRY TREES NEAR THE THOMAS JEFFERSON MEMORIAL; ABOVE: HOLOCAUST MEMORIAL MUSEUM

DISTANCE 1.5 miles (2.5km)

ALLOW 2 hours (more with museum visit)

START Smithsonian Metro station (Independence Avenue exit)

FINISH Smithsonian Metro station (Independence Avenue entrance)

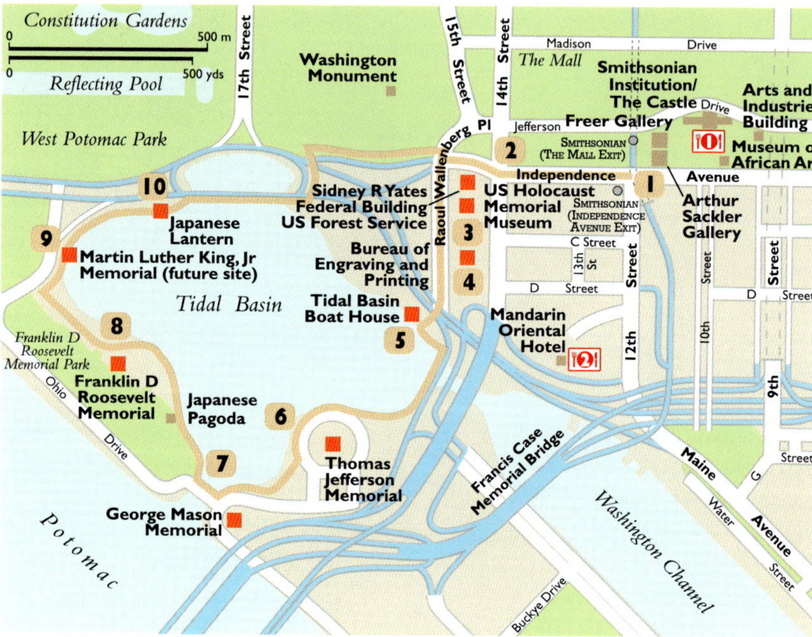

and Naturalization Certificates. Each document is designed and manufactured with 'counterfeit-deterrence' features. On a tour of the facility, you will learn that the average lifespan of a $1 bill is 21 months, and a $100 bill is 89 months. Schoolchildren seem to enjoy purchasing plastic containers of shredded dollars.

BUREAU OF ENGRAVING AND PRINTING;

TEL (FOR TOURS): 1-866-874-2330 (toll-free) or 1-202-874-2330 (local);
www.moneyfactory.gov

4 Continue to follow 15th Street to the end of the block. Carefully cross Maine Avenue, SW and walk over to the Tidal Basin boathouse.

After a severe flood damaged parts of the National Mall and Washington's waterfront in 1881, the Army Corps of Engineers were enlisted to manage the flow of the Potomac River. Accumulation of silt and debris made the river prone to flooding. The Potomac was dredged and the massive amounts of silt removed were used to create the peninsula known as East Potomac Park (to the left of where you are standing), this Tidal Basin, and the land west of the Washington Monument. The original purpose of the Tidal Basin was to flush water from the Potomac River through to the nearby Washington Channel. Today, the Tidal Basin provides the means for taking in the surrounding views by paddle boats, which can be rented during warm weather.

TIDAL BASIN PADDLE BOAT DOCK;

www.tidalbasinpaddleboats.com

5 Follow the path from the boathouse along the Tidal Basin until you reach the Thomas Jefferson memorial.

Very few significant Washington structures have come to life without a degree of controversy. In this case, the Thomas Jefferson Memorial Commission asked US architect John Russell Pope (1874–1937) to submit a design – without holding a nationwide competition. Many decried this approach, claiming that it went against all that democratically minded President Thomas Jefferson (1743–1826) held true. Pope proposed designing the memorial in the style of the Roman Pantheon, which Jefferson himself used for both his Virginia home, Monticello, and the school he founded, the University of Virginia. Washington's arbiters of taste and design, the Commission on Fine Arts, were dismayed by his proposal, though the Thomas Jefferson Commission was savvy enough to bypass their objections by appealing directly to President Franklin D. Roosevelt. He gave his full support to the Commission and authorized the design, a somewhat controversial move for a US president. The memorial was finally unveiled on 13 April 1943, the bicentenary of Thomas Jefferson's birth. Along with a stately bronze likeness of the man himself (he holds a copy of the Declaration of Independence), the memorial contains four panels of famous quotations.

THOMAS JEFFERSON MEMORIAL;

www.nps.gov/thje

WHERE TO EAT

1 CASTLE CAFÉ,
Smithsonian Castle Building,
1000 Jefferson Drive, SW;
Tel: 1-202-633-1000.
Enjoy casual offerings of sandwiches, salads and baked goods in one of the city's landmark structures. After your meal, wander around and soak up the Gothic Revival architecture. $

2 EMPRESS LOUNGE,
Mandarin Oriental Hotel,
1330 Maryland Avenue, SW;
Tel: 1-202-554-858.
For elegance and a view. The light-fare menu features Asian-inspired nibbles and signature martinis. A curry lunch buffet is available during the week. $$

6 Follow the pathway as it runs up a small embankment. At the top, cross Ohio Drive, SW and walk into the garden across the street.

This perfectly poised figure is probably the least known of the Virginians who contributed so much to forge the founding principles of the US government when America gained independence from Britain in 1775. Despite having no formal education, statesman George Mason (1725–92) authored the Virginia Declaration of Rights, the document used as a model for many state constitutions, as well as France's Declaration of the Rights of Man and the United Nations Charter of the Rights of Man. Although he was directly involved in the composition of the US Constitution, he ultimately refused to sign it, because it did not abolish the slave trade and lacked an explicit statement of individual rights.

The sculptor and landscape designer of the memorial's garden reinterpreted an existing flower garden planted here in the 1920s with perennials, wooden benches, evergreens and boxwoods, each a tribute to the formal garden at Mason's home, Gunston Hall. What's particularly pleasing about the depiction of Mason is that a visitor can actually sit down next to Mason as a friend would. A very polite friend, that is, as Mason appears to be immersed in Cicero.

GEORGE MASON MEMORIAL; www.nps.gov/gemm

7 After leaving the memorial garden, return to Ohio Drive, enjoying the view of the Tidal Basin and Potomac River atop the Inlet Bridge. You may be able to see the National Air Force memorial swooping upwards across the river in Virginia. Follow the pathway that takes you right along the Tidal Basin itself. Watch out for low-hanging Japanese cherry trees! Continue along this course until you reach a stairway leading up to the Franklin D. Roosevelt memorial. Walk around the building directly in front of you by first turning right and then left towards the entrance of the memorial itself.

It takes a memorial comprised of four 'rooms' to adequately chronicle the life and impact of America's only four-term president. Franklin D. Roosevelt (1882–1945) guided the country through two monumental events: the Great Depression and World War II. Inscriptions recall his speeches, often conveying what citizens themselves felt. Sculptures, such as the gaunt Depression-era couple and men standing in a bread line, depict a stark reality. Likenesses of Roosevelt himself and First Lady Eleanor Roosevelt embody the strength and resolve each brought to their respective role. Even Fala, Roosevelt's devoted Scottish Terrier, is on hand. Water flowing throughout the memorial evokes both Roosevelt's love of sailing and the healing pools he bathed in while attempting to rehabilitate his polio-stricken legs. When the memorial was unveiled in 1997, many wondered why the country's first disabled president had not been overtly depicted as such. In 2001, a new statue of Roosevelt in a wheelchair was placed at the entrance to the memorial.

FRANKLIN DELANO ROOSEVELT MEMORIAL; www.nps.gov/fdrm

OPPOSITE: REFLECTIONS OF THE THOMAS JEFFERSON MEMORIAL IN THE TIDAL BASIN

8 Exit the Roosevelt memorial and then turn right, following the path along West Basin Drive, SW. Look out for a medium-sized bronze plaque placed in the ground on your righthand side.

This is the future site of the Martin Luther King memorial. Fundraising has been underway for a number of years and a design has been selected. Before his assassination in Memphis, Tennessee, Martin Luther King (1929–68) was the pivotal leader of the Civil Rights movement. A Baptist minister, King led the Montgomery, Alabama Bus Boycott and helped found the Southern Christian Leadership Conference. His eloquence and skill as a speechmaker soon established him as one of the greatest orators of the 20th century. In 1964, he became the youngest person to be awarded the Nobel Peace Prize. His death on 4 April 1968 plunged many US cities into days of violent riots, yet King's legacy of non-violent civil disobedience, his inspiring writings and his steadfast example have proven more enduring. His memorial will be the first on the National Mall dedicated to an African-American.
MARTIN LUTHER KING MEMORIAL SITE;
www.mlkmemorial.org

9 Follow the path to Independence Avenue, SW. Turn right and continue until you discover a large stone lantern on the right, just before the Kutz Bridge.

You are standing next to what may be the oldest man-made object in Washington not housed in a museum. This stone lantern was carved in 1651 in Edo (now Tokyo), Japan. On 30 March 1954, it was presented to the city to commemorate the centenary of the first Treaty of Peace, Amity and Commerce between the US and Japan, signed by Commodore Matthew Perry. Today, it is lit once a year during the National Cherry Blossom Festival, Washington's annual signal that spring has arrived. The indescribably beautiful display of pink and white blossoms reaches its zenith around the Tidal Basin, where thousands of the trees have been planted since the original gift of two trees was made by the city of Tokyo to the city of Washington in 1912. Just beyond the lantern there is a stone containing a bronze plaque. This marks the site where First Lady Helen Taft and the Japanese ambassador's wife, Viscountess Chinda, planted the first two trees, which still bloom each spring.
NATIONAL CHERRY BLOSSOM FESTIVAL;
www.nationalcherryblossomfestival.org

10 Walk across the Kutz Bridge and proceed until you reach the exit to the Tidal Basin car park. At this point, cross the street and then cross the next one too (Independence Avenue). Turn right and continue along Independence Avenue. Almost immediately, look to your right and left. You will be able to see both the White House and the Thomas Jefferson memorial. Follow Independence Avenue, crossing 15th and then 14th Streets. The next intersection will be 12th Street, SW, where you find yourself back at the starting point of the walk.

ABOVE: MEMORIAL TO GEORGE MASON, THE 18TH-CENTURY VIRGINIAN STATESMAN

WALK 4

A Visit to the Memorial Sites

Disputes and unusual occurrences have repeatedly interrupted the evolution from conception to reality of many of Washington's memorials.

Had you attempted this walk in 1880 or earlier, you would have been wading through the Potomac River. However, in 1881 a flood threatened Washington's city centre and the Army Corps of Engineers began a massive civil-engineering project to create the land that now comprises the western end of the National Mall. The Lincoln memorial was the first to be located here, in 1914. Since then, the placement of memorials along the Reflecting Pool has been steady, though the proceedings have been anything but straightforward. The Washington Monument set the precedent, perhaps, and the proposed site for the National World War II memorial was greeted with strenuous objection. Korean War vets grappled with how their service could be honoured as powerfully as the Vietnam War vets who had, after a wrenching process, finally succeeded in erecting their memorial. Even the revered Abraham Lincoln didn't come by his stately seat at the Mall's terminus easily. This walk takes you to all these sites, and more.

1 When exiting Federal Triangle Metro station, follow both sets of escalator steps outside. Proceed straight ahead onto Woodrow Wilson Plaza. Turn left at the silver *Federal Triangle Flowers* sculpture and past the bronze, thumb-like piece *Bearing Witness*, heading out to Constitution Avenue, NW through the arched entryway of the Environmental Protection Agency building. Turn right on Constitution Avenue. Continue and cross 14th Street, NW. At 15th Street, NW cross the street and then follow the path up the small hill to the Washington Monument.

Urban legends abound as to why the marble used to construct the lower portion of this obelisk, in honour of the first US president George Washington (1732–99), looks darker than the stone used for the remainder of the monument. Some have thought it may be caused by floodwater or a result of the US Civil War. However, it is most likely that the responsibility lies with a bizarre political faction called the Know-Nothings, who were the chief suspects in an incident that altered the obelisk's fate. The Washington Monument National Society, which had launched the monument creation as a privately funded project, had made an appeal for building stone as well as financial support. In response to the request, Pope Pius IX offered a block of marble that was originally used to build the Temple of Concord in Rome. On 6 March 1854, the marble disappeared and the Know-Nothings, thought to have anti-Catholic and anti-foreigner sentiments, were accused of stealing the stone. What happened to the marble was unclear – it was either broken into pieces or heaved into the Potomac River – but it was never found and no arrests were made. The incident caused a severe reduction in contributions of both stone and money, and work ground to a halt for 22 years, until 1876. Although the same type of marble was used to complete the construction of the monument, it came from a different quarry and did not weather the same way. Consequently, the stone in the lower portion of the monument is darker than the stone in the upper portion.

THE WASHINGTON MONUMENT;
www.nps.gov/wamo

2 Stand by the Washington Monument, so you can see the Abraham Lincoln memorial straight ahead. Bear to the right, following the path down the hill on which the Monument stands. On your left, just outside the retaining wall, is a short, white column.

If he were alive today, Thomas Jefferson (1743–1826), the third US president, would be pleased to know someone had stopped to acknowledge the Jefferson Pier Stone, which he established in 1804 in order to provide the US with its own prime meridian – one to designate US time as distinct from Greenwich Mean Time. By the mid-19th century, the stone no longer had any function (the meridian of the US was changed to the centre of the Naval Observatory and was later finally subject to Greenwich Mean Time),

OPPOSITE: ABRAHAM LINCOLN, IMMORTALIZED IN MARBLE IN THE LINCOLN MEMORIAL

DISTANCE 2 miles (3.2km)

ALLOW 2 hours

START Federal Triangle Metro station

FINISH Federal Triangle Metro station

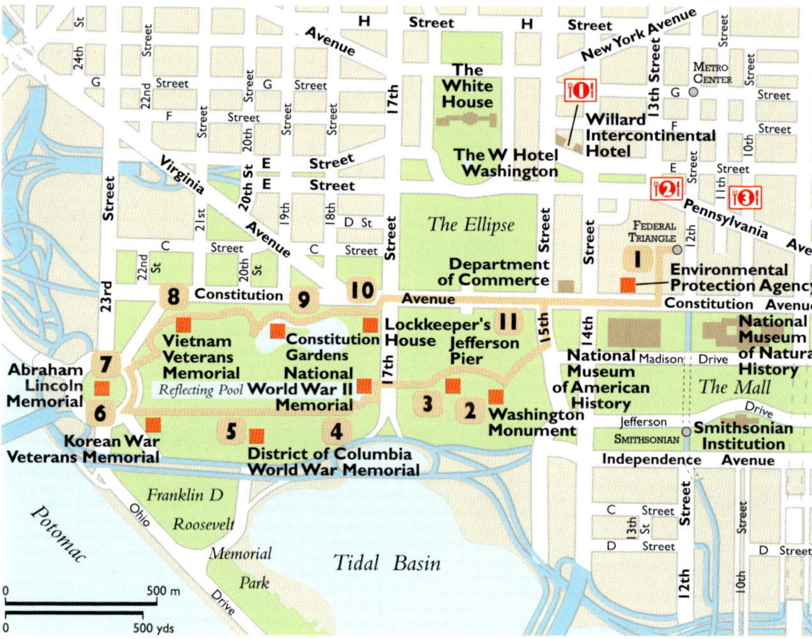

but this spot marks the east–west and north–south axes of the National Mall. Today, it provides an unexpected vista to four Washington landmarks – the White House to the north, the Thomas Jefferson memorial to the south. Look to the west and the Lincoln memorial comes into view; look east to see the US Capitol.

3 Continue along the path until it ends at 17th Street, NW. Cross the street to enter the National World War II memorial.

At the memorial's unveiling on Memorial Day 2004, only a few of the veterans and family members present knew the full extent of the heated debate that had erupted over its placement and design. Many had been enraged by the prospect of a structure blocking the vista from the Lincoln memorial to the Washington Monument. Others insisted that the Mall was already overcrowded with memorials. When architect Friedrich St Florian presented his winning design, some criticized it as echoing the architecture

of the totalitarian regimes US soldiers had fought to defeat; others lamented what they described as warmed-over classicism. In the end, though, the monument did not obstruct the cherished vista, nor did architectural critics universally dismiss it. **NATIONAL WORLD WAR II MEMORIAL;** www.wwiimemorial.com

4 Leave the memorial area, bearing to the left and going past the visitors' information building and toilets. Follow the gravel path parallel to the Reflecting Pool. On your left you will soon see what looks like a white marble temple.

An act of Congress may have authorized the development of the Washington World War I memorial, but it was the citizens themselves, led by newspaperman Frank B. Noyes, who distributed pledge cards and raised the funds. The Doric temple, in honour of veterans of World War I, was designed as a marble bandstand large enough to accommodate the entire Marine Band. John Phillips Sousa himself conducted that band during the unveiling ceremony on Armistice Day in 1931. Subsequent outdoor concerts at the memorial have long ceased.

5 Continue along the gravel path, passing the National Park Service stables. At the end of the path, turn left and walk to the entrance of the Korean War Veterans memorial.

'I wore that type of boots. I carried the radio just like that,' said Bernard Brooks, 62, a Washington resident who served in the Signal Corps during the Korean War. On a sweltering day in July 1995, thousands came to this site to commemorate what is often called the 'forgotten war'. The 19 grim-faced figures encountered here, however, are impossible to forget, particularly at night. Four architects from Pennsylvania State University won the design competition in 1989. They included 38 figures in a column of soldiers moving forwards. Once they realized that their design would have to be altered dramatically to pass review with the various powers that be, they dropped out. They then sued, and lost. Cooper-Lecky Architects of Washington were finally selected for the project, working in tandem with other designers and a veterans' advisory board. **KOREAN WAR VETERANS MEMORIAL;** www.nps.gov/kwvm

ABOVE: THE FIELD OF STARS ON THE FREEDOM WALL AT THE NATIONAL WORLD WAR II MEMORIAL.

6 From the Korean War Veterans memorial, follow the path to the Lincoln memorial.

The construction of this memorial, in honour of the 16th US president Abraham Lincoln (1809–65), began on 12 February 1914, on what would have been his 105th birthday. The public was sceptical, even insulted: the western end of the National Mall was newly created and raw-looking – what kind of tribute would be paid to Lincoln on a site that resembled a wasteland? Seventeen years after the unveiling ceremony in 1922, when black and white audience members had been seated separately, the public had its answer. On Easter Sunday 1939, African-American opera singer Marian Anderson gave a concert on the steps of the memorial that transformed the way many interpreted it, recognizing the part Lincoln had played in the emancipation of slaves (which he achieved in 1863) rather than simply the unifier during the US Civil War. This association of the monument with emancipation and egalitarianism continued to evolve and was crystallized on 28 August 1963, when Martin Luther King delivered his 'I Have a Dream' speech.
LINCOLN MEMORIAL; www.nps.gov/linc

7 Looking across the Reflecting Pool to the Washington Monument, turn left and walk towards the flagpole, which marks the entrance to the Vietnam Veterans memorial.

Little did architecture student Maya Ying Lin know when she entered a design competition sponsored by the Vietnam Veterans Memorial Fund how much her life was about to be transformed. Her entry was the unanimous choice for a Vietnam Veterans memorial in Washington. At the time, she was an undergraduate at Yale University. The black granite wall cut into the earth contains over 50,000 names of soldiers killed and has become one of the most sacred sites in Washington. However, no memorial process has been as fraught with acrimony and misunderstanding: opponents suggested throwing the design out and starting again and the Secretary of the Interior refused to issue a building permit. Finally, the veterans, their supporters and their opponents met to forge a compromise. Lin's powerful black walk of remembrance would remain; representational figures of three servicemen would be added nearby.

8 Follow the path out of the Vietnam Veterans memorial (be sure to look at the Vietnam Women's memorial on your way out). Head towards the pond, bearing to your left and following the path around it until you reach a bridge that crosses over to a small island.

The 56 signatories of the Declaration of Independence are honoured here at the Signers' memorial. This island and pond were unveiled in 1976 as part of the US bicentennial celebration. Ten years later, on the 200th anniversary of the US Constitution, the area was named Constitution Gardens. Look for red-winged blackbirds in the reeds.

9 Leave the island and then follow the path to the stairway. At the top of the stairs, turn left and exit Constitution Gardens onto Constitution Avenue, NW. Turn right and proceed along Constitution Avenue until you see 17th Street, NW.

This stone house, on the southwest corner of 17th Street and Constitution Avenue, is all that remains of a canal that once ran along what is now Constitution Avenue. Erected in 1831, it was the lockkeeper's house at the canal's entrance. Although planned as both functional and decorative, the canal had been lined with timber, making its durability questionable. By the time of the US Civil War (1861–65), the canal had become a garbage-strewn, fetid eyesore. It was filled in and turned into a street soon after the war.

10 Follow Constitution Avenue for two more blocks. Make sure to look to your left for a view of the White House between 17th and 15th Streets. After you cross 14th Street, start to notice the detailed sculpture on the Environmental Protection Agency Building on the left.

In the 1930s, funding was given to adorn these government headquarters with exterior sculpture. Five ornamental panels feature on the Constitution Avenue side of the buildings. Above the entrance, near 14th Street, a woman represents *Abundance and Industry*, while two rams represent *Productivity and Security*; a vase pours forth the *Fruits of Industry*. A little further along the avenue you can see *Labor and Industry,* represented by a male figure and a bull accompanied by a sheaf of wheat and a millstone. The remaining panels are *Columbia* (in the centre), *Commerce and Communications* and *Interstate Transportation*. Notice the frieze that extends the length of the complex, consisting of a wild variety of human, animal and other forms. As you approach 12th Street, NW notice the bas-relief over the entrance to the Andrew Mellon Auditorium. It depicts Lieutenant General George Washington planning the Battle of Trenton, New Jersey.

11 To return to Federal Triangle Metro station, turn left on 12th Street.

WHERE TO EAT

1 CAFÉ DU PARC,
1401 Pennsylvania Avenue, NW;
Tel: 1-202-942-7000.
Charming bistro for breakfast, lunch and dinner; ground-floor cafe. $$

2 LES HALLES,
1201 Pennsylvania Avenue, NW;
Tel: 1-202-347-6848.
Steak frîtes, mussels and other brasserie standbys; patio. $$

3 TEN PENH,
1001 Pennsylvania Avenue, NW;
Tel: 1-202-393-4500.
A very popular restaurant serving Asian-style cuisine. $$$

GRIM-FACED SOLDIERS OF THE UNFORGETTABLE KOREAN WAR VETERANS MEMORIAL

WALK
5

A Walk along America's Grand Avenue

A promenade along Washington's grandest avenue and, arguably, the most famous street in the US should not be missed.

Pennsylvania Avenue is the all-important mile linking the White House to the US Capitol. It is thought the street's name was intended to smooth the ruffled feathers of Pennsylvanian politicians, who considered Philadelphia a more suitable locale for the nation's capital. Ever since Thomas Jefferson walked down Pennsylvania Avenue for his inauguration in 1801, it has witnessed countless parades, marches and demonstrations. Depending on the time of day you choose for your stroll, Pennsylvania Avenue will either bustle with activity – its extra-wide pavements crowded with pedestrians – or appear all but deserted, its grand edifices like slumbering giants, still and shuttered. It's then that you notice the different eras of Washington history reflected along this grand boulevard. Evidence of what was probably its most fascinating time – from the city's founding in 1791 up to the US Civil War years (1861–65) – is sadly gone. However, the late 19th and 20th centuries are well represented, waiting to be appreciated on foot.

1 When exiting Federal Triangle Metro station, follow both sets of escalator steps outside. Proceed straight ahead onto Woodrow Wilson Plaza. Turn right at the silver *Federal Triangle Flowers* sculpture, heading out to Pennsylvania Avenue, NW. Turn left. On the corner of Pennsylvania Avenue and 14th Street, NW is the John Wilson Building.

The offices of Washington's mayor and city council are housed in this 1908 building. Prior to that, a large powerhouse for the electric trams that ran up and down 14th Street was located here. Supposedly constructed to be fireproof, the powerhouse nonetheless burned down in one hour flat during a devastating fire. Ironically, the only wall remaining bore a sign that read, 'Absolutely Fireproof'. The statue outside the main entrance of the John Wilson Building is of Alexander R. 'Boss' Shepherd, who headed a massive public works campaign in 1871, after the city of Washington was granted its first opportunity at self-governance. However, Shepherd's corrupt policies led to the removal of this privilege.

2 Cross 14th Street and then Pennsylvania Avenue. Walk one block past the park on the left. At the intersection of 14th and E Streets, NW is the Willard Hotel.

This is the last example of the grand and luxurious hotels that once lined Pennsylvania Avenue. In 1901, hotelier Henry Willard razed his original property to construct this lavish replacement, but financial difficulties nearly caused it to face the demolition ball in the late 1960s/early 1970s. After being boarded up for 18 years, the decaying lobby and public spaces were completely restored, and the hotel reopened in 1986. Take a look inside and see the results for yourself. Make sure to visit the Willard's Hall of History located just inside the F Street entrance, then order a Mint Julep from the Round Robin Bar.

WHERE TO EAT

1 701,
701 Pennsylvania Avenue, NW;
Tel: 1-202-393-0701.
Contemporary continental cuisine and live jazz in the evening. $$$

2 THE OCCIDENTAL,
1475 Pennsylvania Avenue, NW;
Tel: 1-202-783-1475.
Known for fine dining since 1906; outdoor seating. $$$

3 W HOTEL ROOF TERRACE,
15th and Pennsylvania Avenue, NW,
Tel: 1-202-661-2400.
Hip bar; views of the White House and Washington Monument. $$$

3 Cross 14th Street, turn right and cross E Street. Step up onto Freedom Plaza.

Freedom Plaza, designed by architect Robert Venturi in 1980, is named in honour of Martin Luther King (1929–68),

OPPOSITE: ORNATE LOBBY OF THE WILLARD HOTEL ON PENNSYLVANIA AVENUE

DISTANCE **1.5 miles (2.5km)**

ALLOW **1 hour (more with site visits)**

START **Federal Triangle Metro station**

FINISH **Archives-Navy Memorial-Penn Quarter Metro station**

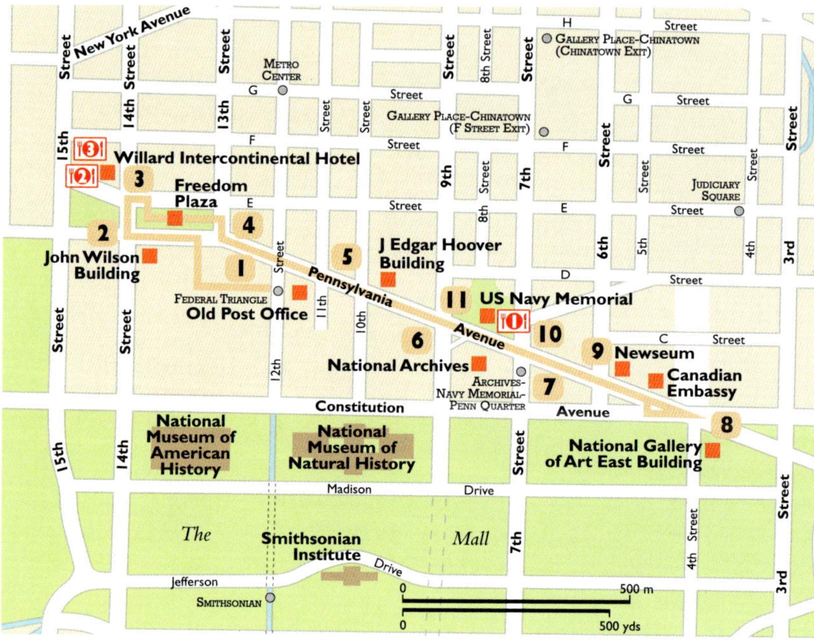

who finished work on his famous 'I Have a Dream' speech at the Willard Hotel in 1963. As you walk across it, notice the inlaid rendering of the central part of the city plan of Washington, which was designed by French-born American architect, engineer and urban designer Pierre Charles L'Enfant (1754–1825) in 1791. Around the city plan, there are quotes about Washington from famous people carved into the paving. Venturi had originally proposed tall, stone pylons and large-scale models of the White House and Capitol, but these were never built. The plaza is a popular venue for outdoor concerts, rallies and, unofficially, skateboarders. A time capsule, which contains the slain civil-rights leader's robe, Bible and other memorabilia, is buried here and is scheduled to be opened 15 January 2088.

4 Walk across Freedom Plaza, then cross 13th Street. Continue on Pennsylvania Avenue to the intersection of 12th to the Old Post Office building.

Pennsylvania Avenue was the city's first commercial thoroughfare, lined with shops, markets and a financial district. By the end of the 19th century, however, the corridor had begun to decline. In an attempt to improve its prospects, Congress authorized construction of a combined Post Office Department headquarters and City Post Office building. In 1899, this striking Romanesque Revival building was completed, its clock tower, 315ft (96m) high, becoming an instant landmark – you can still take a lift to the top. The Post Office Department left in 1930 and the threat of demolition loomed over the building. Finally, in the early 1980s, a group of preservationists persisted in having it restored. Moreover, their campaign, known as 'Don't Tear It Down' grew into the DC Preservation League, which continues to carry the flag for preserving the city's buildings.

OLD POST OFFICE TOWER;
SUMMER: MON–FRI 9–7.45, SAT–SUN 10–5.45;
WINTER: MON–FRI 9–4.45, SAT–SUN 10–5.45;
www.nps.gov/opot

5 **Walk down Pennsylvania Avenue. The buildings on the south side of the street are located within the Federal Triangle, an enormous construction project undertaken by the federal government in 1926. Its goal was to reclaim what in the 19th century had been the city's seamy Red Light District for a triangular-shaped precinct of government headquarters. The six limestone buildings with red-tiled roofs are the result. At the intersection of Pennsylvania Avenue and 10th Street, NW is a building from a different era, the J. Edgar Hoover Building.**

The Federal Bureau of Investigation has been headquartered in this imposing, impenetrable fortress since 1974. US lawyer John Edgar Hoover (1895–1972), the building's namesake, was director of the Bureau for 48 years. Highly regarded while he was alive, various allegations tarnished Hoover's reputation after his death. His leadership spanned a staggering eight presidential administrations, encompassing Prohibition, the Great

ABOVE: ROMANESQUE REVIVAL ARCH OF THE OLD POST OFFICE TOWER

Depression, World War II, the Korean War, the Cold War and the Vietnam War. Especially during the 1960s, Hoover was accused of exceeding and abusing his authority, investigating individuals and groups because of their political beliefs rather than suspected criminal activity. It is because of Hoover's long and controversial reign that FBI directors are now limited to 10-year terms.

6 Cross 9th Street, NW and then turn right and cross Pennsylvania Avenue. Look for a stone tablet near the corner of 9th Street and Pennsylvania Avenue.

In 1941, President Franklin D. Roosevelt (1882–1945) met with his friend Supreme Court Justice Felix Frankfurter in his office. Roosevelt told Frankfurter, 'If they are to put any memorial to me, I should like it to be placed in the centre of that green plot in front of the Archives building. I should like it to consist of a block about the size of this' (meaning his desk). In 1965, Roosevelt's request was granted. Thirty-two years later, a second $48 million Franklin D. Roosevelt memorial was unveiled at the Tidal Basin (see Walk 3). Inside the National Archives, visitors can view the original Declaration of Independence, US Constitution and Bill of Rights. The building was designed by architect John Russell Pope (1874–1937) and opened in 1935.

NATIONAL ARCHIVES;
SPRING AND SUMMER: DAILY 10–7; AUTUMN AND WINTER: DAILY 10–5.30;
www.archives.gov/nae/visit

7 Cross Pennsylvania Avenue at 7th Street, NW. Continue past the building situated at the tip of the Federal Triangle: the Federal Trade Commission. Cross 6th Street, NW, passing the National Gallery of Art West Building on the right. Across 4th Street, NW is the National Gallery's East Building.

In a city of conservative, classically derived structures, the National Gallery's East Building is a breath of fresh air. Designed by famed Chinese-born US architect, I.M. Pei (born 1917), historians and critics widely regard it as the best example of modern architecture in the US capital city. Rising gracefully from an awkward trapezoidal site, the building is divided into two triangles – one for gallery space, the other for offices. Even if you don't have time to look around the gallery, it's worth a look inside just to experience Pei's solution first hand – standing beneath the light-filled atrium, with a large mobile by Alexander Calder peacefully turning overhead, is a pleasure in itself. Funding for the gallery, which opened in 1978, was given by Paul Mellon and Ailsa Mellon Bruce, son and daughter of the National Gallery's founder, Andrew Mellon.

NATIONAL GALLERY OF ART;
MON–SAT 10–5, SUN 11–6;
www.nga.gov

8 Outside the East Building, cross Constitution Avenue, NW and turn left, returning to Pennsylvania Avenue. Pass John Marshall Park on the right, to arrive at the Canadian Embassy.

The embassies of the two countries that border the US – Canada and Mexico – sit on Pennsylvania Avenue. (Mexico's can be found on the stretch between the White House and Georgetown.) Architectural elements of the Canadian Embassy, designed by Vancouver-based architect Arthur Erickson (born 1924), pay tribute to neighbouring buildings: the exterior of the embassy is sheathed in white marble; the rotunda echoes those of the Capitol and National Gallery West Building; and the building's three wings are positioned to reflect the geometric minimalism of the National Gallery East Building. At the end of the 19th century, this block of Pennsylvania Avenue was the heart of Washington's original Chinatown. However, in 1931 the community was forced to relocate to its current site along H Street, NW to make way for the construction of a municipal centre. Years later, in the mid 1980s, a portion of that new Chinatown was displaced for the construction of the Washington Convention Center.

9 Next door to the embassy is the Newseum.

When it opened in April 2008, the Newseum injected a rare boost of technological pizzazz and curatorial bravura along what has traditionally been a fairly refined block of Pennsylvania Avenue. When you've finished with the exhibits, which cover five centuries of news history, the view of Pennsylvania Avenue and the National Mall from the observation deck is incomparable.

10 Continue along Pennsylvania Avenue, crossing 6th Street and then 7th Street, NW. In the middle of the block is the US Navy memorial.

The US Navy memorial and the Market Square development on its border were constructed between 1984 and 1990. Preservationists objected when 8th Street, NW was closed off for the memorial, opposing the alteration to the original city plan conceived by Pierre Charles L'Enfant in 1791. Yet the memorial's plaza does at least retain the vista from the avenue to the majestic former Patent Office Building to the north. The former Patent Office Building and the National Archives are the focal points for what has become the best public outdoor space along Pennsylvania Avenue.

11 The Metro station is adjacent to the Navy Memorial.

ABOVE: *THE LONE SAILOR* STATUE AT THE US NAVY MEMORIAL

WALK 6

Great Estates of Georgetown

Impressive mansions and gardens are featured on this walk that introduces you to some of the most historic properties in Washington.

One of the most remarkable aspects of the Georgetown historic district is that it represents a complete town, with commercial, residential and civic buildings still intact. In a densely developed city like Washington, visitors are amazed to discover four Georgetown estates that have retained much of their original acreage. They are located high above the waterfront and bustling commercial corridor on terrain that follows the slope and rise of the old road, where workers used to roll casks of tobacco from rural Maryland down to the inspection station on the banks of the Potomac. The prosperous merchants whose fortunes were made in the tobacco trade built large, freestanding Federal-style houses (1790–1820) along Prospect and N Streets. Further north, however, other wealthy Georgetown families such as the Davidsons and the Peters created expansive estates featuring grand mansions and landscaped gardens. These manorial houses are the subject of this walk. Try to take it Tuesday to Saturday, when the houses are open for tours.

1 Leaving Dupont Circle Metro, turn left onto Q Street, NW and follow it two blocks to Massachusetts Avenue, NW. Cross Massachusetts Avenue and continue on Q Street until you reach the entrance to the Dumbarton Bridge (known as the Buffalo Bridge for the massive animals guarding the approach). Cross the bridge over the Rock Creek as you enter Georgetown. Make sure to look to your right about halfway across for a view to the Washington National Cathedral. Follow Q Street, NW until you arrive at Dumbarton House at No. 2715.

Dumbarton House stands on a tract of land patented in 1703 by an immigrant Scot, Ninian Beall, who named it 'Rock of Dumbarton'. In 1798, a developer bought 4.5 acres (1.8 hectares) of the land and began to construct the house. The First Lady Dolley Madison stayed overnight in the house following the burning of the White House in the War of 1812. When the Dumbarton Bridge was constructed in 1915, the house faced possible demolition, so preservationists had it moved 100ft (30m) to its present site, thus allowing the extension of Q Street into Georgetown. The primly named National Society of The Colonial Dames of America purchased the home in 1928, restored it to its early Federal period character, and bestowed the present name of Dumbarton House. Tours include the music room, parlour and upstairs bedrooms, where visitors can see a wealth of furniture, paintings, textiles, silver and ceramics that were made and used in America's early years.

DUMBARTON HOUSE;
TUE–SAT (TOURS 10.15, 11.15, 12.15, 1.15);
www.dumbartonhouse.org

2 Follow Q Street to 28th Street, NW, then turn right and begin to walk up the hill. When you are about halfway, stop outside the street entrance to No. 1628 28th Street.

Evermay is the last privately owned estate in Georgetown. The house is not open to the public unless you are invited to a party or reception. Built in 1801, its original owner was Samuel Davidson, a Scottish immigrant who made a fortune in real estate. That privacy was of utmost importance to him can be gleaned from the inscription on the bronze plaque that hangs on the 28th Street wall. He begs his neighbours to avoid Evermay 'as they would a den of evils, or rattlesnakes, and thereby save themselves and me much

OPPOSITE: ENTRANCE TO BUFFALO (DUMBARTON) BRIDGE; ABOVE: BUST IN OAK HILL CEMETERY

DISTANCE 3 miles (4.8km)

ALLOW 2.5 hours (or more with museum visits)

START Dupont Circle Metro station (Q Street exit)

FINISH Foggy Bottom Metro station

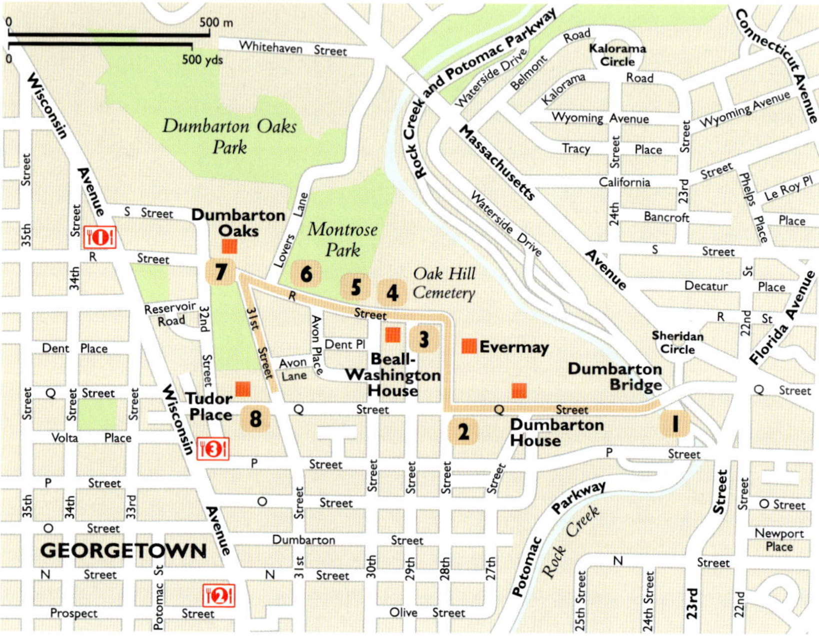

vexation and trouble'. This warning was issued via a newspaper advertisement placed by Davidson. When he died, the residence went to his nephew, Lewis Grant, with the proviso that he emigrate from Scotland and add 'Davidson' to his name. Grant complied and lived out his life on the estate.

3 Proceed on 28th Street, following as it curves into R Street, NW past a cemetery. Cross R Street at 29th Street, NW and stand in front of 2029 R Street.

On 23 July 2001, friends, family and admirers of Katharine Graham, who had died at age 84, repaired to this house (built in 1784) for a reception following her funeral at the Washington National Cathedral. They paid tribute to a woman who had surprised herself when, inexperienced and uncertain, she took over control of the *Washington Post* newspaper following the suicide of her husband. During her tenure the *Post* rose to prominence and Graham became one of the most influential and admired

women of her generation. She was at the helm of the newspaper when it made history with the publication of the *Pentagon Papers* during the Vietnam War and again when two *Post* reporters broke the story that became Watergate and resulted in the resignation of President Richard Nixon. In 1997, Graham published her memoir, *Personal History*, which received critical acclaim, became a bestseller and won the Pulitzer Prize for biography. With her death, a glittering era for Georgetown social and political life came to an end.

4 Cross R Street and walk to the entry gate of Oak Hill Cemetery.

Picturesque Oak Hill Cemetery descends from R Street to the Rock Creek Parkway below via a series of ravines and alternating terraces. Established in 1849, it takes its name from the grove of huge oak trees that provided shade for those who brought picnics here to commune both with nature and their deceased loved ones. The charming Gothic Revival chapel, built in 1850, was designed by Smithsonian Castle architect James Renwick (1818–95). Look for the simple gravestone of Katharine Graham, owner and publisher of the *Washington Post*, on the chapel grounds. Other notables laid to rest here are statesman Edwin M. Stanton (1814–69), Secretary of War under President Abraham Lincoln; architect Adolph Cluss (1825–1905); socialite Peggy O'Neale Eaton (1799–1879), whose marriage to President Andrew Jackson's Secretary of War split the Cabinet in two, and William W. Corcoran (1798–1888), the banker and philanthropist who donated the land for the cemetery.

OAK HILL CEMETERY;
MON–FRI 9–4.30, SUN 1–4;
www.oakhillcemeterydc.org

ABOVE: WISTERIA BLOSSOMS BEAUTIFY A HEDGE AT DUMBARTON OAKS

5 Next to Oak Hill Cemetery is the lovely, rural Montrose Park.

A favourite spot for dog walkers and youngsters with a nanny or parent in tow, Montrose Park was once the site of a mansion by that name built here in 1810. Make sure to read the sign that tells you all about the Parrott rope walk, an operation that took place when rope-making magnate, Richard Parrott, owned the land. Sarah Louisa Rittenhouse, a Georgetown native who had grown up at Dumbarton House, campaigned to turn the acreage into a park. In 1911, the decaying Montrose mansion was razed and a new National Park welcomed the public. To honour Rittenhouse's accomplishment, in 1956 the Georgetown Garden Club placed a bronze armillary sphere near the park's entrance. She is buried in Oak Hill Cemetery.

6 Continue along R Street past Lovers Lane, a path down to Rock Creek Park that separates Montrose Park from the more formal gardens of Dumbarton Oaks at 31st and R Streets, NW.

This estate dates back to 1801, although it would be difficult to tell from looking at the house, which has been altered extensively. The land was part of the 'Rock of Dumbarton' tract owned by Ninian Beall. The original mansion was later transformed by another owner into a fashionable house in the style of the Second Empire (1850–80). In 1920, Robert and Mildred Bliss purchased the property and renovated extensively, stripping away the Second Empire elements. They also enlisted landscape architect Beatrix Farrand to create a formal garden for the estate, a stroll through which should not be missed.

ABOVE: DUMBARTON OAKS, WITH ITS ORNATE PAVED COURTYARD

When they moved to California in 1940, the Blisses gave the bulk of Dumbarton Oaks to Harvard University, which in 1963 commissioned architect Philip Johnson to design the Pre-Columbian Museum, where the Bliss's collection is now on display.

DUMBARTON OAKS;

15 MARCH–31 OCTOBER: TUE–SUN 2–6;
1 NOVEMBER–14 MARCH: TUE–SUN 2–5;
www.doaks.org

7 From Dumbarton Oaks, cross R Street and proceed along 31st Street, NW. Enjoy the splendid brick and clapboard homes you pass before you reach the entrance of Tudor Place, which will be on your right.

Six generations of the Peter family lived here continuously between 1805 and 1983. Their ownership began when Thomas and Martha Custis Peter bought an unfinished house that stood on this site. Martha was the granddaughter of First Lady Martha Washington and her husband was the son of Georgetown's first mayor. They hired William Thornton, first architect of the US Capitol, to complete the house, which he did in 1816. Many consider the finished product to be not only Thornton's masterpiece, but also one of the most important houses in Washington for providing insight into domestic life in the city's first two centuries. The Peters bore witness to such important events as the laying of the US Capitol cornerstone, the burning of Washington in 1814, and the US Civil War. This is one of the best, and most beautiful, places to learn about Georgetown life during the 19th century.

TUDOR PLACE;

TUE–SAT 10–4, SUN 12–4 (CLOSED JANUARY);
www.tudorplace.org

8 To get to Foggy Bottom Metro station, turn right at the exit of Tudor Place grounds and walk downhill on 31st Street to M Street, NW. Turn left onto M Street and follow it to the intersection of 28th Street, NW. Turn right, crossing M Street, and then turn right and proceed along Pennsylvania Avenue, NW. Follow Pennsylvania Avenue to 23rd Street, NW. Turn right onto 23rd Street. The station is on the right.

WHERE TO EAT

1 BISTRO LEPIC,
1736 Wisconsin Avenue, NW;
Tel: 1-202-333-0111.
A perennial favourite with locals, serving classic French bistro fare downstairs; wine bar upstairs. $$

2 MARTIN'S TAVERN,
1264 Wisconsin Avenue, NW;
Tel: 1-202-333-7370.
Traditional American food with a British streak. $$

3 MARVELOUS MARKET,
3217 P Street, NW;
Tel: 1-202-333-2591.
One of Washington's best takeaways, with award-winning chocolate chip cookies. $

WALK
7

Scandals in the Presidents' Back Yard

The 7-acre (2.8-hectare) park north of the White House has been the site of some of Washington's most infamous machinations.

'La Fayette Square was society,' wrote novelist, journalist and Washington resident Henry Adams (1838–1918) '...One found all one's acquaintances as well as hotels, banks, markets, and national government. Beyond the Square the country began'. And what about inside the Square? That's another story, and one that Adams chronicled in 1880 with his anonymously published *Democracy*, a novel about political power – its acquisition, use and abuse set in the elegant enclave of Lafayette Square. It afforded its inhabitants proximity to power and social cachet. It also spawned a remarkable number of scandalous events, a selection of which is introduced on this walk. There's the senator who pioneered the modern political campaign; a suicide that's followed by cold-blooded murder; and the president who refuses to be intimidated by assassins. And let us not forget the secretary who shredded and smuggled top-secret documents. Take the walk on a weekday, when the government offices surrounding the park are in full swing.

1 Exiting McPherson Square Metro station at Vermont Avenue, NW, turn right and walk one block to H Street, NW. Cross H Street and continue along Madison Place, NW to the second yellow house on the left – the one with the wrought-iron balcony.

Benjamin Tayloe, who was a member of one of the wealthiest families in Virginia, built this house in 1828 and lived there for 40 years, keeping a journal of his residency published as *Our Neighbors on Lafayette Square*. It's a pity that he did not live long enough to record events here between 1900 and 1902, when the home was leased by Senator Mark Hanna of Ohio and became known as the Little White House. Hanna was a wealthy industrialist who many believed exerted great influence over Ohio governor William McKinley. As chairman of the Republican National Committee, Hanna promoted McKinley as his party's 1896 presidential candidate. He personally took charge of the campaign, raising an unprecedented $3.5 million, employing 1,400 people, and outspending his opponent, William Jennings Bryan, by 12 to 1. It is considered the forerunner of the modern political campaign. McKinley won the election, and Hanna's close relationship with the now President continued, McKinley partaking in countless 'power breakfasts' at this house in order to confer with Hanna.

2 Next door to the Tayloe House is the entrance to the US Court of Claims and Court of Appeals. Walk up the steps and into the courtyard. On the wall at the far right is a large plaque illustrating the Rodgers House.

Although the assassination of President Abraham Lincoln is one of the most well-known events in US history, what is less known is the scope of the plot hatched by Lincoln's murderer, John Wilkes Booth. His intention was to kill not only the President but to assassinate General Ulysses Grant, Vice President Andrew Johnson and Secretary of State William Seward on the same night. Seward rented the house that once stood on this site while he served as secretary of state. It was here, on 14 April 1865, that he was brutally attacked by would-be assassin Lewis Powell, assigned by Booth to 'slit the throat of the old man'. Powell had entered the house claiming to be a messenger bringing a prescription for Seward, who was recovering from a carriage accident; his attack wounded the secretary of state yet did not kill him. It was Powell, in fact, who would suffer death after being arrested, found guilty and sentenced to death by hanging. Seward recovered from knife wounds that had been inflicted by Powell, as did two of his sons who had also been injured. However, it was all too much for Seward's wife Frances, who died two months later of a heart attack.

3 Return to Madison Place and follow it to the intersection of Pennsylvania Avenue, NW. Turn right, cross Madison Place and stand in front of the sculpture group on the corner.

DISTANCE **0.5 mile (0.8km)**

ALLOW **1 hour**

START **McPherson Square Metro station (Vermont Avenue exit)**

FINISH **McPherson Square Metro station (Vermont Avenue entrance)**

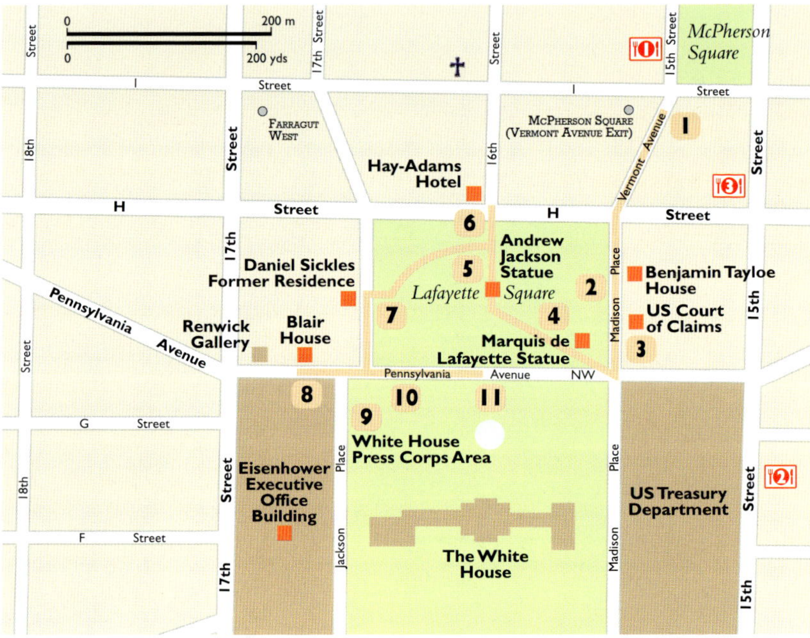

For two weeks in 1824, Washington was abuzz over the arrival of the Marquis de Lafayette (1757–1834), who is depicted atop the pedestal. Congress had finally seen fit to landscape President's Park, as this 7 acres (2.8 hectares) was originally known, because the Marquis – a French military officer and beloved hero to the American public for his service to the US military during the American War of Independence – was due to give a speech here. Following the ceremony, the park was popularly called Lafayette Park or Lafayette Square. Three other foreign-born military men are honoured on the other corners of the park, each having rendered service to the US during the American War of Independence (1775–83).

4 Follow the path from the Lafayette statue into the centre of the park. There you will find the first equestrian statue ever erected in America. It commemorates General Andrew Jackson.

OPPOSITE: FIRST EQUESTRIAN STATUE IN THE US, COMMEMORATING GENERAL ANDREW JACKSON

In 1853, to much fanfare, General Andrew Jackson (1767–1845), triumphant at the Battles of New Orleans and Pensacola during the War of 1812, was honoured with the unveiling of this statue. Jackson later served as America's seventh president (the first ever Democratic president). His inaugural reception is famous for its raucous nature, with thousands roaming through the White House and causing extensive damage. The only means of getting the crowd to leave was to drag tubs of rum punch out onto Lafayette Square.

5 Walk around the Jackson statue to the other side and continue to H Street. Cross H Street to 16th Street, NW. On the left side is the Hay-Adams Hotel.

The hotel is named after the owners of the homes that once occupied this site. The Hay and Adams families built two magnificent mansions designed by US architect Henry Hobson Richardson. However, they were razed in 1926 to make way for the hotel. The owners of the 16th Street house were John and Clara Hay; the H Street residence belonged to Henry and Marion 'Clover' Adams. However, Clover never lived in the house. On 6 December 1885 she took her own life by ingesting potassium cyanide, dying on her bedroom floor in the Adams' rented house one block away. She and her husband were two of the most illustrious and enigmatic residents of Lafayette Square and their Boston Brahmin lineage, keen intelligence and exclusive social circle were of unending interest to their neighbours. A few unsympathetic types placed the blame for Clover's death at Henry Adams' feet, although nothing has ever come from such speculation. In fact, letters written by Clover to her sister Ellen would indicate that Henry regarded his wife with tenderness. An air of mystery continues to hover over the suicide of Mrs Adams nonetheless, many seeking answers at the powerful memorial placed on Clover's gravesite in Rock Creek Cemetery. A copy of the statue depicting an androgynous cloaked figure can actually be seen inside the Court of Claims courtyard on the left side.

6 Cross H Street back to Lafayette Park. Turn right and walk along the path that leads through the park to the other side. Cross Jackson Place, NW and find No. 722 along the terrace.

Today, almost all of the buildings in this terrace accommodate White House offices. However, many were once private residences. A house that once stood on the site of No. 722 was once the scene of a Washington scandal. Congressman Daniel E. Sickles and his young wife, Teresa, lived at this address. In February 1859, an anonymous letter sent to Sickles stated that his wife was engaged in an illicit relationship with his friend Mr Philip Barton Key, son of the man who wrote the lyrics to the US national anthem. 'He has as much use of your wife as you do', the letter declared. Sickles became enraged. Although himself unfaithful to the bonds of marriage, this dual betrayal by his wife and by a man he considered his trusted friend was intolerable. Three days later, upon seeing Barton Key attempt to signal to Teresa across Lafayette Square, Sickles burst through the front door of his Jackson Place house, stormed across the park and shot at Barton Key three times. The hapless suitor died soon after, and Sickles gave himself up to the law. The resulting trial was a national sensation, particularly when the verdict was given against the congressman: not guilty due to temporary insanity, the first time such a defence had been used successfully in the US.

7 **Looking at No. 722 turn left and follow Jackson Place to Pennsylvania Avenue. Turn right and proceed to 1651 Pennsylvania Avenue, called Blair House – the building with the green awning extending from the entrance.**

While renovations were carried out at the White House between 1947 and 1951, President Harry Truman and his wife, Bess, moved out temporarily to Blair House. On 1 November 1950, two Puerto Rican nationalists began to shoot their way inside the building, determined to assassinate the president. A quick response by the White House police prevented their plan from being carried out, yet one officer, Leslie Coffelt, was killed. The plaque closest to the entry gate pays tribute to him. Security for President Truman became tighter, although Truman did not understand all the fuss. To the alarm of the Secret Service, he had stuck his head out of the second-floor window of Blair House during the attack to see what was going on. Later, he wrote to a friend, 'I've been shot at by experts and unless your name's on the bullet you needn't be afraid'. Today, Blair House serves as guest quarters for visiting heads of state who are in Washington for an official meeting with the US president.

8 **Cross Pennsylvania Avenue and stand in front of the grandiose Eisenhower Executive Office Building.**

The original occupants of this massive building, built in the Second Empire style (popular in the US between 1850

WHERE TO EAT

1 GEORGIA BROWN'S,
950 15th Street, NW;
Tel: 1-202-393-4499.
Upscale southern cooking at its best. The Sunday brunch is bountiful. $$

2 OLD EBBITT GRILL,
675 15th Street, NW;
Tel: 1-202-347-4800.
Voted 'best place to talk politics', this restaurant has an American menu for plain and fancy tastes. $$

3 LE BAR,
Sofitel Lafayette Square;
806 15th Street, NW;
Tel: 1-202-730-8700.
A chic urban setting featuring light French fare. Popular for after-work drinks on the outdoor patio. $$

and 1880) were the State, Navy and War Departments. When they all moved to new headquarters, every inch of space inside became White House offices. A secretary named Fawn Hall worked in room 392. It was notorious in the late 1980s for the 'shredding parties', where secret documents were destroyed. Hall's superior was Lieutenant Colonel Oliver North, a notable figure in the Iran-Contra scandal, which involved arms sales to Iran and funding of Contra militants in Nicaragua. How ironic that Hall's smuggling of confidential papers out of her employer's office caused President Ronald Reagan to form a task force that eventually put both North and Hall on trial. In March 1989, having been granted immunity in exchange for her testimony, Hall testified against North. She told of shredding documents, at one point claiming, 'Sometimes you have to go above the law'.

9 Facing the Executive Office Building, turn left and walk past the entry gate to the White House grounds. Just past the fence is an area filled with camera equipment.

Located just outside the White House's West Wing lobby and press briefing room, television correspondents use this area for 'stand-ups' while they report the news of White House scandals. Constant use over the years caused the spot to become muddy and grass refused to grow, so, in 1998, the White House installed honeycomb grating and gravel to create what is known as Pebble Beach.

10 Continue along Pennsylvania Avenue until you are standing looking at the White House.

This famous edifice has witnessed many a reputation tarnished by scandal. A handful of occupants have suffered the ignominy of being removed from office. The process begins with impeachment, in which a public official is accused of wrong-doing by the House of Representatives. Next comes a trial by the Senate, after which a president can be forced out of office. Andrew Johnson (17th US president 1865–69) was the first president to leave office as a result of impeachment. In the wake of the Watergate debacle, President Richard Nixon, who had been president since 1969, avoided impeachment by resigning in 1974. Former White House intern Monica Lewinsky, who told a confidante about her affair with Bill Clinton (president 1993–2001), caused a storm of gossip and legal prosecution that resulted in a graphic 453-page report to Congress, providing details of the intern's hopes, dreams and sexual proclivities. Bill Clinton soon became the second US president to be impeached. However, the charges of perjury and obstruction of justice ended with his acquittal.

11 To get back to the Metro, cross Lafayette Park, past the Andrew Jackson statue, back to H Street. Turn right and proceed to the intersection of H Street and Vermont Avenue. Cross H Street and follow Vermont Avenue one block. The station will be on the left.

OPPOSITE: THE EISENHOWER EXECUTIVE OFFICE BUILDING, AN EXAMPLE OF SECOND EMPIRE ARCHITECTURE

WALK 8

A Walk through the Corridors of Power

The US Capitol represents the heart of America's democratic government and the geographic centre of Washington.

This walk leads you around Washington's most famous architectural icon, the US Capitol, and past the buildings housing America's legislative and judicial branches of government. You will discover that Capitol Hill does indeed describe a rise in the ground upon which the monumental edifice stands. Take this walk during the working week, when the streets are filled with members of Congress and their staff. You'll notice impromptu conferences being held on street corners and advice being hastily conveyed via mobile phones. Sleek black town cars and humble city taxis will pick up and drop off lobbyists eager to pitch their cause. It may come as a surprise that such intensive activity takes place amidst a gracious park-like setting, the US Capitol grounds representing some of the most pleasing outdoor spaces in the city. Pay attention to the street signs, too: the Capitol marks the spot from which the principal streets separating Washington's four main areas radiate. You will walk through each of them.

1 Directly across 1st Street, SE from the Capitol South Metro station is the Capitol Hill Club at No. 300.

The concept of a national social club for Republicans was first proposed by New Jersey Congressman James C. Auchincloss in 1950. The organization has occupied this site since 1972. Presidents, vice presidents, members of Congress, governors and state party leaders are among the members who enjoy meals in the Presidential Dining Room or drinks at the Auchincloss Grill. The National Democratic Club can be found nearby on Ivy Street, SE.

2 Looking at the Capitol Hill Club, turn left and continue on 1st Street, crossing C Street, SE. At Independence Avenue, SE, turn left. Pass the Cannon and Longworth House Office Buildings. Next is the Rayburn House Office Building on the left. Each of these buildings contains offices for members of the House of Representatives.

The Rayburn Building was named in honour of Sam T. Rayburn of Texas, a lifelong bachelor and member of the United States House of Representatives from 1913 until his death in 1961. He served as Speaker of the House (leader of the House of Representatives) for 17 years and is regarded as the most effective Speaker in history. In shaping legislation, Rayburn preferred to work quietly in the background rather than be in the public spotlight. As Speaker, he won a reputation for fairness and integrity, refusing to

accept gifts or money from lobbyists. His legendary after-hours 'Board of Education' meetings, held in hideaway offices in the House, were off-the-record sessions where invitees of Rayburn would play poker, sip bourbon and engage in frank political discussion. An invitation to attend was considered a high honour.

3 Continue along Independence Avenue. At the intersection of 1st Street, SW turn right and cross Independence Avenue. Turn left onto Maryland Avenue, SW and look for the entrance to the US Botanic Garden.

Sited here since 1933, this is the offspring of earlier botanic gardens established by Congress. It includes a conservatory, 2 acres (0.8 hectares) of surrounding grounds, as well as a garden across

OPPOSITE: GRANT MEMORIAL; ABOVE: STATUE IN FRONT OF THE RAYBURN HOUSE OFFICE BUILDING

DISTANCE **0.7 mile (1.2km)**

ALLOW **1 hour (more with site visits)**

START **Capitol South Metro station**

FINISH **Capitol South Metro station**

Independence Avenue displaying the Frédéric Auguste Bartholdi Fountain, which commemorates the French sculptor (1834–1904) who created the Statue of Liberty. Always an inviting refuge from the demands of Capitol Hill, the Botanic Garden is especially welcoming on a frosty winter's day.

US BOTANIC GARDEN;

DAILY 10–5; www.usbg.gov

4 Follow Maryland Avenue back to 1st Street and turn left. Almost immediately on your right will be a stunning view of the west terrace of the US Capitol.

Undoubtedly one of the most recognized buildings in the world, the US Capitol has stood on this hillside since the federal government located to Washington in 1800. Beneath its massive cast-iron dome, members of Congress go about their work, which is chiefly to make laws. The body is required to assemble once every year at noon on the third day of January.

A Congress lasts two years and is divided into two sessions. The Senate is composed of 100 members, two from each state; the House of Representatives has 435 members, elected every two years from each of the 50 states apportioned to their total populations. The Commonwealth of Puerto Rico, the District of Columbia and US Territories all have representatives. Take note, however, that although these delegates enjoy most of the prerogatives of representatives, they do not have the right to vote on matters before the House. This reality continues to infuriate Washington citizens, who addressed the matter by revising the District licence plate design to read: 'Taxation Without Representation'.

US CAPITOL GUIDE SERVICE;
MON–SAT 9–4; TEL: 1-202-225-6827;
www.house.gov/house/tour_services.shtml

WHERE TO EAT

1 BULLFEATHERS,
410 First Street, SE;
Tel: 1-202-543-5005.
Watering hole for the House of Representatives since 1980. Casual atmosphere and food. $$

2 THE MONOCLE,
107 D Street, NE;
Tel: 1-202-546-4488.
Where members of the Senate go to devour crab cakes and other American fare. Moderately priced bar menu. $$$

5 Directly across 1st Street is an elaborate memorial to General Ulysses S. Grant.

Ulysses S. Grant (1822–85) achieved international fame as the most important Union military leader during the US Civil War (1861–65). Key battles led by the cool-headed general turned the tide of war in the Union's favour. Moreover, it was Grant who accepted the surrender of Confederate military leader Robert E. Lee that ended the war. Grant served as US president through two terms plagued by scandal and corruption. After leaving the White House, he went bankrupt because of poor business investments. So as not to leave his family financially destitute, and despite intense pain from terminal cancer, Grant completed his memoirs, finishing the book three days before his death. This memorial was completed in phases between 1909 and 1916.

6 Continue to follow 1st Street along the periphery of the Capitol grounds and then to the intersection of 1st Street and Constitution Avenue, NW. Near the corner is the Robert A. Taft Garden Park.

Senator Robert A. Taft (1889–1953) was the eldest son of 27th US president William Howard Taft. By the 1950s, his hard work and reputation for personal integrity had won him the title 'Mr Republican', although most voters apparently considered him too conservative, too regional, and perhaps a bit too dull to be president: he campaigned for the office three times to no avail. In 1957, after Taft's death, a committee led by Senator John F. Kennedy selected him as one of five of their greatest Senate predecessors whose oval portraits should adorn the President's Room off the Senate floor. This memorial was erected in 1959.

7 From Consitution Avenue, turn right and continue across New Jersey Avenue, NW. Cross Delaware Avenue, NE to the Russell Senate Office Building.

In 1972, this building was named after former Senator Richard Brevard Russell. The Russell Caucus Room inside was used for hearings on the sinking of the Titanic in 1912, the Watergate scandal in 1974, and the nomination of US Supreme Court Justice Clarence Thomas in 1991. Russell represented Georgia from 1933 until his death in 1971. At the time, he was the most senior member of the Senate. Although a highly respected colleague and skilled legislator, Russell disagreed with many of his fellow senators regarding civil rights for African-Americans. In fact, Russell repeatedly blocked and defeated civil-rights legislation. As a result, when Russell made a run at the 1952 Democratic presidential nomination, he was shut out of serious consideration by northern Democrats. Nonetheless, Russell proved a valuable mentor to Texas Senator Lyndon B. Johnson, who was US President between 1963 and 1969 and convinced Congress to pass the Civil Rights Act of 1964.

8 Following Constitution Avenue, cross 1st Street, NE and proceed to 2nd Street, NE. On the corner is the Sewall-Belmont House and Museum.

Mrs Alva Belmont acquired this house in 1929. After a divorce and then the death of her second husband, the wealthy widow devoted her money and leadership to the cause of women's rights. She helped found the National Woman's Party in 1913 and that same year organized a huge suffragette rally in Washington, campaigning to gain women the right to vote. During the march the day before Woodrow Wilson's inauguration in March 1913, unruly behaviour among opponents of women's rights required police intervention to keep order. But the march built momentum for the women's suffrage movement, which succeeded in 1920 with ratification of the 19th Amendment to the Constitution.

SEWALL-BELMONT HOUSE AND MUSEUM;
SAT 11–5, TUE–FRI BY APPOINTMENT;
www.sewallbelmont.org

9 Cross Constitution Avenue and bear right onto Maryland Avenue, NE. At the intersection of 1st Street, turn left. Immediately on the left will be the US Supreme Court.

After the Capitol was set fire to by the British during the War of 1812, a large brick building was quickly erected on this site and Congress met there between 1815 and 1819. The Supreme Court, the highest judicial body in the US, was not constructed here until 1935. Over the entrance to the building is a pediment, which contains the sculpture *Liberty Enthroned Guarded by Order and Authority* by Robert Aitken (1878–1949). Nine figures are featured in the sculpture. Liberty, with the scales of justice in her lap, sits in the centre and is flanked by Roman soldiers, who represent Order and Authority. Beyond them are two pairs of historical figures symbolizing Council – on the left are the building's architect Cass Gilbert (1859–1934) and Elihu Root, a noted lawyer; to the right are Charles Evans Hughes (chief justice 1930–41) and the work's sculptor, Robert Aitken (1878–1949). At the far ends, two more figures represent Research: William Howard Taft (27th US president and chief justice 1921–30) and John Marshall (chief justice 1801–35).

SUPREME COURT OF THE UNITED STATES;

MON–FRI, 9–4.30; www.supremecourtus.gov

10 Stay on 1st Street and cross East Capitol Street. Immediately on the left is the Library of Congress Jefferson Building.

In 1800, Congress voted to purchase books and create a library for its use. From 1800 to 1814, the Library of Congress was housed in various spaces in the Capitol until it was burned. Congress then purchased Thomas Jefferson's personal library to replace their losses. In 1897, this freestanding Library of Congress building opened to the public. It is known as the Jefferson Building, and with two additional structures named after Presidents John Adams and James Madison it comprises the largest library in the world. It welcomes visiting scholars, the general public and, of course, Congress. The interiors of the Jefferson Building are as ornate as their exterior would suggest. The octagonal main reading room, where 'the opening of a book becomes a noble rite', to quote architectural historian Martin Moeller, is topped by a dome 160ft (48m) high.

LIBRARY OF CONGRESS JEFFERSON BUILDING;

MON–SAT, 10–5; www.loc.gov

11 To get back to Capitol South Metro, follow 1st Street to Independence Avenue, SE. Cross Independence Avenue and continue to D Street, SE. The station will be on the right.

ABOVE: THE ORNATE INTERIOR OF THE LIBRARY OF CONGRESS JEFFERSON BUILDING

STATUES OF PROMINENT AMERICANS IN THE NATIONAL STATUARY HALL IN THE US CAPITOL

WALK 9

Washington during the Civil War

Everywhere you look in central Washington, the story of the US Civil War (1861–65), so crucial to the history of the city, is waiting to be told.

For the first time, what had been a provincial, unimproved capital became the seat of genuine national power. When the war began in May 1861, Washington citizens were catapulted into a world of action and violence, crowds of strangers and an atmosphere of political and military crises. President Abraham Lincoln (1809–65) created the Army of the Potomac to defend the federal capital and thousands of soldiers came to the area. Along Washington's 7th Street corridor, the places where their lives intersected with the war still stand. Greater 7th Street (or Penn Quarter, as it has come to be known) is one of the few parts of central Washington to have retained its 19th-century character. It is full of activity day and night, just as it would have been between 1861 and 1865, though the wartime hospitals, public markets, stables and boarding houses have since evolved into condominiums, restaurants and theatres. Even so, if you set out on a quiet weekend morning, you'll sense the Civil War spirits close at hand.

I **As you exit the Archives-Navy Memorial-Penn Quarter Metro station, you will see the Prayer of Columbus carved in the granite wall at the foot of the escalator. Poet Walt Whitman (1819–92), its author, was a civilian volunteer during the US Civil War and spent much time in the area you are about to walk through. Outside the station, look for the equestrian statue of General Winfield Scott Hancock directly behind the station exit.**

Known to his Army colleagues as 'Hancock the Superb', General Winfield Scott Hancock (1824–86) became a Civil War hero when he led the Union forces to defeat the Confederate army at the Battle of Gettysburg in 1863. During the charge he was shot from his horse, but he continued to command his troops. General Hancock's dress is typical of a US army officer of the time, in particular the broad-brimmed felt hat worn by Union generals. Such was the admiration of Hancock, and so fervent the desire to commemorate US Civil War leaders, that when this statue was unveiled in 1896 every major official in Washington attended.

2 **Cross 7th Street, NW at Pennsylvania Avenue, NW. To the left is the memorial dedicated to the Grand Army of the Republic.**

The Grand Army of the Republic was a society founded by Dr Benjamin F. Stephenson in 1866. Stephenson conceived the idea of a national society composed of honourably discharged Union soldiers and sailors who were dedicated to assisting disabled soldiers and widows of fallen Union servicemen. Grand Army posts existed in every US state. In fact, the organization wielded such political clout that between 1868 and 1908, no Republican was nominated to the presidency without a Grand Army endorsement. It also played a key part in establishing Decoration Day, which evolved into today's Memorial Day holiday. The Grand Army reached its largest enrolment in 1890, with 490,000 members. In 1956, after the death of the last member, Albert Woolson, the brotherhood was formally dissolved. Its records are archived at the Library of Congress; its badges, flags and official seal at the Smithsonian Institution.

3 **Across from the Grand Army of the Republic memorial is a tall building with two conical towers: the headquarters of the National Council of Negro Women.**

Founded in 1935, the National Council of Negro Women is a consortium of women's organizations that advocates for women of African descent as they support their families and communities. Built as a hotel during the US Civil War, this entire structure was renovated in the 1980s by combining the hotel with the adjacent commercial structures facing Pennsylvania Avenue. Civil War photographer Mathew Brady (1822–96) had a studio on the upper floor of one of the buildings from 1858 until at

OPPOSITE: AMERICAN EAGLE DETAIL ON THE BASE OF THE GENERAL HANCOCK STATUE

DISTANCE 0.5 mile (0.8km)

ALLOW 1 hour (more with site visits)

START Archives-Navy Memorial-Penn Quarter Metro station

FINISH Metro Center station

least 1869. One of the most famous photographers of the 19th century, Brady is frequently described as the 'father of photojournalism'. His Civil War portraits and battlefield images conveyed the horror of the conflict to the American public. In the early days, Brady took his photo studio right onto the battlefields. However, he later employed over 20 other photographers, each of whom was given a travelling darkroom, while he stayed in Washington organizing the operation, perhaps due in part to his deteriorating eyesight. Abraham Lincoln was one of his subjects; his Lincoln photographs have been used for the $5 bill and the Lincoln penny. Although Brady died in New York City, his body was taken to Washington, where he was buried at Congressional Cemetery in the district of Capitol Hill.

4 Walk back towards the Grand Army of the Republic memorial and then proceed to Indiana Avenue, NW. Look at Nos. 637 to 641.

Many of the 19th-century commercial and residential buildings in the city centre were constructed during the boom in development that followed the US Civil War. However, these three structures, dating from 1817 to 1825, represent the streetscape that the thousands of Civil War soldiers marching in and out of Washington would have known.

5 Return to 7th Street and turn right, climbing a small hill. Look for No. 437 on the right.

In 1997, a government employee named Richard Lyons made a remarkable discovery in a sealed crawl space over the third floor of this building: US Civil War artefacts and documents that had been undisturbed for more than 100 years. They identified this structure as the office and residence of Clara Barton (1821–1912), a revered Civil War nurse. When the war broke out, Barton left her position at the US Patent Office and began organizing battlefield relief efforts, bringing supplies to army doctors and nurses. After the war, she located about 22,000 of the 62,000 missing soldiers. She went on to found the American Red Cross in 1881.

6 Continue along 7th Street to the intersection of F Street, NW. Turn left onto F Street at the Smithsonian American Art Museum.

This Smithsonian Museum was originally constructed to house the US Patent Office. Like nearly every other government building in the city, the Patent Office was used for the US Civil War effort. The First Rhode Island Regiment used it as barracks in 1861. Later, it was filled with 2,000 hospital beds for Union soldiers. The famous US poet Walt Whitman was one of the attendants nursing the wounded. The building took on a more festive mood in 1865 as the site for President Lincoln's Second Inaugural Ball. You can walk through the spaces used for this event when visiting the museum and can also find photographs taken by the Mathew Brady Studio as well as portraits of many Civil War-era Americans, including President and Mrs Abraham Lincoln.

SMITHSONIAN AMERICAN ART MUSEUM;
DAILY 11.30–7; www.americanart.si.edu

ABOVE: ENTRANCE TO THE HOME AND OFFICE OF CIVIL WAR NURSE CLARA BARTON

WHERE TO EAT

1 CAFÉ ATLANTICO,
405 8th Street, NW;
Tel: 1-202-393-0812.
Mexican, Latin American and Spanish cuisines come together in a converted fire station. $$

2 SUSHI AOI,
1100 New York Avenue, NW;
Tel: 1-202-408-7770.
Freshly made sushi and udon noodle soups presented in a Tokyo tech-pop dining room. $$

3 ELLA'S PIZZA,
901 F Street, NW;
Tel: 1-202-638-3434.
Brick-oven baked pizza served in a convivial atmosphere. $$

7 Looking at the Smithsonian American Art Museum, turn left and continue on F Street. Cross 9th Street, NW, passing especially fine examples of post-Civil War architecture. Midway on the left side of the street is an alleyway.

If you walk to the end of this alley and look to the right, you view the back of Ford's Theatre. On 14 April 1865, after shooting President Abraham Lincoln in the back of the skull, John Wilkes Booth fled the theatre. He had injured his left leg jumping from the presidential box to the stage. After limping to the horse he had waiting behind the building, Booth made his way along this alley to F Street. Although he managed to escape to Virginia, federal soldiers eventually surrounded the tobacco shed in which he was hiding. When it appeared that he would shoot his way out, the soldiers opened fire. Booth died shortly thereafter.

8 Follow F Street to 10th Street, NW. Turn right and proceed one block. On the right is St Patrick's Catholic Church.

The city's first Catholic church is also the first house of worship of any denomination founded in Washington. St Patrick's has been on this site since 1794, but the cornerstone for the current building was laid in 1872. Mary Surratt, whose son, John, was intimately involved with John Wilkes Booth in the plot to assassinate Abraham Lincoln, was arrested and put in prison two days after the president's death. She operated a boarding house on H Street, NW, where the men had met to plot the attack. Mary Surratt, along with three conspirators, was convicted and sentenced to death by hanging. Following her arrest, Mrs Surratt turned to St Patrick's priest, Father Jacob A. Walter, for comfort. A staunch defender of her innocence, Father Walter walked Surratt to the gallows on 7 July 1865, the day of her execution. Meanwhile, her son escaped to Canada and then went on to England and continental Europe. He was eventually arrested while living in Italy and sent back to the US, where he was put on trial but was later released following a mistrial in 1868.

9 Return to the F Street intersection, cross the road and continue along 10th Street. On the right is Ford's Theatre.

On 23 May 1865, rows of Union soldiers 60 abreast marched down Pennsylvania Avenue past the US president and General Ulysses S. Grant. So great were their numbers that the procession lasted six hours. They had descended upon America's capital to mark the conclusion of the US Civil War. A mournful air hung over the proceedings, however, because less than one week after Confederate General Robert E. Lee had surrendered, the country was stunned by the news that President Abraham Lincoln had been shot while attending a performance at Ford's Theatre on 14 April. Entrepreneur John T. Ford had recently reopened the venue, following a devastating fire. Now he faced a public demanding the closure of Ford's out of respect for the slain president. After receiving numerous communiqués threatening the destruction of the building and bodily harm to the owner, Ford complied. For almost 90 years, Ford's Theatre offered no live performances, instead serving intermittently as a museum, office space and a storage facility. Following a complete restoration, it reopened in 1968 as a venue for live theatre and a national historic site.

FORD'S THEATRE;

www.fordstheatre.org

10 Across the street from Ford's Theatre is Petersen House at 516 10th Street.

Doctors attending the theatre on 14 April immediately rushed to the wounded Abraham Lincoln. They ordered that the president be brought to the nearest bed, which turned out to be inside a back bedroom of this boarding house. It was here, after a sorrowful vigil, that Lincoln died on the morning of 15 April. He joined 620,000 Union and Confederate soldiers who had also died as a result of the Civil War, the deadliest in US history. Washington was about to embark on a period of unprecedented development, transforming from a muddy backwater town to the grand capital originally envisioned by the nation's first president, George Washington (1732–99). The full restoration of the Union, however, was the work of a contentious post-war era known as Reconstruction. The Reconstruction era lasted from 1866 to 1877 and describes the efforts by the federal government to integrate the southern states back into the Union following the Civil War. A key issue was how those states would develop the means of generating revenue and commercial viability after the dissolution of slavery, upon which much of the Southern economy had been based.

11 To get to Metro Center station, exit Petersen House, turn left and walk half a block to F Street, NW. Turn left on F Street and proceed through the intersections of 11th and 12th Streets, NW. The entrance to the station will be on the left at the corner of 12th and F Streets.

WALK 10

The Tragic Death of a Revered President

The streets of downtown Washington lead to the stately residence where an American president once lived and to the boarding house where he died.

As a young man, Abraham Lincoln (1809–65) 'feared of achieving nothing that would make men remember him'. A single gunshot fired ensured that he would never be forgotten. He served as president during the American Civil War (1861–65), the bloodiest conflict – fought between the North and the South – to have occurred on American soil. Washington was the mould in which Lincoln's momentous years in office were cast. Although the area adjacent to the White House has retained little of its Civil War-era character, if you know where to look, the events of Lincoln's time in the city come to life, whether you are studying a 20th-century office building or a Victorian terrace. The busy streets are much as they would have been in the 1860s, when the president himself made his way, except 21st-century Washingtonians benefit from pavements and Tarmac-covered roads, while in Lincoln's day it would have been a muddy slog. However you make your way, the climax of Lincoln's Washington story – that of the first US leader to be assassinated – was tragic.

1 From McPherson Square Metro station at the corner of I Street and Vermont Avenue, NW, cross I Street and then turn right, crossing 15th Street, NW onto McPherson Square.

As commander-in-chief of the US armed forces, President Abraham Lincoln bore ultimate responsibility for the conduct of the Civil War. At the war's outset in 1861, he had witnessed many army and navy officers resign their commission to serve the new 'country' called the Confederate States of America or the Confederacy, which was composed of breakaway southern states. Not so with Major General James Birdseye McPherson, who remained loyal to the president and commanded the Union's Army of the Tennessee. On 22 July 1864, while riding close to Confederate lines during the battle of Atlanta, Georgia, he was shot and killed. This memorial, in McPherson's honour, was unveiled in October 1876.

2 Cross back onto Vermont Avenue, walking past the Veterans' Administration Building. Look for a bronze plaque on the façade.

Those who work in this building are responsible for administering benefits for veterans, their families and survivors. The Veterans' Administration draws its mission statement from President Lincoln's second inaugural address, in which he wrestled with the moral and religious implications of the Civil War. In the speech's final paragraph, Lincoln delivered his prescription for the nation's recovery:

'With malice toward none, with charity for all...let us strive on to finish the work we are in, to bind up the nation's wounds, to care for him who shall have borne the battle and for his widow, and his orphan.'

3 Follow Vermont Avenue to the end of the block then turn right onto H Street, NW. At the intersection of H and 16th Streets, NW turn right and stand in front of the yellow Episcopal church on the corner.

Lincoln's secretary of state William H. Seward was a member of St John's Church, Lafayette Square. The president himself attended Sunday worship here at least once, but it was on weekdays that he would occasionally slip into a back pew on the south side of the sanctuary during evensong. He would wait until the service had begun and leave before it

OPPOSITE: THE PETERSEN HOUSE, WHERE PRESIDENT LINCOLN WAS TAKEN TO DIE; ABOVE: ST JOHN'S CHURCH

DISTANCE **1 mile (1.6km)**

ALLOW **1 hour (more with museum visits)**

START **McPherson Square Metro station (White House exit)**

FINISH **Metro Center station**

concluded so as not to draw attention to himself, such was his yearning for a few private moments of quiet contemplation.

4 Cross H Street into Lafayette Square, the park on the other side. Turn right and follow H Street to where it intersects with Jackson Place, NW. Turn left and walk along the 19th-century terrace until you come to No. 712.

The night Abraham Lincoln was assassinated proved dire for more than one of his Lafayette Square neighbours. Major Henry Rathbone lived at this house during the Lincoln presidency. It was Rathbone and his fiancée, Clara Harris, who had been invited to attend the theatre with the Lincolns on 14 April 1865, and witnessed the shooting of the president by John Wilkes Booth. Major Rathbone attempted to apprehend the assassin, but Booth stabbed him in the arm, causing Rathbone to let go. Booth fled the theatre and escaped. Rathbone never forgave himself and suffered great mental anguish as a result. So complete was his decline that in December 1893, he inexplicably shot and killed Clara and also stabbed himself repeatedly. He spent the remainder of his life institutionalized.

5 Follow Jackson Place to Pennsylvania Avenue, NW. Walk across, bearing left towards the White House.

The largest room in the White House is the splendid East Room, site of receptions, bill signings and concerts. Yet in 1865 it hosted a much more sombre occasion: the funeral of President Abraham Lincoln. It was not the first sorrowful event to take place in that room while the Lincolns resided there. On 20 April 1862, Willie Lincoln died in one of the upstairs bedrooms at age 11, most probably of typhoid fever. Reverend Phineas D. Gurley of New York Avenue Presbyterian Church presided over the little boy's funeral in the East Room. Willie was the second of Abraham Lincoln's four sons to die of illness, and both he and Mrs Lincoln were devastated. These confrontations with death may be the explanation for a dream Lincoln supposedly had three days before his assassination, in which he prefigured his own death. His friend, Ward Hill Lamon, recollected that the president dreamed he was awoken from sleep by wailing in the White House. After leaving his bedroom, he discovered another room containing only an open coffin with a wrapped corpse inside, and weeping soldiers guarding the coffin burst out, 'The president was killed by an assassin'.

WHERE TO EAT

1 BISTRO D'OC,
518 10th Street, NW;
Tel: 1-202-393-5444.
Family-owned restaurant featuring specialities from the Languedoc in France and other bistro fare. $$

2 CEIBA,
701 14th Street, NW;
Tel: 1-202-393-3983.
Contemporary Latin American cuisine served in a colourful dining room inspired by the Yucatan. $$

3 TOSCA,
1112 F Street, NW;
Tel: 1-202-367-1990.
Italian fine-dining with a hallmark of understated elegance. $$$

6 Cross Pennsylvania Avenue into Lafayette Square. Bear to the right, following the path towards the row of buildings on Madison Place, NW. Proceed to the entrance of the US Court of Claims, the large red-brick structure in the middle of the block.

Lincoln's near-neighbour on Lafayette Square was his secretary of state, William Seward, who resided in a large house that once stood on this site. Like Henry Rathbone, Seward had a traumatic night on 14 April 1865. An assassin working in league with John Wilkes Booth, named Lewis Powell, entered the Seward home with the intent of murdering him.

Booth and his cadre of Confederate sympathizers believed that the chaos of multiple murders committed on one night would throw the Union government into disarray, particularly if those killed included the highest-ranking government officials. Despite being stabbed in the attack, Seward survived and recovered from his wounds. He continued to function as secretary of state in the administration of Lincoln's vice president, Andrew Johnson.

7 Looking at the Court of Claims site, turn left and walk to the end of Madison Place. At the intersection of H Street, turn right. Cross 15th Street, NW. Soon after crossing 14th Street, look for New York Avenue Presbyterian Church on the right. The church is at the intersection of H Street and New York Avenue, NW.

In early 1861, President and Mrs Lincoln began to attend the New York Avenue Presbyterian Church and did so frequently throughout the Civil War. The church has preserved its Lincoln legacy by retaining the president's black hitching post that stands outside the stairs leading to the entrance. The family pew used by the Lincolns has been kept in its original condition in the sanctuary, and a stained-glass window depicts the president at prayer.

8 From there, turn right onto New York Avenue. Follow it one block to 14th Street and turn left onto 14th Street. Continue through G Street, NW and then to F Street, NW. Cross F Street and turn right. The first entrance on the left is to the Willard Intercontinental Hotel. To the right, off the lobby, is the Willard's 'Hall of History'.

This passageway conveys the unique niche in Washington history occupied by the Willard Hotel. Threat of assassination compelled Detective Daniel A. Pinkerton to smuggle President-elect Abraham Lincoln into the Willard at dawn on 23 February 1861. He and his family stayed until his inauguration 10 days later, returning to the hotel to watch the inaugural parade. Lincoln paid his bill upon receiving his first pay cheque as president – it came to $773.75.

9 Walk through the hotel's Peacock Alley to the main lobby and then exit through the main entrance onto Pennsylvania Avenue. Turn left and cross 14th Street to E Street, NW. Continue along E Street, past the National Theater, and on to 10th Street, NW. Cross 10th Street and turn left. The second building on the right is Ford's Theatre.

President Lincoln and the First Lady arrived at Ford's Theatre on 14 April 1865, after the play *Our American Cousin* had already begun. The couple was led to the presidential box, where Lincoln was seated in a rocking chair on the left-hand side. At about 9pm, John Wilkes Booth arrived at the theatre's back door, armed with a single-shot derringer and a hunting knife. Booth had actually appeared at Ford's Theatre

as an actor and knew his way around. He entered a narrow hallway between the Lincolns' box and the theatre's balcony, barricading the door. Booth was also familiar with the play and waited for the right moment: actor Harry Hawk would be on stage alone and laughter would muffle the sound of a gunshot. At approximately 10.15pm, Booth opened the door to the box and shot Lincoln in the back of the head at near point-blank range.

FORD'S THEATRE;

www.fordstheatre.org

10 Across 10th Street from Ford's Theatre is the Petersen House at No. 516.

Dr Charles Leale, a young Army surgeon, was attending Ford's Theatre on the night of Lincoln's assassination, and became the first doctor to reach Lincoln after the shooting. He and other physicians on hand quickly ascertained that the wound was mortal and ordered the president be removed from Ford's Theatre to the nearest bed. Lincoln was then taken across the street to this boarding house owned by William Petersen. Lincoln's oldest son Robert arrived, followed by secretary of the navy, Gideon Welles, and secretary of war, Edwin Stanton. While Mary Lincoln wept in the front parlour, Stanton took over the running of the US government from a small room adjacent to where Lincoln lay dying. Nothing could be done for the president, and he died on 15 April at 7.22am.

11 To get to Metro Center station, exit the Petersen House, turn left and walk half a block to F Street, NW. Turn left on F Street and proceed through the intersections of 11th and 12th Streets, NW. The station entrance will be on the left, at the corner of 12th and F Streets.

ABOVE: FORD'S THEATRE, WHERE PRESIDENT ABRAHAM LINCOLN WAS ASSASSINATED

WALK

11

Urban Scavenger Hunt in Penn Quarter

Penn Quarter, bordered to the south by Pennsylvania Avenue, is a vibrant area of the city centre where the 19th century meets the 21st.

Hip hotels, restaurants, luxury condominiums and some of Washington's newest tourist attractions have sprouted up in the area of central Washington recently christened Penn Quarter by developers. That most of these are housed in buildings constructed during the 1800s is what makes this walk an urban scavenger hunt to discover a bygone era – a time when Chinese, German and Italian immigrants lived and worked on and around 7th Street. Unlike other districts in Washington's city centre, Penn Quarter's historic legacy is evident almost everywhere you look, creating an outdoor museum of 19th-century residential, religious and government buildings. These provide the backdrop for a street scene bustling with residents, theatre- and cinema-goers, bar hoppers, and shoppers – especially at night. Yet what makes a walk through Penn Quarter particularly rewarding is discovering the stories behind the buildings – of the people who inhabited them a century ago. Follow this walk route to meet them.

1 Exiting Archives-Navy Memorial-Penn Quarter Metro station, turn right and then immediately right again, walking past a restaurant and bank to 7th Street, NW. Cross the street and continue along Indiana Avenue, NW to No. 641, the Artifactory Building.

Importer Dominick Cardella has used this 1817 commercial building for both work and home since 1972. He is the last businessman in Penn Quarter to live as the 19th-century immigrants once did, with their shops on the ground floor and their living accommodation above the shop. Cardella's emporium for African and Asian artefacts takes up the ground floor, he rents the first floor to an attorney, and lives in a spacious, light-filled loft on the second floor. If the shop is open, do stop in and say hello. Also, peek into No. 637 two doors away. It was formerly Litwin's Furniture, operated by the same family since the 1920s, when family-run furniture stores proliferated in the area. Although a national sandwich chain has taken over, the vintage Otis elevator has been preserved.

2 Double back to 7th Street and turn right. Continue to the intersection of F Street, NW, turn left, and proceed to the Hotel Monaco on the left.

This building, designed by architect Robert Mills (1781–1855), who also designed the Washington Monument, served as the city's General Post Office between 1842 and 1897. German immigrants who started arriving in the

city from the 1850s on might have sought a job in one of those offices; for people who had held positions as clerks, accountants or even messengers back home, a major government agency like the post office offered good potential employment. In 2000, the then-vacant building underwent a stunning restoration to turn it into a luxury hotel.

3 Across F Street from the Hotel Monaco is the Smithsonian Museum of American Art and National Portrait Gallery.

Construction for this structure, designed by Robert Mills and originally the US Patent Office, began in 1836. In addition to its employees, the building drew more than 100,000 visitors annually as the de facto national museum, before the Smithsonian Castle was completed in 1855. Boyd's *Washington City Directory* wrote, 'You may see the models of most

OPPOSITE: ENTERING CHINATOWN; ABOVE: LILLIAN AND ALBERT SMALL JEWISH MUSEUM

DISTANCE **1 mile (1.6km)**

ALLOW **1.5 hours (more with museum visits)**

START **Archives-Navy Memorial-Penn Quarter Metro station**

FINISH **Judiciary Square Metro station (F Street exit)**

everything that has ever been invented or grown out of the Yankee brain'. For a young German immigrant renting a room on 6th Street, NW, the Patent Office provided inspiration. Emile Berliner, with no background in science but blessed with a patient landlady who allowed him to string wires between the house and the barn out at the back, invented a microphone that captured the human voice via magnetic current: it revolutionized telephone technology. Berliner later developed a means of recording sound vibrations on the sides of a groove spiralled onto a flat disk: this evolved into the long-playing record. He filed patents for these as well as his other inventions at this building.

SMITHSONIAN AMERICAN ART MUSEUM;

DAILY 11.30–7; www.americanart.si.edu

4 Double back to 7th Street and turn left. After you cross G Street, NW, notice the Chinese characters on the shop fronts, signalling that you have

entered the Chinatown district. The name of the bank on the corner of 7th and G Streets is Oriental Business Association (OBA). Surprisingly, it was founded by German rather than Chinese immigrants. The pediments of Nos. 714 and 718 7th Street still bear the names of the original immigrant business owners and residents. Proceed to the intersection of 7th and H Streets, NW.

The world's largest single-span Chinese arch designates the heart of what was once a small but thriving Chinatown. Chinese immigrants first arrived in Washington in the 1880s, having journeyed from the western states, where work had become scarce and discrimination common. They initially settled along Pennsylvania Avenue, not far from the US Capitol, but in 1931 the community was forced to relocate to the H Street area to make way for the construction of a municipal centre. Later, in the mid 1980s, part of the new Chinatown was again displaced to enable the construction of the Washington Convention Center. Although most Chinese-American families have since moved out of the city centre to live in the suburbs, their restaurants and shops have remained in this district. A current form of economic prosperity for the Chinese-Americans is the express bus service that they operate between Washington and New York City.

5 Turn left onto H Street and continue to 8th Street, NW. Turn right on 8th Street and proceed to the imposing Greater New Hope Baptist Church.

In the mid-19th century, Washington's Jewish population was largely of German origin. The first Jewish congregation formed as Washington Hebrew in 1852. Eleven years later, the members purchased a church located on this site, altering its appearance to reflect the Jewish faith. By 1897, Washington Hebrew was able to replace that building with the one you see today (although it is missing the original onion domes that topped the towers). The synagogue was the largest in the city and a vital resource for the many Jews who lived in the area. When many of its members opted for life in the suburbs, Washington Hebrew built a new synagogue in northwest Washington, selling its former home to Greater New Hope Baptist Church in 1954.

6 Looking at the church, turn right and proceed to I Street, NW. Turn right again and follow it across 7th Street, to the intersection of 6th and I Streets, NW.

By the early 1860s, Washington Hebrew Congregation began to introduce reform practices into the services, allowing women to sit with men and using English or German for the sermon and some prayers. When the congregation bought an organ in 1869, 38 members resigned to form a more traditional Orthodox congregation called Adas Israel. In 1908, having outgrown their small wooden synagogue, Adas Israel moved into the gracious domed building on the corner. Like Washington Hebrew, Adas Israel's members also relocated to the suburbs in the 1940s and 1950s, inspiring

WHERE TO EAT

1 MATCHBOX,
713 H Street, NW;
Tel: 1-202-289-4441.
The brick oven is always busy baking New York-style pizza. $$

2 OYAMEL COCINA MEXICANA,
401 7th Street, NW;
Tel: 1-202-628-1005.
Chef José Andrés creates innovative dishes inspired by the urban fare of Mexico City. $$

3 TEASIM,
400 8th Street, NW;
Tel: 1-202-638-6010
Simple and delicious Bento boxes from Japan, curries from Thailand, and tandoor breads from India. $$

construction of a third worship space in northwest Washington. In 1952, the 6th and I Historic Synagogue became the Turner Memorial African-American Episcopal Church. The church remained here for nearly 50 years before putting the building on the market in 2001. The estate agent's brochure described the structure as 'suitable for a nightclub'. Alarmed that such an important reminder of the city's Jewish odyssey was in peril, the Jewish Historical Society worked with three prominent Washington developers with historic ties to the building to purchase it for $5 million. The synagogue was restored to its 1908 state and now offers Friday-evening Shabbat services and Saturday worship, as well as concerts and lectures, echoing its original use as a gathering place for Jewish Washington.

7 Turn right and proceed along 6th Street to the corner of 6th and H Streets. The large apartment house on the corner is Wah Luck House.

More than 200 Chinese-American families, many of them senior citizens, lost their homes when displaced by the construction of the Washington Convention Center on the western edge of Chinatown in the 1980s. Wah Luck House was built in 1982, in exchange for the loss of housing. It is one of the few residences in the area still occupied by Chinese-Americans.

8 Cross H Street and turn left, following H Street one block to 5th Street, NW. Turn right on 5th Street and stand in front of St Mary Mother of God Catholic Church.

This is a remarkable spot in Penn Quarter: a small campus of religious structures developed by German Catholic immigrants soon after arriving in Washington. The Gothic church was constructed in 1890. The rectory next door came next, followed by what used to be St Mary's Orphanage and St Mary's School. (The orphanage building can be seen at the end of the alley that runs next to the school.) Each is a testament to the German Catholics' desire to meet the spiritual and social needs of its immigrant congregation, as well as providing a means of maintaining a German identity. Notice the sign advertising worship in Cantonese, a nod to the Chinese-Americans who eventually moved into the parish.

9 Follow 5th Street to G Street and turn left. Proceed along two long blocks to 3rd Street, NW. You will pass the enormous General Accountability Office headquarters on the left and the stately National Building Museum on the right. At the terminus of G Street at 3rd Street you will see the first synagogue constructed in Washington.

When the 38 members of Washington Hebrew left to form their own congregation, they initially prayed in rented spaces while they raised funds to build a synagogue of their own. By 1876, the congregation had raised $4,800 and built their new synagogue in the heart of the Jewish community – at the southeast corner of 6th and G Streets, NW. The synagogue is the oldest in the nation's capital and among the oldest in the country. The most distinctive feature is the original, semi-circular, protruding Aron Kodesh (Holy Ark), the cabinet at the front of a synagogue in which the sacred Torah scrolls are kept. In 1968, the synagogue was slated for demolition when the Washington Metropolitan Area Transit Authority acquired the entire city block for its new headquarters. The Jewish Historical Society mobilized the community, saving the building with assistance from local and federal governments. On 18 December 1969, the 237-ton synagogue was moved three city blocks to its current site. After it was moved, it reopened as the Lillian and Albert Small Jewish Museum.

LILLIAN AND ALBERT SMALL JEWISH MUSEUM;

OPEN BY APPOINTMENT; www.jhsgw.org

10 Turn right and walk one block along 3rd Street to the small Holy Rosary Catholic Church on the left.

A sizeable number of Italians emigrated to Washington at the turn of the 20th century. Many were skilled masons brought in to build and adorn monumental public buildings, such as the Library of Congress and Union Station. They were frequently shunned by the more established Catholics in the city, prompting the new Italian community to request an Italian-speaking priest. In 1916, this land was purchased and in 1919 work began on Holy Rosary Catholic Church, which from its inception has promoted and preserved Italian Catholic heritage and culture.

In fact, the order of priests serving the church, the Scalabrini Missionaries, has as its purpose the pastoral and social care of migrants from Italy. Italian language classes are offered at Casa Italiana, the parish hall next door to the church.

11 From Holy Rosary, turn right onto F Street. Walk one block and then look for the entrance to the Judiciary Square Metro station. It is located across the street from the National Building Museum.

WALK 12

History and Culture in Foggy Bottom

The Foggy Bottom Historic District, one of Washington's oldest neighbourhoods, is an oasis of calm in the middle of this fast-paced city.

Originally a little port town called Hamburg, Foggy Bottom was later the site of two breweries, a gas works and other light industry. While the district has lost its industrial character, you can still explore Foggy Bottom's alleys and courts and discover the neat rows of houses that blue-collar workers called home. One of the smallest residential areas in the city, Foggy Bottom's historic district is tucked away between the George Washington University campus and the Rock Creek Parkway. It's a place of contrasts between high rises and small terraced houses, peaceful alleyways and relentless traffic. One moment you'll be standing before some of the tiniest houses in Washington, the next you'll be exploring the Watergate complex, one of the city's largest residential developments. The finale to any walk through Foggy Bottom is a visit to the John F. Kennedy Center for the Performing Arts. Time your walk to finish around 6pm, when free daily performances sponsored by the Kennedy Center begin.

1 **Step outside Foggy Bottom Metro station and turn right onto 23rd Street, NW, passing a large bust of the George Washington University's namesake. Notice a dorm named after First Lady Jacqueline Kennedy across the street. She earned a BA here. Proceed to St Mary's Church at 728 23rd Street.**

Two years after the US Civil War (1861–65), a group of newly emancipated slaves formed an Episcopal congregation, called St Mary's, and began worshipping at the refurbished Union Army Chapel, on the site of the present St Mary's Church. In 1887, assisted financially by the congregations of St John's Lafayette Square and the Church of the Epiphany, St Mary's hired Smithsonian Institution architect James Renwick (1818–95) to design this church. The Foggy Bottom district was the recipient of the church's various ministries through the years, including the organization of one of the first Boys Clubs in the city, a clinic for infants, sewing and cooking schools, and facilities for mentally disabled children. It is the oldest African-American Episcopal congregation in Washington.

2 **Continue along 23rd Street to the intersection of G Street, NW. Turn right and then right again on 24th Street, NW. At No. 725 is St Mary's Court.**

Parishioners from St Mary's Church urged the Episcopal Diocese of Washington to create affordable housing for senior citizens here in Foggy Bottom. St Mary's Court is the result of those efforts. Over 150 senior citizens reside here in individual apartments. The Episcopal Diocese continues to sponsor the residence, with the Department of Housing and Urban Development providing the funding.

3 **Follow 24th Street past St Mary's Court to the intersections of I Street and New Hampshire Avenue, NW. Bear right onto New Hampshire Avenue. Continue until it intersects with Washington Circle. Carefully cross the street onto the circle.**

Washington Circle has always been an important crossroads in northern Foggy Bottom, originally connecting the area to Lafayette Park to the east and Georgetown to the west. The vistas down Pennsylvania Avenue and K Street are amazing for around 12 blocks. See for yourself via a promenade around the circle. The equestrian statue of George Washington captures a crucial moment in the American War of Independence: a surprise attack on the British forces at Princeton and Trenton, New Jersey. This was the first memorial to Washington in the city, unveiled in 1860.

4 **Exit the circle onto Pennsylvania Avenue. Follow it one block to 24th Street, NW. On the corner across the street is 2401 Pennsylvania Avenue.**

Examine the exterior of this building closely. The architectural firm of Keyes Condon Florance added a few whimsical touches to this office building, erected

OPPOSITE: FOUNTAIN IN THE MAIN ENTRANCE OF THE MASSIVE WATERGATE COMPLEX

DISTANCE 1 mile (1.6km)

ALLOW 1 hour

START Foggy Bottom Metro station

FINISH Foggy Bottom Metro station

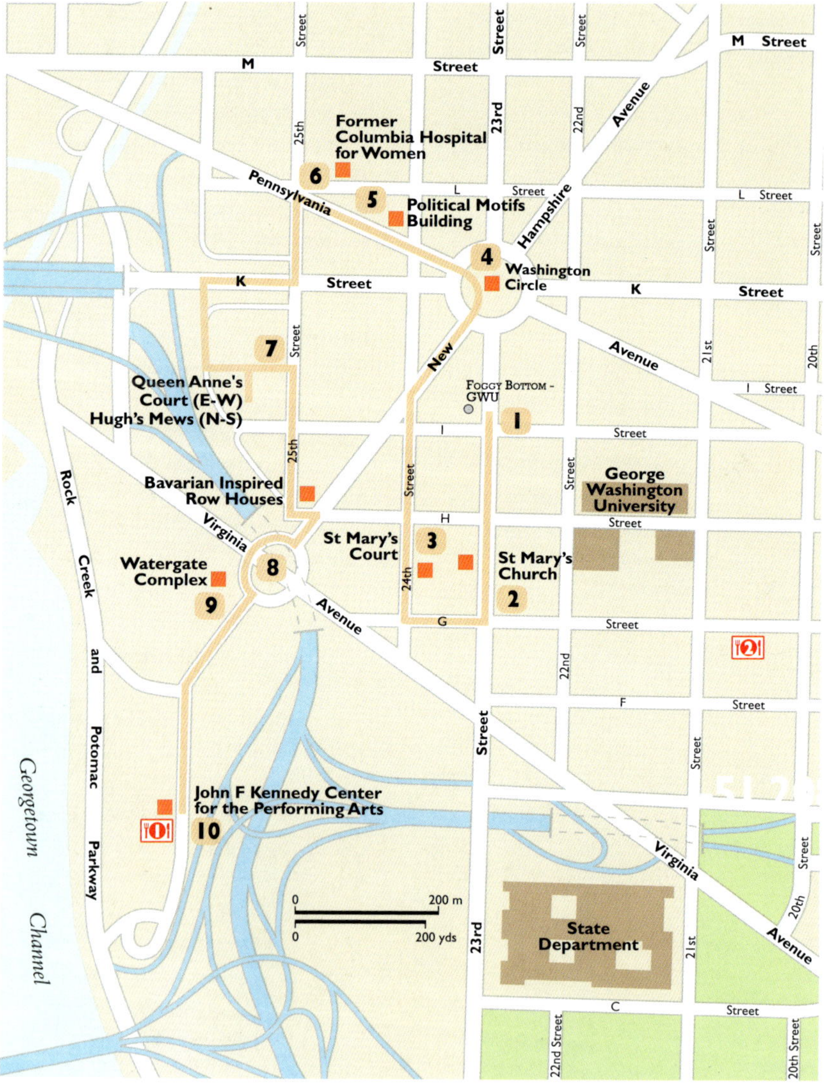

in 1991. What better than political motifs for a building with a Pennsylvania Avenue address? Elephants, symbolizing the Republican Party, and donkeys, for the Democrats, form the brackets holding the cables that support the ground-floor canopies. A stars and stripes 'banner' unfurls along the roofline right into the US and District of Columbia flags.

5 Continue one block to the intersection of 25th Street, NW. Across the street is the Columbia Residences of Washington, DC.

Some of the female homeowners residing in this handsome condominium may have memories of giving birth here when the building housed the Columbia Hospital for Women. The hospital was founded during the US Civil War to assist destitute women, many of whom had arrived in the city seeking information about relatives who were injured or imprisoned. The enormous Ringgold House, built here in 1812, was converted into a hospital in 1872 and was then razed to the ground in 1914, when the structure now occupied by the condominiums was built. Columbia Hospital for Women closed in 2002.

6 Turn left onto 25th Street, NW from Pennsylvania Avenue. Cross K Street and then turn right onto K Street. One block later, turn left onto 26th Street, NW. The first left is Queen Anne's Court. Turn into it and then turn right into Hugh's Mews. At the end of the alley is a group of tiny terraced houses.

WHERE TO EAT

1 KC CAFÉ,
John F. Kennedy Center for the Performing Arts,
New Hampshire Avenue, NW and Rock Creek Parkway;
Tel: 1-202-416-8555.
Upmarket cafe on the roof terrace of the Kennedy Center, perfect for a quick bite before a performance. $$

2 TONIC RESTAURANT AT QUIGLEY'S PHARMACY,
2036 G Street, NW;
Tel: 1-202-296-0211.
Historic drug store on the George Washington University campus, serving comfort food with a twist. $$

During the first half of the 19th century, Foggy Bottom was a working-class riverfront settlement populated largely by Irish and German immigrants. Two breweries and the Washington Gas Light Company offered employment, and these alley houses provided inexpensive accommodation. Once the area's identity had shifted from industry to a precinct of government headquarters, the original homeowners moved on. Houses like these were then occupied by poorer, disenfranchised residents who could not afford to move. Living conditions in the alleys had deteriorated to such a sorry state that by the 1950s, large swathes of Foggy Bottom were selected for urban renewal. Some, but not all, of the alley houses were selected for preservation.

This explains the juxtaposition of the small-scale alley houses to the looming high rises constructed around them.

7 Exit Hugh's Mews and turn right onto Queen Anne's Court. At the intersection of 25th Street, turn right and proceed along 25th Street.

You are passing through the heart of the small Foggy Bottom Historic District. The Flemish gables, tall, narrow lancet windows and peaked lintels adorning the terraced houses on this block were designed to remind the Germans who emigrated to Foggy Bottom in the 19th century of their homeland architecture.

8 At the end of 25th Street is the massive Watergate complex.

Before it became synonymous with political scandal, the term Watergate was a direct allusion to the water gate at the edge of the Potomac River, due west of the Lincoln Memorial and flanking the Arlington Memorial Bridge. The Water Gate Inn once stood near this site and a floating water-gate barge once hosted concerts. The presidential political scandal received its name from the Watergate office building, where Republican operatives broke into the Democratic National Committee headquarters. This huge development was constructed between 1965 and 1971 and included three apartments, one office and one hotel building placed in a garden setting overlooking the Potomac. Italian architect Luigi Moretti (1907–73) was said to have been inspired by the beautiful curvilinear terraces in Bath, England. Unfortunately for local residents, the complex blocks what used to be an unobstructed view of the river. You can glimpse the water if you go into the building, towards the back.

9 Looking at the main entrance of the Watergate complex, turn left onto New Hampshire Avenue, NW. You will pass the Saudi Arabian Embassy on the left and then arrive at the stairway leading to the John F. Kennedy Center for the Performing Arts.

Dedicated in 1971, the Kennedy Center is not only the largest performing arts venue in the city, but also the Washington memorial to President John F. Kennedy, who was assassinated in 1963. It's an active place, with performances every day of the year by groups such as the Washington National Opera and National Symphony Orchestra in addition to ballet, theatre and jazz. Each day at 6pm the Millennium Stage presents a wide variety of free programmes. Visit the gift shop, take a tour, and, without question, take the lift up to the roof terrace and step outside. More splendid, panoramic views of the Potomac riverfront cannot be found.

10 An easy way to return to Foggy Bottom Metro station is to catch a free shuttle bus from outside the front entrance of the Kennedy Center. The red minibuses run from morning until the last performance of the day, transporting Kennedy Center guests to and from the station.

OPPOSITE: THE GRAND FOYER OF THE JOHN F. KENNEDY CENTER FOR THE PERFORMING ARTS

THE JOHN F. KENNEDY CENTER, THE LARGEST PERFORMING ARTS VENUE IN THE CITY

WALK 13

Elegant Circles and Squares

Discover Logan Circle, the city's only unaltered Victorian residential district, just a short walk from the heart of downtown Washington.

Few areas of Washington have witnessed the dramatic change and breathtaking renaissance of Logan Circle, which evolved from rural obscurity to an enclave of elegance, home to wealthy white and later African-American residents. If you're a fan of Victorian Gothic Revival architecture, this walk is for you. If you're fascinated by the dynamics of urban neighbourhoods, consider the residents of Logan Circle: their tenacity and vision preserved the historic district when it teetered on the brink of decline. Today, it is one of the most sought-after addresses in Washington. Impressive restoration and renovation continues, and restaurants and shops multiply. This is a fun expedition to set out on in the afternoon. As the hapless commuters climb into their cars to battle traffic, you'll be following the denizens of Logan Circle home on foot, soon to be walking their dogs in the shadow of John Logan's statue. Then it's on to a cafe or bar for a quick drink before dinner. You'll be finishing your walk just in time to join them.

1 Leave McPherson Square Metro station, 14th Street exit, and turn right. From the corner of 14th and I Streets, NW cross I Street and then turn right to cross 14th Street into Franklin Square. Standing along the 14th Street side of the park is a statue of Commodore John Barry.

From 1920 on, Irish-Americans decided to mark St Patrick's Day by processing from St Patrick's Roman Catholic Church some blocks away to lay a wreath at the feet of this statue. Barry, a young Irish-American sea captain, became the first American naval officer to capture an enemy ship during the War of American Independence (1775–83). Congress erected this monument at the request of Irish-Americans, who attended the unveiling ceremony in the thousands on 16 May 1914.

2 Walk across the park to the other side, which is bordered by 13th Street, NW. The exuberant Victorian Franklin School will come into view. Look towards the top of the building for a small bust of Benjamin Franklin (1706–90), the US statesman, scientist and inventor after whom the school (and the square) was named.

Completed in 1869, Franklin School was designed by German-born Adolf Cluss (1825–1905), one of Washington's most influential and progressive architects. Cluss's ideas on how to build modern, multi-roomed state schools with adequate ventilation and space for students and teachers reflect the influence of the socialist circles he had been part of before emigrating to the US. At the time, the Franklin School was considered to be an outstanding Washington state school located in what was then a fashionable residential area. However, when these homeowners moved out of Franklin Square to the area northwest of the city centre, the district began a slow decline, reaching its nadir in the 1970s and 1980s, when prostitution, pornography and the drug trade infested what was left of the glorious 19th-century built environment. Developers took matters into their own hands in 1990, commencing with a transformation of Franklin Square into a precinct of commercial office buildings.

3 Return to 14th Street along K Street, NW. At the intersection of K and 14th Streets, turn right and proceed on 14th Street until it intersects with Thomas Circle. Bear to the left and travel around the circle until you reach the steps of National City Christian Church.

Thomas Circle, named after General George H. Thomas, whose statue stands in its centre, first developed as a quiet area of handsome townhouses framed by the beautiful Victorian gas lamps that illuminated the circle's perimeter. Located at the intersection of what became three major Washington thoroughfares, Thomas Circle was probably destined to be overtaken by the automobile in the 20th century, as the numerous traffic lanes winding around it prove. The National City Christian Church was completed

OPPOSITE: THE UNSPOILT VICTORIAN GOTHIC REVIVAL ARCHITECTURE OF LOGAN CIRCLE

DISTANCE 1.5 miles (2.5km)

ALLOW 1.5 hours (more with museum visit)

START McPherson Square Metro station (14th Street exit)

FINISH McPherson Square Metro station (14th Street exit)

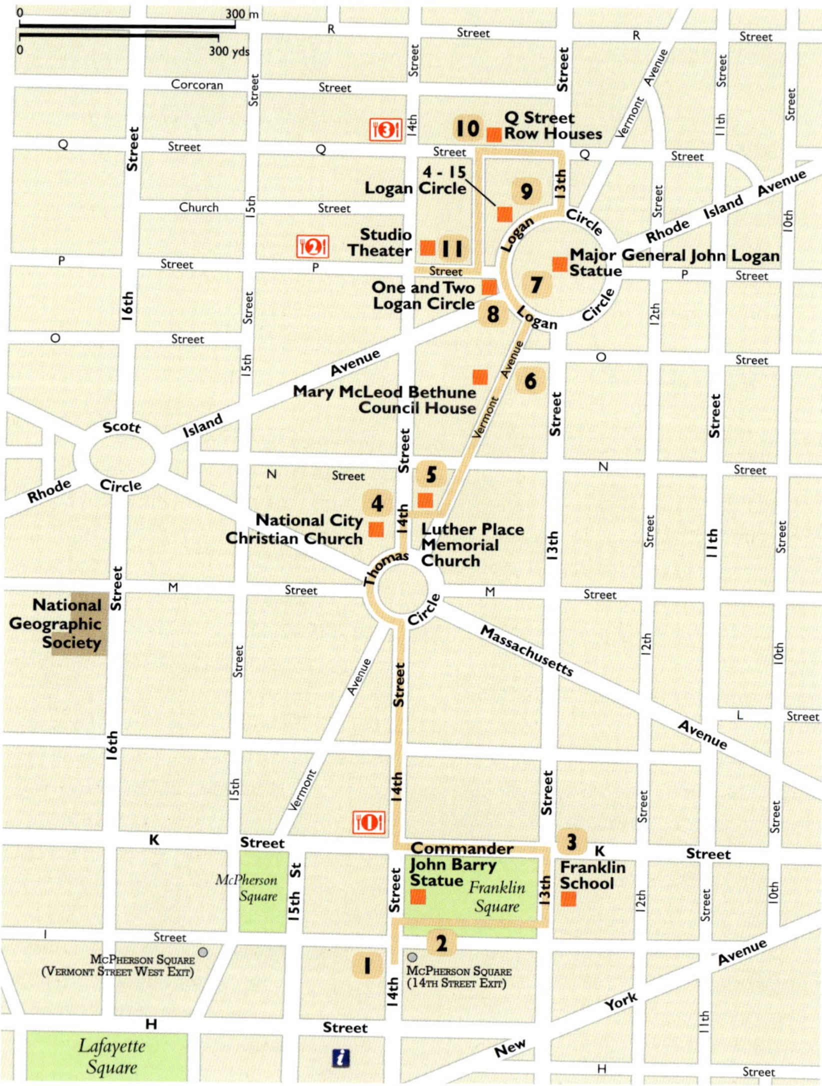

in 1930 by the Disciples of Christ, a Protestant denomination based in North America. The original sanctuary still stands nearby on Vermont Avenue, NW. The limestone edifice cost $1.2 million and was designed by John Russell Pope (1874–1937), architect of the Thomas Jefferson Memorial.

4 **Cross 14th Street to Luther Place Memorial Church.**

Soon after the US Civil War (1861–65), Lutherans in Washington built this church as a memorial to peace. It is the only remaining evidence of the 19th-century Thomas Circle, its High Victorian Gothic Revival style rendering it particularly impressive. The church did not receive its present name until the unveiling of the statue of Martin Luther (1483–1546), German theologian and leader of the Protestant Reformation, in May 1884. It is a copy of a statue in Worms, Germany, and was erected to commemorate the 400th anniversary of Luther's birth.

5 **Facing the statue of Martin Luther, turn right onto Vermont Avenue and begin your walk into the heart of the Logan Circle Historic District. The church on the left, Mount Olivet Lutheran Church, occupies the building first used by the Disciples of Christ for worship. The houses you will pass next were built between 1874 and 1876. Stop in front of No. 1318.**

The Mary McLeod Bethune Council House honours one of the most remarkable African-American leaders of the 20th century. A tireless educator born to former slaves, Mary McLeod Bethune (1875–1955) is best known for founding a school in 1904 that later became part of Bethune-Cookman University in Daytona Beach, Florida. One of the few women in the world to serve as a college president at that time, she was later a member of President Franklin D. Roosevelt's Black Cabinet. In 1935, Bethune founded the National Council of Negro Women, bringing together 28 different organizations to form a council to facilitate the improvement of quality of life for African-American women and

WHERE TO EAT

1 DC COAST,
1401 K Street, NW;
Tel: 1-202-216-5988.
Knock-out dining room serving the coastal cuisines of the Mid-Atlantic, Gulf of Mexico and West Coast. $$$

2 LOGAN TAVERN,
1423 P Street, NW;
Tel: 1-202-332-3710.
Upscale but casual restaurant serving sophisticated comfort food. Don't miss the Bloody Mary menu during weekend brunch. $$

3 RICE,
1608 14th Street, NW;
Tel: 1-202-234-2400.
Imaginative Thai restaurant, with a Zen-like atmosphere. $$

children. She bought this house in 1943, making it the first headquarters of that organization, and lived there until 1949. **MARY MCLEOD BETHUNE COUNCIL HOUSE;** MON–SAT 9–5; WWW.NPS.GOV/MAMC

6 Continue to follow Vermont Avenue until it intersects with Logan Circle. Cross the street to the circle itself, standing in front of the equestrian statue of Major General John Logan.

John A. Logan was a member of the House of Representatives from Illinois when the US Civil War broke out in 1861. He recruited the 31st Illinois Regiment and was promoted to colonel. He became tremendously popular among veterans as someone who would champion their cause. For example, Logan and his wife were instrumental in organizing the first Memorial Day in 1868. A US federal holiday, Memorial Day is observed on the last Monday of May and commemorates US men and women who perished while in military service. The Logans lived at 4 Logan Circle between 1884 and 1885, when this was called Iowa Circle. It was not until 1930 that Congress passed a law changing the name to Logan. The statue was unveiled in 1901. It is unique in Washington in that the elaborate pedestal is made of bronze, not granite. A figure representing Peace is north of the statue; and one representing War on the south. Panels on the east and west sides depict Logan as statesman and general.

7 Across from the Logan statue is a large, white, Second Empire style building at Nos. 1 and 2 Logan Circle.

After the US Civil War, impressive homes such as this began to appear on what had been considered barren land. These substantial adjoining townhouses were built in 1878 and are a typical example of the architectural style known as Second Empire, which was popular with wealthy Victorian-era Washingtonians between the 1850s and 1880s. A hipped or mansard roof, porthole windows and a double entranceway are all characteristic of this style. In 1921, the building was converted to apartments and began a slow period of decline. By the 1970s, the entire area was infested with prostitutes and drug addicts. This was the first property to be restored

ABOVE: LOGAN CIRCLE Q STREET ROW HOUSES

by a developer after years of neglect. The P N Hoffman company purchased it in 1998 and lovingly brought it back to life.

8 From 1 and 2 Logan Circle, cross P Street, NW and look at the houses at numbers 4 to 15 Logan Circle.

Logan Circle has a variety of High Victorian-era residential buildings and is one of only two circles in Washington to have retained its residential character completely. Not all of the houses, however, are original. Can you spot the new construction at 27 to 30 Logan Circle? The row of eclectic homes in front of you, however, is authentic, the façades having changed little since the residences were first constructed. A few remain family homes, though most have been subdivided, a trend that began in the 1940s. From the 1930s, prominent African-Americans began to inhabit many of these homes. No. 8 belonged to Belford V. Lawson and Marjorie M. Lawson, an esteemed lawyer and the first black woman to serve on a local court in Washington. Their neighbour at No. 11 was Charles Manuel 'Sweet Daddy' Grace, founder of the United House of Prayer, an African-American church with millions of members throughout the world.

9 Just after No. 15, bear right onto 13th Street, NW. Proceed one block to Q Street, NW then turn left. Notice the row of brightly coloured houses.

These homes, constructed between 1876 and 1878, are perfect examples of the rows of middle-class speculative houses built throughout Washington in the late 19th and early 20th centuries. They are joined by party walls, and ornamental detail has been placed only on the buildings' facades. Builders often ordered prefabricated materials for these houses from catalogues in order to keep expenses down. This meant that owners of modest means could duplicate, on a smaller scale, the mansions of the well-to-do.

10 Follow Q Street to the intersection of Kingman Place, NW and turn right. The modest homes on this block were built to house lower-income residents who might have worked for the wealthy home owners on the circle. At the intersection of P Street, turn right, stopping at the corner of 14th and P Streets.

The Studio Theater moved to this space in 1987, a pioneer in an area few businesses were willing to consider investing in. This building was formerly occupied by Petrovitch Motors, one of the numerous car dealerships and showrooms that sprang up along 14th Street from the 1920s on. The enormous windows were to provide optimal viewing of the shiny new cars inside.

11 To get back to McPherson Square Metro, turn left and follow 14th Street to Thomas Circle. Bear right, walking halfway around the circle and exiting back onto 14th Street. Cross L and K Streets, NW. The station is at the intersection of 14th and I Streets, NW.

THOMAS CIRCLE, NAMED AFTER GENERAL GEORGE H. THOMAS, WHOSE STATUE IS IN ITS CENTRE

WALK 14

A Feast for the Senses at Kalorama

Kalorama – Greek for 'beautiful view' – certainly lives up to its name, with its natural ambience, elegant mansions and international flavour.

Joel Barlow named the estate he purchased in 1807 Kalorama for the expansive views it enjoyed in its elevated position. The 90 acres (36 hectares) remained intact until 1887, when they were divided into smaller plots. The development that followed retained the hilly character, topography and densely planted trees, with the entire northern boundary of the district overlooking the picturesque Rock Creek Park. Undoubtedly the most beautiful part of Washington, Kalorama has always been a prime residential area, with its urban mansions located on the high ground between Massachusetts and Connecticut Avenues, the enclave seen on this walk. You start by ascending the Spanish Steps to reach the heights where Washington's diplomatic community is evident everywhere you look – many of the residences are occupied by ambassadors or function as embassies. Old phone boxes that once had a direct line to the police or fire brigade punctuate the area and are now considered works of art.

1 Leave Dupont Circle Metro station from the Q Street exit, turn right onto 20th Street, NW and follow it to the intersection of R Street, NW. Turn left onto R Street. At the intersection of 22nd Street, NW turn right. Proceed for one block and you will arrive at the Decatur Terrace Steps (also known as the Spanish Steps), at the intersection of 22nd Street and Decatur Place, NW.

Notice the two police and fire-brigade phone boxes on the corner. These were installed throughout Washington from the 1860s on, before the advent of the 911 emergency services. Too large and heavy to be removed after they became obsolete, the phone boxes have been 'reinvented' by Cultural Tourism DC as works of art. You'll find several on this route. Across the road from the phone boxes is 2145 Decatur Place. Today, the Thai ambassador resides in this house. Notice how the garden terrace and house itself act as a massive retaining wall for the Decatur Terrace slope. Martha Codman was the original owner, her cousin Ogden Codman, Jr having designed the house for her in 1907. Both would have been society celebrities to their Kalorama neighbours: Martha contributed to Edith Wharton's classic book *Decoration of Houses*, which Wharton co-wrote with Ogden. Moreover, Ogden was the architect of choice for the wealthy Vanderbilts and Rockefellers of New York.

2 Climb the Decatur Terrace Steps to S Street, NW. At the top of the steps on the right is 1743 22nd Street, NW.

A noted palaeontologist, Charles D. Wolcott became secretary of the Smithsonian Institution in 1907, just two years after completing this Italianate mansion. The cheerful panda sculpture greeting visitors was one of dozens on display throughout Washington during a public art exhibition called Pandamania.

3 Turn right onto S Street and then left onto Phelps Place, NW. At the intersection of California Street, NW is Our Lady, Queen of the Americas Roman Catholic Church on the left.

The entrance to the church is at 2200 California Street. At 1836 Phelps Place is the entrance to what was St Rose's Industrial School, founded in 1872 to educate orphan girls in home economics and other domestic arts. It is one of the few buildings in Kalorama that was not built as a residence.

4 Turn left on California Street then right onto 23rd Street, NW. On the corner of 23rd and Wyoming Streets, NW is 2300 Wyoming Street.

Anthony Francis Lucas was the original owner of this mansion. A mechanical engineer who had emigrated from Croatia, Lucas was responsible for the first successful oil well at Spindletop oil field in southeast Texas, turning unassuming Beaumont into one of the first oil boomtowns. On 10 January 1901, a gas eruption occurred, followed by a stream of crude oil spewing up nearly 200ft (60m). The eruption lasted nine days.

OPPOSITE: THE WOODROW WILSON HOUSE, WHERE THE PRESIDENT LIVED AFTER HIS TERM OF OFFICE

DISTANCE **1 mile (1.6km)**

ALLOW **1 hour (more with museum visit)**

START **Dupont Circle Metro station (Q Street exit)**

FINISH **Dupont Circle Metro station (Q Street exit)**

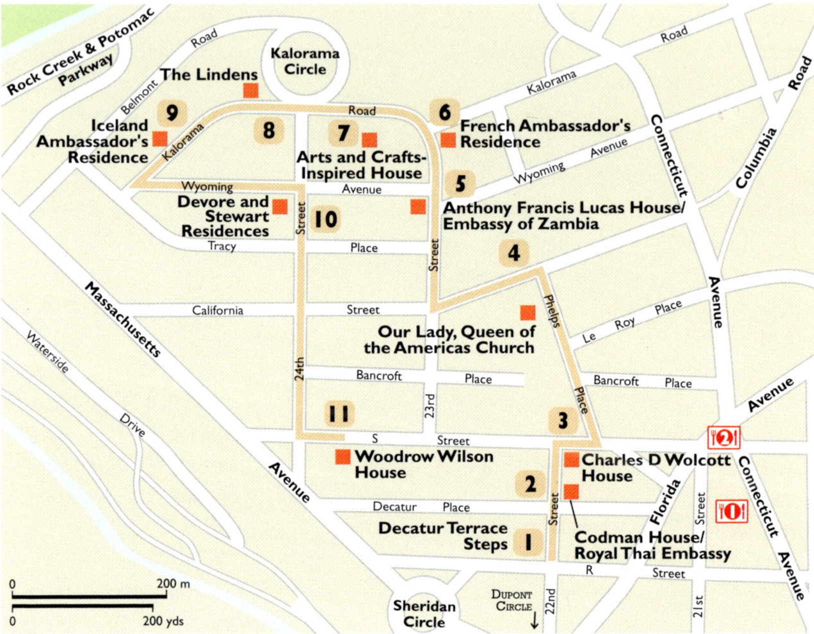

5 Continue along 23rd Street. At the next intersection it becomes Kalorama Road. Soon after the intersection, on the right at No. 2221, is an enormous house that resembles a Tudor country manor.

This is the largest house in Kalorama. It was constructed in 1911 for William Watson Lawrence, a successful businessman from Pittsburgh, Pennsylvania. It was designed by Jules H. de Sibour, architect of many Embassy Row and Kalorama mansions. When Watson died, he was living in New York City and had no heirs, so he willed all his Washington property to his two unmarried sisters who resided here. The government of France purchased the house in 1936 for about $400,000, including furnishings. It has been the French ambassador's residence ever since.

6 One block further along Kalorama Road and across the street is No. 2340.

Built in 1928, this house was designed not as an Italianate or French mansion, but in the Arts and Crafts style. This design style, which strived to revive medieval craftsmanship, originated in Britain in the late 19th century but was popularized in the early 20th century in the US by architect/designers Gustav Stickley and the two brothers, Charles S. and Henry M. Greene.

7 Across the street at 2401 Kalorama Road is the Lindens.

Dating from 1745, the Lindens is the oldest house in Washington. However, it was not built on this site. Instead, the Georgian house was constructed in Danvers, Massachusetts, where it remained until 1936, when the owners Mr and Mrs George Morris moved it to Washington so that they could house their extensive antique collection. The rebuilding probably saved the house, because prior to the move Lindens was crumbling and in danger of being destroyed. Before it was dismantled, the house was carefully documented with precise drawings and photographs so that it could be erected easily in its new position. The Morrises hired Walter Macomber, resident architect at Colonial Williamsburg, to direct the project, which took 34 months to complete.

8 Continue on Kalorama Road to No. 2443 on the right.

The Icelandic ambassador resides in this charming brick house, which dates from 1927. Interestingly, the Embassy of Iceland in Washington also represents Iceland

ABOVE: THE LINDENS, THE OLDEST HOUSE IN WASHINGTON

KALORAMA RD NW
2300
KALORAMA RD NW
2200
23 ST
2000

in Argentina, Brazil, Chile, El Salvador, Guatemala and Mexico. One wonders how often the ambassador is at home!

9 **Follow Kalorama Road until it intersects with Wyoming Street. Turn left and follow Wyoming Street to the end of the block, where it intersects with 24th Street, NW. Stop in front of 2000 24th Street.**

Two daughters of Congressman Alexander Stewart, a lumber magnate from Wisconsin, built this house and the one at 2030 24th Street. One sister hired architect William L. Bottomley to design this two-storey limestone house, named Devore Chase. It is notable for its fusion of two styles – Georgian Revival and 18th-century French – which were popular in Kalorama and nearby Sheridan Circle between the 1880s and 1920s. The other sister hired architect Paul Philippe Cret, who reinterpreted the French country house. Cret was well aware that his building would be positioned between Devore Chase and the Lindens nearby; the spirit of both houses is melded in his design for No. 2030.

10 **Looking at the house, turn left and follow 24th Street four blocks to the intersection of S Street. At 2340 is the Woodrow Wilson House.**

Woodrow Wilson was the only president to remain in Washington after his term in office. He and his wife, Edith, purchased the house in 1921. President Wilson's time here was short-lived, as he died in 1924. However, Mrs Wilson continued to reside here until her death in 1961. Today, this house is a property of the National Trust for Historic Preservation and is operated as an historic museum. The interiors have been maintained exactly as they were at the time of Wilson's death.

WOODROW WILSON HOUSE;
TUE–SUN 10–4; www.woodrowwilsonhouse.org

WHERE TO EAT

1 BISTROT DU COIN,
1738 Connecticut Avenue, NW;
Tel: 1-202-234-6969.
Classic bistro fare served in a fun and often loud atmosphere. $$

2 RUSSIA HOUSE,
1800 Connecticut Avenue, NW;
Tel: 1-202-234-9433.
Eastern European expatriates and more than 90 vodkas make this attractive lounge feel like Moscow on the Potomac. $$

11 **To get back to Dupont Circle Metro station, exit the Woodrow Wilson House, turn right and proceed along S Street. At the intersection of 22nd Street, NW, turn right and walk down the Decatur Terrace Steps. Walk one block to the intersection of R Street, NW. Turn left onto R Street. Turn right at the intersection of 21st Street, NW. Walk two blocks along 21st Street to the intersection of Q Street, NW. The station is located at the intersection of Q and 20th Streets, NW.**

OPPOSITE: GETTING YOUR BEARINGS IN KALORAMA

WALK
15

Duke Ellington's Washington

Until the 1920s, Washington could claim the largest urban African-American population in the US. The U Street area was its heart and soul.

Jazz composer, pianist and conductor Edward Kennedy 'Duke' Ellington (1899–1974), born in Washington's West End, spent his boyhood in an area of town that was populated by leading African-American intellectuals of the day and also families of all economic levels. The businesses that they owned and the houses they lived in are featured on this walk. U Street was dubbed 'Black Broadway' for the numerous theatres, cinemas, nightclubs and ballrooms that were frequented by jazz musicians such as Cab Calloway, Pearl Bailey, Jelly Roll Morton and the Duke himself. Along this route, you'll see great jazz venues as well as several establishments that were among the first in the US to welcome a black clientele and the first memorial to African-American soldiers who fought in the US Civil War. Homes occupied by the Ellington family as Duke grew up are also included, along with the corner where rioting started that extinguished the heyday of the area – but only temporarily. U Street has rebounded to become a must-see corridor for out-of-town visitors and locals alike.

1 From the Metro station exit, turn right and look up at the building directly in front of you. Notice the mural of Duke Ellington by local artist G. Byron Peck. Next, turn left and then cross to the other side of U Street, NW at 13th Street, NW. Proceed to 1215 U Street, the Lincoln Theater.

A recent restoration has returned this theatre to its 1922 glory. When it first opened, the Washington Bee, an African-American newspaper, called it 'perhaps the largest and finest theatre for colored people in the world'. Well-known entertainers performed here and first runs of films were shown. Although the owner of the Lincoln, Abraham Lichtman, was white, he always employed an African-American manager and staff. Behind the theatre once stood the Lincoln Colonnade, a large auditorium that was a favourite venue for sororities, fraternities and other social organizations to hold formal dances.

2 Next door to the Lincoln Theater is Ben's Chili Bowl at 1213 U Street.

Never in their wildest dreams could Ben and Virginia Ali have imagined the beloved place their unassuming chili joint would come to have in the hearts of Washingtonians. The young newlyweds had converted the former Minnehaha Theater into a family-run business in 1958, just as the golden age of U Street was coming to an end. Still, Ben's became the place to be. A decade later, the Alis witnessed and survived the 1968 riots

that engulfed the area following the assassination of Martin Luther King. The area fell into decline soon after. Comedian Bill Cosby gave Ben's a much-needed boost when he held a national press conference at the restaurant to celebrate his number-one-rated television series. Five years of construction for the Metro station across the street in the mid 1990s caused business to drop off precipitously again, yet the regulars never stopped coming and Ben's endured. Ben and Virginia have now retired, but their sons, Kalmal and Nizam, continue to greet the legions of local residents who can't get enough of the old school look and unpretentious food.

3 Looking at Ben's, turn right and continue on U Street to the corner of 12th and U Streets, NW. Cross U Street. You will be in front of the True Reformer Building.

OPPOSITE: BOHEMIAN CAVERNS NIGHTCLUB; ABOVE: BEN'S CHILI BOWL, A CULINARY LANDMARK

DISTANCE 1 mile (1.6km)

ALLOW 1 hour

START U Street/Cardozo Metro station (13th Street, NW exit)

FINISH U Street/Cardozo Metro station (13th Street, SE entrance)

When True Reformer's Hall was constructed in 1902, it was not only one of the tallest buildings north of the city centre, it was also one of the first non-religious structures to be built by an African benevolent organization, the True Reformers. The architect was John A. Lankford (1874–1946), the first black architect to be registered in Washington. Two thousand people could be seated in the second-floor auditorium, which was used for rallies, meetings, dances and theatrical performances. It is also where Duke Ellington played one of his first paid gigs.

4 Cross 12th Street and continue one block to 11th Street, NW. At the intersection of 11th Street, cross U Street and proceed to 2000 11th Street, where there is the Industrial Bank on the corner.

This is the oldest black-owned bank in the city. African-American John Whitelaw Lewis had come to Washington as a

construction worker in the 1890s, but he became the most successful builder and entrepreneur in this part of Washington. By the early 1900s, he had organized a building and loan that was the precursor to Industrial Bank. The Mitchell family took over the bank in 1934 and gave it its name. Founder Jesse H. Mitchell had to train all the bankers himself, because no white banks would hire blacks to gain experience. The Mitchell family continues to operate the bank today.

5 Across 11th Street from Industrial Bank is the Bohemian Caverns nightclub at No. 2003.

John Whitelaw Lewis financed a nightclub on this corner in 1922. Originally called the Caverns, or the Crystal Caverns, it had architecturally rendered stalactites hanging from the ceiling and was a glamorous place that required formal dress. In the 1960s, it was renamed the Bohemian Caverns. Ramsey Lewis and Les McCann both made recordings at this club, and

ABOVE: MURAL OF DUKE ELLINGTON ON THE TRUE REFORMER BUILDING

WHERE TO EAT

1 BEN'S CHILI BOWL,
1213 U Street, NW;
Tel: 1-202-667-0909.
Try the chili and also a half-smoke – a large, spicy hot-dog-like treat that is one of Washington's specialities. $

2 COPPI'S ORGANIC,
1414 U Street, NW;
Tel: 1-202-319-7773.
Brick-oven pizza and light Italian dishes inspired by the seasons. $$

3 DUKEM,
1114 U Street, NW;
Tel: 1-202-667-8735.
The district boasts a large Ethiopian and Eritrean community. Here is one of the best spots to sample the savoury cuisine of those countries. $

'Cannonball' Adderly, Miles Davis and John Coltrane have all performed here.

6 Looking at Bohemian Caverns on 11th Street, turn left onto U Street and proceed one block to the intersection of 10th and U Streets, NW. Cross U Street and walk across the small plaza to the African-American Civil War Memorial.

The only national memorial to honour black soldiers who fought in the US Civil War (1861–65), this bronze sculpture, *The Spirit of Freedom*, depicts Freedom as a woman with her eyes closed and hands over her chest. On the interior of the arc is an extended family being protected by soldiers. The 28,000 names carved on the wall list the 'US Colored Troops' and their white officers. During the US Civil War, greater U Street was the site of major military encampments that became safe havens for freed men fleeing the South. Make sure to stop in at the memorial's Visitors Center, which is located in the True Reformer Building at 12th and U Streets.

7 Leave the memorial, heading towards the rear, and walk along Vermont Avenue, NW until you reach the intersection of S Street, NW. Turn right onto S Street and then turn right again onto 12th Street, NW. Stand in front of No. 1816, which will be on your left.

The first YMCA to provide services to African-Americans was founded here in 1853 by Anthony Bowen, a former slave who had become a civic leader. The building was completed in 1912. It had spacious rooms for reading and recreation as well as a gym, a swimming pool, three floors of dormitory rooms, a dining room and a pool room. It was a vital community centre for African-Americans across the city. Recently restored, it is now occupied by a social service and community centre.

8 Follow 12th Street to the intersection of T Street, NW. Turn left onto T Street, walking one block to 13th Street, NW. At the corner of 13th and T Streets is the Whitelaw apartment building.

Between 1919 and the 1940s, this cream-coloured brick building was the only first-class hotel open to blacks. John Whitelaw Lewis developed the property in 1919, bestowing his name on the finished product, which had been designed and constructed entirely by African-Americans. After Duke Ellington moved to New York City, he would stay at the Whitelaw when performing in Washington, as did musician Cab Calloway and heavyweight boxer Joe Louis. The Whitelaw was elegant, with potted palms and rich carpets in its lobby and an elegant dining room and ballroom. However, desegregation in the 1950s meant that all Washington hotels were open to blacks and the Whitelaw fell into disrepair. By the 1980s, it had been condemned by the government and abandoned: a tree grew through its roof and a fire caused major damage. Happily, the entire structure was restored between 1991 and 1992 and was made into an apartment building.

9 Cross T Street and continue on 13th Street. Look for No. 1805 on the right side of the street and No. 1816 on the left.

These two houses are where Duke Ellington lived as a teenager, when he was beginning to play with local bands. He moved to this area when he was seven years old. His father, known as 'J.E.', was an elegant man who worked as a butler to a socially prominent Washington family. His son grew up exposed to a refined life and manners. In fact, neighbours marvelled at the young man's politeness and stylish dress, a comportment that Ellington maintained throughout his life. His childhood musical influences included the sacred music he heard at church and the popular music played at local clubs, dance halls and pool halls. Ellington once joked that he had two very different sets of education: one in school and one in the pool hall.

10 Continue on 13th Street back to U Street. Turn left onto U Street and proceed one block to the intersection of U and 14th Streets, NW. On the corner to the left is the Franklin D. Reeves Center for Municipal Affairs.

When Dr Martin Luther King was assassinated in April 1968, riots broke out on this site; they raged for three days and destroyed much of the property on 14th and U Streets. The Reeves Center, an initiative of Mayor Marion Barry, was constructed in 1986 to spark an economic revival that had eluded U Street since the three days of violence. Franklin Reeves, the building's namesake, was a well-known local attorney. The project had special meaning for the centre's designer, architect Paul Devrouax. He had stood on the exact corner in 1968 armed with a rifle as a member of the National Guard sent to protect the area during the riots.

11 To return to U Street/Cardozo Metro, cross 14th Street and follow U Street back to the corner of 13th and U Streets. The entrance to the station is on the southeast corner.

WALK
16

Gracious Homes and Vibrant Streets

Discover one of Washington's most dynamic, pedestrian-friendly residential districts, with its lavish 19th-century architecture.

Dupont Circle evolved from a barren wilderness to Washington's most fashionable address at the close of the 19th century. The mansions and elegant terraces remain, many of which are still family houses. Others accommodate museums, bed and breakfasts, embassies or non-profit organizations. This is a cosmopolitan area, where something is always happening, morning, noon and night thanks to the abundance of shops, cafes, bars, restaurants and a bookshop that stays open 24 hours at the weekend. The year-round farmers' market, held on Sundays, is a highlight. Stop by the namesake circle to observe chess players devising a strategy for their next move and bicycle messengers convening for a casual end-of-the-day conference. Wander down one of the residential streets past stunning terraced houses, pausing to admire their lushly planted gardens. The Dupont Circle area has traditionally been a centre of Washington's gay and lesbian community. Each June, the area plays host to Capital Pride, a week of parades, pageants and happy hours. This walk is best taken at a weekend.

1 From the Metro station, cross 19th Street, NW and then turn onto the one-block-long Sunderland Place, NW. At the intersection of Sunderland Place and New Hampshire Avenue, NW is No. 1307 New Hampshire Avenue.

German immigrant Christian Heurich finished building this residence in 1894 with profits made from his highly successful brewery. The company slogan was 'Beer recommended for family use by Physicians in General'. Heurich, at least, must have benefited from following his own advice, because he was still actively managing the business when he died at age 102. The Heurich family inhabited the house until 1955, when they transferred the deeds to the Historical Society of Washington, DC. After moving its headquarters to Mount Vernon Square, the Historical Society sold the house back to descendants of Christian Heurich. The Brewmaster's Castle, as the house is known today, offers tours of the interior, which has been preserved. The breakfast room walls are covered with murals depicting the virtues of beer drinking.

2 Follow New Hampshire Avenue towards the fountain you can see on Dupont Circle.

During Washington's US Civil War years (1861–65), this piece of land was as remote as you could find. That's hard to imagine, given its vitality today. Not until the 1870s did development arrive in the form of wealthy captains of industry and their families, eager to make their mark in high society. Two of the mansions they built on the circle remain, one at No. 5 Dupont Circle and one at No. 1801 Massachusetts Avenue, just off the circle itself. The fountain in the centre of the circle commemorates the eponymous Rear Admiral Samuel Francis du Pont (1803–65), a hero of the US Civil War. Dupont Circle plays host to one of the city's most fascinating pedestrian thoroughfares, day or night. On Sundays, visit the farmers' market at 20th Street and Massachusetts Avenue, NW.

3 Exit Dupont Circle at Massachusetts Avenue near P Street, NW. You'll first pass the Sulgrave Club, which has its headquarters in the Gilded Age mansion at No. 1801 Massachusetts Avenue. Continue to the intersection of Massachusetts Avenue and 18th Street, NW. The National Trust for Historic Preservation is at No. 1785 Massachusetts Avenue.

Jules Henri de Sibour was the architect of choice for many moneyed families who desired a 'party palace' in the nation's capital. In 1917, he received a commission from millionaire Stanley McCormick to create 'the most luxurious apartment building in Washington'. The finished building contained just one unit per floor with only six apartments in total. Its exterior resembles those found on residential buildings in Paris, especially the mansard roof, wrought-iron balcony and rusticated first floor. Washington élites such as Lord Joseph Duveen and Andrew Mellon were both residents.

OPPOSITE: LEAFY DUPONT CIRCLE

DISTANCE **1 mile (1.6km)**

ALLOW **1.5 hours (more with museum visit)**

START **Dupont Circle Metro station (Dupont South exit)**

FINISH **Dupont Circle Metro station (Q Street entrance)**

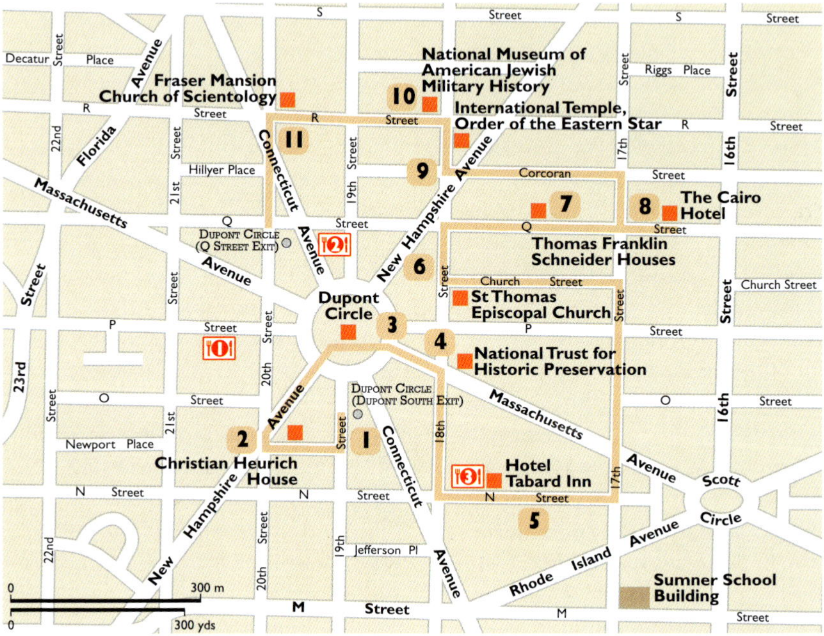

Duveen, an international art dealer, filled his space with an astounding collection of Old Masters art and offered neighbour Mellon the key, thus enabling him to peruse at his leisure. Mellon eventually bought about $21 million worth of paintings and sculptures, donating the collection to the US as the National Gallery of Art (see Walks 5 and 18).

4 Cross Massachusetts Avenue to 18th Street, following it one block to N Street, NW. Turn left onto N Street and proceed to the middle of the block. On the left side is No. 1739.

A place of respite for the pilgrims in Geoffrey Chaucer's *The Canterbury Tales* is the namesake for the Hotel Tabard Inn. Washington residents return again and again for drinks in front of the fireplace or brunch on the garden patio. Legions of out-of-towners wouldn't dream of staying anywhere else. No rooms are alike and the décor throughout is eccentric and homey. Vladimir Lenin watches as you climb the stairs to your room. There's no lift, no room service and no television. But there's no more personable place to sleep or eat in the city. Make sure to try the Inn's signature Route 11 potato chips, which are available at the front desk and in the bar.

5 Follow N Street to the end of the block. At this intersection, turn left onto 17th Street, NW. You'll walk through a restaurant corridor that draws crowds to the al fresco dining tables on fair-weather weekends. At Church Street, NW turn left. Past the modest terraced houses and the Church Street Theater building is the entrance to St Thomas Episcopal Church at 1772 Church Street, NW.

In August 1970, the grand Gothic-style, cruciform church that had been built on this site in 1899 was destroyed by fire. An arsonist was responsible for the blaze but was never caught. The St Thomas vestry voted to remain in the same location – the footprint of the old church was converted to a park, and the Parish Hall (which did not burn) was turned into the worship space used by the church today. At the turn of the 20th century, St Thomas' was a high-society church, attended by the élite who lived in the nearby mansions. However, by the 1960s both the church and the area shed that aristocratic identity and became home to a new population of artists, hippies and activists. The parish became involved in social justice and civil rights, an emphasis its membership maintains to this day.

WHERE TO EAT

1 AL TIRAMISU,
2014 P Street, NW;
Tel: 1-202-467-4466.
This cosy Italian restaurant offers great service and truly delicious pasta. $$

2 KRAMERBOOKS & AFTERWORDS CAFÉ,
1517 Connecticut Avenue, NW;
Tel: 1-202-387-1400.
Local colour in all its glory, open 24 hours at weekends. Casual dishes and luscious desserts. $

3 HOTEL TABARD INN,
1739 N Street, NW;
Tel: 1-202-331-8528.
Even if you don't stop in for a meal at the lovely restaurant, have a drink and a nibble in the bar – there's nothing better on a chilly winter's day in Washington. $$$

6 Turn right onto 18th Street and then right onto Q Street, NW. This is one of the most beautiful residential blocks in Washington.

The varied textures and hues of the stone used in the construction of these terraced houses are particularly magnificent to behold. Many of the houses were designed by Thomas Franklin Schneider, one of Washington's master architect-developers during the late 19th century.

7 At the end of the block, cross 17th Street and continue to No. 1615 Q Street, the tallest building in the city.

Once a fashionable hotel and now an apartment building, the Cairo, designed by Thomas F. Schneider and completed in 1894, is the reason Washington has a building height limit. Even before it was completed, neighbours were protesting about its 160-ft (49-m) rise into the sky. Using the rationale that the city fire service's ladders could not reach that high to extinguish a fire, they successfully lobbied Washington's Board of Commissioners to limit the height of subsequent buildings. A variation of this law continues – as does the debate about whether the law should be abolished or left untouched. One wonders what Schneider would think of the role his innovative building has played in the evolution of the nation's capital skyline. No doubt the condition of the building in the 1960s would have caused him deep distress, its decline all but complete. However, a 1976 renovation restored some of the Cairo's former glory. Today, the building still soars above all others in Dupont Circle.

8 Double back to 17th Street. Turn right and continue one block to Corcoran Street, NW. Turn left and enjoy the walk down one of the first streets in Dupont Circle to be rehabilitated following the area's decline in the late 1960s. The gas lamps and

ABOVE: DECORATIVE DETAIL OF THE CAIRO, ONCE A HOTEL, NOW AN APARTMENT BUILDING

outdoor artwork are a playful mix of period and contemporary elements. At the intersection of New Hampshire Avenue, NW, where Corcoran and 18th Streets and New Hampshire Avenue meet, you'll find yourself standing in front of the International Order of the Eastern Star headquarters.

No. 1618 New Hampshire Avenue was built to be the home of Diplomat Perry Belmont in 1909. He hired a French architect, who laid out the $1.5 million house in a French manner: the bedrooms were on the ground floor and the main public rooms on the first floor, known as a piano nobile. The piano nobile is the principal floor of a large house that has been elevated to afford views and, more practically, to avoid damp. Belmont sold the house during the Great Depression in the early 1930s to the Order of the Eastern Star, a benevolent organization founded in 1850 by freemason, lawyer and educator Rob Morris. The organization is based on teachings from the Bible but is open to both men and women of all monotheistic faiths. The sale was made with the stipulation that the Right Worthy Grand Secretary of the Eastern Star must live in the house. The emblem of the Order is the five-pointed Star of Bethlehem, which you can see on the fence enclosing the grounds.

9 Turn right onto 18th Street and then left onto R Street, NW. Almost immediately on the right is No. 1811.

Although most of the best-known Jewish historical sites are located in Washington's Chinatown, one aspect of the national Jewish identity can be found here, quietly tucked away in Dupont Circle. The National Museum of American Jewish Military History chronicles the contributions of the men and women of the Jewish faith who have served in the US Armed Forces.

NATIONAL MUSEUM OF AMERICAN JEWISH MILITARY HISTORY;

MON–FRI 9–5; www.nmajmh.org

10 Continue along R Street until you reach the intersection of R and 20th Streets, NW.

The ornate building on the corner was originally built in 1898 for George S. Fraser, a New York merchant. Much of the mansion's grandeur has been restored. If you don't mind being proselytized by members of the Church of Scientology, go inside and look at the hand-carved wood panelling decorating many of the rooms. Scientology was founded in Washington by L. Ron Hubbard in the 1950s. He selected the Fraser mansion building to house what is known as the Founding Church. Public awareness of Scientology has increased as a result of celebrity members such as Tom Cruise.

11 To end the walk, cross 20th Street and Connecticut Avenue and then turn left back onto 20th Street. Follow it for one block until you come to the Q Street entrance of the Dupont Circle Metro station.

THE FOUNTAIN IN THE CENTRE OF DUPONT CIRCLE

WALK 17

Grandes Dames of Embassy Row

At the turn of the 20th century, a handful of remarkable wealthy women made a name for themselves on Massachusetts Avenue.

The 1888 edition of *Picturesque Washington* estimated that about one-sixth of Washington's population resided in the city only in winter, during the 'social season'. Washington Episcopal Bishop Henry Y. Satterlee denounced them from the pulpit in 1904, asking 'whether the material advantages that they bring are any compensation for the atmosphere of careless irresponsibility which they create'. From the late 1870s until the Great Depression, northwest Washington became home to the nouveau riche who had been successful in industry, agriculture and finance. Unacceptable in the established high societies of Philadelphia and New York, they flocked to Washington and built extravagant residences. On this walk, you'll meet a group of women from this era. For some, the burden of wealth proved too heavy; others charted a steady course to make enduring contributions to the city. Today, most of their former homes house embassies or private clubs, and the avenue on which they stand has been named Embassy Row.

1 Leave Dupont Circle (Dupont South exit) Metro station, turn right onto 19th Street, NW. Do not cross the street onto Dupont Circle. Instead, turn right again, crossing Connecticut Avenue, NW. The next block will be Massachusetts Avenue, NW. Cross it and then turn right to stand in front of No. 1801.

Like many of their contemporaries, Henry and Martha Wadsworth spent the winter social season in Washington. For Martha, talented amateur pianist and accomplished horsewoman, the height of the experience was the season's finale. She frequently organized an 800-mile (1,285-km) trek on horseback from Washington to her estate in the Genesee Valley of western New York State. Her friends joined Martha on horseback and travelled over several weeks, enjoying picnics, parties and overnight stays at local inns and private houses. The household staff, the luggage and the family dogs travelled ahead by train and car in order to prepare for
their mistress' arrival. Around the time of World War I, Washington's extravagant social scene began to fade and in 1917 the couple stopped using the house. It sat empty for many years until 1932, when Martha Wadsworth's old friend and neighbour, Mabel Boardman, organized a group of socially prominent women to purchase the house and convert it to a women's club. The founders named it Sulgrave Club, in honour of George Washington's ancestral home, Sulgrave Manor.

2 P Street, NW runs behind the Sulgrave Club. Cross it and stand in front of the large white mansion at 15 Dupont Circle now known as the Washington Club.

In 1950, another women's club purchased this residence known as the Patterson House. Constructed in 1901, it was the scene of many a lavish society event hosted by Mr and Mrs Robert Patterson, its original owners. Mrs Patterson maintained a staff of 10 to 15 servants who, until World War I, wore full livery. This refined atmosphere may be why Charles A. Lindbergh stayed at the house while receiving a hero's welcome in Washington following his transatlantic flight, and President and Mrs Calvin Coolidge used the Patterson while the White House was being refurbished. Yet the most notable occupant of the house was actually the Patterson daughter, known as Cissy. After adhering to the dictates of high society, in which she married (and divorced) a European count, Cissy embarked on life as a wealthy, well-connected single woman. Her friend, renowned newspaper publisher William Randolph Hearst (1863–1951), encouraged her to take up journalism, eventually appointing her editor of the *Washington Herald*. By 1942, Patterson had taken over both the *Washington Times* and the *Washington Herald*. The two papers were combined to form the *Washington Times-Herald*, Cissy became its editor, and she increased her reputation as one of the most influential Washingtonians of her day.

OPPOSITE: ONCE A FAMILY HOME, 2020 MASSACHUSETTS AVENUE IS NOW THE INDONESIAN EMBASSY

DISTANCE **1 mile (1.6km)**

ALLOW **1.5 hours (more with museum visits)**

START **Dupont Circle Metro station (Dupont South exit)**

FINISH **Dupont Circle Metro station (Q Street entrance)**

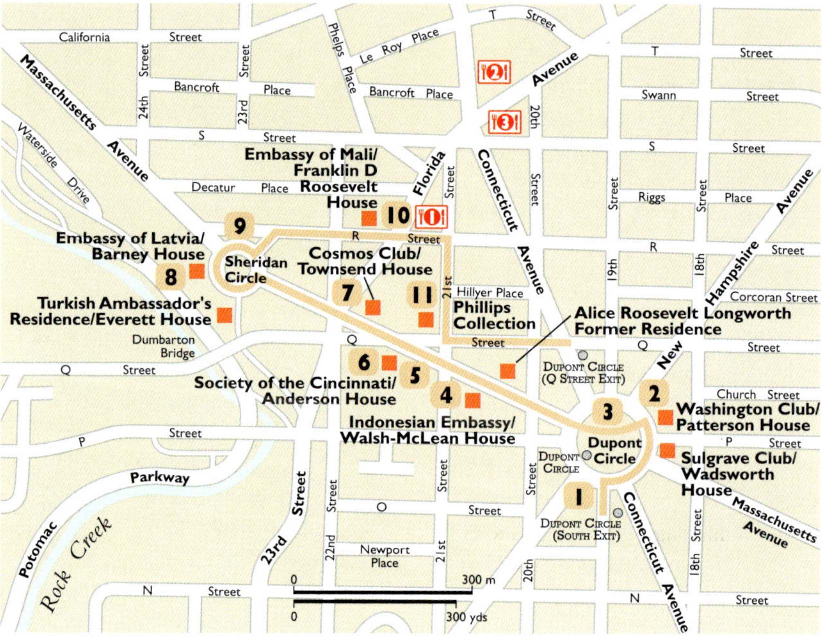

3 Cross the street onto Dupont Circle itself. Walk past the fountain and cross to the other side, exiting the circle by crossing the street onto Massachusetts Avenue. Walk about one block to No. 2009 on the right.

Of his daughter Alice, Theodore Roosevelt (26th president of the US, 1901–09) once observed, 'I can either run the country or I can control Alice. I cannot possibly do both.' Roosevelt's oldest child was one of the most rambunctious, freewheeling children ever to roam the White House. By the time she reached adulthood, Alice had honed her capacity to shock and flout convention. The house at 2009 Massachusetts Avenue was her home following the death of her husband, Republican speaker of the House Nicholas Longworth. It became a salon, drawing politicians, writers, film stars – anyone who kept Alice entertained. When she died in 1980 at age 96, Alice was declared to be 'the other Washington monument'.

4 Continue along Massachusetts Avenue, noting No. 2020 across the street, now the Indonesian Embassy.

Father Struck It Rich was the title of the memoir written by Evalyn Walsh McLean, who grew up in this mansion and later inherited it from her parents. Her father, Thomas Walsh, made his fortune in Colorado gold mines. His daughter was the quintessential 'poor little rich girl', who embraced the highlife with gusto. In 1908, Evalyn eloped, against her family's advice, with the handsome heir to the *Washington Post* fortune, Edward ('Ned') Beale McLean. In 1911, the couple purchased the Hope Diamond, a 45-carat deep blue stone, which was said to be cursed. Although her friends urged her to keep the diamond concealed, Evalyn often wore it in public. Was she tempting fate? The effects of lifelong alcoholism led to an early death for her estranged husband; her son, Vinson, died from injuries in a car accident at age nine; her daughter, Emily, suffered a drug overdose; and Evalyn herself died at age 60 of pneumonia. Her unlucky jewel is now on display in the Smithsonian Museum of Natural History.

5 Remain on Massachusetts Avenue, crossing 21st Street, NW. Across the street from the statue of Mohandas Gandhi is 2118 Massachusetts Avenue, the Society of the Cincinnati.

In 1896, while serving at the US Embassy in Rome, Larz Anderson met Isabel Weld Perkins, a young debutante from Boston. At age five, Isabel had inherited 17 million dollars from her grandfather, William Fletcher Weld, making her the wealthiest woman in the world. She and Larz were married and embarked on a life of luxury combined with public service and adventure. They travelled widely across the world, becoming among the first Westerners to visit countries such as Tibet and Nepal. When she became a widow, Isabel deeded this property and its contents to the Society of the Cincinnati – a patriotic organization of which Larz had been a lifelong member – for use as a headquarters and a museum.

SOCIETY OF THE CINCINNATI;
TUE–SAT 1–4; www.societyofthecincinnati.org

WHERE TO EAT

1 RESTAURANT NORA,
2132 Florida Avenue, NW;
Tel: 1-202-462-5143.
Deliciously prepared organic produce, meats and dairy products served in a former grocery store. $$$

2 BUCA DI BEPPO,
1825 Connecticut Avenue, NW;
Tel: 1-202-232-8466.
Southern Italian culinary legacy in all its kitschy American glory. $$

3 THAIPHOON,
2011 S Street, NW;
Tel: 1-202-667-3505.
Thai noodle dishes, curries and soups. $$

6 Continue along Massachusetts Avenue until you reach No. 2121, the Cosmos Club.

The first house on this site was built in 1871 by a property speculator. In 1900, Richard Townsend, his wife Mary and their daughter Mathilde moved here from Lafayette Square. Although Mrs Townsend disliked the house, a childhood superstition led her to believe that evil would befall her if she ever lived in a new house, and she could not bring herself to tear down the original. Instead, the Townsends built around the old edifice, incorporating it into a lavish mansion. Mrs Townsend rested easy at first, but her anxiety levels must have risen when, a year after moving into the house, Richard fell from a horse, fractured his skull and died. She seems to have coped by continuing to entertain in grand style: her expenses for social events often exceeded $240,000 a year. In 1950, the property became the private Cosmos Club, where professionals in the arts and sciences meet to exchange ideas.

7 Cross Florida Avenue, NW and stay on Massachusetts Avenue until you reach Sheridan Circle. Cross Massachusetts Avenue in front of the Greek ambassador's residence at No. 2221. Turn right and follow the road to 23rd Street, NW. Almost directly across 23rd Street is No. 1606, the Turkish ambassador's residence. Notice the charming portrait of Isabel Anderson (see Step 5) concealed in the red police phone box on 23rd Street.

The money that paid for this – one of the most spectacular homes on Embassy Row – came from the crimped bottle cap for soda pop and beer bottles, invented by Edward H. Everett. He gave architect George Oakley Totten free rein in design, insisting cost was of no concern. The resulting home continues to be used today for grand social functions by the Turkish ambassador. Everett's second wife was operatic soprano Grace Burnap. Together, they hosted 'Evenings with Music', accommodating several hundred guests. Attendance at one party in the 1930s was estimated at 3,000. The *Washington Sunday Star* reported, 'footmen in mulberry livery with white silk stockings and pumps with silver buckles were everywhere".

8 Return to Sheridan Circle and turn left. The Spanish Mission-style building at 2306 Massachusetts Avenue is the Latvian Embassy.

When she built this relatively modest home on Sheridan Circle in 1901, free-spirited Alice Pike Barney made an important contribution to Washington's art scene. The building served as her home, her art studio and Washington's ad hoc cultural centre, where Alice hosted theatrical productions and art exhibitions. She had been inspired by years spent in France studying painting, much to the disapproval of her husband, Albert. Alice ignored his protests, spending less time with him and more time with her artist companions and two daughters. In 1901, she presented her first solo exhibition at the Corcoran Gallery of Art, in

ABOVE: HEADQUARTERS AND MUSEUM OF THE SOCIETY OF THE CINCINNATI, A US PATRIOTIC ORGANIZATION

Washington. During World War I, Alice Barney convinced Congress to fund construction of the National Sylvan Theater in the grounds of the Washington Monument. She also raised money for Neighborhood House, which offered social services to immigrants in southwest Washington. Today, three branches of what is now called the Barney Neighborhood House continue to provide social services in the city.

9 Continue around Sheridan Circle, crossing Massachusetts Avenue and proceeding along R Street, NW. Follow R Street across 22nd Street and then look for No. 2133, the Embassy of Mali.

Franklin and Eleanor Roosevelt lived at this address from 1917 to 1920, while Roosevelt was assistant secretary of the navy. In autumn 1918, Eleanor discovered that her husband was having an affair with her social secretary, Lucy Mercer. Eleanor offered Franklin a divorce, yet partly because divorce was considered a disgrace in their social circle and partly because it would have badly damaged his political career, Franklin asked to stay married and agreed never to see Lucy again. The incident profoundly altered their relationship and was a major factor in Eleanor's search for friendship and fulfilment in social and political activism independent of her spouse. Despite their parallel lives, however, by the time the Roosevelts reached the White House in 1933, they were able to function highly effectively, Eleanor playing an integral role in the Roosevelt presidency.

10 Follow R Street across Florida Avenue. Note Restaurant Nora as you continue on R Street. Chef Nora Pouillon is one of the grand dames of the Washington culinary scene, having converted a grocery store into one of the city's best restaurants. At the intersection of 21st Street, NW, turn right, cross R Street and proceed on 21st Street to the Phillips Collection, which will be on the right.

Artist Marjorie Acker married Duncan Phillips in 1921 and resided with her husband on the third floor of his family's spacious house. That same year they opened the main floor to the public as the Phillips Collection, the first museum of modern art in the US, comprising art acquired by Duncan and (later) Marjorie. When the collection outgrew this space, the Phillips made their entire house into a museum, building a new house for themselves in northwest Washington. At their new home, the couple acquired paintings on loan, hung them and 'tested' them. If after two months they were still excited about the piece, they bought it and sent it to the Phillips Collection. That artwork can be viewed today, as well as a number of Marjorie's paintings.

THE PHILLIPS COLLECTION;
TUE–SAT 10–5, THU 10–8:30, SUN 11–6;
www.phillipscollection.org

11 From the Phillips Collection, turn right. Walk to the end of the block to the intersection of Q Street, NW. Turn left onto Q Street. The Metro station is at the end of the block.

OPPOSITE: THE PHILLIPS COLLECTION ART GALLERY, THE FIRST MUSEUM OF MODERN ART IN THE US

WALK 18

The Best-kept Smithsonian Secrets

If you enjoy exquisite gallery space, rare treasures, appealing outdoor viewing areas and unexpected treats, this is the walk for you.

Take this walk on a hot, sultry day when the cool, quiet spaces will provide much-needed relief. The most popular (and usually most crowded) of the Smithsonian museums – the National Air and Space Museum, the National Museum of Natural History, and the National Museum of American History – are more than worthy of repeat visits. Consider, though, that the Smithsonian Institution encompasses 19 museums, nine of which can be found along the National Mall. This walk is an opportunity to explore that cultural bounty via less familiar venues. The route travels inside serenely beautiful gallery space located both above and below ground, through lush Victorian-era gardens as well as inside two sculpture gardens. Every stop has been selected to reveal an unusual or little-known aspect of the Smithsonian experience. It's a rewarding way to acquaint yourself with some of the best painting, sculpture and landscape architecture in Washington in a short period of time and without the crowds.

1 After leaving Smithsonian Metro station by the Mall exit, turn right, crossing Jefferson Drive, SW, and approach the Italian Renaissance-style building to your left.

The Freer Gallery of Art, founded by Charles Lang Freer (1854–1919), houses a world-renowned collection of art from China, Japan, Korea and Southeast Asia. Not your cup of tea? Enter nonetheless to enjoy the elegant museum building and its sublime interior courtyard. Also, make your way back to the gallery that houses the lavishly ornate Peacock Room. This dining room was once part of a London townhouse owned by Frederick R. Leyland, a wealthy ship owner from Liverpool, UK. He commissioned the US artist James McNeill Whistler (1834–1903) to decorate the room, but unfortunately Leyland was not happy with the result and arguments ensued. Freer purchased the Peacock Room in 1904, and it was dismantled and taken to his house in Detroit. After his death it was taken to the Freer Gallery in Washington.

FREER GALLERY OF ART;
DAILY 10–5.30; www.asia.si.edu

2 From outside the Freer Gallery, turn right and walk over to the charming, leaf-topped kiosk next door.

Just because many who enter this building appear to be Smithsonian employees doesn't mean the general public is not welcome. Indeed, the S. Dillon Ripley Center houses gallery space expressly for visitors, and there are often exhibits covering a particular theme, event or American ethnic group. A peek inside also affords you the chance to see how the Smithsonian Institution administration functions behind the scenes. Its popular Smithsonian Associates program is based here, as well the Traveling Exhibition Service. For those with youngsters, check the schedule of events for the Discovery Theater. Dillon Ripley (1913–2001), the centre's namesake, was secretary of the Smithsonian Institution from 1964 to 1984.

S. DILLON RIPLEY CENTER;
DAILY 10–5.30; www.si.edu/ripley

WHERE TO EAT

1 GARDEN CAFÉ,
National Gallery of Art
(West Building, Ground floor),
7th Street and Constitution
Avenue, NW;
Tel: 1-202-712-7454.
An indoor garden setting complements the artful menu that is often inspired by whatever major exhibition is on view. $$

2 MITSITAM CAFÉ,
National Museum of the American Indian,
4th Street and Independence
Avenue, SW;
Tel: 1-202-633-1000.
Imaginative and delicious native foods from the major US regions, presented with a contemporary twist. $$

OPPOSITE: THE CIRCULAR CEILING AT THE NATIONAL MUSEUM OF THE AMERICAN INDIAN

DISTANCE 0.5 mile (0.8km)

ALLOW 1 hour (more with museum visits)

START Smithsonian Metro station (Mall exit)

FINISH Archives-Navy Memorial Metro station

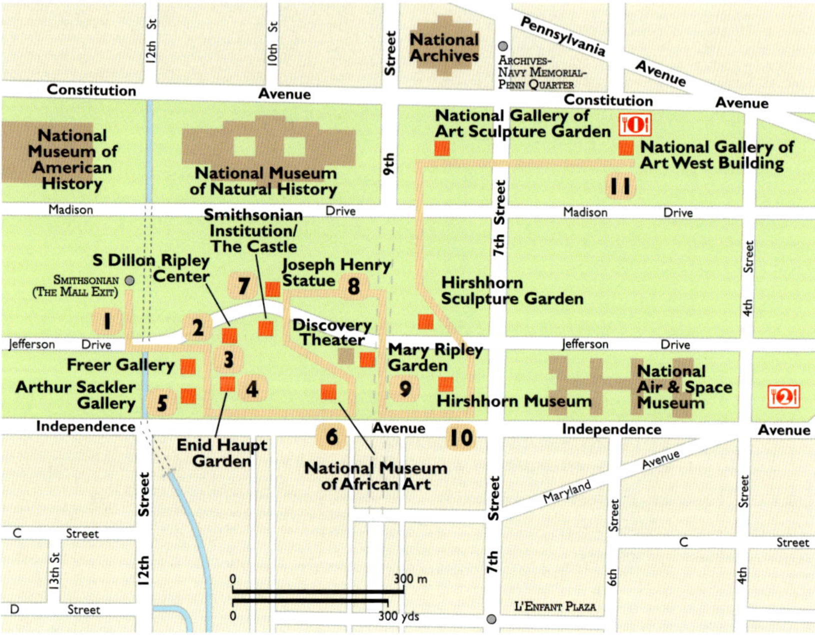

3 Exit the Ripley Center and turn right into the Enid Haupt Garden.

S. Dillon Ripley conceived this quadrangle to accommodate museum space. During Ripley's tenure, Dr Arthur M. Sackler pledged part of his enormous collection of Asian and Near Eastern art, but the Smithsonian had nowhere to display it. Likewise, the Museum of African Art had outgrown its terraced-house quarters on Capitol Hill. In 1982, Congress appropriated the funds to construct the two museums. They are underground, so are not visible from street level, but you can see their entry pavilions on the right and the left. The formal garden atop the museum space was created in 1987 – a gift from New York benefactress Enid Haupt.

4 Follow the garden walk to your right, heading towards the Arthur Sackler Gallery. Notice the Moon Gate Garden located next to the museum's entry pavilion.

Arthur M. Sackler (1913–87) was a New York psychiatrist, medical researcher and publisher who donated 1,000 objects from his personal collection to the Smithsonian in 1982. The building interconnects underground with the Freer Gallery. Next to the Sackler Gallery is an intimate garden with a circle-in-square fountain, based on the Temple of Heaven in Beijing. Two 'moon gates', 9ft (2.7m) high, complete the setting.

ARTHUR SACKLER GALLERY;

DAILY 10–5.30; www.asia.si.edu

5 From the Sackler Gallery, walk across the garden to the National Museum of African Art.

Traditional and contemporary art from the African continent is on display here. A common characteristic of many of the objects is that they were used in everyday life. The museum also offers you the chance to listen to the sounds of Africa in the form of live Radio Africa broadcasts as well as podcasts. Adjacent to the museum building is a series of fountains and canals terminating in a *chadar*, or water wall, inspired by the Moorish Alhambra gardens in Granada, Spain.

NATIONAL MUSEUM OF AFRICAN ART;

DAILY 10–5.30; www.nmafa.si.edu

6 From the museum, follow the path along the garden's parterre towards the Smithsonian Institution entrance. Enter the building and walk through the main hall towards the opposite entrance. To the right of the entrance way is the James Smithson Room.

In 1826, British scientist James Smithson (1765–1829) made out his Last Will and Testament declaring that he would entail his estate to his nephew. If the nephew died without an heir, however, even though Smithson had never visited the US, the money was to go 'to the United States of America, to found at Washington, under the name of the Smithsonian Institution, an establishment for the increase and diffusion of knowledge'. The said nephew died without offspring, and the inheritance – valued at half a million dollars – came to the US. Although he died in Italy, Smithson's remains were eventually brought to the US, where they have rested ever since. What exactly motivated him to make the bequest to the United States remains a mystery.

SMITHSONIAN INSTITUTION/ THE CASTLE;

DAILY 8.30–5.30; www.si.edu/visit/infocenter/sicastle.htm

ABOVE: THE SMITHSONIAN INSTITUTION'S FIRST BUILDING, POPULARLY KNOWN AS THE CASTLE

7 Exit the Castle building, cross Jefferson Drive and walk down the steps. To your immediate right is a statue of a man on a pedestal.

No doubt a majority of passers-by behold the dignified man standing in front of a building called Smithsonian and identify him as James Smithson. But look closely at the name carved on the pedestal and you will see the inscription 'Joseph Henry'. An eminent American scientist, Joseph Henry (1797–1878) was the first secretary of the Smithsonian Institution and held the position for 34 years. (One of the job's perks was an apartment in the east wing of the Castle.) When he died, such was his stature that the US president, the cabinet, the chief justice and associate justices of the Supreme Court, as well as members of both houses of Congress attended the funeral. US sculptor William W. Story (1819–95) embedded an electromagnet in the pedestal upon which Henry leans, honouring one of the physicist's primary areas of research.

8 Climb back up the steps and cross Jefferson Drive again. Turn left and walk along the Castle grounds, passing the festive Arts & Industries Building. Turn right into the Mary Ripley Garden.

One of the loveliest spots in the city at any time of year, the Mary Ripley Garden was created in 1987 to commemorate the wife of Smithsonian secretary S. Dillon Ripley. Its formal layout, wrought-iron furniture and dense, varied plantings provide a hint of how the National Mall outside once appeared. A 1850s plan proposed by landscape architect Andrew Jackson Downing (1815–52) turned an under-utilized piece of land into a vast Victorian garden complete with flowerbeds, a flower

ABOVE: THE DOUGHNUT-SHAPED HIRSHHORN MUSEUM, CENTRE FOR CONTEMPORARY ART AND CULTURE

meadow and winding carriage paths. The sweeping, open vistas you see today – while included in Washington's original city plan designed in 1791 – were not achieved until the early 20th century.

9 Exit the garden back to Jefferson Drive. Turn right almost immediately onto the grounds of the Hirshhorn Museum. Follow the path around the building, past the main entrance, and then a bit further until you come to a tall sculpture made from aluminium tubes.

There's more to 'Needle Tower' than meets the eye. Notice the stones placed on the ground beneath it. Stand on them and look up to see the familiar, five-pointed shape that resembles the Star of David. The doughnut-shaped Hirshhorn Museum is a centre for contemporary art and culture, presenting exhibits, lectures and films. Erected in 1971, it was constructed on the site of the former Army Medical Museum, which was razed and relocated in order to allow the art collection of industrialist Joseph Hirshhorn to secure a home on the National Mall. Famous for its collection of artefacts and photographs detailing US Civil War medicine, the Army Medical Museum tended to shock the viewing public and, probably for that very reason, was well attended. In fact, the potential loss of the collection to the Hirshhorn building caused such a stir that the exhibits were relocated to the campus of Walter Reed Army Medical Center.

HIRSHHORN MUSEUM;
DAILY 10–5.30; http://hirshhorn.si.edu

10 Continue to follow the path around the Hirshhorn Museum back to Jefferson Drive. Cross Jefferson Drive and follow the steps down into the Hirshhorn Museum Sculpture Garden. Walk through the garden and out of the opposite entrance back onto the National Mall. Walk straight across the Mall towards the National Gallery of Art Sculpture Garden. Walk through and exit at the corner of 7th Street and Constitution Avenue, NW. Cross 7th Street and walk towards the 7th Street entrance of the National Gallery of Art West Building.

The National Gallery of Art exhibits one of the rarest pieces of art in the US: a Leonardo da Vinci. Painted between 1474 and 1478, the double-sided painting Ginevra de' Benci is the only work by this Tuscan master in the US. The young Ginevra was captured on canvas probably around the time of her marriage at age 16, and is currently to be found in Gallery 6.

NATIONAL GALLERY OF ART;
MON–SAT 10–5, SUN 11–6; www.nga.gov

11 To get to the nearest Metro station, leave the gallery's entrance on 7th Street, NW, turn right and proceed to the intersection at Constitution Avenue, crossing the street. Continue on 7th Street to Pennsylvania Avenue, NW. Cross Pennsylvania Avenue and then turn left to cross 7th Street. The entrance to the Archives-Navy Memorial-Penn Quarter Metro station is to the right.

CANDELABRA HANGING FROM THE CEILING OF THE SMITHSONIAN FREER GALLERY OF ART

WALK 19

The Kennedys in Georgetown

Fashionable, high-status residents such as the Kennedy family helped to establish Georgetown as the social and political centre of the US capital.

Georgetown continues to enjoy a reputation as the home of the influential élite, but it didn't come by this identity until the 1950s. Prior to that time, it had suffered the vicissitudes of its economy – based first on tobacco trading and then industry – and was a motley area comprised of wealthy merchants, middle-class shopkeepers, free and enslaved African-Americans and poor white immigrants. The Kennedy era in Georgetown coincided with a movement by many connected to the government to live close to the city centre as well as a desire to preserve the area's historic character. The Kennedys conferred a social and political status on Georgetown that had not existed to that point. They marked some of their best times in Washington here as well as a few of the more heartbreaking. This walk pays tribute to those events by visiting homes where the Kennedy family lived, a church where they worshipped, and residences of others impacted by their tenure. Note that all the houses on this route remain private residences.

1 Exiting Foggy Bottom Metro station, turn left and proceed to Washington Circle. Turn left and walk around the circle, exiting onto Pennsylvania Avenue by bearing left. Follow Pennsylvania Avenue to the intersection of 28th Street, NW. At this point the street changes its name to M Street, NW. Follow M Street six blocks to the intersection of M and Potomac Streets, NW. Dean & DeLuca at 3276 M Street will be on the left.

Joel Dean and Giorgio DeLuca opened their first market in SoHo, New York City, in 1977. Since then, Dean & DeLuca has become famous for its bread and cheese, first-rate foods and high-quality cookware and accessories. Outposts of the food emporium can now be found in California's Napa Valley, Kansas City and Charlotte, North Carolina.

2 From Dean & DeLuca, cross M Street, NW and proceed up Potomac Street, NW. At the intersection of N Street, NW turn left. Midway along this block on the left side of the street is 3260 N Street, NW.

While renting this house, built in 1828, John F. Kennedy began his campaign for his seat in the US Senate. In spite of the strong public support for Republican Dwight Eisenhower, Kennedy won what had been a close campaign. While living here, Kennedy attended a dinner party at the home of Georgetown friends, where he met a striking young woman named Jacqueline Bouvier, who was later to become his wife.

3 Continue along N Street, crossing 33rd Street, NW. On your right will be No. 3307.

The William Marbury House was constructed in 1812 and purchased by John F. Kennedy in 1957. He took the deed of the house to the hospital and presented it as a gift to his wife, Jacqueline, who had just given birth to their first child, Caroline. John Kennedy, Jr was also born while they lived here. Mrs Kennedy is reputed to have decorated the house three times during their first year of residence, while her husband focused on winning the presidential campaign of 1960. After his victory, the doorway of this house became instantly recognizable because of the cadre of reporters who waited across the street day and night for word from the president-elect about cabinet appointments and other administration news.

4 Cross the street to 3302 N Street.

One of the bronze plaques on the east side of this house commemorates Helen Montgomery. When her neighbour across the street was elected US President, Montgomery took pity on the constant swarm of news reporters standing in the cold waiting for a story to break, so she and her father, Charles, offered food, a warm room and use of the telephone to these journalists. In appreciation, John F. Kennedy himself presented the plaque to Miss Montgomery on Inauguration Day, 1961. She died in 1975.

OPPOSITE: THE FEDERAL-STYLE TOWNHOUSES OF COX'S ROW IN GEORGETOWN

DISTANCE 3.5 miles (5.6km)

ALLOW 3 hours

START Foggy Bottom Metro station

FINISH Foggy Bottom Metro station

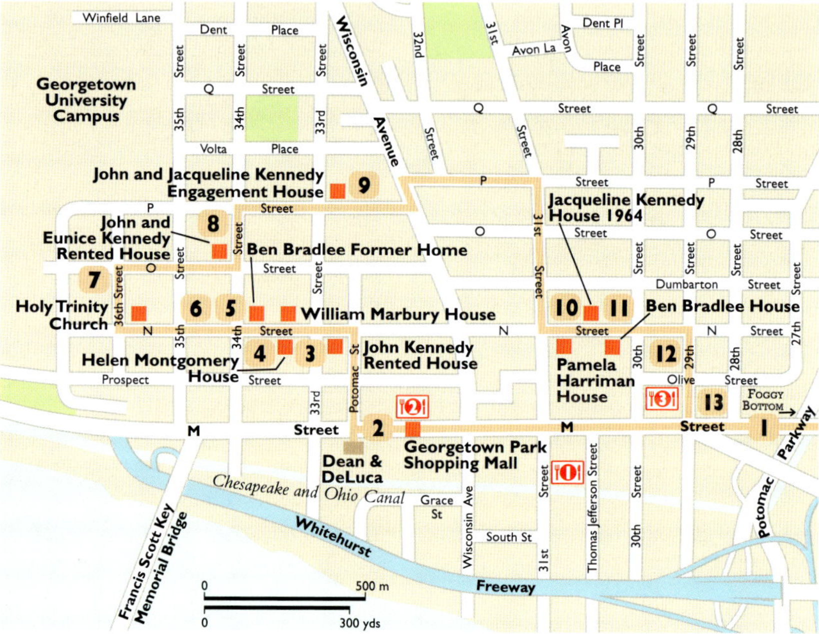

5 Just a little further on N Street on the right is No. 3321, former home of Ben Bradlee.

Newsweek magazine's Washington correspondent Ben Bradlee enjoyed a close friendship with Senator John F. Kennedy. The two first met when wheeling their infant children around in their prams. Bradlee kept notes of their intimate conversations, with Kennedy's knowledge, and these records became the basis for a behind-the-scenes book revealing the human side of the JFK presidency published by Bradlee following Kennedy's death. *Conversations with Kennedy* was described as providing an insight into what Kennedy was really like, although Mrs Kennedy apparently objected to the book's profanity and ended the friendship with the Bradlees. Another difficult moment in the Bradlee–Kennedy relationship took place in 1964, when Bradlee's sister-in-law, Mary Pinchot Meyer, was found murdered on the C & O Canal towpath.

Meyer had been a friend of Jacqueline Kennedy, and a sensational diary she left at the little studio apartment above Bradlee's N Street home indicated she had also been a lover of John F. Kennedy. Her murder was never solved.

6 Follow N Street across 34th and 35th Streets, NW. Stop in front of the Holy Trinity Church, Chapel of St Ignatius Loyola, at No. 3515.

The Kennedy family often worshipped at Holy Trinity Church. This building, now called St Ignatius Chapel, was the original church, constructed in 1794. The present sanctuary is around the corner, on 36th Street, by the Holy Trinity School. This is a Jesuit parish that has always enjoyed a close relationship with its institution neighbour, Georgetown University.

7 Turn right onto 36th Street, NW. At the intersection of 36th and O Streets, NW you will get a glimpse of the Georgetown University campus. Turn right onto O Street, cross 35th Street and take the next turn left onto 34th Street. Look for 1400 34th Street, which will be on your left.

Senator John F. Kennedy rented this house with his sister, Eunice, who gave up her share of the rent when she became engaged to Sergeant Shriver. JFK then moved to a smaller house at 3271 P Street, NW in the eastern part of Georgetown. He did not yet know that he would soon be married, just four months after Eunice. Eunice

WHERE TO EAT

1 CAFÉ LA RUCHE,
1039 31st Street, NW;
Tel: 1-202-965-2684.
Casual bistro near the C & O Canal, with outdoor garden seating and hard-to-resist desserts. $

2 CLYDE'S OF GEORGETOWN,
3236 M Street, NW;
Tel: 1-202-333-9180.
Washington institution that continues to please due to its extensive menu of sandwiches, soups, salads, pasta, meat and fish dishes. $$

3 MENDOCINO GRILLE,
2917 M Street, NW;
Tel: 1-202-333-2912.
Restaurant/wine bar offering seasonable, sustainable ingredients along with an award-winning wine list starring selections from California and the northwest. $$$

Kennedy Shriver's daughter, Maria, became the wife of actor–politician Arnold Schwarzenegger.

8 Continue on 34th Street until you reach the intersection of P Street, NW. Turn right onto P Street. Soon after you cross 33rd Street, stop in front of 3271 P Street.

John Kennedy was living in this house when he sent a telegram to a female photographer who was working for

After the assassination of her husband in 1963, Jacqueline Kennedy moved with her children, Caroline and John Jr, from the White House to this temporary residence, where they lived for four months before finding a home of their own. It was offered for their use by Averell Harriman, a business tycoon and Democratic Party stalwart. In 1971, Harriman married Pamela Churchill Hayward (1920–97), an English-born socialite who had been married twice before: first, to Randolph Churchill (Winston Churchill's son), then later to Broadway producer Leland Hayward, with whom she remained until his death. On marrying Harriman and moving to Washington, Pamela quickly became a renowned Georgetown hostess and consummate party-giver. She soon became an influential figure in Washington's Democratic Fellowship and was eventually appointed US Ambassador to France by President Bill Clinton.

the *Washington-Times Herald*. Jacqueline Bouvier was the 'Inquiring Photographer' for the paper and had been sent to London to cover the coronation of Queen Elizabeth. The telegram was Kennedy's proposal of marriage. She accepted, and the two spent many hours here planning their wedding, which took place the following September at Hammersmith Farm, the Newport, Rhode Island estate owned by Jacqueline's family.

9 Walk along P Street, crossing the busy Wisconsin Avenue, NW. Keep on P Street until you get to the intersection of 31st Street, NW, where you will turn right. Follow 31st Street through the intersections of O and Dumbarton Street, NW. When you come to N Street, turn left. Stop in front of 3038 N Street.

10 Cross the street to look at No. 3017.

Known as the Laird-Dunlop House, notable Georgetown residents have lived here since it was built around 1799. One inhabitant was Robert Todd Lincoln (1843–1926), American lawyer and politician and the oldest son of President Abraham Lincoln, who purchased the home in 1915. Its current owners are former *Washington Post* Executive Editor Ben Bradlee and his journalist wife, Sally Quinn.

ABOVE: THE CHAPEL OF ST IGNATIUS LOYOLA, WHERE THE KENNEDYS USED TO WORSHIP

11 Across the street you'll find 3014 N Street.

Built before 1800, this house was once a 19th-century academy for young girls. In 1964, it became the home of the widowed Jacqueline Kennedy. Her attempt to remain in Georgetown, a place she loved, was to no avail. Throngs of curious people camped out on her narrow street night and day, just to catch a glimpse of her. After only 10 months in this house, she moved to New York City.

12 Follow N Street to 29th Street, NW. Turn right and proceed until you reach M Street, NW, the commercial heart of Georgetown.

In this commercial district you can find a variety of eateries and outposts of well-known US retailers such as Kate Spade, Pottery Barn, Urban Outfitters and Banana Republic, to name but a few.

13 To return to Foggy Bottom Metro station, turn left at the intersection of 29th and M Streets. Follow M Street to 28th Street, where it changes its name to Pennsylvania Avenue. Follow Pennsylvania Avenue to Washington Circle, bearing right to walk around the circle. Exit the circle by turning right onto 23rd Street, NW. The station will be on the right, halfway down the block.

ABOVE: 3017 N STREET BECAME HOME TO THE RECENTLY WIDOWED JACQUELINE KENNEDY FOR 10 MONTHS

WALK 20

The Haunted Houses of Lafayette Square

The ghosts and spirits of military heroes, young girls, a tragic slave, First Ladies and a US president fill the well-known enclave of Lafayette Square.

Beneath the political history of the capital city of the US churns a haunted legacy borne from desperate suffering and violent death. A gloomy supernatural cloud hovers darkly over a 7-acre (2.8-hectare) park more accustomed to the purposeful step of civil servants and the carefree gait of visiting high-school students than the restless wanderings of ghosts, forever bound to the place where their death occurred. Start at the first private residence constructed on Lafayette Square, which has been disturbed by the ghost of its first owner almost since the day he died. The spirit of a courageous First Lady is known to revisit her final Washington residence, and when an up-and-coming military officer witnessed a horrific assassination, his Lafayette Square home seemed to fall under a bloody curse. Even the White House has been associated with spooky encounters. You'll conclude the walk at what is considered the most ghost-filled place in Washington, the Octagon House.

1 From Farragut West's 17th Street exit, step out onto I Street, NW. Turn right and walk to the corner of I Street and Connecticut Avenue, NW. Follow Connecticut Avenue to the end of the block, then cross H Street, NW. You will now be standing in front of the Stephen Decatur House Museum.

A shadowy, amorphous form is said to move out of the front room to the left of the main entrance and make its way towards a door at the back of the house. A man dressed in military garb from the early 19th century has been seen on the stairway. Is he also the source of the horrendous crashing sounds that resonate, seemingly out of nowhere? Many employed at this house museum believe so. Commodore Stephen Decatur and his wife, Susan, built this fine Lafayette Square residence in 1819. It was soon the scene of glittering parties attended by Washington notables. Decatur, the country's naval hero, was one of the most famous men in the US, destined, many assumed, for additional glory. But alas, Decatur's ambition was snuffed out abruptly. On 22 March 1820 he died in this house from wounds received in a duel. His unhappy, frustrated ghost has made its presence known ever since.

STEPHEN DECATUR HOUSE MUSEUM;
MON–FRI 9–5; TEL: 1-202.842.0920;
www.decaturhouse.org

2 Follow the path parallel to H Street, NW across to the other side of the park. At the corner of H Street and Madison Place, NW is a yellow house.

Statesman Daniel Webster assessed First Lady Dolley Madison as 'The only permanent power in Washington, all others are transient'. Beloved and admired, Mrs Madison ushered in an era of elegance at the White House, hosting weekly gatherings that were so vital to the city's social and political life. She was there when, in August 1814, British soldiers invaded the city and set fire to nearly every government building, the White House included. Not one to panic, Mrs Madison ordered her staff to remove as many treasures from the building as possible to prevent them from falling into British hands. Most iconic was a full-length portrait of America's first president, General George Washington, painted by Gilbert Stuart. That it continues to hang in the East Room of the White House is a testament to Dolley Madison's fortitude and courage. After she and President Madison retired from public life, Dolley later found herself back in Lafayette Square, residing in this corner house from 1837 to 1849, where she died at age 81.

OPPOSITE: THE WHITE HOUSE IN GHOSTLY GUISE; ABOVE: FIRST LADY DOLLEY MADISON

DISTANCE **0.5 mile (0.8km)**

ALLOW **1 hour (more with site visits)**

START **Farragut West Metro station (17th Street exit)**

FINISH **Farragut West Metro station (18th Street entrance)**

A few years after her death, gentlemen leaving a nearby men's club at night began to notice a woman on the front porch sitting in a rocking chair. Her serene countenance revealed that she was none other than the spirit of their favourite First Lady rocking peacefully in the moonlight.

3 Turn around and walk along the path passing behind the memorial honouring Brigadier General Thaddeus Kosciuszko. Stop at the equestrian statue in the middle of the park.

This is the first equestrian statue ever erected in the US. Placed here in 1853, it commemorates the victories of Major General Andrew Jackson during the War of 1812 fought against Britain. Jackson went on to become the seventh president of the US. When his political career ended, he spent the rest of his life at the Hermitage, his Tennessee estate, where he died in 1845. Twenty years later, lusty laughter was reported in a bedroom located on the third floor of the White House. Those seeking slumber in the Rose Room (or Queen's Bedroom) were often startled by the sound, definitely made by a man yet sounding like it came from nowhere in particular. First Lady Mary Todd Lincoln was one of the first to attribute the laugh to former President Andrew Jackson. What his supernatural association with the bedroom might be is anyone's guess, though the bed slept in by overnight guests was indeed a piece of furniture in the White House when Jackson was president.

4 Looking at the Jackson statue, turn left and follow the path to the other side of the park. Turn left onto Jackson Place and proceed to No. 712.

At the end of the 19th century, many inhabitants of Lafayette Square would have been nervous about walking in front of this house, so convinced were they that a curse enveloped it. Numerous people claimed to hear low, sorrowful moaning coming from within. During the Civil War (1861–65) it had been the home of dashing Major Henry Rathbone. It was the major and his fiancée, Clara Harris, who attended the theatre with President Abraham Lincoln and his wife on the fateful evening of 14 April 1865, when they witnessed Lincoln's assassination. Rathbone, moreover, had been wounded by the president's murderer, John Wilkes Booth, as the former tried to stop the latter from escaping Ford's Theatre. Clara attended her injured betrothed. It was only later that she realized her evening dress was soaked with blood, a gruesome reminder of the evening's tragedy. Rather than dispose of the dress, Clara inexplicably kept it, storing it in a bedroom closet at her family's summer home in upstate New York. She and Henry were married and had children, yet their life together proved doomed. Rathbone never recovered from the guilt he felt at failing to save the president or apprehend his assassin. In 1870, he resigned from the army and set off with his wife and children on a futile quest for a mental cure. His friends and family quietly began to fear for his sanity; Clara

WHERE TO EAT

① EQUINOX,
818 Connecticut Avenue, NW;
Tel: 1-202-331-8118.
Chef Todd Gray offers a tempting tasting menu at his modern American restaurant. $$$

② KINKEAD'S,
2000 Pennsylvania Avenue, NW;
Tel: 1-202-296-7700.
A mainstay of Washington dining for the simple reason that chef Robert Kinkead specializes in superb seafood. $$$

confided that she wished to leave him but could not bear the disgrace of a divorce. Then, on Christmas Eve morning in 1883, their tragedy found its climactic moment. Rathbone shot Clara and stabbed himself six times. He survived his wounds but spent the remainder of his life institutionalized in Germany. Years later, his son, Henry Riggs Rathbone, returned to the summer house in New York and destroyed the bloody gown, convinced that it had been the source of his parents' doom.

5 Follow Jackson Place to Pennsylvania Avenue, NW. Bearing left, follow the path until you are standing in front of the White House.

Spirits and ghosts abound in America's most famous residence. Random episodes are common – for example, First Daughters Jenna and Barbara Bush reported opera music coming from the fireplace in their bedroom – as are habitual occurrences, such as the appearance of the ghost of the slain President Abraham Lincoln. First Lady Abigail Adams, the original inhabitant of the house, had her staff dry laundry in the unfinished East Room. Many have reported seeing her spirit moving from the East Room into other parts of the house, her hands outstretched as if she's carrying a load of laundry. Those holding quiet conference in the Blue Room have slowly become aware of violin music playing. Mary Todd Lincoln once said to a friend, 'My, how that Mr Jefferson does play the violin,' referring to America's third president, who used to practise in that room. During a news conference in 1987, President Ronald Reagan shared a story with news reporters about an incident in the Lincoln bedroom, when Lincoln's ghost was sighted sitting on the bed. 'I haven't seen him myself,' said Reagan, 'but every once in a while our little dog Rex will start down that long hall, just glaring as though he's seeing something.' Reagan added that the dog would also bark repeatedly as he stopped in front of the Lincoln bedroom. 'And once I went down and opened the door, and I stepped in and turned around for him to come on. He stood there still barking and growling and then started backing away.'

THE WHITE HOUSE;
GROUP TOURS AVAILABLE (ARRANGEMENTS TO BE MADE IN ADVANCE);
www.whitehouse.gov

6 Looking at the White House, turn right and walk to the end of Pennsylvania Avenue, past the grandiose Executive Office Building on your left. Turn left at 17th Street, NW and proceed to New York Avenue, NW. (The Corcoran Gallery of Art is at the intersection.) Turn right onto New York Avenue and continue to the Octagon, located on the corner of New York Avenue and 18th Street. After viewing the front of the house, turn right and walk a bit up 18th Street, turning right into the garden found at the back of the house. Here is the perfect place to contemplate this building's haunted legacy.

The wealthy, influential Tayloes of Virginia built this home between 1799 and 1801. It became their year-round residence in 1817. Colonel John and Mrs Ann Ogle Tayloe had 15 children, 13 who lived to adulthood, so why so many tales of tragic deaths giving rise to ghosts should have attached themselves to this one site and one family remains a mystery. Certainly, the 12 men who determined to stay overnight in 1888 to disprove the existence of Octagon ghosts reconsidered their scepticism when, to their horror, the house was suddenly filled with three female shrieks. Could it be the agonized ghost of a slave woman who once worked in the house and who may have been secretly murdered? Why would the bells hanging in the kitchen ring of their own accord? Why, when a visiting gentleman attempted to silence them, was he lifted bodily from the floor? And what of the magnificent spiral staircase that winds its way from the main floor all the way to the top? A doctor making a house call here in the 1950s encountered a man on the stairway dressed in an early 19th-century military uniform. The mysterious soldier may be looking for one of the Tayloe daughters, who supposedly loved a soldier named Richard Manners. Racing to a rendezvous with him in the garden one night, the girl tripped and plunged over the stairway railing to her death. Her ghost is said to appear on the stairway on 'the night when the silver light of a full moon filters in through the windows'. Other accounts describe a quarrel between Colonel John Tayloe and one of his daughters that took place on the stairway. Again, the body of a young women careens over the stair rail and is discovered listless on the floor below. Was it an accident? Was it suicide? Was she pushed? It was certainly sinister, because when this ghost manifests itself the sounds of whispers in angry tones are heard, followed by the sound of falling.

THE OCTAGON;
GROUP TOURS AVAILABLE (ARRANGEMENTS TO BE MADE IN ADVANCE);
www.archfoundation.org/octagon

7 To return to Farragut West Metro station, exit the garden and return to 18th Street, NW. Turn right and follow 18th Street five blocks to the corner of 18th and I Streets, NW. The 18th Street entrance to the station will be on your left.

WALK 21

An Oasis of Peace and Calm

Nestled atop a leafy rise in northwest Washington are enormous Victorian homes bejewelled in architectural splendour.

When you feel the need to escape the pavement and office buildings of busy downtown Washington, there is no better course of action than to take the Metro to Cleveland Park. Walking the shady, curving streets in this part of town makes you feel like you're strolling through a New England summer resort. Decorative details proliferate on the late 19th-century houses, with their timber frames and cladding and sporting turrets, towers, oriel and bay windows, steep gables and tall chimneys. It's not hard to imagine yourself sitting on one of the verandas sipping lemonade. An art deco moment – with a look at one of the last period cinemas in Washington – precedes your entry into the world of Queen Anne-style magnificence, when you climb up the Newark Street hill to see home after home built as summer residences for wealthy Washingtonians between 1860 and 1910. Finally, you'll visit one of the most stunning sites in the city: Mount St Alban and the Washington National Cathedral.

1 As you leave the Cleveland Park Metro station's west exit, notice Sam's Park and Shop, an early car-oriented shopping centre, across the street. Turn right and walk to the Uptown Theater. It will be on your right at 3426 Connecticut Avenue, NW.

Opened by Warner Bros. in October 1936, the historic Uptown Theater – an old-style 'movie palace' – was the creation of architect John Zink, who designed numerous art deco and art moderne cinemas across the US between 1930 and 1945. The Uptown boasts the largest film screen in the city. In 1968, Stanley Kubrick's *2001: A Space Odyssey* premiered here and enjoyed a 51-week run. In 1997, the Uptown hosted the re-release of the *Star Wars* saga. So intent were Washington residents to experience the trilogy at the Uptown, on opening day the queue of ticket-buyers wrapped around the block, turned the corner, and continued several blocks away.

2 Continue along Connecticut Avenue past the Uptown Theater. You will pass the Cleveland Park branch of the District of Columbia (DC) Public Library. When trams began to run along Connecticut Avenue in the late 19th century, the Cleveland Park Company – a residential developer – built a waiting area where the library now stands. Turn right onto Newark Street, NW walking uphill and then on towards No. 3035.

Newark Street was the first road to be developed in what became a new Washington suburb. It looks very much the same today as it did when this Queen Anne-style house was constructed in 1898. Robert Thompson Head was the architect and is responsible for at least 17 houses in the area. Most of the family houses were built between 1894 and 1930.

3 Follow Newark Street to Highland Place, NW. Turn right and stop in front of 3141 and then 3155 Highland Place, both located on the right side of the street.

Both of these residences were designed by architect Robert I. Fleming in 1895 and were the first to appear on Highland Place. In 1894, landscape architect Frederick Law Olmsted advised the federal government on how best to extend Washington's streets beyond the city's original boundaries. Olmsted recommended that the streets that run through Cleveland Park between Connecticut Avenue and 34th Street, NW conform to the natural terrain. This is why streets like Highland Place meander rather than adhere to the strict grid pattern found throughout much of Washington. No. 3209 Highland Place, built in 1906 in the Georgian Revival style, was the first brick house to be constructed in Cleveland Park.

4 From Highland Place turn left onto 33rd Place, NW. On the corner of 33rd Place and Newark Street is 3301 Newark Street.

OPPOSITE: NO. 3035 NEWARK STREET

DISTANCE **1 mile (1.6km)**

ALLOW **2 hours**

START **Cleveland Park Metro station (west exit)**

FINISH **Olmsted Woods**

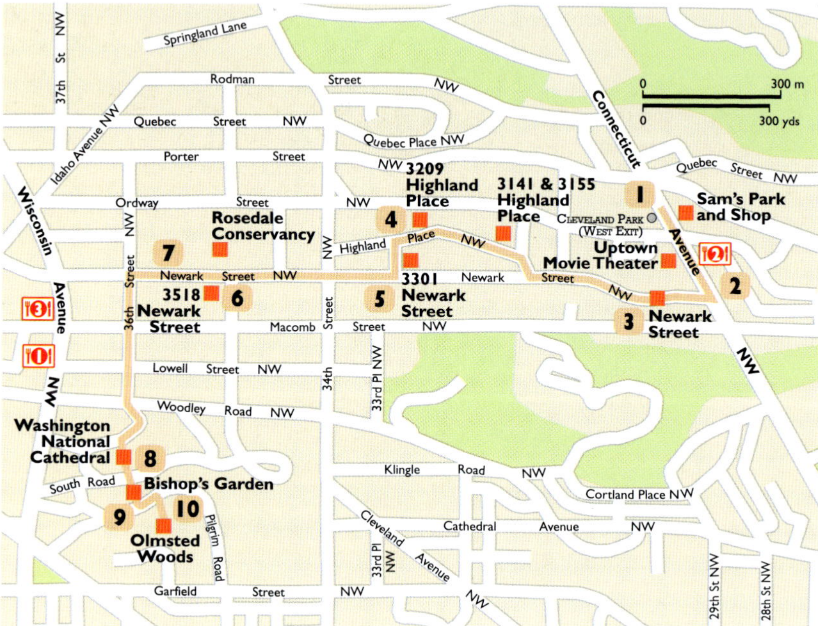

Paul Pelz, designer of the Library of Congress, was one of two architects for this Italian-villa-style residence built by the Cleveland Park Company. John Sherman was the company's president and made a point of hiring Pelz and other well-known architects to create an enclave of unique and impressive properties. Sherman and his artist wife, Ella Bennett Sherman, designed some of the residences themselves. The area you will walk through next was subdivided into a grid pattern in 1894. The curving streets and irregularly shaped plots of land on which the houses in Highland Place were built give way to a more uniform look. The Cleveland Park Company developed many homes in this part of town.

5 Continue on Newark Street to the intersection of 34th Street, NW. Cross 34th Street with caution (there are no traffic lights). Stay on Newark Street until you reach a small gate at No. 3501 on the right. You'll see a stairway of stones ascending the hill to the Rosedale estate.

The oldest house in Cleveland Park is Rosedale, located on the rise above the meadow. The original stone structure dates from about 1740, but in 1794 General Uriah Forrest and his wife, Rebecca, bought the property and added a timber-framed extension. Forrest had fought in the War of American Independence (1775–83), was later Mayor of Georgetown and then a member of Congress. His descendants lived in the house until 1917. By 1959, Rosedale had become a dormitory for girls attending the National Cathedral School. Later, it was used by the non-profit organization Youth for Understanding, which used the house from the late 1970s until 2000. The Friends of Rosedale was founded to ensure the property did not fall into the hands of developers eager to obliterate its historic character and open spaces. In 2004, following an intense fundraising effort and much legal wrangling, the citizens of Cleveland Park purchased the property, creating a land trust known as the Rosedale Conservancy. The Forrest farmhouse has been restored to virtually the same floor plan as existed in the early 1800s, after the Forrests' extension work was carried out.

ROSEDALE CONSERVANCY;
MON–FRI, 7–SUNSET;
www.rosedaleconservancy.org

6 Across the street from Rosedale on Newark Street is No. 3518.

The stone wall that runs just beyond this property is all that remains of Red Top (also known as Oak View), President Grover Cleveland's summer home. Cleveland was one of many wealthy Washingtonians who traded the heat of the city for the shade and serenity of the highland area north of the city centre. Cleveland's tenure here gave this district its name. He bought a stone farmhouse and updated it by adding wooden Victorian porches, a shingled roof and a distinct double chimney. The house was razed to the ground in 1927 and the stones from the house were used to build this wall.

WHERE TO EAT

1 CAFÉ DELUXE,
3228 Wisconsin Avenue, NW;
Tel: 1-202-686-2233.
American bistro that serves familiar dishes such as meatloaf, chicken pot pie, and pasta with a twist. $$

2 DINO,
3435 Connecticut Avenue, NW;
Tel: 1-202-686-2966.
Dino Gold and his wife, Kay, preside over this homey Italian cafe featuring pasta, light dishes and an inventive wine list. $$

3 TWO AMYS,
2715 Macomb Street, NW;
Tel: 1-202-885-5700.
A wood-burning oven yields authentic Neapolitan pizza at this wildly popular Cleveland Park favourite. $$

7 **Proceed along Newark Street to the intersection of 36th Street. Turn left on 36th Street and continue through the intersections of Macomb and Lowell Streets, NW and then Woodley Road, NW. Cross Woodley Road and climb the short hill onto the grounds of the Washington National Cathedral.**

On 6 January 1893, Congress granted a charter to the Protestant Episcopal Cathedral Foundation of the District of Columbia, allowing it to establish a cathedral and institutions of higher learning. In September 1907, the foundation stone was laid on land called Mount St Alban, the most commanding spot in the city. President Theodore Roosevelt and the Bishop of London addressed the crowd of 10,000. By 1912, the Bethlehem Chapel had opened, but it was not until 1976 that the nave and west rose window were completed; Queen Elizabeth II was present for the dedication. The west towers were completed in September 1990, concluding 83 years of construction. Today, the cathedral and its campus are a hive of activity that includes daily worship services, concerts, exhibitions, talks and guided tours. The legacy of the stone carvers whose work adorns the exterior of the structure in the form of gargoyles and grotesques is the topic of an especially popular tour. Look out for Darth Vader!

WASHINGTON NATIONAL CATHEDRAL;

MON–FRI 10–5.30, SAT 10–4.30, SUN 8–6.30; www.cathedral.org/cathedral

8 **On the south side of the cathedral is the enchanting Bishop's Garden.**

This terraced landscape features an impressive array of box as well as a recreation of a monastery herb garden from the Middle Ages. Tours of the garden take place on Wednesdays 1 April through to 31 October at 10.30am, except in August. You can pick up a self-guide booklet at the Herb Cottage.

9 **Beyond the Bishop's Garden at the base of the Cathedral is the 5-acre (2-hectare) Olmsted Woods.**

This is one of the few old forests left in the city. The area has been kept free from development since landscape architect Frederick Law Olmsted Jr designed the cathedral gardens and grounds. The All Hallows Guild, a volunteer group, acts as caretakers of the woodland. Since 1997, the group has been restoring the refuge bit by bit, adding an ecologically sensitive walkway, improving water run-off techniques and adding new plantings.

10 **To get to the nearest Metro station, you'll need to take a bus. From the National Cathedral grounds, walk to the intersection of Wisconsin and Cathedral Avenues, NW, where you will see a waiting area for the Metrobus. Any Metrobus numbered 32, 34 or 36 headed in the direction of Friendship Heights will take you to the Tenleytown Metro station, where you can board the red line trains heading into the city centre or Maryland suburbs.**

OPPOSITE: STATUE OF GEORGE WASHINGTON INSIDE WASHINGTON NATIONAL CATHEDRAL

WALK 22

Blazing the Sculpture Trail

Three-dimensional artistic expression, from the amusing to the sublime, can be discovered amongst courthouses, fountains and inside a garden.

Outdoor artwork can be found throughout America's capital city, yet perhaps nowhere in such abundance as the area known as Judiciary Square. Why should a place known for its courthouses be the source of so much public artwork? Only the lawyers and judges know for sure, but suffice to say that you will run into some giants of jurisprudence along this route – after you've encountered a 'temple' to an egotistical dentist and two anonymous chess players. The National Gallery of Art East Building – which is itself an outdoor sculpture – provides inspiration for a series of contemporary pieces gracing the museum grounds. Even a federal government agency gets in on the act with a pair of sculptures that embody the art deco movement of the 1930s. You'll conclude at the National Gallery Sculpture Garden, only a decade old and already a favourite outdoor venue. For a quiet ramble away from the populace, take this walk at the weekend, when the courts are closed. Otherwise, for a glimpse of Washington's judicial or municipal hustle and bustle, plan to get there on a weekday.

1 Exit Archives-Navy Memorial-Penn Quarter Metro station and walk straight across the US Navy Memorial. Notice that you are walking across a map of the world, symbolizing the breadth of a navy's influence.

This memorial was unveiled in October 1987, on the 212th birthday of the US Navy. The most recognized element is probably this statue, *The Lone Sailor*, a composite of the famous Navy bluejacket. The founders of the memorial envisioned the sailor to be around 25 years old, a senior second-class petty officer. His bronze form was created by Stanley Bleifeld, himself a Navy veteran. Artefacts from eight US Navy ships were mixed with the bronze used for the statue. In both form and meaning, then, *The Lone Sailor* embodies the history of the US Navy and its sailors. Before moving on, look at the 26 bronze reliefs framing the memorial that illustrate naval service.

2 Walk down the steps of the memorial, turn left and walk along Pennsylvania Avenue, NW. Cross 7th Street, NW and walk onto the plaza on the other side. Bear left towards the little temple-like edifice.

In 1849, a Connecticut-born dentist named Henry Cogswell headed west to California, hoping to take advantage of the Gold Rush. He invested in property and mining stocks and shares and struck it rich. A loyal adherent to the Temperance Movement, Dr Cogswell decided to donate a fountain to any municipality that would accept one to ensure that passers-by would be able to quench their thirst with water rather than the demon booze. He had the fountains built in his hometown of Bridgeport, Connecticut, underwriting the $4,000 cost to manufacture each one. The fountains varied in size and design, though all featured sculptured marine and animal life; some even featured a bronze portrait of Dr Cogswell himself. Washington's fountain, built in about 1880, was spared that ornamentation in favour of two entwined dolphins and a water crane. Ironically, during the Prohibition in the 1930s the fountain was the domain of a bootlegger known as 'Skats', who reportedly used the fountain as a distribution point for his homemade gin. Later, in the 1960s and 1970s the area immediately adjacent was home to a highly successful purveyor of booze.

OPPOSITE: *PRINZ FRIEDRICH VON HOMBURG* AT THE NATIONAL GALLERY OF ART; ABOVE: THE US NAVY MEMORIAL

DISTANCE **1 mile (1.6km)**

ALLOW **1.5 hours**

START **Archives-Navy Memorial-Penn Quarter Metro station**

FINISH **Archives-Navy Memorial-Penn Quarter Metro station**

3 Closer to Pennsylvania Avenue on this same plaza you will see a tall, three-sided granite shaft.

A veterans' organization, the Grand Army of the Republic, erected a shrine to its founder, Dr Benjamin F. Stephenson, a surgeon in the US Civil War (1861–65). Sculptor John Massey Rhine created the piece in 1909. The Grand Army was a national society composed of honourably discharged Union soldiers and sailors and was dedicated to assisting permanently disabled soldiers as well as Union widows. It passed out of existence in 1959 when Albert Woolson, the last remaining Union veteran, died at the age of 109.

4 Just beyond the Stephenson Grand Army of the Republic memorial you can see a light-coloured stone building, which is a bank. Walk to the back of it.

The National Bank of Washington building was constructed in 1889 and designed by Washington architect James

G. Hill. A portion of the building is used by the Argentine Naval Attache. The back of the bank building delights those who notice the trompe l'oeil mural.

5 Bear right towards Indiana Avenue, NW. Follow it to 6th Street, NW, crossing that street and continuing on Indiana Avenue past the Moultrie Courthouse. After you cross the intersection of 5th Street, NW proceed half a block.

This marble statue of America's 16th president, Abraham Lincoln (1809–65), was unveiled in April 1868, three years after his assassination by John Wilkes Booth. Almost immediately after Lincoln's death was announced, a fundraising campaign began to erect a statue in front of the City Hall in Washington. Sculptor Lot Flannery received the commission for what became the first public monument to Lincoln. Unlike the more famous depiction of the president at the Lincoln Memorial, where his monumental size and solid stance evoke his legacy as the leader who held the country together during its darkest years, here the viewer encounters the man who served first as lawyer and then as statesman.

6 Cross Indiana Avenue and make your way through the open terraced space known as John Marshall Park. After you descend the steps to the park proper, notice the small bubbling fountain on the right paying tribute to a natural spring that once flowed in Judiciary Square.

It is not surprising that the memorial dominating John Marshall Park should be none other than the site's namesake. Marshall (1755–1835) was one of the most renowned, influential chief justices of the Supreme Court as well as the founder of judicial review. He served on the court for 34 years, strengthening American Constitution law through myriad far-reaching decisions. Marshall remains a giant – if not the giant – of American jurisprudence. To the left of the John Marshall statue are two

ABOVE: *THINKER ON A ROCK* AT THE NATIONAL GALLERY OF ART

WHERE TO EAT

1 PAVILION CAFÉ,
National Gallery of Art (Sculpture Garden),
7th Street and Constitution Avenue, NW;
Tel: 1-202-289-3361 (extension 5).
Enjoy gourmet salads and sandwiches on the patio overlooking the sculptures and fountain. $$

2 D'AQUA,
801 Pennsylvania Avenue, NW;
Tel: 1-202-783-7717.
Freshly prepared seafood is the star of this light-filled Italian restaurant. The outdoor seating overlooks the US Navy memorial and the majestic National Archives. $$$

gentlemen seated on a short retaining wall. They have been engaged in the eleventh move of their chess match since this sculpture was placed here in 1983. The position on the board is taken from an actual game played in 1855 by chess sensation Paul Morphy and his boyhood friend Charles Maurian. Sculptor Lloyd Lillie, however, depicts a scenario in which, at least this time, the chess master would not be savouring victory.

7 Continue through Marshall Park to Pennsylvania Avenue, NW. Turn left and proceed to the plaza in front of the E. Barrett Prettyman Federal Courthouse.

The ceremonial wig worn by this stern-looking figure provides a hint that the lawyer depicted was British. His name was Sir William Blackstone, and he holds a copy of his milestone work, *Commentaries on the Laws of England* (published 1765–69), which clarified English law and aided the individuals who drafted the United States Constitution. This statue was given to the US by the wife of sculptor Paul Wayland Bartlett to celebrate the ties that bind the US and Britain. Mrs Bartlett's original intent was to make the statue a gift from the American Bar Association to the English Bar Association. However, it was discovered that the sculpture, at 9ft (2.7m) high, was too large to stand alongside the other statues in the Hall of Courts in London. Mr Wayland was accommodating and designed a smaller replica for England.

8 Cross Pennsylvania Avenue at 3rd Street, NW. Turn right and walk along the north façade of the National Gallery of Art East Building.

Completed in 1976 and designed by world-famous architect I. M. Pei, the National Gallery of Art East Building has sprinkled its exterior grounds with a variety of contemporary sculpture, the most arresting being *Prinz Friedrich von Homburg, Ein Schauspiel, 3X* by American artist Frank Stella and created 1998–2001. It is a whirlwind of curving aluminium and fibreglass. The title of the work refers to the 19th-century play *Prinz Friedrich von Homburg*, written by the German writer Heinrich von Kleist. Outside the entrance to the East Building stands *Knife Edge Mirror Two Piece* by British artist Henry Moore (1898–1986). Each summer, the National Gallery staff give the piece a good scrubbing to minimize the detrimental effects of its outdoor location. It's an elaborate undertaking: at least six people work for a minimum of three days using mechanical lifts, scaffolding and ladders.

9 Return to Pennsylvania Avenue, turn left, and proceed to the intersection of that street and Constitution Avenue, NW. Proceed and cross 6th Street, NW, continuing along Constitution Avenue to the Federal Trade Commission Building.

This structure is sometimes called the Apex Building for its position in a large precinct known as the Federal Triangle. It is endearing, however, that the true apex is not the building but the daycare playground in its grounds. Two limestone statues, each 12ft (3.6m) high, flank the façade. *Man Controlling Trade* reflects the art deco style of the 1930s and depicts a man controlling a horse, symbolic of the Federal Trade Commission controlling monopolies. Michael Lantz, a young Works Progress Administration instructor from New Rochelle, New York, won the competition to design two sculptures for the Apex in 1942. The Works Progress Administration (WPA) was the largest of the New Deal reforms created by President Franklin D. Roosevelt (1882–1945) in the 1930s.

10 Follow Constitution Avenue across 7th Street. Cross 7th Street and enter the National Gallery of Art Sculpture Garden using the entrance found at 7th Street and Constitution Avenue.

Washington's most recent full-scale viewing ground for outdoor sculpture opened in 1999. Depending on what time of year you visit, you will see either ice-skaters gliding across a frozen rink or arching jets of water spewing forth from a fountain. Abstract and representational work can be found here by such artists as Claes Oldenburg (born 1929), Magdalena Abakanowicz (born 1930), Barry Flanagan (born 1941) and Roy Lichtenstein (born 1923), whose painted aluminium *House I* is a favourite. It is not unusual to be standing near another popular piece, *Typewriter Erase, Scale X*, and hear people from an older generation attempting to explain to their youthful companions how exactly this object was once used. An entrance from a Paris Métro station adds a whimsical element to the patio adjacent to the cafe. Free jazz concerts take place on Friday evenings from May to September.

11 To return to Archives-Navy Memorial-Penn Quarter Metro, exit the National Gallery Sculpture Garden via the entrance near the corner of 7th Street and Constitution Avenue, NW. Cross Constitution Avenue via 7th Street and continue one block to Pennsylvania Avenue, NW. Cross Pennsylvania Avenue and walk half a block along 7th Street.

WALK 23

Washington's Niche Museums

This walk is perfect to take on a cold, rainy day or when the oppressive humidity of Washington's summer makes touring outdoors less desirable.

One could easily spend days roaming through the galleries of the Smithsonian museums lining the National Mall. Yet worthy of your time though they are, a surprising array of smaller institutions can be discovered scattered throughout the city. The four museums included in this walk all focus on a particular subject and are situated in Washington's Penn Quarter, which translates into abundant opportunities for food, drink and entertainment after a morning or afternoon of exhibit viewing. Begin in the heart of Penn Quarter with what must be Washington's smallest museum and one dedicated to that smallest of objects, the bead. Trade the world of handicrafts for a microscope and genomes at one of the city's newest museums, dedicated to explaining breakthroughs in scientific research to the layman. Then honour the life and death of the everyday American hero, the police officer, at a visitor centre and memorial located amidst Washington's federal and city courts. Finally, celebrate architecture and the art of building construction when you enter one of the most spectacular spaces in the city.

1 Exit Archives-Navy Memorial-Penn Quarter Metro station and head along the path that wraps around the US Navy memorial. Turn right onto D Street, NW, then stop at the intersection of 7th and D Streets, NW.

In 1983, 12 bead enthusiasts founded the Bead Society of Greater Washington. By 1995, the organization had created a museum, with individuals contributing to the collection, and set up various national bead societies. A centrepiece of the viewing experience is the Bead Timeline of History, which employs beads and beaded ornaments to 'bridge geographic, socio-economic, and cultural divides suggesting common ground among diverse communities'. An advantage of the Bead Museum's small size is that a knowledgeable staff person is always close at hand, willing to offer explanations or answer questions – and probably working on a beading project to boot!

THE BEAD MUSEUM;
TUE–SAT 12–6;
www.beadmuseumdc.org

2 Next door at 700 7th Street is the National Law Enforcement Officers memorial visitors centre.

This gift shop and information centre complements the National Law Enforcement Officers memorial located a few blocks away. You will see photographs of the memorial itself, including a wall-length mural of the opening ceremonies in 1991 and a rare photo of the memorial site and its surroundings as they appeared

in 1890. Touching mementos left at the memorial by friends and loved ones are on display. An interactive video system allows visitors to read brief biographies and view a photograph of the individual police officers honoured, along with their respective location on the memorial walls. Exhibits such as one about the life and times of Wyatt Earp (1848–1929) – the American folk hero and officer of the law in various Western frontier towns, best known for his involvement in the Gunfight at the OK Corral – provide a historic context to American law enforcement; 'The Deadliest Day in Law Enforcement History – September 11, 2001' presents its dangers in stark relief.

NATIONAL LAW ENFORCEMENT OFFICERS MEMORIAL (VISITORS CENTRE);
MON–FRI 9–5, SAT 10–5, SUN 12–5;
TEL: 1-202-737-3213;
www.nleomf.com/TheMemorial/visitorscenter.htm

OPPOSITE: THE NATIONAL LAW ENFORCEMENT OFFICERS MEMORIAL; ABOVE: THE BEAD MUSEUM

DISTANCE **1 mile (1.6km)**

ALLOW **1 hour for walk (plus at least 2 hours to include museum visits)**

START **Archives-Navy Memorial-Penn Quarter Metro station**

FINISH **Judiciary Square Metro station**

3 Cross 7th Street at D Street. Turn left and walk one block to E Street, NW. Take note of Ticket Place, where you can purchase discounted tickets to many Washington theatre performances. On reaching E Street, NW, follow it to the end of the block. Cross 6th Street, NW. At the corner of 6th and E Streets is the entrance to the Marian Koshland Science Museum.

Since it opened in 2004, this museum has sought to engage the general public in 'science behind the headlines'. The Koshland was set up in memory of one woman's passion for science – immunologist and molecular biologist Marian 'Bunny' Koshland (1921–97). She once wrote in the *Annual Reviews of Immunology* that she chose science as a career because it was a means of making lasting, if not immortal, contributions to humankind. True to her calling, she went on to conduct groundbreaking research in the behaviour of antibodies. Her husband, Daniel

Koshland (1920–2007), also a renowned molecular biologist, partnered with the National Academy of Sciences to found this museum through a monetary gift he made to continue his wife's legacy.

MARIAN KOSHLAND SCIENCE MUSEUM;

DAILY (EXCEPT TUE) 10–6;
TEL: 1-202-334-1201;
www.koshland-science-museum.org

4 From the museum, turn left and walk along E Street, crossing 5th Street, NW. Look across 5th Street to see the large globe balanced atop the National Academies Building. Continue on E Street for half a block. You've now entered an area of the city known as Judiciary Square.

In this quiet district of Washington, the US honours its police officers – the men and women who day in and day out patrol the streets, who have regular contact with citizenry of all sorts, and who valiantly enforce the laws that shore up big cities and small towns alike. The memorial was unveiled in 1991 and occupies 3 acres (1.2 hectares) of Judiciary Square, the place that has been the site of the federal and city judicial buildings almost since Washington's founding. At the entrance are statuary groupings of an adult lion protecting its cubs. Sculpted by Raymond Kaskey (born 1943), they symbolize the protective role played by law officers in today's society. Inscribed on marble walls along the paths are the randomly placed names of more than 17,500 officers who have been killed in the line of duty, dating back to the first known death in 1792. At an annual candlelight vigil held each year during National Police Week (in May), new names of fallen officers are added.

NATIONAL LAW ENFORCEMENT OFFICERS MEMORIAL;

www.nleomf.com

5 Walk across the National Law Enforcement Officers memorial from E to F Streets. Notice the entrance

WHERE TO EAT

1 BURMA,
740 6th Street, NW;
Tel: 1-202-638-1280.
Located upstairs, this no-frills Burmese restaurant offers especially tasty appetizers and Asian salads. $

2 HIGH NOON,
National Building Museum,
401 F Street NW;
Tel: 1-202-628-0906.
Even a humble sandwich is raised to new heights when eaten in the spectacular space that is the National Building Museum's Great Hall. $

3 JALEO,
480 7th Street, NW;
Tel: 1-202-628-7949.
José Andrés is one of Washington's first celebrity chefs. He made his name initially by creating the tapas served at this restaurant. $$

to the Judiciary Square Metro station. Cross F Street.

One step inside will quickly reveal why this building always plays host to a presidential inaugural ball. It is one of the most stunning, soaring spaces in Washington. Prior to becoming the National Building Museum in 1980, the building was used as government offices. The 1,200ft- (365m-) long exterior frieze that wraps around the entire building depicts a parade of US Civil War military units, hinting at the original function of the building. Designed in 1881 by civil engineer and US Army General Montgomery C. Meigs, it housed the Pension Bureau. From the beginning, it was praised as a marvel of engineering. A guided tour of the building (highly recommended) will reveal features such as the ingenious system of windows, vents and open archways that allow the structure's Great Hall to function as a reservoir of light and air. Today, visitors to the National Building Museum can explore exhibits dedicated to architecture, design, engineering, construction and urban planning. The museum shop is one of the best in the city.

NATIONAL BUILDING MUSEUM;
MON–SAT 10–5, SUN 11–5;
TEL: 1-202-272-2448; www.nbm.org

6 To end the walk, exit the National Building Museum at F Street, NW. You will find the entrance to the Judiciary Square Metro station just across the street.

ABOVE: THE STUNNING INTERIOR OF THE NATIONAL BUILDING MUSEUM

WALK 24

International Washington

West of the White House are the institutions that bring the international community flooding into America's capital city.

Here is an insider's walk of Washington. Few visitors, or locals for that matter, take the time to notice the hundreds of employees who pour out of the Farragut West Metro station each day on their way to work at the World Bank and International Monetary Fund. What these seven blocks lack in architectural charm or historic structures, they more than make up for in accessibility. Unlike the diplomatic community along Embassy Row, where the policy is look but don't drop in, the international agencies featured on this walk provide venues expressly for the public to visit, so take this walk during the working week when the offices are open. This route, though, isn't all about work and office buildings: you'll wander through a park or two – even a tiny sculpture garden – and you'll see a beautiful row of stately Beaux Arts headquarters. A stroll through the George Washington University campus, with its large population of international students, concludes this outing through an area of Washington where all the world's nations seem to be represented in the passers-by.

1 Exit Farragut West Metro station onto 18th Street, NW and turn right, crossing I Street, NW. Halfway down the block on the left is Taberna del Alabardero.

One of the most beautiful dining rooms in Washington, Taberna del Alabardero ('Tavern of the Palace Guards') began its life in Spain over 25 years ago, when Father Luis de Lezama rented a 16th-century townhouse near the Royal Palace in Madrid. Despite having no prior training in the restaurant business, he began serving meals to great acclaim. In 1989, Lezama crossed the Atlantic to open Taberna del Alabardero in Washington. Other outposts of the restaurant can be found in Seville and Benahavis in Spain. Those craving an escape to Old World Spain via the US capital city need only head through the doors of Taberna del Alabardero for sherry, tapas and incomparable paella.

2 Continue on 18th Street to the intersection of H Street, NW. Turn right and then turn left onto 19th Street, NW. After crossing Pennsylvania Avenue, NW you will cross H Street again. Continue on 19th Street until you reach the International Monetary Fund at No. 700.

An international organization of 185 member countries, the International Monetary Fund (IMF) was founded to promote monetary cooperation as well as to provide temporary financial assistance to countries. Its IMF Center, at 720 19th Street, helps to heighten public awareness of the organization's role in the global economy via permanent and changing exhibits, a bookstore and gift shop.

IMF CENTER;
MON–FRI 10–4.30;
www.imf.org/external/np/exr/center

3 Return to H Street and turn right. The World Bank is located at 1818 H Street.

Conceived during World War II at Bretton Woods, New Hampshire, the World Bank initially helped rebuild Europe after the war. Its first loan of $250 million was to France in 1947 for post-war reconstruction. Such activity has remained a focus of the bank's work, though its mission has evolved to include the alleviation of global poverty. Being an international enterprise, 40 per cent of the staff work abroad.

OPPOSITE: HEADQUARTERS OF ORGANIZATION OF AMERICAN STATES (OAS); ABOVE: THE WORLD BANK HQ

DISTANCE 1.5 miles (2.5km)

ALLOW 1.5 hours (more with site visits)

START Farragut West Metro station (18th Street, NW exit)

FINISH Foggy Bottom Metro station

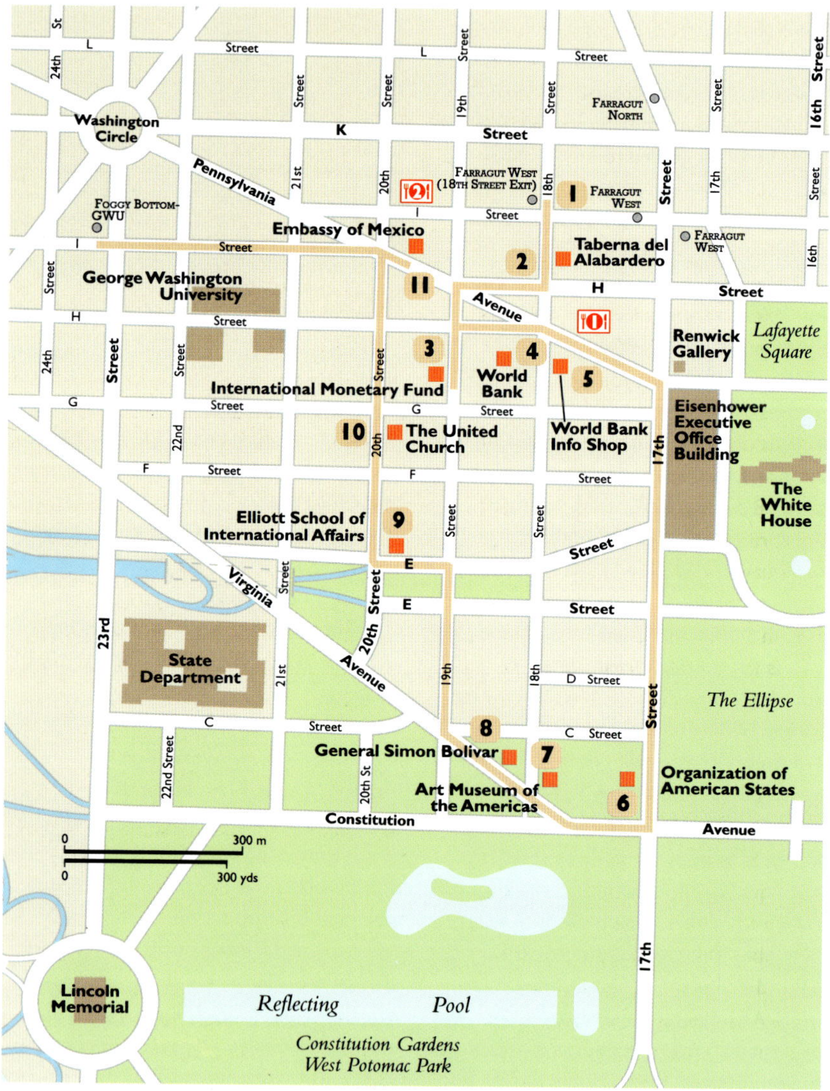

4 Follow H Street to the intersection of 18th Street. Across the street on the corner is the World Bank Info Shop.

The public can delve into the mission of the World Bank by visiting InfoShop. World Bank publications are available for perusal or purchase and computer work stations allow users to browse World Bank websites and databases. Shop staff will even provide a guided tour of its resources.

WORLD BANK INFOSHOP;
MON–FRI 9–5; www.worldbank.org/infoshop

5 Turn right onto Pennsylvania Avenue from InfoShop and then right again onto 17th Street, NW. For the next five blocks, you'll pass majestic edifices constructed in the Beaux Arts style at the turn of the 20th century: the grandiose Eisenhower Executive Office Building is first, followed by the Corcoran Gallery of Art, the Red Cross headquarters and the Daughters of the American Revolution. At the intersection of 17th Street and Constitution Avenue, NW is the stately Organization of American States.

A 1966 sculpture of Queen Isabella I of Spain (1451–1504) greets visitors arriving at the Organization of American States (OAS). She is remembered in the US as the queen who pawned her jewels to finance the first voyage of Christopher Columbus in 1492, popularly described as the 'discoverer' of the New World. The OAS, which was set up in 1948, functions as a forum for strengthening democracy, promoting human rights and confronting shared problems such as poverty, terrorism and illegal drugs in the Americas. There are 35 member states from North, Central and South America, as well as Caribbean nations. Proceedings are conducted in the four official languages of the OAS – English, Spanish, Portuguese and French.

WHERE TO EAT

1 BREADLINE,
1751 Pennsylvania Avenue, NW;
Tel: 1-202-822-8900.
Whatever you select at this busy takeaway, make sure it includes the delicious bread baked on the premises. The sandwiches, salads and soups are all excellent. Closed at weekends. $

2 KAZ SUSHI BISTRO,
1915 I Street, NW;
Tel: 1-202-530-5500.
One of the top spots for sushi in the city. Japanese businessmen vie for one of the six chairs at the bar to watch chef Kaz and his staff prepare the day's selection. $$

6 Turn right onto Constitution Avenue and then right again onto 18th Street. At the corner is the Art Museum of the Americas.

In 1976, the OAS established this museum as a tribute to America's bicentenary. The building was designed by architect Paul Cret in 1912, originally

as the residence for the OAS Secretaries General. The museum's permanent collection of 20th-century Latin American and Caribbean art is one of the most significant in the country. Make sure to amble through the small sculpture garden found in the grounds. **ART MUSEUM OF THE AMERICAS;** TUE–SUN 10–5; www.museum.oas.org

7 Across 18th Street from the museum on Virginia Avenue is an equestrian statue of General Simon Bolivar.

At 27ft (8m) high, this bronze figure of General Simon Bolivar (1783–1830), unveiled in 1959, is one of the largest equestrian statues in the US. It was designed by Austrian-born US sculptor Felix W. de Weldon, who also created the Iwo Jima Memorial near Arlington National Cemetery in Virginia, just across the Potomac River from Washington. Bolivar was one of the most important leaders of Hispanic America's successful struggle for independence from Spain. He participated in the foundation of the Gran Colombia, a nation forming the liberated Spanish colonies, becoming its president from 1821 to 1830. The Gran Colombia dissolved in 1831, yet Bolivar's legacy contributed to the independence of present-day Bolivia, Colombia, Ecuador, Panama, Peru and Venezuela.

8 Facing the statue, turn left on Virginia Avenue and then right onto 19th Street. Proceed to a small park bounded by E Street, NW on both its south and north. Turn left on the northern side and look for 1957 E Street, which will be on the right.

One of the primary reasons that undergraduate and graduate students select Washington for their education is the opportunity to earn a degree from George Washington University's Elliott School of International Affairs. In 1898, what was then Columbian College opened its School of Jurisprudence and Diplomacy, the precursor to the Elliott School. At the time, the study of international affairs was considered useful for

ABOVE: BRONZE EQUESTRIAN STATUE OF SIMON BOLIVAR

training future diplomats or international lawyers. By the 1920s, emphasis on international business was added. Today, the university prepares its students not only for careers in public service, perhaps with the US State Department, but also in the private sector and non-governmental organizations such as the World Bank and International Monetary Fund (IMF). Degree courses include the Master of International Policy and Practice and Master of International Trade and Investment Policy. Regional study programmes cover Europe, Russia, Southeast Asia, Latin America, Canada and the Caribbean. The Elliot School has professional and education partnerships with over a dozen universities around the world.

9 Continue on E Street to 20th Street, NW. Turn right and proceed one block. At the corner of 20th and G Streets is the United Church.

In 1833, the Evangelical Concordia Congregation built a red-brick Romanesque Revival church on this site to accommodate the German immigrants who had begun to arrive in Washington; many took up residence in this area known as Foggy Bottom. A few years later, a small group of Methodists established the Union Methodist Episcopal Church nearby. By January 1975, the two congregations had decided to merge, forming the United Church, or *Vereinigte Kirche*. A German-language worship service is held twice a month.

10 Proceed on 20th Street until it intersects with Pennsylvania Avenue. Turn right and look for No. 1911 across the street, the Embassy of Mexico.

The two countries that border the US each have an embassy on Pennsylvania Avenue, with Canada's located between the White House and US Capitol. In addition, both nations have numerous consulates and other facilities across the US. A portion of the Mexican Embassy is housed in what remains of the Seven Buildings, a row of houses once considered the most prestigious residential address in Washington. After they were developed in 1796, the residences were home to government officials and foreign ministers, who valued the property's close proximity to the White House and Georgetown. The State Department operated from one of the buildings when the federal government arrived in 1800; President and Mrs James Madison lived in a unit while the White House was being rebuilt following its burning by the British during the War of 1812. By the 1890s, many of the houses had begun to be used commercially. In 1959, some of the units were razed for an office building, and, in a rather unfortunate finale, the two surviving houses were enveloped by the massive office complex now in use as the Mexican Embassy.

11 To end the walk, double back to 20th Street and turn left onto I Street. Foggy Bottom station is three blocks away.

THE ATRIUM OF THE WORLD BANK HEADQUARTERS

INDEX

Adams, Abigail 146
Adams, Henry 50, 54
African-American Civil War Memorial 110
American Civil War 61, 66–71, 72, 73, 110
Art Museum of the Americas 169–70
Arthur Sackler Gallery 130, 131
Artifactory Building 79

Barney House 124, 127
Barry, John 93
Barton, Clara 69
Bead Museum 161
Ben's Chili Bowl 107, 110
Berliner, Emile 80
Bethune, Mary McLeod 18, 95–6
Birch Funeral Home and Stable 10
Bishop's Garden 153
Blackstone, Sir William 158
Blair House 55
Bohemian Caverns 109–10
Bolivar, Simon 170
Bomford Mill 13
Booth, John Wilkes 51, 70, 76–7, 145
Bradlee, Ben 138, 140
Brady, Mathew 67–8, 69
Brewmaster's Castle 113
Bureau of Engraving and Printing 23–4

Cairo Hotel 116
Canadian Embassy 42–3
Capitol Hill 14–19, 58–65
Capitol Hill Club 59
Cecil Place 12–13
cherry trees 22, 27, 28
Chesapeake & Ohio Canal 9–11, 12
Chinatown 43, 81
Church of Scientology 117
Cleveland, Grover 151
Cleveland Park 148–53
Clinton, Bill 57
Cluss, Adolf 47, 93
Cogswell, Henry 155
Columbia Residences 87
Constitution Avenue 35
Cosmos Club 124

Dean & DeLuca 13, 137
Decatur Place 101
Devore Chase 105
Dumbarton House 45
Dumbarton Oaks 48–9
Dupont Circle 112–19, 122

East Capitol Street 17–18
Eastern Market 19
Eisenhower Executive Office Building 55, 56, 57
Ellington, 'Duke' 106, 107, 108, 111
Elliott School of International Affairs 170–1
Emancipation Monument 18, 20–1
Embassy Row 120–7
Enid Haupt Garden 130
Environmental Protection Agency Building 35
Everett House 124
Evermay 45–6

Federal Bureau of Investigation (FBI) 41–2
Federal Trade Commission Building 159
Foggy Bottom 84–91
Folger Shakespeare Library 17
Ford's Theatre 70, 71, 76–7
Franklin D. Reeves Center for Municipal Affairs 111
Franklin School 93
Fraunz House 18
Freedom Plaza 39–40
Freer Gallery of Art 129, 134–5
French Ambassador's Residence 102

Georgetown 8–13, 44–9, 136–41
Grace Episcopal Church 12
Graham, Katharine 46–7
Grand Army of the Republic Memorial 67, 156
Grant, Ulysses S. 51, 61, 62
Greater New Hope Baptist Church 81

Hancock, General Winfield Scott 67
Hanna, Mark 51
Harriman, Pamela 140
Hay-Adams Hotel 54
Henry, Joseph 132
Highland Place 149, 150
Hirshhorn Museum 133
Holy Rosary Catholic Church 83
Holy Trinity Church (St Ignatius Chapel) 139
Hoover, J. Edgar 41–2
Hope Diamond 123
Hotel Monaco 79
Hotel Tabard Inn 114–15

Industrial Bank 108–9
International Monetary Fund (IMF) 167
International Order of the Eastern Star 117

J. Edgar Hoover Building 41–2
Jackson, Andrew 52, 53, 54, 145
Jefferson, Thomas 25, 31, 38, 63, 146
Jefferson Pier Stone 31–2
Jewish Washington 81–2, 83
John F. Kennedy Center for the Performing Arts 88, 89, 90–1
John Marshall Park 157–8
John Wilson Building 39
Johnson, Andrew 51, 57
Judiciary Square 154, 157, 163

Kalorama 100–5
Kennedy, Jacqueline 85, 137, 138, 140, 141
Kennedy, John F. 62, 136, 137, 138, 139–40
King, Martin Luther 28, 34, 39–40, 107, 111
Korean War Veterans Memorial 33, 36–7
Kutz Bridge 28

Lafayette, Marquis de 52
Lafayette Square 50–7, 142–7
Laird-Dunlop House 140
Library of Congress Jefferson Building 63
Library Court 16
Lillian and Albert Small Jewish Museum 83
Lincoln, Abraham 18, 34, 51, 66, 68, 70, 71, 72, 73–4, 75, 76–7, 145, 146, 157
Lincoln Memorial 34
Lincoln Park 18
Lincoln Theater 107
Lindens 103
Logan, John A. 96
Logan Circle 92, 95–7
Lucas, Anthony 101
Luther Place Memorial Church 95

McKinley, William 51
McPherson, Major General James 73
Madison, Dolly 45, 143, 145
The Maples 15
Marian Koshland Science Museum 162–3
markets 13, 19, 112, 113
Mary McLeod Bethune Council House 95
Mary Ripley Garden 132–3
Mason, George 27, 29
Mexican Embassy 43, 171
Montgomery, Helen 137
Montrose Park 48

National Air Force Memorial 27
National Archives 42
National Bank of Washington 156–7
National Building Museum 164–5
National City Christian Church 93, 95
National Council of Negro Women 67–8
National Democratic Club 59
National Gallery of Art 42, 133, 158–9
National Law Enforcement Officers Memorial 161, 163
National Mall 22
National Museum of African Art 130, 131
National Museum of American Jewish Military History 117
National Trust for Historic Preservation 113–14
National World War II Memorial 32–3
Naval Lodge Building 15
New York Avenue Presbyterian Church 76
Newark Street 149, 150–1, 153
Newseum 43

Nixon, Richard 57
North, Oliver 57

Oak Hill Cemetery 47
Octagon 147
Old Post Office 41
Old Stone House 13
Olmsted Woods 153
Organization of American States (OAS) 169
Our Lady, Queen of the Americas Church 101

Patterson House/Washington Club 121
Penn Quarter 78–83, 160
Pennsylvania Avenue 38–43, 85, 87
Petersen House 71, 77
Phillips Collection 126, 127
Powell, Lewis 51, 75
Prayer of Columbus 67
Pre-Columbian Museum 49

Rathbone, Major Henry 74–5, 145–6
Rayburn Building 59
Robert A. Taft Garden Park 61–2
Robert Peter House/Ritz Carlton 11–12
Rodgers House 51
Roosevelt, Alice 122
Roosevelt, Eleanor 127
Roosevelt, Franklin D. 27, 42, 127, 159
Rosedale 151
Russell Caucus Room 62

S. Dillon Ripley Center 129
St John's Church 73–4
St Marks' Episcopal Church 16, 17
St Mary Mother of God Catholic Church 82–3
St Mary's Church 85

St Mary's Court 85
St Patrick's Catholic Church 70
St Thomas Episcopal Church 115
sculpture trail 154–9
Sewall-Belmont House and Museum 62
Seward, William 51, 73, 75, 76
Sickles, Daniel E. 54–5
Signers' Memorial 34
6th and I Synagogue 82
Smithsonian American Art Museum 69
Smithsonian Institution/The Castle 131
Smithsonian Museum of American Art and National Portrait Gallery 79–80
Society of the Cincinnati 123, 125
Stanton, Edwin M. 47, 77
Stephen Decatur House Museum 143
Studio Theater 97
Sulgrave Club 113, 121

Taberna del Albardero 167
Tayloe House 51
Thomas Circle 93, 98–9
Thomas Jefferson Memorial 25
Tidal Basin 22, 24–5, 28
True Reformer Building 107–8
Truman, Harry 55
Tudor Place 49

United Church 171
Uptown Theater 149
US Botanic Garden 59–60
US Capitol 58, 60–1, 64–5
US Court of Claims and Appeals 51
US Forest Service 23
US Holocaust Memorial Museum 23
US Navy Memorial 43, 155
US Supreme Court 62–3
Veteran's Administration Building 73
Vietnam Veterans Memorial 34

Wadsworth, Henry and Martha 121
Wah Luck House 82
Walsh-McLean House 122
Washington, George 31, 85
Washington Circle 85
Washington Harbor 11
Washington National Cathedral 153
Watergate 88
White House 57, 75, 146
Whitelaw apartments 110–11
Whitman, Walt 67, 69
Willard Hotel 39, 76
William Marbury House 137
Wilson, Woodrow 105
Woodrow Wilson House 105
World Bank 167, 169, 172–3
World War Memorial 33

ACKNOWLEDGEMENTS

The Automobile Association wishes to thank the following photographers, companies and picture libraries for their assistance in the preparation of this book.

Abbreviations for the picture credits are as follows – (AA) AA World Travel Library

Front Cover AA/Clive Sawyer; 3 AA/Clive Sawyer; 7 AA/Clive Sawyer; 12 Carolyn Crouch; 14 Alamy/David R. Frazier Photolibrary,Inc.; 17 Topher Mathews; 19 Alamy/Chuck Pefley; 20/21 photolibrary.com/North Wind Picture Archives; 22 dcstockimages.com/Randy Santos; 26 dcstockimages.com/Randy Santos; 29 Alamy/Florida Images; 31 AA/Clive Sawyer; 34 Getty Images/Richard Nowitz; 38 Courtesy of InterContinental Hotels Group; 41 dcstockimages.com/Randy Santos; 43 dcstockimages.com/Randy Santos; 44 Carolyn Crouch; 45 Alamy/Nikreates; 47 Corbis/Kelly-Mooney Photography; 53 Corbis/John Aikins; 56 photolibrary.com/Christy Kanis; 58 dcstockimages.com/Randy Santos; 59 dcstockimages.com/Randy Santos; 63 AA/Clive Sawyer; 64/65 dcstockimages.com/Randy Santos; 66 Alamy/Rich Iwasaki; 69 Carolyn Crouch; 72 Alamy/Rough Guides; 73 Getty Images /AFP; 77 Collinstock/Carol M. Highsmith; 78 dcstockimages.com/Randy Santos; 79 Carolyn Crouch; 84 Alamy/Wim Wiskerke; 88 AA/Clive Sawyer; 90/91 Houserstock/Dave G. Houser; 92 AA/Clive Sawyer; 96 dcstockimages.com/Randy Santos; 98/99 dcstockimages.com/Randy Santos; 100 SuperStock/James Lemass; 103 Carolyn Crouch; 104 Carolyn Crouch; 106 Alamy/Rough Guides; 107 Getty Images /AFP; 109 Alamy/Nikreates; 112 dcstockimages.com/Randy Santos; 116 Susan Isakson/Alamy; 118/119 dcstockimages.com/Randy Santos; 120 Alamy/Carrie Garcia; 125 Carolyn Crouch; 126 Alamy/Michael Ventura ; 128 Getty Images/Jonathan Nourok; 131 AA/Clive Sawyer; 132 Houserstock/Dave G. Houser; 134/135 Alamy/Stock Connection Distribution; 140 Alamy/Chuck Pefley; 141 drr.net/Chuck Pefley; 142 National Geographic/Getty Images; 148 Carolyn Crouch; 154 Carolyn Crouch; 155 Collinstock/Carol M. Highsmith; 157 drr.net/Elliott Teel/Dcstockphoto; 160 Carolyn Crouch; 161 Carolyn Crouch; 167 Collinstock/Carol M. Highsmith; 170 Alamy/Photov.com/Hisham Ibrahim; 172/173 Alamy/Wim Wiskerke.

Every effort has been made to trace copyright holders, and we apologize in advance for any unintentional omissions or errors. We would be pleased to apply any corrections in any following editions of this publication.

Other titles in the series:

Printed in Great Britain
by Amazon

32354801R00076

For Philip and Eamon

CONTENTS

A Note from the Author viii

How to Catch a Bullet in a Plate and Other Tricks to Astound 1

Florrie and the Mysterious Death of a Fat Rascal 14

Auld Bride 21

Beryl in the Dark 28

The Silent Mrs B. 40

Snow Day 49

And so it Begins 58

A Face for Murder 81

Jackie Robson's Last Race 93

Endnote 119

Acknowledgements 121

A NOTE FROM THE AUTHOR

Short stories capture a moment so very well. A few pages and the reward is a glimpse into a soul. The short stories I've pulled together in this collection are loosely crime short stories in the broadest definition with some more sinister than others. A couple focus on the impact and consequences of crime rather than on the crime itself. Many involve women sleuths attempting to make sense of the world. (Good luck with that I say.) But whether they are cosy, horror, or mystery - all the stories here are meant to entertain, and my best hope is you enjoy reading them as much as I enjoyed writing them.

Jude x

HOW TO CATCH A BULLET IN A PLATE AND OTHER TRICKS TO ASTOUND

He never performed the trick at a matinee show as he didn't like to worry the children in the audience. At least there was that, Mrs Conway thought, as the red blood pooled around her best boots. And she would sponge her skirt with salted cold water when this whole to-do was done with, she decided, as she knelt beside the dying man. That way she might perhaps save it.

Underneath the pancake make-up, Dong Hongming's face was bone white. Screwed up in agony, as he lay splayed on the oak planks of the stage.

Mrs Conway had seen death too many times nursing at the front in the Great War. The magician wasn't dead yet. But he soon would be. Yes, the skirt she might save, but not the man.

And they both knew it.

There had been silence at first from the audience as, with a sharp cry, Hongming had fallen to the floor clutching his chest. A beat, while they craned forward in their seats waiting for him to rise and then bow. Instead, a stagehand dropped the

curtain with a swoosh and a bang, and now, beyond the heavy velvet, the screaming of the audience wasn't letting up.

Mrs Conway kept the chalky cloth pressed against the gaping wound in the performer's chest, feeling the pulsing blood cool against her skin. He'd taken the bullet in his right lung, she guessed. And judging by the spreading crimson beneath them, it had gone straight through and out the other side.

Blood bubbled at the corner of his mouth as the magician himself fought for breath, and his terrified eyes locked onto hers as if begging her to breathe for him. And it was just him and her, even as the magician's assistants wailed and the magician's wife wept, calling the name, *'George!'* over and over.

For a second, she wondered if this could possibly be one of the magician's tricks. He wasn't Chinese. He merely pretended to be. His real name was George Bannister and his entire life was an illusion. Was this death the same? But experience told her otherwise. There was no artifice here. No cornflower and cochineal. No invisible threads. This dying was his final performance.

Bannister 's long fingers clutched her wrist. The man who had been known as Dong Hongming wanted something from her. But then, in Mrs Lettice Conway's experience, the dying always wanted something from the living. To see their mother. To be forgiven for their sins. Or simply more time on this earth.

The magician wanted an answer to the question: Who killed Dong Hongming?

Mrs Conway gave him a brisk nod. She was curious about that herself.

. . .

The next morning, over her breakfast cup of tea and slice of bread and dripping, she gave the matter some thought.

The magic trick required a team of four on stage, including Bannister, his wife and his two assistants. As well as four volunteers from the audience.

The night she'd watched it from the wings, two young soldiers had been brought up on to the stage and handed a rifle. Each man took a good hard look at his weapon and then gave a self-important nod that they passed muster. With a flourish, Bannister celebrated by igniting a spoonful of gunpowder at the front of the stage to appreciative *oohs* and *aahs* from the audience. Everyone liked a bang and a flash and a wallop, Mrs Conway had thought at the time, though one of the soldiers flinched as if he'd long since had his fill of such things.

That was the cue the magician's wife, Ivy, had been waiting for. Out in the auditorium, she asked a woman in the stalls to select two round bullets from a box. These were handed to the woman's husband to mark with a knife. Job done, Ivy had carried these bullets up to the stage in an ornate gilded cup which she'd handed to one of the soldiers.

Centre stage, Bannister had proceeded to charge the first rifle's barrel with gunpowder and push in a cotton wad to compress it. He gestured over the soldier and took the cup from him before dropping one of the bullets into the barrel of the rifle and ramming it home with the rod. He went through the exact same palaver with the second rifle.

Their responsibilities over, the soldiers returned to their seats and Bannister passed the loaded rifles to his two scowling assistants who had been waiting with arms folded and dressed as his executioners.

Bowing to the audience, the magician took up a willow pattern plate, walked with ceremony across the stage and stood at some distance from the 'firing squad', holding the plate away from him.

The crowd fell silent. How many of them thought about the sons and brothers and fathers that had fallen in the line of fire? Too many, Mrs Conway presumed.

The night she'd watched the illusion, the firing squad fired the rifles, and the magician staggering back a step had seemed to catch the bullets on the plate, with a distinct *'ping... ping'* as they hit it. The bullets when inspected were indeed declared to be the same bullets as the fellow in the audience had marked with a knife. '*The scoundrel's a genius,*' Mr Dixon, the theatre manager, said standing next to her. Old Laurie, the stage manager, had snorted his contempt, but she'd agreed with Dixon's verdict.

Now she considered the trick all over again. Both how it was meant to work, and how it had been altered in order to kill the magician.

Of course, she thought as she slipped a bottle of cough elixir into her capacious handbag and settled her best hat in the mirror, the one she'd sewn a sprig of violets to, it could have been an accident. She turned her head this way and that, allowing herself to admire the violets. Accidents do happen.

She closed her front door and turned the key in the lock. Her first step then was to rule out accidental death. For it to have been an accident, something would have gone wrong with the trick.

Bannister's wife's, Ivy, was boarding with a theatrical landlady a few streets from the theatre. Mrs Conway picked up a corned

beef pie from the corner shop and a packet of tea. You didn't visit the grieving with hands hanging.

'How are you holding up, dear?' she said as Ivy opened the door to her.

Mrs Conway barely recognised Ivy out of her costume. A mousy little thing, she thought then checked herself. There were rumours about the magician and the theatre manager's daughter – a luscious girl with an hourglass figure. But the magician probably needed a wife small enough to fold away into his illusions.

'That trick was cursed, Lettie,' Ivy said, moving away from the door and back into the room. Wringing her hands, she began to pace. 'He's not the first magician to die doing it and he won't be the last.'

Mrs Conway settled herself into the good chair and hoped Ivy would stop pacing long enough to make a pot of tea.

'George got it from the chap he used to work with – the Great Lorenzo. I never met him. It was before my time. And you never hear about him these days, but years ago, he was a headline act.'

Bannister was notorious for stealing his tricks, Mrs Conway knew. He'd steal them, re-work them, and claim them as his own.

'Lorenzo warned him that it was cursed. He said the trick tempted Death to come knocking. But George said the others who died must have been careless, and my George was never careless.'

'How did the trick work then, Ivy? It'll all come out at the inquest.'

Ivy came to a halt at the table. Finally she sat, and her skinny fingers crawled over to the greasy paper that held the

meat pie, sidling under it, to pick at a pastry crust. Tentative, she broke off a wave of pastry from the crown and carried it to her lips. She nibbled at it till it was gone, then used the same greasy fingers to check the corner of her mouth for crumbs. Or evidence of her appetite.

'The fact is that cup with the two marked bullets has a false bottom.' Ivy reached for a knife and plunged it into the pie. The woman was all but starving, Mrs Conway thought. 'When the soldier passes him the cup. My George palms the marked bullets for later, then he loads the rifles with two of our own bullets which were in the bottom of the cup. He only drops the marked bullets on the plate once he's been "shot".'

That made sense, Mrs Conway thought.

'So, the guns are loaded with real bullets?'

Fat tears began to slide down Ivy's thin face.

'Oh, yes. They're real, alright. But George cleaned those guns every night before we went home. And he checked the mechanisms over again before every show. They weren't rusty or dirty. That's how I know.'

She hesitated then raised her chin. 'He wasn't an easy man, Lettie. All of this China rigmarole was a strain on him. Pretending to be something he wasn't. And we weren't happy. I believe he killed himself.' She started to sob. 'He did so love a full-house.'

It was raining by the time Mrs Conway said her goodbyes. A good job, she'd brought her umbrella. According to Ivy then, she could rule out accidental death. But what about suicide?

. . .

The porter had the night off so the stage manager let her in. He shuffled through to his backstage office and she followed. Old Laurie had a silver beard that went up to his cheekbones and a cough that said he'd be lucky to make it through the winter. She fished the bottle of elixir out of her bag. She made it herself for him, broiling herbs and mixing it with the best honey she could find and the best cognac she could afford.

'You're too good to me, Mrs Conway,' he said and she pecked him on his withered cheek.

She hadn't known what to do with herself on her return from France. There was no husband, and without a husband, there was no prospect of a child to comfort her. Her parents were long since dead. The only joy she had from life was her weekly trip to the theatre. The bright lights of the stage, and the laughter and applause of strangers had taken her out of herself. Made her feel less screamingly alone.

Of course, she could have gone back to nursing but she couldn't face any more suffering and pain. She had 13s and 9d a week as a war widow and her savings were gone when one day she'd plucked up the courage to walk through the stage door. Despite herself, her eyes had filled with tears as she'd explained to the old man that she needed a job somewhere less real than the world she had come back to.

And he had introduced her to the theatre manager and vouched for her.

Cough linctus was little enough thanks.

She found the firing squad in their dressing room.

Joe was 17 with a broken nose and as ugly as 19-year-old Jim was handsome. Jim, she knew from the dancing girls who

had tried in vain to catch his eye, had tried to join up but had failed his medical because of a dicky heart.

Now he sprawled, pale-faced and golden-haired on the day bed, the younger boy upright in the hard seat across from him, as if keeping watch. Both looked miserable. And judging by their dishevelled state, they had spent the night in the dressing room.

'The inspector said not to talk about it, Mrs C.' Joe said as he noticed her in the doorway. A note of wariness in his voice.

'He means don't talk about it outside the theatre to strangers,' she said, closing the door behind her. She gestured Joe over to the day bed and took his seat. 'We're family.'

The boys shot each other a look and Jim shrugged as if to say how much worse could it get. He swung his long shapely legs around and sat upright.

'Being a performer is the only thing I ever wanted to do, Mrs Conway.' Jim's beautiful face took on a doleful expression. 'But Bannister taught us nowt and he paid us nowt.'

'He called us apprentices, but he only ever used us as skivvies,' Joe said, his fists clenched. 'When anyone can see Jim should be a star.'

Jim shrugged. 'The fact is the bastard didn't even want us skivvying for him anymore. The night before he died, he said he'd had enough and he was bringing in new boys.'

He thought his assistants would pay him out by betraying him the same way he paid out the Great Lorenzo, she thought.

'Joe's clever though,' Jim said with pride. 'He figured out most of the tricks – even the plate and bullet one. Didn't you, Joe?'

Joe nodded. 'The guns are rigged, Mrs Conway. Mr Bannister loaded them alright, but the bullets drop into a second chamber where the ramrod is supposed to go. It's

blocked off though, so when the gun fires, the bullet stays in the chamber. Except this time, it didn't. This time, one of the guns fired like a regular gun.'

'Joe and I were going to try our luck in Hollywood,' Jim said. 'But are we for the noose, Mrs Conway?'

'They don't hang innocent men.' Not often, anyway she thought to herself. 'Perhaps Mr Bannister fiddled with the gun himself?'

Joe looked hopeful, as if she'd offered them a way out, which he was keen to take. But then he shook his head. 'He'd put a guinea down on an accumulator at Aintree. You wouldn't do that if you were going to top yourself.'

'So it was an accident?'

'I don't see how. He was always most particular about those guns and everyone knew it.'

She opened her eyes wide. Her mother always said they were her best feature. Clear and grey. 'But if it wasn't suicide and it wasn't an accident. What was it?'

Without even knowing what they were doing, they reached out to grip each other's hands.

'Murder.' They said it in unison.

The stage was still set for the magician's act. Old Laurie had done his best to scrub the worst of the blood from the planks but the stain remained. Over there, had stood the firing squad of Jim and Joe, boys who hated Bannister. Two chalk Xs to mark the spot where they should stand. And behind them, had stood his wife Ivy, whom he betrayed.

Resentful of her husband's infidelity, had poor, starving Ivy snapped and decided to murder him?

Could one, or both, of the boys really have fixed up one of

the rifles and then had the nerve to fire it in front of a full house?

And what of Mr Dixon the theatre manager? Had he perhaps heard Bannister had seduced his daughter?

She turned to regard the sandbags erected to protect waiting performers or stagehands from stray bullets. Then again, she reminded herself, it was a set and there could be no stray bullets. Because the bullets stayed in the rifles. She glanced at the floor. A cross was chalked on the boards. The spot where the magician stood just last night. Bannister had been around 5ft 10 inches, she estimated. And he'd been shot through the lung, the bullet passing straight through him. Which meant the bullet should be right there. She placed her index finger over a ragged hole in the hessian of the sandbag. She wheedled the tip of her finger into it, expecting the tip of her nail to find the bullet. But there was only sand.

Even as she pushed a little deeper, there was a polite cough. She pulled her finger out of the hole and turned to find the police inspector who had been called in last night, watching her from the wings.

'The bullet should be there, you're quite right,' he said.

The inspector tip-tapped his way out on to the stage, and she realised one 'tip' was the iron ferrule of his stick, and the other his right leg. Walking wounded, she thought. The war had marked them all one way or another.

'You're quite the amateur sleuth.'

Mrs Conway rose to her full height of 5ft 1 inches. 'I'm sure I don't know what you mean, Inspector,' she said, and felt a flush start up in her cheeks.

'I'm sure you don't,' the inspector said with what might have been a smile although it was difficult to make out under the moustache. 'Well, when you discover who we're to hang, you can find me in the teahouse round the corner. My treat.' And he disappeared – tip-tapping his way into the shadows.

Mrs Conway was not entirely sure how to feel about the encounter with the inspector. He hadn't exactly called her a nosy baggage. But he had implied it. Even so, she was not averse to the idea of a cup of tea and a sticky bun in the teashop he had mentioned. As it happened, it was one of her favourites. And the inspector's collar she had noticed had been rather grubby. Not how a wife would have sent him out in the world. Not how she would have sent him out in the world.

As she left the theatre, Laurie called out *'Goodnight'* to her and she waved back. Lovely Old Laurie. He'd been the one to thrust a cloth in her hands as she knelt by the dying magician. A cloth covered in chalk, as she recalled. A cloth soon saturated in blood.

Old folk always looked so harmless. As if they had been old forever. Unrecognisable from who they had been decades before. But he had told her once when they had been sitting together in his office that he had been on the stage himself years before. A headline act. He'd pointed to a framed theatrical bill on the wall. But when she'd left him the cough elixir, she couldn't help but notice that he had taken it down. Doubtless, he had tucked it away in the bowels of the theatre. Some place safe and nowhere it could be found. A disappearing act.

As for Jim and Joe, she figured they were safe enough.

Especially when the police finished examining the pair of rifles, and found no evidence of tampering. That the guns were as sound and well-maintained as they'd ever been.

Because that would explain the missing bullet. The bullet that had passed through Bannister and been dug out from the sandbag.

Why dig out the bullet otherwise? Perhaps because the murderer had stood in the wings and used a pistol to shoot Bannister.

Which would only have been possible had the magician been standing in a particular spot.

Six inches further to the right of his normal spot. Both feet planted on an X chalked on to the stage by someone who knew every inch of the theatre.

Someone who had wiped away the original X from the stage with a cloth and then chalked up a new mark. Someone who had made sure the chalk was washed out of the cloth with fresh blood. And dug out the rifle bullet from the sandbag in the moments immediately after the shooting when all eyes were fixed on the dying Bannister. That way no one would realise the bullet was not the round bullet that had come from a muzzle loaded rifle. But the bullet from a handgun.

A handgun held by someone in the wings. Standing where no one could see him. Not the audience. Not anyone on the stage. Not anyone else in the wings.

As for why? The Great Lorenzo had always said the trick was cursed, but Bannister had never listened. Nor had he ever looked hard enough at the old stage manager everyone called Old Laurie. After all, it had been a long time since Bannister had stolen his best trick.

On the threshold of the stage door, Mrs Conway considered the waiting inspector with his broad shoulders and the

glint in his eye. The offer of a sticky bun and how it was obvious to all that he was in need of a capable wife. But it was raining again and the darkness was drawing in. If she fancied a sticky bun, she could buy her own. She opened her umbrella and stepped into the night.

FLORRIE AND THE MYSTERIOUS DEATH OF A FAT RASCAL

On the morning in question, in the year of 1926, anyone glancing from the first floor window of Bettys café would have noted first, the falling rain, and second, the bustling progress of Miss Margery Dalrymple along the Stray, past the Obelisk commemorating the fallen dead, and across the road—narrowly avoiding both a motor car, which honked, and a horse and cart, which did not.

On the threshold of the café, Miss Dalrymple shook the raindrops off the canopy of her umbrella and closed it. She did not stop to admire the window displays of finely iced wedding cakes and confectionery. She did not stop to buy a pound of loose-leaf Ceylon tea and a gold-ribboned, silk-lined box of buttercream and hand-piped fondant fancies that were a private vice.

Instead, she almost knocked over the aspidistra in her haste and took the staircase at a trot. For Miss Dalrymple was determined to be first with the news that she had heard from a 'most reliable' source that there was a dead body in the Royal Baths. Moreover, the body belonged to one Randolph

Cummings. And that he had been found 'floating and belly-up' in the sulphurous waters. Facts she announced as she settled, damp and breathless, in her usual place at her usual table with her usual friends.

At this, there was a tutting and a shaking of heads among the three ladies at Table 9.

'And the waters are generally so restorative,' Mrs Winifred Brown said, a note of disappointment in her voice.

'One can have too much of a good thing,' the Colonel remarked from the neighbouring table as he snapped open his copy of the *Harrogate Advertiser.*

There was a moment of silence. A genteel reluctance to speak ill of the dead. Before the Vicar's wife, pressed the palms of her hands against the damask tablecloth and leaned in closer. It was widely known that Cummings was a 'thoroughly bad lot', she confided to her congregation, and would be missed by no one 'aside from his bookies'.

'I imagine they'll send flowers,' she said. 'Perhaps chrysanthemums in the shape of a three-legged horse?'

As the café filled around them, the ladies – who had been companions since their schooldays – settled to a most agreeable conversation. (Misfortune being something to be thoroughly enjoyed, provided it happened to someone other than oneself, or one's dearest friends, and only occasionally in Harrogate.)

'An accident, perhaps?' Mrs Brown wondered, her pale blue eyes wide. 'Perhaps the gentleman in question fell asleep – as one can in the bathtub.' Her friends exchanged a glance with one another and then over at the Colonel, who put away his newspaper and accepted his role as their fourth companion. No one but Mrs Brown believed that Mr Cummings had slept himself into the great hereafter.

'No, Winnie,' said Miss Dalrymple in a decisive tone. 'I believe it must be murder. Most foul. And in Harrogate too.'

There was the chink of china as a golden-haired waitress placed a silver coffee pot and a plate of Yorkshire ham and scrambled eggs in front of the Colonel, who grunted with satisfaction. 'Thank you, dear girl,' he said, tucking his napkin into his collar.

'You're very welcome, Colonel,' Florrie said.

The Colonel had lost his only son in the Great War and his wife to influenza, so Florrie always made sure he was served promptly and with a smile as wide as she could give him. She was still smiling as she crossed to Table 9 in two quick steps. 'What wi't murder and all t'bother, shall I come back in a minute, ladies?' she asked.

The friends sat up a little straighter in their seats. It would not do to appear to be gossiping about murder, as opposed to conversing on engaging topics of mutual interest and of a serious nature, such as the weather.

'Actually, we're quite ready, Florrie,' said Mrs Brown with what might have been a blush. 'A pot of China tea and a Yorkshire curd tart, I think. Curd is always so fortifying in trying times.'

Florrie duly wrote down the order in her best copperplate hand, doing the sums as she did it - 3d for the tea and 1½ d for the curd tart. As she did so, Mrs Brown noted with approval the crisp starched apron and cuffs, and the sparkling white cap and collar that lit up the lovely face as if with a spotlight.

As for herself, she was so very pleased to be in the elegant surroundings of Bettys with such an unexpectedly interesting topic for discussion. She was rather tired of ruminating on the whereabouts of Agatha Christie, the disappeared lady crime writer, that had dominated newspaper reports of late. The

Colonel had grown obsessed, which was most trying. He swore blind he had seen the lady walking in Valley Gardens and passed the time of day. No one believed him of course.

The rest of the order came much as expected for Florrie. House tea and seed cake for the vicar's wife, while Miss Dalrymple, having once travelled to the continent, preferred coffee with cream and a lemon puff.

'Was Mr Cummings in here yesterday, Florrie?' asked Miss Dalrymple, her gaze sharp. 'Do you know the gentleman I'm referring to? Stout fellow. Wall eye. Now I consider the matter, I do believe I've seen him here on several occasions.'

Florrie's expression was as pleasant as ever as she slid the notebook and pencil back into her apron pocket. 'I doubt it, Madam. As you know, Bettys is an exclusive establishment that only attracts the best kind of person.'

Miss Dalrymple nodded, apparently satisfied, and Florrie slipped away. She didn't judge the ladies for their speculation as to the murder at the Baths. In any event, they were hardly the only ones. Rumour had spread as other patrons arrived, and within the hour the entire café was agog with conversation and supposition.

Pausing only to wind the gramophone occasionally, Florrie glided this way and that, setting down teapots and porcelain crockery. The tea room around her humming with Mozart and the whys and wherefores of the murder. And Florrie's morning passed in a blur of madeira cakes and hot buttered scones. Putting down cheese straws and nut slices amid questions as to whether the dead man had owed money, and if so, how much.

Serving poached eggs and toast, sardine sandwiches, and veal and ham pies in the moments between firm and avowed

statements that Cummings was not just a womanizer but a most notorious gambler.

A dozen Florries reflected in the large mirrors on the walls carried three-tier cake stands loaded with Chocolate Leopolds and Sarah Bernhardts to table after table of amateur sleuths, each puzzling as to exactly why Cummings had been at the Royal Baths at all. Perhaps to meet a fellow ne'er-do-well? Certainly not for the good of his health.

The fact was, Florrie could have told them a great deal about Randolph Cummings. He had not been what you'd call a gentleman. Not at all. Indeed, he had made her flesh creep. And he had never left a tip – not once.

When Chef had first caught sight of him sitting like a huge toad at the corner table in the café, he'd described Cummings as an infernal rogue and a rascal. A fat rascal at that. *Good men died because of that man,* he'd told her.

Apparently, he had known him from their days in the Army. She'd been surprised when he'd said so, as Chef did not generally like to speak of the Great War. Though Florrie's widowed mother said he had been awfully brave and had all kinds of medals to prove it. *A proper young hero,* Mother had said.

Mother hadn't wanted to take in a lodger at all. *Needs must, our Florrie,* she'd said, her face grim. But when Chef came knocking, with a mourning band around his sleeve and a tweed cap twisting in his hands, she had welcomed him in like a son.

In the seventeen months since, Florrie too had grown fond of Chef. Or *Dearest George,* as she called him in her mind. And Dearest George had not approved of Cummings one least little bit.

Not of his behaviour in the trenches.

Nor of his lewd and unsavoury comments to Florrie whenever she had to serve him in the tea room.

Still less, when he took to hanging around after the café was closed and following her home through the dark streets, calling and whistling her. And worst of all, falling silent and moving faster, till she had smelled his sour breath and she had taken to her heels and run the last stretch full tilt.

Florrie turned her head and behind her hand gave a small yawn. She'd been late to bed last night. Not least because it had been up to Florrie to wash and dry Chef's shirt, soaked as it was – what with the rain. But as she had rubbed the shirt up and down the sudsy wash board, the sulphur smell of the Baths hit her. Still, it was a familiar enough smell in their house, she thought turning the handle of the mangle, ever since her mother took a job there as a cleaner. Which meant, of course, that her mother had the big brass key to the spa's back door.

Chef had been whistling as he arrived home after his 'constitutional'. Arrived back close to midnight with his shirt wringing wet, and hung the big brass key to the Baths on its hook by the stove. Mother had said nothing. Just patted his cheek and nodded. Mother was never one for a fuss. Told Florrie to wash whatever George needed washing while she draped his jacket over a chair and heated up a pan of milk for cocoa. Then when Mother had gone up to bed, Florrie and George had sat by the fire like an old married couple. The smell of fresh laundry on the wooden clothes horse beating back and winning against the memory of the sulphur stink.

And for the first time, George had drawn his chair close to Florrie's. While he was out, he'd had an idea, he said, for a new dessert for the Betty's menu. An *île flottante* like he'd once eaten in Paris. A scoop of meringue floating in a crème anglaise, served with a drizzle of caramel and berries.

'For the meringue, the egg whites must be beaten just hard enough,' he'd said. 'While the trick to the crème anglaise is in the rum, Florrie. The rum makes anyone believe they're floating, even when they're drowning.' He was planning to suggest it to the owner, Mr Frederick Belmont, at the first opportunity. And he had taken her hand in his. Like it was nothing and like it was everything. She could feel it there yet.

And for some reason, she had gone to sleep dreaming of a towering snowy-white wedding cake, studded with iced roses and silver leaves, latticed brackets on every corner. Just like in the window.

As for the *île flottante*, with all the excitement about the death of Randolph Cummings, Florrie wasn't sure if Chef had mentioned it to Mr Belmont yet. All she knew was that it sounded perfectly delicious. George was so clever, so talented. She really had no idea where he got his ideas.

AULD BRIDE

I never wanted to come back. Deep down, I knew I shouldn't and yet, I came here anyway.

The quayside was colder than I'd imagined possible as I clambered off the boat. A wind sweeping in from across from the North Atlantic with one intent, to blow the marrow from my bones and leave them hollow. Even in my thermals and goose down jacket, I shivered.

Everything was arranged. They'd told me a chap called Malcolm would be waiting for me. And sure enough, as I looked to the end of the quay, the headlights of a black SUV flashed on and off. I raised my hand in greeting. By rights, I should have started walking towards the car, and yet I stayed rooted to the spot, staring at the cliffs and the churning sea flecked with white foam. The stone houses some way up the road. And I thought about every time my father had warned me that this island was not for me. That nothing good ever came out of this place. *Except you, my darling,* he'd say. And

whatever happened I was never to go back. *There's nothing there for you. Are you clear about that, Elodie? Absolutely, Daddy,* I'd say.

I knew the story, of course. My mother had died when I was six months old. A fever, he said. Bereft, my father swaddled me up, packed a suitcase, and left on a supply boat one dawn. His own parents were long since dead and he told no other soul he was leaving.

And throughout my childhood, even into my early twenties, I never wanted to go back to the island. I was never curious. Until my father died, and I saw the job advertised: Marketing manager, Auld Bride Whisky Distillery: £60,000, six weeks holiday, accommodation provided. *Only suitable for someone happy at the idea of remote island living,* it warned. I liked the outdoors and the occasional whisky, and the job would be a massive step up from being a marketing assistant. But it wasn't the money, so much as the idea that took hold. Because my father shouldn't have done what he did. He shouldn't have got ill, and he shouldn't have died, and he certainly shouldn't have left me. And this right here was his punishment, because now I was standing where he said I shouldn't ever go. The recklessness of it thrilled me.

Then again, he'd only ever wanted the best for me.

And there was still time to change my mind. As the engine of the boat roared into life again, as the captain's mate unwound the rope from the metal cleat embedded in the concrete, and tossed it down into the well of the boat, I considered retreat – calling for the captain to take me back with him.

But, as if he suspected as much, Malcolm was right there in front of me. His calloused hand over mine, taking the case from me with a grunt, swinging my rucksack onto his own back, and it was too late. There was no going back. Instead, I

watched as the boat pulled away, picking up speed as it cut through the choppy water, lifting and falling, sea birds wheeling in the air above as it headed back to the mainland.

I cursed as I hurried to catch up. Shona was waiting to meet me, he said. Everyone was waiting to meet me.

Her arms were wide as I pushed open the door of the distillery. It made me hesitate. Did she mean to hug me? My father was not a tactile man, so Shona's warmth made me panic. I stumbled, almost falling at the threshold and Malcolm's strong fingers gripped my wrist to keep me upright. Smiling at my reticence, she lowered her arms.

We had never met. Only talked on Zoom during the interview when I'd confessed that I'd been born on the island. But now she spoke with the warmth of someone who had known me a lifetime. 'Elodie McKenzie, come home to us.' And a cheer went up from the workers.

I couldn't help myself. I grinned. Who doesn't have that reaction when they're cheered? But then, I didn't know what it was they were cheering.

I lost track of how many hands I shook, how many tearful hugs the women gave me. *Dougie's child,* I heard more than once. I felt a flush of pleasure that my father was remembered here. And sadness that he couldn't see he'd been wrong not to come back. And, if I'm honest – and why wouldn't I be now – there was anger, too. That he'd kept me away so long.

I should have run then, of course. But I had no idea what was to come.

Later, in her office, a peat fire blazing in the hearth, Shona sat me down in a leather armchair, and placed a whisky glass in front of me. With some ceremony, she reached for a bottle and

poured both of us a drink. Her eyes narrowed as she watched me take my first sip. They were amber I realised, the same colour as the whisky she'd poured, and the flames from the fire flickered in them.

'What do you think, Elodie McKenzie, child of Douglas and Moira McKenzie, grandchild of Fraser and Anne McKenzie?'

That was new, my father never discussed his family. The people here would know more about my own heritage than I did. A moment of disquiet before the burn of the whisky hit me.

Over the years, I had tasted various whiskies. A Laphroaig after a country walk, a Talisker on a date. A whisky cocktail in a nightclub. And each and every time, it was as if voices whispered to me but I couldn't make out the words. But this whisky was the truth. I heard all of it, and understood what it had to say to me. That it was the rain that fell from the sky. And the barley that grew through me and around me. I'd yet to swallow it but I knew the heat that had passed over it, because I was that heat. And I was the peat and the smoke, and the oak cask around it. The noise and the silence of the years of waiting. Knew that the whisky was me and I was the whisky.

Swallowing the fire of it, I struggled to catch my breath the whole time Shona talked, and I thought it was to give me time to come back to myself.

The Auld Bride distillery was a ghost distillery, she told me. There'd been 'aquavite' brewed in a monastery on the island as early as the 16th century, with a distillery opened by the laird in 1701. Business was good, but tastes change and the distillery closed in 1994. That was the year my father left the island. Was that the reason for his bitterness? That the island first took his wife and then his living when the distillery closed its doors?

Shona was still talking as I zoned back in. Three years ago, a bottle of the 1912 Auld Bride came up at auction and fetched £56,000. I blinked then. For one bottle? I queried. Shona nodded. My eyes went to the bottle we'd been drinking. I could have sworn it too was a 1912.

'We're going to do it again, Elodie,' she said, turning the bottle away from me an inch. 'With your help.' She pulled out a smaller flask from a drawer. But when she poured this and lifted the glass to the light, the liquid in it was crystal-clear. 'In the oak barrels, it turns to Auld Bride. It's a different creature without the ageing.' I went to take the glass from her, but her hand stayed mine. 'Tomorrow,' she said.

I never did get to the accommodation I'd been promised with its stove and its views over the sea. Apparently, the roof was leaking. Instead, Shona took me home with her. It could have been awkward, but she made it seem like the most natural thing in the world.

I dragged myself to bed and slept for twelve straight hours. The next day I came down to salted porridge and a pot of tea you could stand a spoon up in. And then Shona drove me back to the distillery. It was raining, but even so people lined the road. Each man, woman and child straining to see into the car.

I panicked then, I admit. But Shona patted my knee. Said not to worry. The islanders were pleased to see me. It was a mark of respect.

And what could I do but trust her.

The morning passed slowly. They told me the landline and internet connection had gone down, so I'd little to do but wait in my dusty office for a tour of the distillery. Shona had promised to come for me at twelve, and I hoped the tour

would inspire me with ideas for a marketing campaign. Truth to tell, I also hoped it would reassure me. Malcolm had bolted the huge distillery gates behind us as we drove in and now islanders stood six deep outside them. I could catch the low thrum of their murmurs even through the leaded window.

I called to Fiona, the elderly secretary outside my office. What was happening?

But she waved a hand. Shona was sorting things. She'd said the same about the lack of signal on my phone. But I must need another cup of tea? I'd shrugged okay and went back to the bookshelves I'd been idly scanning.

That was when I found the *History of Whisky*. It was at the back of the lowest shelf in the darkest corner. I sneezed as I pulled it out and carried it across to my desk. Something told me not to let Fiona see it, so I met her at the doorway when she brought me tea in a bone china cup, a triangle of sugared shortbread balanced on the saucer. *So kind*, I said.

I closed the door and went back to the book on my desk. I turned the pages with care, the tea forgotten.

Auld Bride Whisky.

It was a short entry and much as Shona had told it. The monks. The distillery and laird. The geography and geology of the island that helped lend the whisky its distinct flavour. Then I turned the page. An addendum on the superstition of the Auld Bride.

'Originally, this author understands the whisky was known as 'Auld One's Bride'. According to legend, no fisherman could catch so much as a sprat in his nets, and the crops had failed year after year. The islanders were starving when the local laird summoned the Devil. They made a pact. The Devil would help them brew unforgettable whisky they could trade for gold. In return for which, every generation of islanders must drown a girl

of the Devil's choosing in an oak barrel full of clear spirit. The girl to become his bride in Hell. Witnessed by each and every islander, the laird signed his name in blood. The first bride the devil chose was his youngest daughter.'

My mouth dried and I stood up from the desk. My father had left this place for a reason. Because he knew the evil here. And the islanders had laid the perfect snare. There'd never been a job for me. No picturesque cottage with a stove and windows overlooking the sea. If anyone enquired, they'd say I'd never arrived, and that I must have thought better of it. I had no father and no mother to search for me. My London friends would wonder and then they would forget me. I'd be gone from this earth and no tears wept for me.

I was chosen.

I hear the scrape of the gates over the cobbles, and the islanders streaming through. Malcolm already stands outside the door. When I finish writing this, I'll leave these pages pressed between the pages of the history, and hide the book again as best as I'm able. As they pull me to the open barrel, I'll fight them harder than they expect me to fight them. Fight against the drowning and the Devil.

I expect to lose.

BERYL IN THE DARK

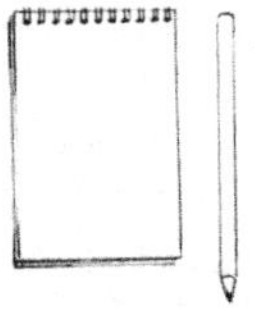

Widowhood isn't bad. Truth to tell, I decided that before the sudden death of my beloved husband, and I take comfort from how quickly I adapted. Naturally, I'm lonelier with Arthur gone, and in bed, my feet are colder, but I have Radio 4 when the silence gets too loud, and last year I bought a pair of cream angora bed socks which helped considerably. It's probably a good thing my sexual urges are long dead – not that they were ever that strong. But I did my wifely duty for Arthur and he appreciated my efforts. Once a fortnight, he'd bring a box of Terry's All Gold in from the car, and I knew his needs that night wouldn't be entirely satisfied by the orange cream. I always preferred the caramel crunch.

It's a miserable day – never quite got light – and if that journalist wasn't hanging around by the front door, I'd be tempted to slip out and treat myself to a box of chocolates. These days, I allow myself the odd binge and to hell with the consequences for my hips – I've arrived at the age where extra flesh is no great burden. Indeed, it's some comfort to feel your-

self to be a substantial figure – there's less chance of being blown away by the wind.

She arrived just past one, and every half an hour on the dot, she calls me on her mobile phone. I've turned off the answer phone so she can't leave a message again which irritates her. She's a slip of a thing called Emily Walsh, and I'm glad to say, she seems reconciled to failure – her hard little face is tight and bad-tempered on those occasions she leaves the car, bundled up in her oversized, red, waterproof coat, to pee behind the hawthorn hedge. Doubtless, she'd like to go back to her London newsroom and drink Fairtrade coffee, but whoever else she's calling on that phone won't let her. It's all well and good for them, she's thinking. They're not the ones wasting their lives away, buffeted by cold winds in across the fields from the North Sea and soaked to the marrow by the unforgiving Norfolk rain. She should have got herself a proper job. I've no time for journalists – even the pretty ones – the lies they told about Arthur.

I can last three weeks without leaving the house in the event of invasion, epidemic or siege. There are plenty of tins – sardines, ravioli and beef stew, I bake my own wholemeal bread with sunflower seeds from packets, and in the freezer as well as single servings of pork casserole and meat and potato pie in handy foil trays, there's milk, all swollen and grey-looking in those enormous plastic bottles. I never use those containers in the kitchen, instead, I decant milk into a small, rose-blown china jug that was once my mother's. She'd fetch her own milk from the dairy in an earthenware jug and carry it home up the high street, never spilling a drop. I'd do that myself if I had a choice – so much nicer than a trip to the supermarket, though I admit those places have their uses. I bought a plastic bucket of jelly spiders and snakes when I went in last week ready for

Halloween. I've no neighbours to speak of, but the woman at the farmstead up the track brings her twins down trick or treating. Last year, the boy came as a vampire and the girl a green-faced witch. Macabre of course and a thoroughly silly American habit, but the children were charming. They had black cauldrons for the chocolate coins I gave them all wrapped up in gold paper – the woman was most grateful. She's what they call a 'single parent' I suspect. That's to say, I've never seen the children's father. Nice manners though. I always insisted on nice manners when I was teaching. My class knew to hold open the door for me and stand up when we had a visitor in class, they said 'Sir' and 'Miss' and quite right – the world would be a better place if everyone had better manners. Arthur had lovely manners. Exquisite. When he came in late at night, and woke me, he was always so apologetic.

I'm old – you'd think she'd show some pity, but none of it. She's back, knocking at the door and peering in through the windows. There's someone who could learn better manners. I've drawn the curtains – knock away dearie. I never did mind the dark. Not even when Mammy locked me in the cupboard when she caught me in some childish wickedness. I acted as if I did of course – to get out quicker, but she never caught on. I'd be hollering and crying something fearsome, but inside my own head, I was laughing at her. Emily's put another note through the door asking me to talk to her – terrible handwriting. It's on headed paper. They must travel with headed notepaper – how very old-fashioned. She must keep it in the glove compartment – I've not noticed her go to the boot. I'm surprised they don't e-mail me, but perhaps they think I'm too old for a computer. I rather like the computer. It's astonishing what you can find on the internet these days – I spend hours looking through it all. I don't buy anything too hardcore of

course, and I'm careful to erase my history. Best of all, I've picked up a couple of lovely recipes for jam – one with lime and ginger, most unusual. Like those photographs with the dogs. It seems ridiculous to think I'm a cyberspace astronaut, but here I am, helmet on, 'following' famous names and bored housewives in Maine, both. Everyone looking to connect. It might help if they got out more of course. I make that point to them on occasion, although they don't like it.

I looked up my little Emily sitting out there with such ill grace. She'd be surprised how much I know about her – articles, old school, her twittering, an hour ago she accepted me as a friend on Facebook. Obviously, I don't use my own name with these things – I'm a thirty-year-old mother of two, living in Cornwall with an interest in crafts. The last bit is true as it happens. She's popular enough – 382 'friends' but then she would have that number if she accepts just anybody. She gets annoyed with her mother for commenting on what she gets up to. The mother's probably mortified. She's wiling her time away with her laptop out there - it must have one of those dongles you can connect up to the internet with. I just hope she isn't using my wireless connection.

Emily's been depressed lately – from the heavy hints, I'd guess an affair with a married man went wrong. Judging by her photographs, she'd be advised to spend more time working and less time getting drunk and sleeping around – that way, they might want her back in the office occasionally. No manners and even fewer morals. I've known enough women like her.

For a moment there, I thought she might be about to leave – she started the car but she's switched it off again. She's cold – turning on the heater and letting it run a while. What I don't want her doing is asking questions in the village. Forget free speech, privacy should be enshrined as a human right. I only

ask to live out my days in peace, Lord. Surely that's not over-ambitious. I had enough excitement to last me a lifetime when Arthur was arrested, and in the run-up to the trial. It's not much to ask – to spend the rest of my life as 'that nice woman who came in the other day.' Nobody would recognize me. There was a time when I was glamorous – a head-turner. Arthur maintained I reminded him of Elizabeth Taylor. He was very gallant like that. I shudder to think what he'd say if he saw me now, but you can hide anywhere with a good perm and an elasticated skirt. Perhaps not if you're a man. He'd understand. He always understood me perfectly. I had my vices and he had his. Doesn't everybody? That's what the police didn't seem to understand. The young lady in the car for instance, smokes. That is what I call a nasty habit. These days there's no excuse for smoking – it may very well shorten her life but she seems oblivious. I have a good mind to go out and tell her to stop throwing her cigarette butts out of her window. She winds it down an inch and flicks out the butt still burning then winds up the window again sharpish to keep the rain out. The twins will see them lying there when they come trick or treating – it's no kind of example for them. I wonder what they'll come as this year. I sincerely hope she's gone by then, and doesn't pester the mother who seems like a very nice woman even if she is divorced.

It's not the most salubrious of addresses my solitary house by an abandoned garage, but I like it more than I thought I would. They built a by-pass and the garage became uneconomic. There was compensation and the garage owner sold the remains of the petrol station along with his house. It's obviously quieter than it used to be but behind the copse of trees, juggernauts rumble through and cars, back and forth, going nowhere I want to go. I've never lived by the sea, though

we had it in mind for our retirement, but the sound must be similar – a dull roar of engines and road, water and shingle. I don't even mind the way at night lights wheedle their way through the curtains and across my ceiling as desperate drivers pull in thinking they can get petrol, and pull out again cursing when they realize it's a ghost town garage, the pumps as useless and stubby as rotten teeth. I lie awake for hours waiting for these foolish travellers – their confusion makes me smile. I was always something of an insomniac and the older I get, the less sleep I need. Arthur on the other hand slept like a baby. He'd have his bath and clean his teeth, and once he was in his striped pyjamas, he'd be asleep within seconds. I used to wonder how he managed it when he had so much on his mind. Perhaps he used sleeping pills and never told me? He didn't tell me everything. Breakfast was the time he'd make his confessions. I forgot to put the cat out last night. That sort of thing.

This house serves my purpose. I found it on the internet and it was cheap at £49,000. I'd plenty left to live on once I'd sold the old place. Gerald saw to that. Gerald managed everything for me after his father died. He had the house sold in two weeks – at a huge discount of course. Some developer razed it to the ground – such a waste. They'd have been better off painting it all the way through. It's amazing the difference a lick of paint makes to the atmosphere in a room. Gerald brought me round the cheque, kissed me on my cheek and hasn't spoken to me since. Like his father, once he puts his mind to something, there's no budging him. I considered sending him a postcard telling him where I am, but he wouldn't reply so I hardly see the point. He has his own life, and I respect his decision. From the moment they're born, you know there'll come a day when they leave you. Gerald planned

to change his name and move away from the area. The bank was very understanding.

It's snug since I had the central heating put in, and the new kitchen was a good decision. The bathroom was old-fashioned with a scratched-up, claw-foot ceramic bath and a high cistern for the lavatory with a long chain, but I liked it that way so I've let it be. There's two bedrooms – my own and one at the back which I keep as a hobby room – for crafts, pergamano, decoupage, and card making. I sit there snipping and cutting, lost to everything. Apart from the craft table, I didn't bring much with me – everything new. A fresh start – Gerald disposed of it all. Even the cat went – I'm not sure where. Gerald was never fond of her. I'd like to think he kept some memento of his old mum and dad but frankly, I doubt it. If Arthur was living here of course, the house wouldn't be enough for him, he'd be digging out a basement room. He liked his basement did Arthur. He could have been a professional builder, the time and energy he spent in our basement. Our rockery was the envy of the avenue. And he dug out a goldfish pond several times only to change his mind at the last minute and fill it in again.

This is the first time I've lived on my own. When Mammy died so tragically, I was already engaged. Arthur moved straight in and we brought the wedding forward. I was twenty-two and he was nineteen – too young they'd say these days, but I felt as old as the hills even then. Now, there's only myself to please and no nay-sayers. I won't have it that there are no consolations to widowhood. There's church. I always enjoyed a nice church service though Arthur was never that keen. There's a lovely one in the village. Norman. Beautiful kneelers – I've never tried cross-stitch but I'm willing to give it a go. I'm told it's therapeutic. I've become quite a regular at vespers, and a reliable pair

of hands helping out at the coffee mornings in aid of the lifeboats and the unfortunates caught up in the latest natural disaster. Flood or famine, count me in to hand round the macaroons. The vicar can take a hint as well which was a pleasant surprise. He offered to drop by but I don't want strangers in the house. I put him off. Politely. He understood completely. I told him: 'I'm sure you have enough old dears to visit, without adding me to your list, vicar.' He was relieved – needy parishioners can be a nightmare to men of the cloth. To all intents and purposes, I'm a widow, retired to the county where I holidayed as a child. Unfortunately I have no children of my own – God's will. I almost believe it myself.

I've done a six-week writing class as well. That was an eye-opener. The things those women were willing to share with the class whilst writing about the seasons changing astonished me. What goes on during the menopause is not a matter for the iambic pentameter. And as for the gossip after class when they all trooped off for coffee together – as Mammy always said: 'If you don't have anything nice to say, don't say anything at all.' Arthur and I would sit in silence for hours on an evening as we watched television together, and at half past seven we'd have a nice cup of tea and a chocolate biscuit. If he didn't fancy what was on, he'd go down to the basement to tinker around with whatever he had down there.

The reporter is hammering on the door like a lunatic. She's losing the plot entirely. As if I would answer the door to a madwoman. I did the right thing buying a house in the middle of nowhere – goodness knows what the neighbours would think. I'm irritated though that she found me. If it happens again, I may have to move on and I'd almost decided to get chickens – Black Rocks. They lay a lovely brown egg. You never seem to get a proper brown egg these days. I'm going to

do some hoovering so I don't have to hear her carry-on. I've hoovered today already. I always do my jobs first thing in the morning, working down from the top of the house to the bottom – bedrooms first, a quick going-over in the bathroom, a hoover round and a spit-and-dust. The kitchen I always keep straight. Nothing worse than a grimy sink. There she's stopped. Perhaps it was her blood-sugar. She's had nothing to eat all day and time's getting on.

Thank goodness, she's leaving, finally. I was beginning to get quite annoyed with her. I was shaking as I cut myself that last slice of seedcake, almost cut my finger. And that can get quite bloody. At least I can open the curtains now and drink my tea in peace. It's almost time for the evening news. Arthur's cellmate is on, maintaining Arthur made an arrangement to pay his family £5,000 if he didn't call the prison guards while he hanged himself. Easy money if you ask me and a bit too late for his conscience to come calling. The wife was glad enough of it at the time. Greasy hair tied back in a ponytail, a cigarette hanging out of her thin-lipped mouth, three snotty-nosed children hanging off her. The very picture of a convict's trollop. Did he tell her what he had to do for the money? I thought not at the time, though she was no fool, there was a feral intelligence in those beady eyes of hers. She had a good look round the car park once she opened the boot of the car as agreed by the menfolk. Morrison's 1pm – money in the boot wrapped in a plastic bag. Arthur warned me to make sure I wasn't seen. Then something spooked her because she banged shut the boot and shovelled those children into that car so fast I doubt she even strapped them in. Doubtless she spent the money on drugs rather than food and shoes for the children – she was the type. I wondered afterwards whether the money was well-spent, whether the cellmate would have stopped Arthur

hanging himself anyway. Unlike Emily, Arthur wasn't exactly popular at the time, but I couldn't risk him incriminating me at the trial. He understood that when I explained it all to him at visiting. He could see I was frightened – my hands trembling on the Formica table. He worshipped me, there's nothing he wouldn't have done to take that fear away. His gaze was fond. 'Beryl lovie. Don't you fret,' – he murmured and I thought I felt his breath warm on my skin for the last time.

Emily's back. She must have parked the car around the corner out of sight. Would you credit it and bearing flowers? What an old chestnut. As if a bunch of tired dahlias would make me break my silence. You stupid, stupid girl. I don't even like flowers, and just look at the time. The lady up the lane will be here within the hour. Alright, you've brought this on yourself. I'm opening the door. The look on her face as I open the door is almost worth the inconvenience. She virtually falls over her own pixie boots to get back up the path. 'Alright my dear, come in.' I go into the kitchen and switch the kettle on. 'Go into the lounge and take a seat while I make you a cup of tea – you must be freezing.' She doesn't need a second invitation. The chance to look round my lounge without me watching her. No photos. Nothing personal. A copy of the *Spectator*. I warm the pot, swirling the boiling water round its belly, ladling in the loose tea. I have a special mix reserved for visitors, and bring it through on a tray with my bone china jug of milk. It's a shame I ate the last piece of cake earlier, but there's home-made shortbread, fork-pricked and gritty with sugar. She shakes her head. Tea is fine. Of course, tea is fine. I watch her drink it. 'Drink up,' I instruct her and she swallows it down. Have another cup and then we'll talk. We talk and it's more of a relief than I expected it to be. I tell her all about it.

We met in the working men's club. Mammy with her port

and lemon, myself newly qualified, stiff with boredom, and there he was through a fog of curling tobacco smoke and conversation. A messiah in a black satin shirt strumming a guitar trying to make them listen to his song. They didn't hear him, but I did. He wasn't as educated as I was. Not as intelligent but I helped him, improved him, polished him till he shone – not that his talent ever got the recognition it deserved. His virtues were never recognized in the factory where he ended up. He and I both hoped he'd be made manager but he never got there, never got past floor supervisor. Perhaps he was too weak. Not enough of a leader for them. But they didn't see him as I saw him. Arthur knew what he wanted. He was a man with appetites. Not even orange creams were enough. That first time, I made a suggestion he went on a little hunting trip – brought back what it was he needed – he wept at my feet with gratitude. I'd bring him a cup of tea while he worked. The girls always looked so relieved when I appeared at the door, and so very disappointed when I handed Arthur a digestive and took a seat to watch. He was a craftsman in his way. I tell Emily every last detail although she's rude enough to fall asleep, drool hanging out of the corner of her pink lipsticked mouth, slumped in the corner of the settee like a ratty old cushion. My arm around her, I take her weight as we stagger up the narrow stairs to the back bedroom. Occasionally, she falls to her knees with a grunt, and I have to pull her up the last few stairs by her hair but she doesn't complain. I get her into the bedroom and lie her on the spare bed, tying her ankles together with pretty pink silk ribbon and her wrists and ankles behind her back with pale blue. Yellow silk links the ankles to the wrists. I use my craft knife to slice the ribbon once I've pulled it from the cardboard spool – a small razor blade cut on the diagonal that slides up and down its plastic holder. Scraping the knife along

the dangling strands of colour leaves ringlets of ribbon. Arthur always admired my finishing touches. She'll be out for a while yet but for safety's sake, I knot the black tights I've taken off her, slide them between her teeth and use them as a gag. 'Congratulations dear – you have what you'd call a scoop,' I tell her, but she lies there mute, her eyes closed.

There's her car of course but that doesn't worry me unduly. I could drive it down to Norwich early tomorrow morning and leave it unlocked in the hope it would disappear. I'd have to get the train back and a cab home but there'd be time to do some shopping. Everybody knows how little old ladies like to shop. And there's room in the freezer for more pie. Or there's the quarry lake which can't be more than a mile away. That I could do tonight. It doesn't leave me quite so long with Emily, but long enough I expect and too long as far as she's concerned. Perhaps that might be tidier. There's no trace of my special tea after twenty-four hours and I'll be careful not to leave any other marks on her. She drives herself off the edge. Quarries are notoriously dangerous places. It might well be weeks till she's found – if at all. And if she is? Depressed you see. Unstable. Too much time to think sitting in her car in the rain outside the widow's house. No, I never spoke to her.

Right on cue, the doorbell goes and there they are, the nice woman from up the track and her two charming children. They're dressed as monsters – the boy as Frankenstein and the girl as a ghoul. Every bit as charming as they were last year, the mother looking more tired than ever. 'I wonder my dear whether you ever need a baby-sitter,' I ask, and her eyes light up.

THE SILENT MRS B.

Thirteen years had passed since Violet Bainbridge had spoken. She regretted her last words. 'Cup of tea, officer?' So dull. Surely, your last words should be an insight into living, which future generations could remember. On consideration, if she had another go-round, she would advise listeners to 'jiggle it', as it had been her experience if something mechanical went wrong, a jiggle could work wonders. Of course, that wasn't profound either. Perhaps then, her parting advice should be 'Love like there's no tomorrow', because in her experience sometimes there were no tomorrows.

Naturally, there were moments she missed conversation. But not enough to break the silence which brought her clarity and comfort. Anyway, it had been too long. She didn't think she could speak now even if she wanted to. But that didn't mean to say she couldn't communicate. Communication, she had learnt, did not necessarily require words.

Violet reached for the tin of corned beef and used its key to saw away its lid. She turned it upside down on the chopping

board and picked up the knife. The onions were already in her cast iron pan, glossy and fat with oil, the potatoes sliced and drowning in her white bowl. The knife slid through the meat. How large had her mother cut the pieces? She paused for a second considering the issue. The length of her fingertip up to the first knuckle perhaps. The meat would break up in the pan anyway. She scraped it from the board and pushed it around the frying pan with a spatula, seasoning it to her taste, and picturing her mother's frown of concentration as she cooked. *'A bit of help's worth a lot of pity, our Violet',* Mam would say, kissing her forehead, before wrapping an apron twice around and handing her a wooden spoon. Violet pressed down the cooked beef and onions and poured yesterday's cold gravy over it, before laying the slices of potatoes in concentric circles. Forty minutes, she thought. A meal meant to feed a family which cost less than a coffee on the high street these days. Her mother was no fool.

A grilled avocado next, she decided, cutting the fruit apart and easing out the stone with a spoon. The breadcrumbs, mixed with paprika and parmesan were already prepped and the grill on. She covered the surface of the avocado, taking care to fill the hollow with the mixture. The first thing she had ever cooked for her husband. Would he remember what she'd privately called 'The Avocado Wars'? His mother asking time and time again, if Violet had ever eaten it. *'An acquired taste, dear.'* No girl good enough for him, and certainly not Violet from a two-up, two-down with an outside privy. Saying to Tony that she'd like to cook a meal for the three of them one night. And Sheila, exiled from her own kitchen, sitting at the dinner table in her best silk blouse, desperate to find fault. A chicken roasting in the oven. A black forest gateau bursting

with tinned black cherries and whipped cream, pressed over with splintered dark chocolate. *'Right fancy,'* her father's verdict as she left. *'Watch the old trout don't curdle it.'* Laying down the grilled avocado on the placemat. A statement. That she loved Tony and she was going to marry him. *'I don't know if you've ever had avocado this way before,'* she'd said, her tone pleasant. *'I'll give you the recipe if you like, Sheila.'* And a look had passed between the two women. An understanding which, over the years, deepened into respect and finally, to their mutual surprise, love. Deep enough to bring the old lady into her home and care for her, to wash her and wipe her and feed her beef tea and pressed tongue sandwiches. To hold her in her arms as she passed from this world.

The avocado took only minutes. The oxtail was a different matter. When Tony had been at the start of his career in the bank and she'd been a teacher, they'd eaten it once a fortnight. They'd been saving for a deposit so only cheap cuts of meat went into her basket. Five hours, she remembered as she placed the chunks of oxtail into the casserole and scraped the sliced carrots, shallots and crushed garlic in after. She rifled the wine rack and found a fruity Valpolicella. Too good to cook with really. But it wasn't as if they were watching the pennies anymore. And thank the Lord that she had four ovens in her kitchen, bearing in mind all she had to do today. She set the second oven to 140 degrees and the timer for five hours. 'You're a genius,' Tony used to say, kissing her fingertips as he took the first mouthful of the rich oxtail stew, the meat falling from the spurred spine in strands, the gristle and cartilage dissolved into something silky and almost sweet.

Then there had been the early years in Sweden when Tony took a posting abroad. Having to leave her family and friends and job behind. Finding solace and meaning in rosemary and

garlic studded reindeer, wrapped around in thinly sliced Coppa; the golden striped, pink fleshed Arctic char in white wine and dill, and the smoked salmon she laid out and sprinkled with brown sugar before dribbling over the oil and lime juice stiff with chives and tomatoes and lime zest. Reading recipes and cookbooks in bed, like Tony read his biographies of great men. And while he re-lived battles and mountains climbed, she planned dinners to please him, to impress his colleagues, and to prove to herself she existed.

Today, the reindeer was already on the long kitchen table, alongside the marinading salmon and the arctic char. Each reminding her of who she used to be. Of how she used to feel about Tony and how he used to feel about her. The bittersweetness of lime forever associated with loneliness and the glittering snow; the gamey flavour of garlic-infused reindeer of Tony's growing distance from her.

But then, she'd had her daughter Flora, and Flora was enough. Flora was everything. They came back home and Tony was a good father. And through Flora they found each other again. At breakfast, watching her eat porridge and cinnamon rolls, waiting for her kiss goodbye and the cheery wave through the window. Then later, over dinner, hearing about her day – her friends, her triumphs and disasters. The dinners of tagliatelle Flora loved, covered in tomato or cream sauces, fajitas they would stuff with paprika chicken tangled in red and yellow pepper strips – spitting-hot on a cast iron griddle. Handmade pizzas and Chinese stir-fry. The vegan year. The glowering judgment Flora heaped on them for their choices. And dutifully, Violet had mastered the sprouting beans and pulses. Because anything that made Flora happy made her happy. Serving medjool dates stuffed with nut butter and sprinkled with cacao powder for no other reason than to see

her daughter's smile. Flora's *'You have to try it, Daddy'*, and Tony's point-blank refusal.

The fajitas and the dates, the tagliatelle and a wok of stir-fry already sat on the table. This is everything I am, Violet thought. Everyone I loved and everything I ever had to say is here in this food that took me a lifetime to cook.

She picked up a date and bit into it, her mouth filling with the exotic nutty sweetness. Flora. Who went to university and never came back. Whose death at 18 was a tragedy, everybody said so. Except Violet who said nothing. Not one word. She didn't speak, because what was there to say. And she figured her silence was better than a scream.

But even so, after the first few months, she went back out into the world. The local shopkeepers knew her. She would point or write them notes. And she left casserole pots and foil-covered plates on the doorsteps of her neighbours when she heard of a loss or a grief, when a husband left, when a house teamed with children, when an elderly neighbour came out of hospital. Beef and ale stews bulging with thyme and horse-radish dumplings. Ham boiled and then roasted with mustard and demerara sugar, speared with cloves, on a bed of savoy cabbage and surrounded by floury boiled potatoes. Meals meant to give courage and strength. Each one tailored to a need she noticed, or a particular sadness she glimpsed. Potted shrimps heated and covered with cream mixed with brandy, Worcester sauce and a shameless dollop of ketchup, her speciality for divorce or a broken heart. Kidneys sautéed in butter and finished with red wine and mustard for a hollow-eyed mother whose grown child disappointed. A chicken pie pressed between two slices of white bread for those she sensed needed comfort, but she couldn't guess at why.

The pots and the platters were always returned washed.

Sometimes she would open the door and there'd be flowers on the step or a card. Best of all, she'd lift off a lid and inside would be a child's scrawled *Thank you, Mrs B* or a picture of a smiling face. She kept them all, pressing them under magnets of places she and Tony travelled – Pisa, Paris, Portugal. Her fridge door fluttering with other people's gratitude as she pulled it open. But in reality, she should thank them, she thought. Because who else was there to feed these days, but herself and a man who had lost his appetite for food, for her, and for life itself. Without Flora. Without his darling girl, Tony didn't know how to be. He was fading out of existence. Thinner every day. Greyer. So small and pale that soon, he would be invisible. In the first year, he'd been strong. For her sake, she knew that. Then, as inevitable as winter, he'd suffered a breakdown. And when he recovered, he'd lost himself in work. Three months ago, he had retired and was now busy dying each and every day.

You can't starve yourself to death, she wanted to say.

But couldn't get the words out.

You can't leave me here alone. Her eyes spoke for her. But he saw only his newspaper and the television and the lawn he cut on Sundays.

So she had decided to speak to him with food.

I love you.

I'm still here.

Stay.

The message spelled out in a white chocolate ganache and strawberry cake she'd first made for his 40th. Now displayed alongside the beef tea she'd made his dying mother, and the nut butter their daughter had loved. A shot glass full of salt tears standing alongside a cottage pie – the only thing she'd cooked in the early months with Flora gone. Violet had

planned this for weeks. Her kitchen table an altar to all the evenings spent in front of the fire considering recipes and watching old films together. No crime dramas for them. No missing children or dead girls. Pouring all she didn't say with words, into the food meant to tell him that she was trying to stay alive too. That it was a fight. Like the Avocado War. Against an enemy even more dangerous than his mother. Against Death itself.

Leaning against the sink, Violet opened her mouth but no sound came, not even a scream.

Instead, she crossed over to the fridge – flutterings – and pulled open the door. Lifted out a bottle of vintage Veuve Cliquot. Paused, while she considered it in her hand. Hesitated. Then pulled out another. She went to their wine fridge in the pantry and pulled out four more. Six. Twelve. Filled ice buckets and put out champagne flutes. Took out stacks of plates and the best silver cutlery. Damask napkins. More glasses. More wine. Red and white, uncorking the red, chilling the white.

She sat down at the laptop on the desk against the furthest wall and drafted a simple invitation. *Violet and Tony, Drinks/food. 6pm tonight! Please come!* Her hand trembled as she read the invitation. The neighbours she had never spoken to. Only ever fed and smiled at. Only ever taken their children's drawings and stuck them to her fridge. Would they think it strange? Would they turn up? But she was committed now. She pulled on her coat and crossed this way and that with her pieces of A4 paper.

The first to ring the bell was Belinda (divorcing – kidneys in red wine and mustard). 'Oh my word! It smells a-may-zing,

Mrs B!' she said, holding out her arms to Violet who found herself moving into them. Next up, Sam and Emma (redundancy – Hungarian goulash and noodles.) By 6.15pm the kitchen was heaving with conversation and laughter. The oxtail casserole out. The corned beef pie. The roasted chicken. Violet almost didn't hear Tony come in. It was only the cheer from her guests that made her glance across. Standing in the doorway, her husband's face was puzzled, as if wondering if this was his house. His eyebrows raised, he looked for Violet in the crowd. And she willed him not to turn and run. His gaze switched to the table and his brow furrowed. He moved a step closer till he was right up against it. He breathed in and she wondered what he was smelling. The rabbit fricassee of their honeymoon in the Borders? The Chicken Maryland of their family trip to Florida? She took up a fork from the table and dug it into the corned beef. 'A bit of help's worth a lot of pity, our Violet',' she said, and her voice was cracked and croaky. Hearing her, his eyes widened and she carried the fork to his lips. He took in the forkful and chewed and swallowed. His gaze never shifting from her.

There was silence now in the kitchen, even the children were hushed as Violet dug into the grilled avocado, breaking through its parmesan crust. 'I'll give you the recipe if you like, Sheila.' Tony's mouth twitched into a smile and opened like that of a small child.

She took up a date loaded with nut butter and Tony's eyes filled with tears. Her's too. His mouth stayed shut as if he couldn't bear to remember the girl they had lost. But she kept the date there, bumping stickily against his lips. 'You have to try it, Daddy',' Violet said. And with her other hand she wiped her own cheek dry. Tony bit into the date and chewed, and she

knew the sweetness and the loss he tasted. There was colour in his cheeks when he'd finished.

'Delicious,' he said.

He looked round at the unexpected guests that filled his kitchen, and gestured to the food, then took Violet's hand in his. 'Please everyone, dig in. My wife, as you know, is a remarkable cook.' He kissed her fingertips.

SNOW DAY

Virginia Cafferty rapped so loudly on the window that the child she'd been watching dropped her chalk in fright. Maisie was a vandal in Virginia's opinion. Hopscotch on the public sidewalk was little better than a desecration of the neighbourhood. Virginia had her own chalk, of course, which she used on her walks to draw circles round the litter that was dropped and the foulings by dogs. But that was altogether different. That was a public service. One for which she should, by rights, be commended by the town mayor.

In the early dawn, when the mood came upon her, Virginia would zip up her sheepskin-lined ankle boots, button up her thickest tweed coat and patrol the streets. The chalk clutched in arthritic fingers, she'd stoop to write LITTER LOUT by the discarded food wrappers and tin cans. And FOUL!!!! by the poop, wrinkling her nose and careful that her sleeve didn't graze the stinking mess. It would have been quicker and simpler to pick up the offending garbage, but she was willing to admit that it would also have been a deal less satisfying. It was, after all, her duty to alert the lazy and the slack-jawed to

the fact she was alive to their misdemeanours. Occasionally, she considered making her rounds in the daylight, but she wasn't convinced the rabble would understand her motivation, and to be frank, she loathed the idea of becoming a public spectacle if one of the miscreants challenged her or, worse yet, laughed at her. No, it was safer when there was no one about.

This morning, it was Maisie's turn to be taken to task and it was Maisie who stared back at her. Huge dark eyes and a look of indignation on her round face. The child was seven, and in Virginia's opinion, desperately noisy and a great deal too full of herself. Always in sneakers and the same denim dungarees, knocking and hollering for the other children to come play and shrieking with laughter when they did. The first out on the street after school and the last one to trail home at night. Not a nice child, in Virginia's opinion. She imagined herself drawing a chalk circle around the girl and writing the words TOO LOUD next to her. Her own mother would have made Maisie go without supper and learn by rote improving Bible verses from the Old Testament. EMPTY VESSELS. Yes, Mother would have soon knocked Maisie into shape, one way or another.

'Go on with you!' She gestured at the girl through the window, shoo-ing her off the sidewalk outside her house and across the road towards her own home. She knew why Maisie crossed the street. Maisie's house had no garden, only a small fenced-in yard at the back and the narrowest of sidewalks out front. It was a strange, sagging, excuse-of-a-house, which looked as if it had been thrown together by a builder who hated his job and resented whoever might go on to live there.

Having given Virginia's command due consideration, the girl poked out a pink tongue, picked up the white stick of chalk, and skipped away. OUTRAGEOUS thought Virginia.

NO RESPECT. She considered phoning Maisie's mother to demand an apology from the child, not least because white splinters and powder now blotted the sidewalk where the chalk stick must have broken when it hit the ground. Just what she had been trying to avoid. SPOILATION. It really was too bad.

Her hand went to the phone where it sat on its crocheted doily next to her armchair. Hovered there. She lifted the handset. Put it down. Then again, it was past supper time and Maisie's mother would probably be drunk. Because that was the other thing about her dawn walks. Another civic service she contributed, free and gratis – organising her neighbours' recycling. People were so cavalier about mixing plastic and cardboard. It took only a few minutes to sort one from the other. And it was so informative as to who bought what. Not to mention the amount of junk food they gobbled up. Obviously, as she smoothed out and folded the cardboard, it was almost impossible to avoid noticing the empty bottles in the green plastic boxes that were put out for the refuse collectors every second Thursday of the month.

BOOZEHOUND. She chalked a ring round Maisie's mother as she watched her stumble out of her door, down the porch steps, and up the street. Virginia knew where she was going. The convenience store two blocks away. Virginia even knew what she would buy – two bottles of Californian rosé at $4.99 a piece. The woman got through seven bottles of the rosé a week. Out of curiosity, she'd bought one herself a couple of months ago. Although a pretty enough colour, it tasted like stale flower water and it was nothing she ever wanted to taste again.

Her gaze went to the downstairs window as the blue light from the TV came on in the gloom and she imagined Maisie sitting on the couch watching cartoon dogs and cats. Did chil-

dren still find cartoons as entrancing as they used to? She had no idea. She did know this much though, children should not be left in the house alone – there really was no excuse for it.

Virginia's lips went to a narrow line. And Maisie was definitely alone, she knew that for a fact, because Maisie's father walked out on his family last year. Virginia had been woken by the screaming and the slam of the front door, then the splutter and roar of his beaten-up jalopy as it took off. Not been seen since. QUITTER, Virginia thought, drawing the chalk ring around her memory of Maisie's dad. ROTTER – to leave his little girl alone like that.

With her half-done crossword on her knee, she sat watching the flickering light of Maisie's TV. Should she call someone – the police perhaps? But then again, Maisie's mother would be back soon enough. Perhaps she should go over and check on the child? Her heart started to beat faster as she considered the idea. It wouldn't do for Maisie's mother to accuse her of interfering, and everyone knew drunks were quick to take offence. But she couldn't in all conscience do nothing. With a certain relish, she gave up on her original plan to watch her favourite TV programme – a particularly gory British detective series – and settled down to watch Maisie's house instead. She drew a chalk line between herself and where she imagined Maisie to be sitting and chalked the word VIGILANCE along it.

This way, if a bad man broke in or smoke and flames started to pour from under the eaves, she would rush to Maisie and drag the child from the villain or from the burning building. HERO, she wrote above her own head, sipping at a schooner of sweet sherry. *'Really, it was nothing,'* she imagined

telling the local news reporter. *'Anyone would have done the same.'* Both of them knowing that to be a lie.

The clink of bottles alerted Virginia to the mother's return. Swaying, the young woman leaned against the porch as she attempted to fit her key in the door and Virginia noticed the lounge go dark, imagined the TV switching off, a pause long enough for a child to scamper upstairs, and then a first floor light go on in what she guessed to be Maisie's bedroom. The key found the lock and Maisie's mother half fell into her hallway. As she did, Virginia lifted her eyes. Maisie stood at her window staring directly down at Virginia, her round face a pale blur. Instinctively, Virginia lifted her hand. I'M HERE, she told her. NEVER FEAR. But Maisie drew her curtains together with what Virginia imagined to be a snap, and the chalk line blew apart into so much dust.

The night was a long one. In her second-best flannelette nightgown, stretched out in her feather bed, at first Virginia felt too warm under the quilt she had made herself, and then too cold. Laying first one way and then another, bringing out her arms and legs then curling up, but nothing felt right. Everything about her body creaked and hurt. Finally, she crossed her arms over her chest, closing her eyes as she would lay in her coffin – as she would lay in her grave. And as she listened to the ticktock of the grandfather clock in the hallway and finally surrendered herself to sleep, above all things, she wanted to be young again.

It snowed during the night, and as soon as she woke Virginia felt the itch in her blood to be out in it. As a girl she had loved snow. But the risk of a fall at her age was too frightening. A broken hip. A spell in hospital. A bout of pneumonia. And that would be the end of independent living. Growing old was no fun, she thought, entering the kitchen – itself lit up

by the fallen snow outside, the branches of the old apple tree heavy with it. From somewhere the memory came of an old snowball fight and her brother's hand in hers. Dead now. Poor Teddy. All of them dead. Everyone she had ever loved and who had ever loved her. Really, what was the point of her? She shook her head as if to dislodge the past, filling the coffee maker with water and spooning in the fragrant, ground coffee from a battered tin. PULL YOURSELF TOGETHER, VIRGINIA CAFFERTY.

A bowl of oatmeal might be best, bearing in mind the weather – and perhaps she would treat herself to a drizzle of syrup in it? Mother never allowed syrup or honey or brown sugar. *A waste,* she'd say and smack Virginia's hand away. *Not for the likes of you.*

As she did every day, Virginia took her breakfast in the dining room, although it was the coldest room in the house. The mahogany table was laid with a white linen cloth, the good silver and the best china. An African violet in the centre and a silver framed photograph of her mother across from her. For a moment, Virginia regarded her place setting then stood up and went back to the kitchen, opening the pantry door and reaching in to take hold of the unopened glass jug of maple syrup. *There's only me left, Mother. If not now, then when?* She closed the pantry door, headed back down the corridor, and sat at the breakfast table. Heady with recklessness, she unstoppered the jug.

In the hallway, the grandfather clock struck quarter of the hour. And in the dining room, Virginia waited for life to get sweeter.

At first, nothing happened, as if the syrup had decided to stay where it was. As if her mother was right, and it wasn't for the likes of her. Virginia waited it out. Ticktock. Ticktock.

And then in a slow amber river, the syrup dropped from the lip of the jug into the bowl of oatmeal. NOT ENOUGH, Virginia thought, putting down the jug to stare into the amber lagoon. Sucking a stray drop of syrup from the pad of her thumb, with her other hand she reached for the creamer, swirling the cream into the syrup, round and around. *Not nearly enough to make up for all those years without.*

Unusually, she didn't carry her empty bowl out to the kitchen. TROLLOP, she wrote, glancing back at the unwashed dish. Instead, she went through to the parlour, standing on slippered tiptoe, pressing her forehead against the cold glass as she leaned forwards to see what she could see of the new world.

The children hurly-burly piled out of their houses, all but mummified in scarves and gloves and wearing heavy winter boots. SNOW DAY, Virginia thought settling herself in her usual seat by the window, drawing a rug over her knees. But for the first time in her forty years in the house, she felt self-conscious as she stared out. She had every right to sit in her own parlour, she reassured herself. No one had any right to think she was a NOSY OLD BAT. Not at all.

Her cheeks flushed as she made a show of shaking out and opening the local paper she had scoured the day before. And out of the corner of her eye, she sensed as much as saw Maisie jump down the steps of her porch to join her playmates. At least she had galoshes on today. She waited for the child to acknowledge her, but Maisie appeared not to notice the old woman in the window. As ever, her voice was louder than the others and her laugh at a higher pitch. LET THEM KNOW YOU'RE THERE, MAISIE, Virginia thought. QUITE RIGHT. After an hour or two, the rest of the children went in,

called home by parents wanting them to get warm and eat their lunch, Virginia guessed. But Maisie stayed out.

Alone, the child played directly in front of Virginia's house, but for some reason Virginia found she didn't mind. The girl could hardly be expected to play out in the road, she thought to herself. As Maisie rolled the snow up and down the sidewalk, her feet slipping and sliding under her, Virginia found herself wondering if she mightn't happen upon Maisie's mother at the convenience store. If she mightn't ask her to carry home her shopping, and in return it would only be a neighbourly thing to do if she brought over a nourishing stew to thank her? Perhaps the woman was floundering, abandoned by her husband that way? Perhaps she was lonely and frightened and could be encouraged if someone reached out a hand? Seven bottles of wine weren't so many to give up. It was certainly something to think about.

For the first time, Maisie's eyes met hers, and Virginia nodded. CARRY ON, she thought. The child's focus was a THING OF WONDER as she patted and shaped the snow. At one point, Maisie had dashed back home and come back clutching a bundle. She settled the scarf and the baseball cap, the stick arms and bits of coal for the eyes. Finally, she took a step back, the snowman's smile complete. Maisie stood alongside, flushed and exhausted. She looked up at Virginia and beamed. TWO SMILES. The child's and the snowman's, Virginia thought, and both meant for her. Two more than on any other day in she couldn't think how long. Maisie pointed and called, and Virginia leaned closer to the glass again. 'I made you a friend,' Maisie shouted.

FRIEND. Virginia chalked the letters up in her mind. Drawing a circle around the snowman first, and then the girl.

Tears prickled her eyes, and Virginia reminded herself she

was required to breathe again. She held up a finger as if to say WAIT THERE, then hurried out of the living room, the chalk crunching under her slipper on the parquet floor of the hallway. Her hand on the wall to support her, she flung open the door and the cold fresh air rushed into the house almost knocking her over. Blinking in the winter sunlight, her gaze found Maisie. And Virginia felt swept away by the most unfamiliar feeling of what she realised was gratitude.

AND SO IT BEGINS

Michael

He was writing a letter. It was the seventh one he'd written. '*I thought you should know...*' he wrote, balancing the piece of paper against his exercise book, trying to keep his writing neat like they said at school. Easy to read. The lettering big in case she couldn't see well. He wasn't sure about the address. That was the problem. He was posting them out to the list he'd made from the phone book. But would any of the letters find her?

He stopped writing as Brendan rolled over, and creaking, the bunk beds swayed away from the wall then slammed back again. One night soon, Michael figured it would sway, pause, then keep right on going till it crashed to the floor taking them with it. It would only take the smallest push.

It was cold in the room. Both boys had gone to bed fully dressed. Last week, Mrs McGyver turned off the radiator. It was healthier that way, she said. Too much heat was bad for

children – it was all there in the *Daily Express*. She'd waved a copy of the paper at them from the doorway in justification. In his sleeping bag with its broken zip trapped under him, Michael shivered. Freezing to death was bad for children too, he thought.

Mrs McGyver

What was it I needed to do? I know there was something. Bugger. My memory is a shocker. Mind, hardly surprising with everything I've got on looking after those kids. They drag them up these days I tell you. These single mothers they've no respect. Of course, they're going to end up with children who are worse than they are. Like the two I've got now. They never told me the handicapped one was a bed-wetter or I'd never have taken him – no wonder the grandma's in hospital with her heart. What happened to his mother? That's what I want to know. Took one look and did a runner, I bet. No, it would've been better all round if they'd drowned him at birth like dad used to say. Kittens. Runts. Handicapped kiddies. Even Mum when she turned the nervous-Nelly type. Not a sentimental man, my dad. You certainly felt the wooden spoon all right if you didn't speak up and act sharpish. Now I think about it, I can't say I miss the old bugger.

Course nowadays, you can't lay a hand on kids however they provoke, or those do-gooders are all over you. Pathetic. Public servants they are. I pay their wages but they've no respect either. No gratitude for what I'm doing for those boys. Always wanting more food. New shoes for God's sake. Well, that's not my job. I teach them independence that's what I do. Resilience. No one else would have them I know that. Without

me fostering them, they'd be in an institution. It's a cushy number with me right enough. Nice respectable house. Fitted carpets. Pets. Rules so they know where they are.

But I've had it with that North kid. I'm getting shot. He's trouble right enough. Watching me. I can see it all going in. He'll end up behind bars, mark my words. But I'm ready for him. He's the type to tattle on – put me and Mr McGyver in a bad light. If I could just win the national lottery – four million would do it. I'd be shot of this lot sooner than you could say 'No publicity'. Head out for Marbella – buy myself a place with a pool. Wouldn't see me for dust right enough. Obviously, I'd set the girls up with their own semi-detached over here and they could fly out for holidays. I'd have to do that. Not that they deserve it. Not that they ever call. And Jeff could keep this house. I nearly had House yesterday thinking of it. Closest I've come for a couple of weeks – only needed a legs eleven – and then there was the £500 I won three years ago from the scratch cards. Born lucky I was. Dad always said so. How I ended up here with this lardy lump laid next to me, I do not know. I was a looker in my time right enough – throwing myself away on this sly no-mark – like Dad said. It makes me angry just thinking about all I do for this family and the little thanks I get. Taking those children off the streets out of the kindness of my heart. Out of my Christian goodness. I'm sure there was something I should've done.

Michael

'Mickey,' Brendan whispered from the bottom bunk. In the first few days they'd tried it with Brendan on the top bunk and Michael below. It didn't work – Michael felt sorry for

Brendan still wetting the bed at his age, but he'd spent one damp night too many to keep it that way round.

Michael let his breath out through his teeth, to quieten his companion. Mrs McGyver's wheezy whistling had been going for a good ten minutes but her snoring had only this minute started up. Rasping and guttural. The occasional violent snort which might yet wake her.

'I'm right hungry, Mickey.'

Brendan's attempt to whisper more quietly came out even louder than before. Michael wasn't sure what the matter was with the other boy. According to their schoolmates, he was a 'spacker', a 'knacker', and a 'right drongo'. He was none of those things when Michael was around. He was Michael's friend. As such, he was entitled to respect, Michael explained to his classmates as he pounded their faces with his fists. They were getting the message all right.

Now he thought about it. He was as hungry as Brendan. That was nothing new, but at least at home, he was able to steal money from his mother's purse – enough to buy a burger at least or a greasy bag of chips. Once, there'd been a ten pound note, he'd agonised over it. She'd spot the fact it was gone and it would mean a beating – then again, the money would feed him for the week. He took the note and the beating, which broke his arm in three places. He told his teacher Mrs Lang that he fell playing football on the rec, and she'd nodded, but he could tell she didn't believe a word of it. As a rule, he liked Mrs Lang – when she wasn't being nosy. Liked school – when he wasn't in trouble for fighting. But he quit going. It took a week but they found him anyway. Knocked at the door – two policemen and a social worker – and bundled him screaming into a car. His mother too drunk or drugged up to care.

That was the first time he was fostered into an emergency placement as far as he could remember, and they were okay in retrospect – a retired nurse and her doctor husband. He liked her at least, but they didn't want him back after he kicked holes in the bedroom wall. The second, he could barely remember – only the fact they had a gummy toddler called Tilly and they never left him alone with her. The third set he never bothered making eye-contact with, because he wasn't speaking at the time. The McGyvers were the fourth, and by far the worst. Not least, because it was five months and counting. Brendan was lucky. He was only six weeks in – respite care while his granny was in hospital. Michael hoped for Brendan's sake, granny made it out.

'Love these poor mites like my own,' Mrs McGyver assured the social worker when she'd brought round Brendan. What she loved, Michael knew, was the money. She considered the £98 a week she got for fostering Michael and the £196 for Brendan who had 'special needs', payment for her trouble, rather than a way to feed and clothe the boys. And, once the door was shut on the social worker, she made it clear she wasn't spending the allowance, or the 'pittance' that Mr McGyver earned delivering medical supplies to chemists on their good-for-nothing behinds.

The pecking order in the back-to-back of 18 Rum Street, Peckham, was clear from the start. Mrs McGyver. The McGyver husband. The McGyver dog Bonzo – a bow-legged, mean-spirited Staffordshire. Only after the dog, came the McGyver twins Janice and Janette who'd had the good sense to move far away and never visit. Then came anyone Mrs McGyver ever met, followed by Brendan who was worth more, and Michael who was worth less.

Ever since he could remember, ne'er-do-wells and druggies had drifted in and out of whatever dump he and his mother were living in – each place worse than the last. Occasionally, the bleary-eyed and sentimental patted empty pockets for fifty-pence pieces to give him which they'd spent long ago. But most ignored him. Didn't even see him to ignore him. He was the invisible boy. And it was safer that way, because there were those who were mean with need – others who were angry and blazing. Worst of all though were the silent and downright dangerous. Like the dealer who'd cut his mother after she attempted to short-change him. The dealer had held her up against a wall and drawn a blade along her cheek as she'd screamed. Michael thought he must have been about seven. He'd launched himself across the room and the dealer had knocked him to the floor, and laughed as he kicked him in the belly. Once. Twice. Three times. His mother wailing like a banshee, crimson blood oozing between her fingers of the hand held against her cheek, but making no attempt to come between them.

Yes, Michael had learned how to read people. A narrowing of the eyes. The two frown marks deepening over the nose. He figured the latest social worker had her doubts about the McGyvers. That she'd believe him if he complained. Get them moved into a group home, but who's to say what would happen to Brendan then? It probably wouldn't be the same home, and he was reluctant to part from the younger boy. His own mother was in prison for another stretch – nine months, six with good behaviour. When she got out, he'd go back home to her. He knew she'd want him, because she'd need the child benefit that came with him, and she was good at making promises. A good liar. The court always seemed to believe her.

That this time, she'd turn things round. Keep clean. Please, don't take her boy away. He was all she had in this world. Hands clasped. Huge blue eyes brimming with tears. He believed her himself sometimes. Let himself, because he wanted to. Yes, she'd get him back and till then, he'd sit it out in McGyver-land and keep Brendan from the worst of it. Because somebody had to look out for the little guy, and nobody else was volunteering.

When the McGyver snoring hit the regular rhythm he'd been waiting for, Michael slid out and down from the bed. The bunk beds swaying like a rotten tree in the wind. He checked his jeans pocket for the tin opener then held his index finger to his lips for Brendan to stay quiet, and the younger boy raised his own index finger to his lips, his eyes opening wide and sincere. Good as gold, he promised.

Bonzo

Sound. Furry critter? Eat? Dark. No Boss-Missus. No Walk-Man-do-shite-bloody-now. Intruder? Danger? Bark? Bad dog. Bad dog. Listen Bonzo. Good dog. Fart. Snuffly noise. Food? Hunger. Hunger. Want. Want. Boy. Listen. Fart.

Michael

Michael took the stairs two at a time, missing the ninth and the third which always whined for pity. The house was better at night. The fug of Mr McGyver's sweat and farting dog less intense. He pushed open the kitchen door and Bonzo bared his teeth, growling far back in his throat, before the stump that passed for his tail began thumping against the kitchen floor. Michael and Bonzo had a deal. Bonzo would

let Michael steal food, providing Bonzo got a piece of the action.

Brendan

Try to be good. Try to be good and not wet the bed. Try. Don't wet the bed. Don't wet the bed. Be brave and make granny proud. *It won't be for long pet. They'll look after you for me just till I'm right again.* Granny.

Michael

He eased round the door and pushed it almost shut behind him. Treading carefully – Bonzo had been known to do his business in the kitchen – he headed across the lino to the larder. Mrs McGyver padlocked the fridge. She said it helped her willpower if she had to take off the padlock, but North thought it was a message. *The food is mine, because I'm somebody and you're nobody.* She had, however, yet to lock up the cupboards with their cardboard trays of tinned fruit, 'value' beans and dog food. Instead, she kept the tin opener in her handbag, but he'd lifted one from the Co-op weeks before. Tucked it in his windbreaker. Walked out whistling. Stealing was wrong, he knew that – knew the difference between right and wrong. He'd be good when he was grown up and could afford to be.

He eased out one tin of dog food from the bottom tray, one of beans, and closed the cupboard door behind him. The McGyvers were both huge. They shopped in bulk from some discount warehouse on a trading estate a few miles away. They drove there once a month. Went out smiling. Came back flushed and quarrelsome. Shouting at Michael and Brendan to

carry in the shopping from the car. Immense packets of teabags and cornflakes. No names he ever recognised from the telly or from real shops. Dozens and dozens of rolls of toilet paper. Giant boxes of washing powder as if they ran a laundry. And tray after tray of tinned goods. He'd read a comic once about a zombie apocalypse. Zombies took over the world and ate the brains of any human being they could find. The humans who survived were keen on two things: smashing zombie heads and raiding supermarkets for tinned goods. He figured the McGyvers would do okay up against zombies. He could only hope that by the time they got down to the bottom tray of beans or worse yet, the peaches, both he and Brendan would be long gone or he'd be positively praying for the zombies to come knocking.

Enough with the zombies, he told himself. If he took any longer, Brendan would come looking for him and that would definitely wake the McGyvers.

He dipped into his back pocket for the tin opener, before sawing round the dog food and easing open the metal lid. Bonzo whined, his claws clicking on the lino as he shifted his weight from paw to paw.

Upstairs, there was silence where there should have been the rasping saw of the McGyver sinuses.

Michael held his breath. He looked up at the ceiling – the lid of the dog food at half-mast.

And she was off again.

He closed his eyes, his breath gusting out from between his lips.

Opening them again.

Something was off.

Light gleamed from across the kitchen.

The streetlight was reflecting from something on top of the fridge.

Michael placed the can of dog food on the counter to move closer – Bonzo moving with him.

He went up onto his tiptoes to reach it down.

It was a large foil dish, heavier at one end than the other.

The smell of beef hit him.

It was the remains of a meat pie left over from the McGyver's dinner. He'd smelled it cooking as he and Brendan sat in the lounge eating their sandwiches. His mouth had watered then and it was watering now, even though the pie was cold and the gravy had congealed on the bottom of the tin.

Bonzo whined again.

He wasn't rushing this. It was too important. With outstretched arms, Michael carried the pie back across to the counter with the dog food, thinking hard all the while.

Was it a trap?

He came down to the kitchen every three nights. Any more was pushing his luck, he reckoned. Had Mrs McGyver figured out what he was doing and left the pie as a test?

Michael used a fork to scrape out the dog food into the bowl and Bonzo fell on it, moving the bowl across the lino with the urgent force of his tongue. Michael flipped the lid of the bin and pushed the empty can down into the bottom under the potato peelings and teabags already in there.

Mrs McGyver wasn't that clever, he decided.

When she found out he was stealing food, she would hit the roof. Because if there was one thing she enjoyed even more than Bingo and pie, it was ranting and raving.

What was different about today then?

Cheese. Ham. Tuna in rotation. Today was cheese. Two slices

of white bread – a scrape of margarine, a thin smattering of grated orange cheese that tasted of feet. 'You've a hot meal at school,' she told them when they arrived. 'No one on God's earth needs two hot meals a day.' As usual, he and Brendan had eaten the sandwiches as they watched a quiz show on TV, while the McGyvers ate their tea together in the kitchen. Usually, after tea, Mrs McGyver would throw them out of the lounge to 'have-a-nice-sit-down-God-knows-I-deserve-it' and leave her husband with the washing up. But tonight, the phone had gone. Mrs McGyver's sister calling to complain about her ex-husband and his floozie. She must have been about to lock up the remains of dinner in the fridge when she'd been distracted by the prospect of someone else's misery.

Michael did a quick check on the padlock – she hadn't been so distracted that she'd failed to lock up the fridge. He wasn't that lucky.

His eyes went back to the pie as he ran through his options. He could forget all about it. He thought back to the tenner he stole from his mother and his arm started to ache with the memory of the beating. It was too obvious, and there would be Hell when she realised it was missing. He should put the pie back on top of the fridge. No harm done.

But who feeds kids cheese sandwiches at night while they eat hot pie? Michael felt a slow burning anger start up in his chest. And Brendan wasn't like him – he wasn't used to being hungry. How would a tadpole like Brendan ever get to grow bigger if he wasn't fed properly?

He was doing it.

The question was how?

He stared at the dish. He could take up the whole pie and, together with the beans, he and Brendan could go to bed with food in their bellies for this one night. But in the morning, even if he threw the foil dish out the bedroom window, she'd

find the pie missing and they'd both be blamed. He wasn't having Brendan cop it.

He could eat his share of the pie standing here, carry up the rest for Brendan, and then leave the dish upside down on the floor and the dog would be blamed, but chances were, she'd beat the dog which hardly seemed fair. Bonzo nudged him in apparent agreement, and the animal's wet nose against his bare foot almost made Michael yelp.

He had a better idea.

He went back to the cupboard.

Michael slid a fork under the flaky pastry lid and lifted it, clean off. It lay upside down on the scratched veneer of the table, its pale belly slashed with knife marks from the pie maker.

In the gloom, the meat and gravy in the foil dish looked black and dangerous and succulent.

Bugger Mrs McGyver, he thought, closing his two fingers together to spoon up a mouthful of cold beans. In the space where there had been beans, he lay the seven pieces of beef from the pie – four for Brendan, three for him – he'd already had that spoon of beans to make room for the meat, so that was fair. He closed the lid on the tin of beans so that nothing would fall out when he carried it back upstairs, licked his fingers clean of the bean juice, and in the tray where there'd been steak, forked out the meaty chunks from the second can of dog food, filling the pie with them, before again burying the can in the bin. It was his job to take it out in the morning so it should be safe enough.

He put his nose to the meat – he'd smelled worse – before lifting the pastry lid, righting it in the air, and crowning the pie. Good enough to eat and serve the McGyvers right.

There was a growl from Bonzo as the electric light went on with a snap, and as the door closed, Michael felt the blood stop running in his veins.

'I bloody knew you was robbing us, you thieving little git.' Mr McGyver's immense belly pushed against his vest, bulging over the striped cotton pyjamas. His shining face was tight and smug under the harsh kitchen light. 'I should report you to the police.'

This was bad. Mr McGyver would tell Mrs McGyver and there would be Hell to pay.

His foster father's eyes went between the can of beans and the pie.

'You can't eat the pie. She'll know it was you. The beans is different. You can get away with the beans, but you have to put the pie back.'

Michael did a rapid recall. The empty cans of dog food were both in the bin. The lid was down on the beans. The pie was for all intents and purposes on the counter. McGyver thought he'd caught him about to clear the dish.

He worked to keep his face blank. If McGyver realised the pie was topped up with knacked horse and entrails or whatever it was dogs ate, he was dead where he stood. He had to blag it.

'We're hungry.' He made his voice sound reasonable. Tried to keep the panic out of it.

McGyver nodded. He didn't seem surprised.

'You're growing lads – the pair of you. I've told her you need more food, but she's a woman of firm opinions is my wife. Not one to understand that a man has needs.'

The beady eyes behind their jam jar glasses watched Michael's face. They had a look he'd seen before and run from. An assessing wanting look. Michael was suddenly glad the bedroom was cold. Glad he was fully dressed. He

scowled. Pushed the pie as if he didn't want it anymore. Who would?

But there was still the can of beans and meat to give him away.

He picked it up, and made for the door. But McGyver blocked his way.

'You're a clever lad, Michael. Resourceful. You and I should come to an understanding.'

There was a sheen of sweat on his upper lip that Michael could see now he was closer.

'You help me out when I give you the say-so, and I'll let you have the odd bit of cash that you can use to treat yourself to fish and chips, or a nice pizza even.' McGyver took a step closer to Michael and the smell of bad breath and dirty feet came with him. McGyver's sweaty hand closed over Michael's wrist and made to drag it down to his crotch. Michael moved back, pulling his hand away, curling his fingers into a fist, and McGyver closed the gap between them. His face had contorted. The pretence of pleasantry gone. 'You stupid boy. No one cares about you, don't you know that yet?' He raised his hand to strike him. Michael braced himself – time slowing. He'd been hit before. He could survive it. There were worse things. But the blow never landed. Instead, there was a muffled scream from McGyver as Bonzo attached himself to his calf.

The dog didn't seem keen to let go. Michael grabbed the tin of beans and beef, pushing past McGyver to take the stairs three at a time regardless of any noise. Panting, he slammed the door shut behind him.

Brendan was waiting. His eyes still big – brimming with unspilled tears. His hands peeping over the top of the sleeping bag.

'I wet the bed Mickey,' he whispered.

. . .

The boys got themselves up in the morning. Michael went down first, sliding the empty bean can into his school bag hanging in the hallway, taking out the black bin bag, and then hauling Brendan's sleeping bag and rubber sheet from the washing machine to hang outside on the line, pegging it with plastic pegs. Through the kitchen window, he could see Mrs McGyver cooking eggs and bacon for the morning fry-up. He looked up at the sky. If it rained, he'd spend another night freezing. Once he'd heard McGyver go to bed last night, he'd tiptoed downstairs for the second time with the reeking sheet and sleeping bag in his arms. In his basket, Bonzo had whimpered as he'd opened his eyes. A scrap of torn striped cotton lay on the floor next to the basket. Michael had pushed the sheet and sleeping bag into the drum of the washing machine, thrown in a cup of powder and set it going. Then he'd knelt next to the dog, pressing his forehead against the dome of warm skull, and Bonzo rallied enough to lick his nose, before farting explosively.

Upstairs again, he'd helped Brendan get dry and changed, then wrapped him in his own sleeping bag, lying top to toe in the same bunk and willing himself to sleep. Even with the cold. Even with the threat of Mrs McGyver's rage yet to come, it didn't seem as bad with the beans and beef in his stomach.

When he got back into the kitchen, Mrs McGyver was scowling as she poured their ration of cornflakes into their bowls, but the scowl was no more heartfelt than usual. The two plates of eggs and bacon were spitting and flaming under the grill. Michael glanced up at the pie. It was still in its dish on

top of the fridge. Underneath the table, Bonzo licked his hand, and he scratched the dog between its ears. Was it possible that McGyver hadn't told her he was stealing food? If he hadn't, it wasn't because of any sense of loyalty, it was because McGyver didn't want his wife knowing anything at all about last night.

The door opened and in limped the man himself. A low rumble started in the dog's chest – the vibrations travelling up Michael's arm. He patted Bonzo's back to quieten him – the dog was in enough trouble on Michael's account. But McGyver ignored both Bonzo and the boys as he took his seat. With huge padded hands, Mrs McGyver slid the plate of eggs, bacon and greasy triangles of fried bread in front of her husband.

'We should do a stock-take in the larder Cynthia,' he said to his wife's back as she started to fish for teabags in the His Lordship and Her Ladyship matching mugs. 'Before we go back to Macro, so we know we're buying exactly what we need.' McGyver rested his fists on the table, a knife upright in one, a fork in the other, and stared at Michael. A glare of unadulterated hatred. 'And I'll take that left-over pie with me for my lunch. I've a lot of deliveries today. I don't want it wasted.'

Brendan's coat was half off him as they slammed their way out the house. It had started to spit with rain. No point hoping Mrs McGyver would bring in the sleeping bag. God he was tired. He'd have to sleep through lessons.

Brendan bumped into him, accidentally on purpose and giggled. He was in a weird mood this morning. Michael stopped walking long enough to pull up the younger boy's coat onto his shoulders and tugged him onwards. They were

going to be late. Again. By his reckoning this was his tenth school. They'd no sooner settle, than his mother would be off. But the schools he went to when he was in a care home or fostered were the worst. Teachers looking at you like you were scum, or worse yet, like they felt sorry for you. He hated strangers feeling sorry for him. Thinking they knew everything there was to know about him.

It took Michael a second to process what it was Brendan was waving in front of him.

It was a Mars Bar. Flatter than it should be, but still a Mars Bar. Had Brendan stolen it? They hadn't been in the corner shop, and anyway Brendan wasn't like that. He said his granny taught him stealing was bad and he was resolute on the matter. Michael had to tell him the food he brought up at night wasn't stealing, it was borrowing.

The younger boy tore off the black wrapper and held the chocolate bar under Michael's nose for him to take a bite. Michael bit and the boy's grin widened.

Brendan

'Nice one, Brendan mate.'

Brendan liked Mickey more than he liked anyone in this world apart from his granny. But he didn't want to think about his granny because she was in hospital getting well again, and he wanted to see her so badly that thinking about her made him sad.

As they walked on, he nibbled the chocolate from the side. It lasted longer that way. Mickey was silent, but he was like that sometimes. Brendan figured he missed home too. Still this morning, he had been able to do something for Mickey, instead of Mickey always doing something for him. He was going to

leave the toffee goo till last. That was the best bit. He could make it last for ages if he tried. Ages and ages. Maybe till they got to school? Even though he'd just eaten cornflakes, he was still hungry. He missed the porridge his granny always made him, missed the blue and white striped bowl she served it in, and the golden syrup she poured over it in the shape of a 'B' and the 'wee blueberry surprises' she'd stirred into it.

'So?'

Brendan shook his head. He must have not been listening. His stomach tightened. Everyone got cross with him when he didn't listen. But it was only Mickey he reminded himself. Mickey never got cross with him.

They were almost at the school gates, he noticed. He wasn't feeling as worried about school these days. He hadn't liked this school at all when he first got to the McGyvers. The children weren't kind. Not like Mickey.

'I said, where did you get the Mars Bar from?'

'Mr McGyver gave it to me just before we left. He said I was a good boy and good boys needed special treats sometimes, and it was our secret.'

Michael

Michael stopped in his tracks. He put his arm up to his mouth and wiped the taste of caramel off his tongue onto his arm.

'Brendan.' His voice was louder than it should have been, he realised, but he couldn't help it. He took hold of the boy by both his upper arms and swung him round to face him. Brendan's face was a mask of fear. 'Did McGyver make you do anything for it? Tell me the truth.'

The younger boy shook his head.

'Only say thank you. But I said it Mickey. I did. Am I in trouble? Did I do something wrong?'

The boy's huge eyes seemed to fill his face. Michael made himself let go. Brushed him down as much to keep his own face hidden, then looked at Brendan and smiled, though he didn't feel like smiling

'Listen to me, Brendan. You're not in trouble. But you have to listen to me, because this is important. McGyver's a dirty pervert. Do you know what that means?' He searched for some comprehension in the younger boy's face. 'Brendan, did your granny ever tell you not to get into any strange man's cars? Did she tell you not to go off with them even if they offered you sweeties or to show you puppies or whatever?'

What Michael took to be understanding sparked at the back of Brendan's eyes.

'She said I was never to get in a car or go with a stranger, because they were bad men. Bad. That I was to yell for help and run away as fast as I could and not listen to them. Should we yell for help and run away Mickey?'

Briefly, the idea of running away spooled across Michael's brain. He'd never be able to keep Brendan safe on the streets. They'd be caught and returned.

'If McGyver gets you alone and says he wants you to do anything at all – like touch you, or hold his willy – you bang it as hard as you can with your fist like I showed you how to punch those lads in school. Will you do that?'

Brendan nodded.

'Let's tell someone he's a bad man, Mickey.'

Michael considered their options. Nothing had happened to Brendan yet, so it would be Michael's word against McGyver. If he was believed, they would both be taken away and separated and Brendan would be alone in the world. If he

wasn't believed and Michael knew how well adults could lie, then the worst possible thing would happen: he'd be taken away to a group home and Brendan would be left alone and at the mercy of the McGyvers.

To the relief of his teacher, Michael sat quietly in his seat all day, a look of furious concentration on his face.

He knew one thing. He didn't have long.

Tuesday, he skipped school, swearing Brendan to secrecy and trusting the McGyvers not to care even if school rang to complain. He stole a bike – temporarily. He'd bring it back as soon as he'd finished with it and no harm done. He followed the McGyver van. Local routes. In and out. Fifteen drops mostly to small, independent chemists. Mr McGyver liked to chat. Make the delivery. Get them to sign. Hand on the counter, lean in, pass the time of day with the chemist or the prettiest sales assistant, occasionally he'd even drink a cup of tea. Michael got the impression he was a regular. Wednesday, he wrote a note in his best handwriting and said he was sorry but Michael was very poorly, signed Mrs Cynthia McGyver. While Brendan was taking it to the school office, McGyver parked up with the back of the van to a brick wall, took out what he needed and strolled to the chemist. Michael was moving towards the backdoor of the van before McGyver had made it into the shop. He wasn't going to be greedy – not at first. He slit the bottom of the nearest cardboard box and slid out three white boxes of oxycontin. One of his mother's favourites. By the seventh delivery, the van was emptying and Michael had to reach right to the back to scoop up a small

oblong box of morphine patches and a large box marked diazepam. Thursday, Mr McGyver went too far afield to follow so Michael wrote more letters. On Friday, he razored the bottom of every cardboard box to hand and took out a smaller box from each, then taped each box up again with tape he'd shoplifted from the newsagent. No one would notice till they'd unpacked the boxes and checked them against the contents list. His pockets rattled as he rode the bicycle home.

When the police arrived, he was on the top bunk reading a copy of the *Daily Express*, but he heard them. Brendan was doing what he'd been told to do by Michael – sitting watching the TV and 'not budging one inch' till he was told he could. Not even when Mrs McGyver shouted at him for being a useless lump. Not even when the police arrived. Not even when they pounded upstairs, Mrs McGyver shrieking after them. Straight to the master bedroom. Straight to the bed. Under the bed. As if they'd known, and as the police pulled out the empty cardboard tray covered with pill packets, he heard an almighty yell.

The door flew open and McGyver went for him, clawing at his ankle to pull him closer and off the mattress. Michael pulled back to the corner, bracing himself, lifting himself, letting the walls take his weight for a second as he pushed off. It wasn't his fault. The policeman was right there in the doorway. He saw everything.

Sgt Andy Nash

We took our eye off the ball, I admit it. We couldn't believe the bloke had been so thick. It was like a druggie's wet dream under that bed. I've never seen so many pills. God knows how

long he'd been at it. And he didn't look the type to lose the plot that way. Big fat bloke he was, but he could move fast enough when he wanted to. At first, I thought he was trying to leg it out the house, but he wanted the lad in the bedroom next door. It's all in my report. I think we should be able to do him on an assault charge, intention to cause actual bodily harm to a minor, as well as the stealing. The boy didn't know what was going on. He scrambled into the corner. His hands went either side of the wall. The only thing in his head was getting away from his attacker and there was literally nowhere for the poor bugger to go.

The Good Lord only knows how he wasn't hurt too. That pile of clothes and sleeping bags on the floor must have broken his fall. Lucky for him they were there like that, but they didn't do McGyver much good though. The frame of the bunk bed caught him a real nasty one. Pinned him to the floor. Nearly knocked his head off, broke three ribs and both his legs, and him still calling the boy all the names under the sun even as the paramedics were carrying him out.

The kid's no angel I'm willing to bet – his type never are – but he's well out of that house. And I don't reckon he'll miss the woman. She was a piece of work that one. Hard-faced. Said she had no idea what was under the bed. But who'd believe that one? She won't be getting any more kiddies to foster, that's for sure. She'll have to go get a job like the rest of the world. But as for the older lad, well he never looked back when we walked him and the young one out the house and put them both in the social worker's car. Just put his arm round the kid. Wanted to know if he was doing okay. Told him he'd done great and his granny would be proud of him. Said he'd found the hospital his granny was in and he'd been in to see her that morning. He'd make sure Brendan got to see her, and that his

granny was giving social services what for just as soon as Michael gave the word. She was coming to get Brendan whatever the doctors said. What did they know. Said for Michael to tell Brendan she'd cook him porridge tomorrow morning. It would have broken your heart to see that little kid's smile I tell you. Ten feet wide.

Then the lad asked us if his mother was out of lock-up yet.

A FACE FOR MURDER

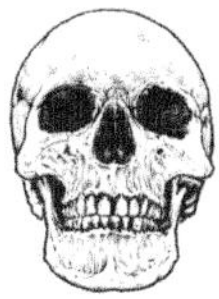

Hey everyone, thank you so much for joining me. My name is Ashley Tootles. This is 'A Face for Murder', and wow! I mean – wow! I'm really pumped about today's show.

Okay, so while I apply my latest glamour make-up look – and take note, we are heavy on the smoky eye today – I'll be telling you all about the murder of Maisie Carter. AKA – The Girl Who Ran Away. Cue the sinister music! (Sienna is wrangling the tech for me. Don't mess up, Sienna! I'm kidding – she's super smart.)

Right, to celebrate our one millionth subscriber, we decided to do something special. As you know, we're all about putting the beauty into True Crime. And usually while I apply my make up, I talk you through the details of a real life True Crime case. This time – wait for it – we went out on the road and did our own investigation into Maisie's murder! We are loco, huh!

Do you like what I'm doing with my foundation? Yep, you're right. Guilty as charged. I'm using the exact same primer as I applied on my Jack the Ripper show. But, shoot

me. Or should I say – stab me! – I know for a fact this particular foundation goes on really well over it. (Quick reminder: all the products are listed at the bottom of the video.)

We chose the Maisie Carter mystery for this special treatment, because I felt really upset when her body was found last month. I didn't just think 'Hooray, here's another murder mystery that my subscribers are going to love'. No! Because I'm not a monster. I'm interested in monsters, sure I am. But then, you are too, because you wouldn't be here otherwise. I am super aware of the need to be sensitive. Victims are people too. And they have families, and those families, they're nearly all of them people too. And friends. People also. I get that. Which reminds me, sometime soon, I'll be doing a 'Get Ready with Me' make-up show with products all aimed at sensitive skin. One to watch out for if you're prone to breakouts.

And I think part of my upset was her age. I mean look at that photo. Maisie was gorgeous, and not that there's a good age to be murdered, because there really isn't. But 17! That sucks big time. Talking of age, I need a truckload of concealer today, don't I? That's because it's been party central here since the conviction of Annie the Cannibal out in Sydney, Australia. Life sentence. Whoop, whoop! Am I right? I don't want to fat shame Annie, because frankly, I don't think that's a very nice thing to do to another woman, but seriously, I hope she gets some help with her appetite in prison. I don't just mean what she eats. I mean how much she eats, right!

What do you think? Is that enough concealer? No more tequila for me, it goes straight to my eyebags.

And don't worry, before we uploaded this video, we told the detective in charge of the investigation everything we found out, and she was thrilled. If you're watching this DI Sharon Oates – you're welcome.

Let's start at the beginning. So, 21 years ago in 2001, Maisie Carter runs away from home. Or that's what everyone thinks. Her dad Frank is a farmer on the North Northumberland coast. He is super strict. Her mum Val is 10 years younger than Frank, and everyone we met up there told us what a lovely person she is. (Val is still alive, but unfortunately she has dementia now). This is a photo of the farmhouse where the Carters lived. It's pretty grim right? And it's three miles outside the nearest village, a place called Seaport.

Maisie is super talented and wants to go to art school, but the problem is – she never turns up to her first A level exam. When her art teacher rings up to find out why, Maisie's mum tells him that the night before there was a quarrel, and that Maisie got upset. Val later tells police that the minute she puts down the phone, she runs up to Maisie's bedroom, and finds revision books open on the desk but her rucksack and purse, favourite clothes, makeup and art portfolio are all missing.

Val is super upset. She rings the police to tell them Maisie has run away after a row about £200 going missing from a biscuit barrel in the kitchen. The police come to the farmhouse to talk to Val and Frank, and to Maisie's older brother Jackie. Val says she believes her daughter left the house around quarter to one in the morning, because that's when she heard the farm collie dog bark. Eighteen-year-old Jackie, however, says he got home from Newcastle just past one, and seeing her light was still on he knocked on Maisie's door. She didn't open it, just told him to get lost. At this point, the police aren't worried, but they decide to drop by Maisie's school and talk to her girlfriends – Lauren, Emma and Fiona. Sienna, can we have the photo?

Lauren is Head Girl and editor of the school newspaper.

She's the blonde in the 'Little Miss Bossy' tee-shirt on the driver's side of the Mini.

Emma is the one with bad skin leaning up against the passenger door. It's actually her car. (While I think, I'm going to add a fantastic glycolic spot treatment to my product list.)

Fiona is the one with the glasses and plaid shirt by the open boot. Sidebar: she's had laser treatment now, so no spectacles. She still has the same haircut though. I don't know why.

The three friends are still really tight and initially, they didn't want to talk to us. They kept saying things like 'Leave it to the police. Blah blah! What's this got to do with mascara? Duh!' Luckily for us, Lauren's eldest daughter is a fan of the show and told her mum it might help find Maisie's killer. She even looked out that photo for us!

The three friends all tell the police that Maisie didn't get on with her dad and that her brother used to beat up on her. Fiona says that Maisie couldn't wait to leave home and had regularly suggested they run away to London. Fiona advised Maisie to stick it out so she could take up her place at art college. Fiona even took out her phone and showed us a self-portrait of Maisie, which she still has hanging above her fireplace in her living room in Chelsea.

Just going to apply the blusher now. Big brush, see. Then, blend like you're a psycho trying to fit in.

We know that in the weeks following Maisie's disappearance, her family travel down to London looking for her. They put up posters and go round hostels. But no one has seen Maisie. After a year, Jackie joins the army. After three years, Lauren marries her childhood sweetheart Sam. And why wouldn't you – the guy's family own a stately home. Plus he's cute, huh?

Emma goes into the family funeral business.

And Fiona becomes a big City lawyer in London.

No one hears from Maisie – ever. Ten years ago, Frank dies after a heart attack and Maisie's mother tries to find her all over again. Contacts the Salvation Army this time. Nothing. But at least, Jackie comes back from the army and takes over the farm.

Okay, so this is where it gets interesting.

Last month, there's a huge storm over North Northumberland. Power lines are down. Roofs are off. Trees are felled. Including an ancient oak tree on the Carter farm. A tree which is in a field close by a stone wall. A field way distant from the farmhouse, but pretty close to a lane which locals use as a cut-through. And when the oak tree comes down, the roots tear out of the ground, and the whole thing topples over. Kerboom. The next morning, it's chaos. But when Jackie goes walkabout to assess the damage on the farm, what does he see tangled in the roots of the uprooted oak?

I'm going to apply my eyeshadow now. Don't you love these colours. Kinda reminds me of a black eye. In a good way.

A skull.

He knows straight away. It's Maisie. When he rings the police. That's what he tells them. Let's listen to the recording we managed to get hold of. (Don't ask me how. Sienna's a wonder.)

'I think I just found my sister's body.

Can you tell me your name and where you're calling from?

Oh my God.

Sir, can you tell me your name.

My name's Jackie Carter. We thought she'd run away.'

He sounds shocked right. Not shocked enough for the police though. They turn up to the farm. Go out to the tree, and yes, there are skeletal remains in the ground. They re-open

the investigation into Maisie's disappearance. Except now, it's a murder investigation.

Just to say, I'm not that into contouring at the moment. I think it's had its day. But I will still do a stripe here and here down either side of my nose and a highlight stripe on my nose and chin. But you have to keep it subtle, right?

Anyway, along with what's left of Maisie after twenty years, the forensic team also discover fragments of canvas and clothing, scraps of leather, as well as an old mobile phone which they go to work on. The fragments indicate that Maisie had indeed packed up her belongings, and that she was in the process of running away. Except Maisie never made it.

The police bring Jackie in for questioning. Jackie says he never beat up Maisie. He caught her with drugs one time and took them off her. When she tried to get them back, he pushed her away. He says he loved Maisie, but she was often 'a giant pain in the arse' and 'a compulsive liar'. Obviously, he denies killing her.

Meanwhile, the post-mortem comes back. Don't ask how, but we have a copy! You catch more flies with honey, Sienna always says. I have no idea what that means. But she's a machine. So, the pathologist has checked the teeth against Maisie's dental records, and confirms the body is hers. The report says that Maisie *'suffered damage to the side of her skull consistent with a single blow'* and a broken wrist which they speculate could have happened when she fell. The pathologist also points to a large stone found in the shallow grave, which has trace elements of dried blood on it. He says the injuries are consistent with the theory that the stone was the murder weapon.

Sienna and I start wondering if someone caught Maisie running away. Maybe her super strict dad? Well, Frank isn't

around to ask. And Maisie's mum is away with the fairies. But Jackie said his father was convinced Maisie had run away from home, that he blamed himself, and was left a broken man by it.

We went back to talk it all through with Maisie's friends.

Lauren was a straight-A student, but had decided to take a year off before she went to uni. She gets a job in the café attached to Sam's stately home and within a few months, she's engaged to him – they're married by the time she's twenty-one. We asked her about the drugs Jackie mentioned. Was Maisie involved with the wrong kind of people? Had she bought drugs she couldn't pay for? Was that why the money was missing from the biscuit barrel?

Lauren admits that the four girls used to smoke cannabis together regularly and had taken ecstasy a couple of times. Sam had a supplier in Newcastle, and whatever he didn't use – he sold on to friends. She says that Maisie didn't owe Sam or anyone else money, but that yes, as Jackie said, she wasn't always a nice person. For instance, her nickname for Sam was 'Dim Sam'. And she was a liar. For instance, the week she was murdered, Maisie had told lies about Emma stealing from the dead at her dad's funeral home.

Hold on. Fake eyelash emergency. Give me a second. There you go.

When we talk to Emma, she claims the other three girls were prettier, smarter and more popular. That they weren't always nice to her, but that she had a car and was useful to them. She used to come out from the village to take Maisie to school every morning, for instance. Even so, she says Maisie was a bully, and that she regularly refused to sit next to her in form, because she claimed that she smelled like dead people. Emma said she ended up spending a fortune on shower gels and perfumes. When Sienna asks about the argument, Emma

says Maisie had accused her of stealing diamond earrings from a corpse, but that on the very evening she disappeared, she'd called to apologise, describing it as a 'wind-up'. Maisie had confided that she and Fiona were going out, and that the pressure of keeping the relationship a secret was getting to her.

Oh, and while I think. We have a sponsor to thank for their support today. Just Fabulous! is a monthly subscription service that for as low as £10 a month gives you access to premium beauty and skincare products at discounted prices. If I didn't already have beauty companies literally begging me to use their products, I would almost definitely probably take out a subscription to Just Fabulous! Check out their socials, guys. And use the code AFACEFORMURDER for 10% off your subscription.

At school, Fiona was already 'out' by the way. Maisie, however, wasn't. Fiona admitted that she was passionately in love with Maisie and had been for years, but Maisie didn't feel the same way. In fact, for a long time she'd suspected that Maisie was two-timing her with Sam, not least, because she'd seen him give Maisie a stack of money.

So, what we have is a brother, who may or may not have been violent with his sister some time before her death.

Lauren, who had cause to be jealous, because rumour had it Maisie was sleeping with Sam.

Emma, who was bulled by Maisie and wrongly accused of being a thief.

Fiona, who loved Maisie, but who believed she was being betrayed by Maisie.

And 'Dim Sam' himself. Why was he giving Maisie money? Had she threatened to expose his drug dealing to his family or to the police? That was Sienna's theory, anyway, so we put it to

him, and Sam didn't deny it. Just called the pair of us some very bad names.

We had to buy a whiteboard.

Jackie might have had the opportunity to kill his sister, but he didn't have an obvious motive.

Each of her friends however had their own reasons to kill Maisie.

What about the opportunity though?

The farm was three miles outside the village. Forensics indicated that Maisie had brought her bag outside the farmhouse. Was she waiting for a lift?

Both Sam and Emma had cars. Had Maisie persuaded one of them to pick her up and drive her to the local train station, or better yet Newcastle train station an hour away? When they arrived, did an argument blow up about the bullying, or the drugs?

Neither Lauren nor Fiona had their own cars, although Lauren sometimes borrowed Emma's car. We saw her about to drive it in the photograph of the three of them. Fiona had a bicycle but couldn't drive a car. Could she have cycled out to the farm with the intention of persuading Maisie to stay? And did tempers become heated?

We know Maisie had an exam the next day. Indeed, her revision books were open on her desk when her mother went into her room. But, as Sienna pointed out, why revise if you're going to run away?

After twenty years in the grave, it took time for the police to salvage the received text messages and the record of the calls in and the calls out. The night of her death, Emma and Maisie did indeed talk.

But Maisie didn't call Emma to apologise. I believe she called Emma to accuse her of the theft of the £200 cash from

the biscuit barrel. After all, Emma had the chance to steal the money when she gave Maisie a lift to school that morning. Perhaps Emma took it – not because she was a thief – but because she wanted Maisie to know how it felt to be wrongly accused.

But Maisie wasn't so easily brought to heel. I think she accused Emma – rightly this time – and then told one of her famous lies. Perhaps that her mother Val had seen Emma steal the money? Understandably, Emma panicked.

The other call that came into Maisie's phone that night was from a number listed under 'Dim'.

Twenty years ago, Sam was quite the ladies' man. I'm guessing Emma called him in hysterics. To calm her down, he suggested they'd go talk to Maisie together. Then Emma could give her back the £200.

Somehow, he persuaded Maisie to come out to the oak tree. Maybe he told her he had drugs for her? Or more blackmail money? I don't think Sam and Emma went there with the intention of murdering Maisie. But when Maisie refused to listen to Emma's pleading...

Hold on while I line my lips. You need a steady hand.

... a panicking Emma picked up a piece of the crumbling dry stone wall and...

Okay, where is that lipstick brush. Ah, here we go...

... smashed Maisie over the head with it.

These two aren't exactly Rose and Fred West.

So Sam reached out to the girl who always knew exactly what to do – Lauren. And, as ever, Little Miss Bossy took charge. Lauren snuck out of her own house, and drove Emma's mini over to Fiona's house. She explained the situation, and together the two of them drove to the oak tree. Just how organ-

ised was Lauren? Organised enough to pick up a couple of spades from the garden shed? I think so.

Lauren and Fiona chose to help. Lauren, because Sam would have to marry her now. But if he went to prison, her dream of a big house and a wealthy husband was over.

As for Fiona? Is it too much to believe Maisie's death came as something of a relief?

The others certainly needed Fiona on board for Lauren's plan to work. Fiona was a regular visitor to the farm. Which is why Maisie's mother paid no heed when the dog barked and then quietened as she let herself into the house. When Jackie knocked on his sister's door and was told 'Get lost, Jackie', he presumed it was his sister. It was, in reality, Fiona packing up Maisie's things, because it had to look as if Maisie was running away.

I'm guessing, afterwards, the four of them made a pact. That if Maisie's body was ever found, they would point the finger at each other. Knowing as time passed, the evidence such as it was, would never be enough to incriminate one of them on their own.

After all, it's twenty years ago and no one can prove there was ever a call between Dim Sam and Lauren that night.

And their plan would have worked, if only Fiona hadn't kept Maisie's portfolio. The rucksack of clothes and make-up, the purse, all went into the grave with Maisie. But not the portfolio. She even had Maisie's self-portrait framed, remember. After all, Maisie's art was all she had left of the girl she'd once loved. The girl she still loves perhaps. Unfortunately for Fiona, Maisie's old art teacher kept detailed records of his students' work and the contents of their portfolios. We checked with him.

I'm sure all four old friends are watching today's show, and

I'm guessing Fiona will be the first to confess her part in the mystery of Maisie Carter's disappearance. I suspect she's still sad about how it went down. We'll be sure and do an update in the event of a trial. We took advice on this show from lawyers. They warned us someone might sue. Of course, it would help their case if they were innocent. If Fiona doesn't have that portfolio stashed in her attic some place. See you in court, guys.

Okay, so that's it for today. Really hope you like this date night glam look. Join us next time on A Face for Murder when we'll be examining the case of Dr Crippen. And the look I'll be going for is sun-kissed Californian beach babe. See you soon, true crime nerds! Keep it criminal and keep it beautiful.

JACKIE ROBSON'S LAST RACE

It was scarcely dawn when Mary Robson, her hair in blue foam curlers under a silk scarf, lifted the wooden gate half-hanging off its hinges and pushed it open. Still holding it, she took one, two, three heavy steps down into the allotments.

Her destination was at the far end and although she knew the place well enough, she felt her nerves start up. Even as she began to pick her way along the rutted path, she glanced back and considered heading home.

It had seemed like such a good idea to get it over and done with. But it was too early and the wind was knife-sharp. There weren't enough folk around and she was being foolish. And this, exactly this, was how the monsters came for you.

She peered over the lollipop stick fences and across the gardens of spring cabbages and leeks, scanning for young tearaways lurking by the lean-to sheds. Leaping out from raspberry canes to beat passing pensioners till their wrinkled faces turned puffy and black and blue. Till the whites of their eyes bled red, before they died on a trolley in a hospital corridor, ignored by striking nurses too busy shopping at a food bank to care. Their

geriatric minds filled with a firm conviction that cellulite was a sin and that the migrant crisis gave you cancer.

Mary would admit that it was difficult to keep the stories straight sometimes. Especially since most of them came via her best friend Jean, a devoted hypochondriac, who took the *Mail* every day for the purposes of self-diagnosis and conversation that started *'I read a piece in the* Mail *the other day…'*.

A figure in the distance turning the soil raised a hand in greeting, and she waved back. Wondering briefly if he was burying a body to be here so early.

Jean was a tonic, but sometimes the catastrophes her friend recounted with such relish left Mary with an acute sense of unease. As if the world might be drawing to a close and there was nothing, but nothing, to be done about it.

Not today, she thought, as she drew in a breath that smelled of chilly dawn air, cut grass, and good earth. Today, she had a jumpstart on the apocalypse.

But as she turned the key in the padlock and loosened the chain draped through the mesh gate of the aviary, she felt gloom sweep over her.

Under her breath, she cursed at the fact that she was here and Jackie wasn't.

Expected to go back and forth, when she should be putting the 1,000 pieces of her jigsaw heart back together. When she should be sleeping on his side of their double bed so she could dream he held her in his arms. When she should be lying to her daughter, Deirdre, over in Adelaide, Australia that really, all things considered, she wasn't doing badly.

As for the idea of Jackie seeing her like this! Out in her rollers, buffeted by a North-Easterly wind, when she could have been getting ready to slide down the town with Jean to have a latté and a cinnamon roll. Yes, Jackie would laugh

himself silly. Then again, Jackie wasn't around anymore to laugh or to cry.

'My Bonny Mary' he'd called her from the start. Although, truth to tell, she'd never been that bonny. Not like her sister Veronica with her bouncing auburn curls. Or her own mother either. No one could gainsay her mam had been a beautiful woman in her day. When she was young, her own homeliness used to grieve her and she'd sob into her granny's pinafored chest, desperate with envy and wanting.

'None of that lasts, hinny,' her gran would say as she'd stroke her arm. And whilst others minded as the wrinkles came on and their waists thickened, Mary never minded any of it. Welcomed the years if anything. And, of course, there'd been her Jackie. Jackie with his gentle ways. Jackie with that daft lopsided smile of his. That first kiss at Whitley Bay, and as her knees went from under her she clung to him, convinced for the first time and forever, that there were better things than being bonny.

The cooing of the pigeons was coming on now as if they knew she was getting closer and they'd be fed soon.

'Some widows get left big houses and pots of money,' she scolded the dead man. *'A posh bungalow in Ponteland. A river cruise down the Danube. A first-class ticket out to see Deirdre and the kiddies.'* She'd never even seen the youngest. But Jackie made no reply even though she listened for it. There was only the bill and coo and flutter of the hungry pigeons.

The thing she'd never said. Not once. Not in all the years was that they unnerved her. His pigeons with their beady eyes. The claws. The feathers, which she'd read had once been scales. The flapping and the dirt.

But there was no Jackie now to chase out the mouse in the larder, or catch between his calloused hands the spider in the

bath and carry it gently out into the garden. Or tend the birds. '*Big girl pants now, Mary,*' she said as she lifted the latch to the cree.

And the birds rose, their outstretched wings beating against the air, to fly this way and that in the confines of the wooden shed. And her heart beat in time with the flapping, slapping wings, thudding in her chest.

Kerboom. Flap. Slap.

Kerboom. Flap. Slap.

'*Steady*', she told herself. '*Steady, Mary.*'

And her heart quietened. Just a notch. Still, it quietened.

Her eyes moving from bird to bird in case of attack, she took off her anorak, hung it on the back of a deck chair, and sniffed. It didn't smell as bad in here as she'd thought it might. Then again, Jackie's pal, Tom, had been looking after them for the last five weeks. She wondered how often he'd been cleaning them out. Jackie would clean them out twice a day. Morning and evening. Twice a day! It was a dismal thought. She sniffed again. Under the scent of warm birds and cold air was the smack of eucalyptus and Jackie himself. Like a hunting dog, she traced it to a piece of rag tied to a brass hook. She pulled it from the hook and raised it to her nose. Eucalyptus. Closing her eyes, she heard a low moan and realised it had come from her. Local news on the radio, a chicken roasting in the oven, and the smell of Jackie's hands as he washed them in the kitchen sink. Eucalyptus. Occasionally the fresh smell of mint. Or the sweet summer scent of lavender. A man who refused to wear aftershave for fear it upset the birds!

She knotted the cloth around the hook again and wiped her fingers up and down her trousers. They were going straight in a boil wash when she got home.

She simply wouldn't look at the birds, she decided as she

coaxed the empty pink fingers of the rubber gloves over her own, pulling them down at the wrist to make a proper seal.

The pigeons could do their thing and she would do her thing.

Truth to tell, she was surprised to find herself here. But it had got awkward with Tom. After the funeral, clutching a pint and a side plate with one too many slices of beef, he'd hinted at it. But she'd been too forlorn to puzzle out his meaning, and others had nudged him aside to offer their own consolations. Two days, and he'd phoned on the pretext of seeing how she was getting on, and asked outright. Told her Jackie would want someone to have the birds who knew what they were doing. As if he knew what Jackie would have wanted, better than her who'd been married to the man for the last forty-nine years. And she'd been offended. She'd admit it. Said she was grateful for what he'd done but she wouldn't trouble him anymore. That No, she wasn't giving up Jackie's birds. Not yet anyhow. That she'd knock on very well with the pigeons till she decided what to do with them. Anyway, she'd need to talk to Deirdre – as if Deirdre cared. There was someone at the door and she'd better go. And he'd hung up on her.

Of course, she regretted it even as she'd put down the phone. Rang Jean and cried, saying it wasn't like she wanted the dirty things.

And Jean said *'Mind, Tom Cartwright always was a funny beggar,'* and *'Still, I'd have thought better of him.'*

And she was caught. So here she was, going on instinct and half-remembered scraps of do's and don'ts from down the years. She should have listened harder. But she'd had her detective stories and her puzzle books. And Jackie? Jackie'd had his birds.

She had to keep the place clean though, she knew that much.

Shuddering, she blocked out the idea of feathers running with lice. And germs swinging from perch to perch like monkeys in the jungle. *Pretend you're David Attenborough,* she told herself.

Should she empty the loft before she started? Get the pigeons flying. But they hadn't turned on her. And at least they were a bit of life around the place.

She used a stiff brush and started on the nesting boxes and perches that ran the length of the back wall. Then the perches at the front. Each pigeon needed the security of its own perch, Jackie used to say from the comfort of his armchair next to the gas fire.

She hummed *Onward, Christian Soldiers* as she reached for a scraper Jackie had fixed to a broom handle.

Marching as to war as she pushed it along the wooden floorboards that ran the length of the cree.

With the cross of Jesus and she swept the pigeons droppings and sand into a dustpan and tipped it into a black binbag.

She picked up the metal feeders and flicked open the cage, emptying them out before scrubbing at them with a brush and a squirt of antiseptic spray, then dried them with a clean tea-towel she'd brought along specially. She kept a pin-neat house smelling of Zovirax and shining with polish. There would be no pigeons of hers catching that avian flu Jackie was always on about. Avian flu! She shook her head. Whatever next. As if one pandemic wasn't bad enough. The metal shining to her satisfaction, she reached for the brass scoop and plunged it into the hessian bag of corn mixed with tic beans and chicken feed, lifting it and throwing it into the feeders so it fell like spring rain hitting a tin roof. Then took a handful of grit and threw

that down as well. Careful not to get any on the 12-volt battery and small electric clock Jackie kept for his races.

She moved on to the next section. Trying to remember why Jackie kept them apart. Paired birds and young birds, she thought. And the young birds divided into hens and cocks. If left to themselves, racing pigeons paired for life, she knew that much. And approved.

Jackie had made this cree himself out of scraps of wood and rolls of mesh, adding to it over the years. It had a pitched tiled roof and a wooden floor, with three sides around it and the south facing wall of mesh. An opening high up let the birds fly in and out as they wanted. She knew he'd paid for this and that over the years. Most of it out of his winnings. And he'd done a fine job. Even in the storms the year before, storms that had wrenched trees from the ground and whipped away roofs, the pigeon loft stood strong. The daft ha'porth had all but run down the morning after to check, and come back beaming. And she'd made him tea to warm him up, and wished the wind had blown the damn pigeons out and across the North Sea.

'Now then, who've we got here,' she said, unlatching a nesting box. For a second, she hesitated, then lifted out a pigeon and held it away from her between rubber gloved hands. The small bird felt like a cork, she thought, floating on the sea. She brought the pigeon closer, tucking her right hand into her armpit and wriggled it free of its glove. Gently, she stroked her index finger over the grey plumage of its back. The feathers were like warm silk, she thought moving to the iridescent green and purple collar and over the piebald head. The bird's gleaming round orange eyes regarded her as she turned it this way and that. 'He promised I'd go first, birdie. We had a deal.' Ringed legs between her fingers, the pigeon rested quiet. Listening.

And she opened her hands, and the pigeon flew to a nearby dowling perch. Pulling off the other glove she rolled them into a ball and tucked them into her trouser pocket.

She could admit it now when it no longer mattered anymore. It was more than nerves kept her away from the cree over the years. She'd hated these birds. Jackie had never so much as looked at another woman. But these pigeons were her rivals. Rivals for his affection, for the touch of his calloused hands, and for his time.

'Hours he spent down here,' she told the birds as if they needed telling. Days spent away training them. And even sat with her watching *Death in Paradise*, she'd look across and she'd know his mind was on his pigeons. On the lift and spread of them in the sky. That he was flying with them and away from her.

And now...

And now when the future was done with...

She caught her breath at the thought of it.

When he had no future, when he was dead and gone and mouldering in the grave, leaving her lost and alone...

Now, she begrudged each second he'd spent down here and away from her. Especially after he retired when the sadness came on him and he seemed to have no patience with her. And she hadn't said he was under her feet. Because she would never say such a thing. Not in so many words and not often anyhow. You kept a marriage strong with kindness, she believed. When they said something that pained you, out of ill temper or cussedness or tiredness, she was never one for a cutting retort. Or a raised voice. Instead, she'd return harsh words with a cup of tea and a slice of lemon drizzle. With a *'pet lamb'* or a *'love'*.

He missed Deirdre, she knew. *'She'll not come back,'* he'd said, when she'd first gone. She hadn't even made it over for the

funeral. Not that it stopped her having opinions. So Mary was trying to keep busy, like Deirdre said she should.

She'd started clearing out his clothes. A waste not to get more wear out of them. He'd had three lovely suits, top-notch wool cloth, specially tailored for his barrel chest and short legs. It wasn't that she expected a medal, but the dopey baggage in the Oxfam shop had no idea of the price they'd been new. '*We just don't get much call for suits like this,*' she'd said eyeing the trousers, and Mary had felt herself flush with rage on Jackie's behalf. The anger rising in her so fast, her hands trembled and she'd had to reach for the counter and cling to it for fear she'd slap the woman otherwise. She'd been minded to fold the suits back up and walk out with them. Frankly, only the fact they'd weighed so heavy and she'd be carrying them back up the cruel hill home again had stopped her. Later, safe back in the kitchen as the kettle boiled she thought what she should have done was whip them down the High Street to the Cat Protection League.

Careful with the door, she let herself out of the loft and went to the old brass tap, running the water clear before putting the bottle under it. The cold bled through the plastic and into the marrow of her fingers. But it was bearable. Providing she rubbed them with gel and did the exercises the doctor recommended. He wanted her to have injections into the joints, but she'd put it off while Jackie was so poorly. In case something went wrong and she couldn't nurse him. The doctor had understood. Or didn't care. Or both. She turned off the tap and carried the water back to the pigeons, before pouring it into the bowls and it made a kind of music.

'It's all fetch me, hand me, carry me with you lot,' she said to the birds. But really to Jackie.

A feeling of defeat came over her as she sat on the deck

chair. Bone tired, she thought. The pigeons needed too much from her. They needed air or they would sicken and die, to be kept dry, to be kept at an even temperature. Safe from avian flu. Safe from soaring hawks and greedy cats. Widowhood offered little enough consolation. Surely if nothing else, it meant being able to rest. Surely, she had a right to that. To cinnamon buns whenever and wherever she wanted them? And not caring if some other living thing sickened and Death came knocking?

Even as she thought it, there was a sharp rat-a-tat-tat on the wooden door of the loft. And around her there was the rise and flurry and fall of pigeons. Tom stood in the doorway scowling – feathers falling between them like ash.

'You should have flown the birds before you fed them,' he said in a voice stiff with disapproval. 'They've a routine.'

'Know-it-all,' she thought. Furious suddenly, like a light going on. Furious at him for catching her out, at the pigeons for not telling her, at herself for not knowing all there was to know.

'You'd best mind out the door then,' she said as if it was him stopping up the birds. With a snort, he stepped away and she stood, flapping her arms up and down. 'Go on then. Go on then.' Moving among the pigeons, her cheeks hot, stamping her feet and waving her arms, she tamped down the feeling she must look part-pigeon herself right this second. Like she was trying to launch herself. And failing.

But in a rush and a flurry they moved towards the door and she thought *'Hah!'* and *'Look at that!'* and *'Well, I never.'* She moved with them, clearing the stragglers and at the threshold braced herself for more of the old man's glowering disapproval.

But Tom's eyes were on the birds themselves as they flew out and upwards into the fresh air, the pattern of them, the

flock wheeling up and around and over the common land alongside the allotments. She stepped into the fresh air, and gazed at the birds swooping and turning overhead. The thrumming beat of their wings. The air around her still electric with their release and lift, and she laughed at the sudden freedom, her own and the birds.

The thought came on fast – she'd rollers in her hair.

Another.

Why return? To something little better than a cage? She'd said that once over supper one night not long after they were married. And my word, but Jackie took offence, she told Jean later. On his dignity he was, as he poured tea from the Brown Betty pot in his tartan flask. Not spilling a drop. His words coming slow. He'd said it wasn't a cage. It was a home he'd built for them and they knew a good thing when they had it. Pigeons were clever that way. And he'd left without kissing her goodbye.

'I've bad news,' Tom said.

'Bad news' is what the doctor said to them. And she'd taken Jackie's hand in hers. Like he was a kid, like they both were. Jackie was gone. What could bad news do to her now?

'The council's gone and sold the allotments and we're all of us getting a notice to quit.'

It took her a second to take in his meaning, but Tom kept talking. The words tumbling out. Fast and hard and knocking one into the other.

'We have to clear out. Everyone. All the gardens.' He waved his right arm to take in the allotments. 'All the birds.' Then his left, taking in the pigeon cree. 'It's over.' Held both hands out to her, empty, palms up.

And she was bereft, all over again.

The news would have killed Jackie, she thought. Stone cold

dead. But he wasn't here. At least there was that. He was already stone cold dead and gone. He wouldn't know men in hard hats and high-vis jackets would come and tear down his beloved pigeon loft. Wouldn't have to find another hideaway. Wouldn't have only his medical appointments and ferrying her hither and thither to get him out of the house. And she wouldn't have to come down here and run herself ragged keeping the pigeons clean and fed and watered. She could spend as much time as she liked in the town with Jean, hearing all the best ways to swerve dementia and cellulite if cancer didn't get you first.

But if she'd have known, she could have dragged his body down here, let the pigeons fly free and burnt Jackie and the cree together. He'd have liked that she thought. It would have tickled him. Or she could have dug a hole and buried him and his cree in the earth like an Anglo-Saxon king.

'How long have we got?' she said.

Tom took up the outdoor broom propped in a corner, and started to sweep feathers and droppings from the hardened earth outside the cree. Bang the brush head, sweep, bang, sweep. Short sharp violent sweepings that hurt to watch. Mumblings.

Then, 'Ten days,' he said.

Mary thought she'd misheard him. He couldn't have said ten days. No council would give allotment owners only ten days to clear out. These were allotments men and women had worked for over fifty years. They kept local families fed.

Tom scratched at the stubble along his sagging cheek with tobacco-yellowed fingers. 'We didn't want to bother Jackie with it. Not with him as bad as he was.'

They had waited for her husband to die. Waited like she'd been waiting. By the side of his bed at home and then

by the side of his bed in the hospital ward. A hospital ward where a poor soul called Billy wailed and cried and shouted obscenities till the nurses sedated him and Jackie could die in peace.

'Then you had the funeral to arrange and what have you,' he said.

By *'what have you',* Tom had to mean dealing with the crucifying, crushing despair of her loss, the howling grief of life without the man who had been her life. Pain which he found too hard to name but which she had to bear.

'How long have you known?' She wanted the full picture now.

A pause as Tom turned the broom head on its end and knocked it clear of the dirt, then placed it back in the corner.

He started counting on his fingers. Running through the days? The weeks? And he counted slowly.

'Six months,' he said.

It was over then. Jackie gone. The thing he loved best in the world apart from her. Apart from Deirdre in Adelaide. Gone. They would batter this little world he had built into kindling and splinters. Nothing would be left of him but the woman who had loved him and when she died, nothing would be.left of him at all. Apart from Deirdre, who, let's be honest, didn't count.

'What about the pigeons?' she said.

Tom turned his head and then moved his whole body as he followed the birds' progress overhead. His back was to her when he spoke. 'You'd best be rid. I'll take them off your hands.' He glanced at her once and then away again. 'I said I would and the problem's mine, not yours. Jackie wouldn't want it any other way.'

Had Tom tried to get the birds so she would mind less

when the diggers and the bulldozers came? She'd misjudged him?

'I'll come by tomorrow for the birds. I've always kept mine in my garden so it could be worse. For me, anyhow.' As he spoke, he glanced up. One of the pigeons was circling overhead as if deciding whether to come home or not. As if waiting for Tom to leave.

Mary sensed him move off towards the gate as she reached for the whistle she wore around her neck since Jackie's death and started blowing. The piercing blast hurting her ears. Come on. Come on, she called up. While you still can.

The birds looked the same to her. But as the first of them landed on the ground close by, she recognised its piebald feathered head. It was the bird she'd nursed earlier. And to her own surprise she felt her spirits lift.

It took another forty minutes for the rest of the pigeons to return. Technically, she could have left them to it, but Jackie always liked to see them back in. So she stayed. What else was there to do? Took out her foam rollers, ran her fingers through the curls. Stayed calling and whistling like a lunatic. But who was there to see but the birds and they didn't judge.

Ten days, she thought about it as she stomped home. As she let herself in the back door. Called out, 'Hello, pet, only me.' knowing there was no one to hear her. As she dumped the bag of blue foam rollers and red ring binders that she had taken from the loft on to the kitchen table. As she unknotted the silk scarf at her throat, unzipped the padded anorak and turned on the central heating. Early. But she was perished and there was no Jackie to tell her they weren't made of money. She inspected her shoes for the last leavings of bird muck and left them on a

piece of old wallpaper by the front door, then slid her feet into her slippers with a sigh.

She washed her hands for a long time with the good soap she usually kept for guests. And lifting her hands to her face, breathed in the scent of late summer roses. A menthol after-note of eucalyptus to punch her in the heart.

She hadn't bothered much with food of late, and certainly not a cooked lunch, but today she was famished. The new potatoes went on to boil, a pinch of salt in the spitting, roiling water, and the lamb chops on foil under the grill as she pulled out the first ring binder and flipped it open. At first, she couldn't make head nor tail of it. A jumble of numbers, names and dates. But as she flicked through it became clear enough. They were Jackie's breeding records. The identification numbers and names of each cock and hen. The cocks all sportsmen, the hens all with the name Mary in there somewhere. Their dams and sires, the dates each egg was laid, each bird was hatched and weaned. A photograph too of each bird, and strangely, each bird's eye. The birds he'd trained and raced. Those he had lost and how – cat, sparrow hawk, powerlines and wires, in sickness, in training, in a race. So many small losses, she thought. Jackie had been brave to persevere. Their medications, vaccinations, and those he'd given away. But none to Tom, she noted.

She flipped back through the pages. On the back cover he had stuck a race calendar for the year ahead. A year he'd never see. The shame of it, she thought, because his birds won races. More races than she'd known about. And there were pound signs by some of them. He'd always handled the bills – insisted on it, so it made sense he could slide a few hundred into their account here and there. But over the years, he'd won thousands, and she'd have picked up on that, surely? Or had he

given it straight to Deirdre? She didn't need to ask, because she knew the answer to that. Of course, he had. He'd give that girl the shirt off his back and leave his own wife scrimping and saving.

'Jackie man,' she said. *'It's a good job you're dead or I'd wring your neck.'*

But even leaving aside the money he'd kept from her, all this work, she thought. All this love and scrupulous attention to feather and seed detail. Only to die and the birds to go to scrawny, know-it-all Tom. It didn't sit right. She turned on the grill.

Tom meant well, she supposed. Not just Tom. The fact Jackie was dying. The fact Jackie was dead and there was the widow to tell. It must have been a topic of conversation at the allotment society's meetings. Men deciding they knew what was best. She'd grant them the fact it would have upset Jackie to know. But if they'd told her, perhaps she could have done something to make the council think again? Written letters and what not. Gone to see her councillor. The MP maybe. But ten days? It was too late for all that now.

It wasn't too late for one last race for Jackie's birds though. She could do that much. For Jackie and the birds. For her too. See what it had all been about.

The lamb chops were done and the potatoes were on the plate. Bright green petit pois. As she ran her finger down the calendar. Saturday, Brighton to Newcastle, 350 miles. Two day's time. She'd need the pigeons away tomorrow.

It was a downright ridiculous thought to enter Jackie's pigeons in a race. Wasn't it? The thinking of a lunatic. Grief had addled her mind she decided, picking up her knife and fork.

But she was still doing it.

. . .

She went back out to the allotment after her supper. Her mind too busy to fear delinquents or birds. Let them fly. Cleaned them again. Fed them. Watered them. And all the time, ticking over with the cheek of it. The cheek of her.

One last race.

Tom's house was on her way home and there was no answer when she knocked. Perhaps he didn't answer the door at night? Nervous of strangers and ne'er-do-wells selling squeegees and hard luck stories. Not that they'd get much soot from Tom.

The wicket gate to the path that ran along the side of his house was ajar. She pushed it open and peered into the garden to the aviary and his loft. Bought, she thought, looking at its edges. Top of the line. While overhead, a CCTV camera swivelled and then fixed on her. He took his home security seriously did Tom.

A wait.

More waiting.

Then the rattle of a chain and the drawing of bolts.

'I'll sort the transfer of ownership once I've the birds if that's why you're here.'

The old man's arrogance set her teeth on edge.

'We've ten days,' she said.

'I told *you* that. Tomorrow, it'll be nine.'

'But there's time. So, I've an idea to enter them for a race. On Saturday.'

He stared at her as if she had grown another head.

'You can't do that.'

Mary dropped the pleasant smile. It was wasted on the old man anyway. 'They're my birds.' She knew what he wanted to

say. He wanted to tell her they were his birds now. But felt he couldn't risk it.

Tom's eyes narrowed. 'It costs good money to enter a race. You've money to throw away, have you? Alright for some.'

She felt a flare of panic. She most certainly did not have money to throw away. Jackie's funeral had cost more than £4,200 and she had done it as cheaply as she could. And it wasn't as if it was money well spent. She'd buried him alright but there was no sense of closure. She'd felt not one whit better after it than she had before.

'I've enough put by to enter a few birds in a race.'

'You'll be making a fool of yourself and of the birds.'

Why Jackie was ever friends with this man she didn't know.

'That's on me. All I came to say was to leave the birds where they are until the day before the council's due.'

He gave a wheeze which she took to be something between a laugh and a grunt before he slammed the door.

If he'd been a different kind of man, he'd have offered to help, she thought, staring at the door. She'd half expected him to. A different kind of man would have said that was a fine idea for the pigeons to race one last time in memory of Jackie. But that wasn't Tom.

Panic took her by the throat again. How did you race a pigeon?

In her mind, she heard Jackie's throaty chuckle. *'You need a very small saddle.'*

'This is all your fault,' she said.

She was so preoccupied as she turned to go that she almost didn't hear the rustling. Then it came again. She peered at Tom's wheelie standing sentry by the wicket gate. Was there a rat in there? In which case, she should leave well enough alone.

She walked on. But it could be a cat. Turned. Next door's cat perhaps that had got itself trapped in the bin. Walked back towards the bin. Stretching out her arm, she took hold of the handle and threw back the lid.

Inside, the black bin bag moved. Dear God. If it was a rat, she was going to scream so loudly, the glass in Tom's windows would shatter.

Inch by inch, she pulled apart the black bag. A seed bag folded over. Nudged apart the folds of heavy brown paper.

It wasn't a rat.

She peered closer.

Inside, a dying pigeon gave a last flutter of its wing and lay still. The pigeon lay on top of a small heap of dozen or so other bloodied birds, their heads hanging at odd angles, their eyes cloudy. She took a step back, her hand at her mouth and as she did, heard the whirr of the CCTV camera move again. She stared up into the lens then back at the feathery corpses.

Pigeons died. Of course, they did. It was the way of the world. Living and dying. Maybe these pigeons got sick and died of natural causes? But one had been alive when Tom had bagged it up. At the very least, he hadn't cared enough to check. But if there was sickness in his loft, surely he wouldn't have been so fierce-keen on bringing in new birds? He'd made it clear that he wanted Jackie's birds. She wasn't fooled by his talk that Jackie would have wanted the birds looked after. Tom was greedy for them.

But pigeons needed space. They couldn't be kept too close or they sickened and died. Jackie's birds were good strong birds with impressive pedigrees. She could see that much from his records. And she was willing to bet that they'd be better than any bird of Tom's. So he'd made space for the newcomers. She swallowed the nausea she felt at the idea of the gnarly tobacco-

stained fingers pushing pigeons into the sack, before wrenching and snapping their necks in the papery darkness.

And now she considered the matter. Where were the young birds Jackie had mentioned in his records? He'd been breeding them. There should have been at least a dozen birds around a month old, ready to take from their parents and start training. Surely, at least one or two of those she might have expected to see with the parent birds? But there'd been none. What was the betting Tom had put his own rings on them, then carried them off, expecting her to be none the wiser?

But she'd have her work cut out proving it. Tom would claim the young birds were his all along. The rings would prove it. And he'd argue he had no reason to steal them because Jackie's birds would be his soon enough. The arrogance of the man.

Because now she came to it. Jackie loved those birds and he had known he was dying. That he didn't have much time left to him. But he'd never told her that he wanted the birds to go to Tom. Why not? He'd never made any provision for them. Of course, he didn't know the council was coming for the cree. Perhaps that would have changed things for him? But he'd trusted her with them. Trusted her to do what she thought best.

She stared down the lens of the camera and shook her head, from side to side. *'I know what you did, you mean old buzzard,'* she said in so many words. As for the rest of the flock, the pigeon thief – the killer – could dream on. She'd no idea what she would do with her pigeons. She knew only one thing. Tom wasn't getting anywhere near the rest of them.

. . .

Back home, Jackie's records spelled out the loss. There was always the chance one or two baby birds might not have hatched or had died for some reason. But as far as she could make out, during the five weeks he'd acted as caretaker, Tom had stolen a dozen young birds. Two of which had been marked on the page with red asterisks which she presumed meant Jackie had hopes for them.

One battle at a time she decided. She had to focus on the race. Then a permanent home for the pigeons. Then she'd be back knocking on Tom's door for the return of the young birds. She'd shame them out of him. Just see if she didn't.

As for the race, from what she could make out Jackie's fastest pigeon was named Lord Paul Gazza. It was a year old and had won at least half a dozen races. Another likely contender was Sir Kevin Keegan, five years old with an impressive list of wins. A picture caught her eye. If she was reading the books correctly, the piebald-headed bird she had nursed, the one that had returned first to the cree yesterday, was called Baroness Mary Martha, a seven-year-old hen whose own ancestor Elizabeth, Duchess of Neville had flown with the RAF in the war. Mary had heard Jackie tell the story before. That his grandfather had bred racing pigeons he'd given up to the war effort. Baroness Mary Martha had never won a thing. She deserved her day in the sun though, Mary thought. The Baroness was going to the races and Mary was going with her. She might even buy a hat.

Jackie's club met at six every Friday in the upstairs room of the Dun Cow. Aside from the noise of pigeons in baskets lined up on a table and the bass beat from the public bar downstairs, the room fell to silence when she walked in.

'It's Jackie's wife,' she heard from one of them.

A bald, silver-bearded man whose name she thought was Harry, rose from his chair and ambled over to her. His tread so heavy she could feel his approach through the soles of her shoes.

'Now then, Mary,' he said, leaning over her. 'What can we do for you, pet?'

Harry had been a Detective Inspector in Northumbria Police, it came to her. Long since retired. She remembered the squeeze of his huge hand outside the church. White chrysanthemums in the shape of a dove and a card which read: *Fly home, Jackie. From all your pals at the North Durham and District Racing Pigeon Club.*

'I'm wanting to enter pigeons in tomorrow's race.' She sensed a ruffling and a flurry from the men across the room as they turned in their seats to take her in. Like pigeons in a loft, she thought. Aside from the pints of bitter in front of them.

Harry raised an eyebrow and made a face she could imagine him making in an interview room. An expression that said I've heard everything now. He looked back at the other members and then at her again. His eyes were kind, she thought, but they'd seen too much.

'We're sending them off tonight. The wagon's due in an hour. You'd need to get them down here sharpish. And the clock with them.'

She opened her handbag and took out the clock. Placing it on the table between them like a challenge, then moved back to the doorway. She pushed it open and reached through for the three wicker baskets she had persuaded the cabbie to let her bring in the back of the taxi with her.

All eyes were on her, she knew. But at least there'd been no witnesses to her performance in the cree as she attempted to

work out which bird was which. Holding up the photos to the birds, comparing stripes and the length of tail feathers, catching them, squinting through her reading glasses at the metal rings around their legs.

Harry waved across a younger man with a clipboard and gestured him to the clock. There was a scandalised murmur from the club members.

'You'll have to fill out this form,' Harry was all business now. Serious, as befits the secretary of the North Durham and District Racing Pigeon Club when faced with a new member. He fetched her a chair and dutifully, she sat down, pulled out her glasses, took the pen he offered and filled out her membership application. He reached out his hand to her and she took it. 'Let me be the first to welcome you to the club,' he said. Across the room, she heard a smattering of applause and glanced over, shy suddenly.

'Right,' he said, 'We'll call the membership fee quits because Jackie was up to date. For the race though, there's an entry fee of £5 a bird. Transport costs and the like down to Brighton which works out at another £18. We also run a sweepstake between us £1 each. Are you good with all that?'

She nodded.

'The birds are already in our system. We set the race up on your clock, scan the rings so they're entered into the race, and check all the numbers tally. The wagon comes for them tonight and takes them to the liberation site. And we're off to the races.'

Meanwhile his hands were in the basket pulling out Lord Paul Gazza. 'Weather permitting, they fly at six tomorrow morning.' He held the pigeon away from him, bounced him as if weighing him, spread first one wing and then the other, looked at his eye and used his thumb to

open the beak, stroked the tail and turned it over to look at the pink skin of its belly. 'He's a lovely bird, alright,' he said with approval as he held it over the pad. A bleep as it read the microchip. 'Jackie knew his stuff.' He eased it back into the basket, and went through the same rigmarole with Sir Kevin Keegan. 'Cheer up, Kevin Keegan,' he half-sang to the bird.

'And you've not doped them up or fed them steroids?' His face set stern. Before he winked. She spared him a smile for his effort as he opened the basket for Baroness Mary Martha. He frowned this time as he ran his hands over her. 'She's smart but she's small for this,' he said. 'They don't all make it, you know.' He didn't want her upset, she thought.

'She's tougher than she looks,' Mary said and hoped it was the truth.

'Set your clock back up in your loft and their times will register automatically when they get back home,' Harry said.

'If they get back,' she thought.

'I'll come and take a look tomorrow. Make sure it's as it should be. Then once the birds are back, you're like the rest of us. Living on your nerves till late on while the organisers work out who's won.'

Turned out all she had to do was wait.

Her eyes were on the kitchen clock. Counting it down. The fastest would make it home within five or six hours, Harry said. And the winner would be down to velocity. Something about distance divided by time, and average speeds.

The garden chair was awkward to carry, especially with the hatbox. But she needed it for Jean later, so she managed. She had it all planned out – she'd clean and feed the rest of them,

slip home for a couple of hours, and then come back with a Thermos and sandwiches. Jean said she'd bring cake.

She smelled the smoke before she saw it. The ruination of the cree. Scorch marks on the ground, the wire fencing twisted in the heat. A pounding in her ears. Her eyes watering with the smoke. From somewhere an allotment owner. Then another.

Vandals, she heard the word. An arm around her as she stepped through the swinging gate. The link chain on the ground blackened and coiled like a snake.

Teenage delinquents.

But she knew the truth.

Glimpsed Tom across the common watching the commotion. And the birds all dead. Jackie's pigeons gone. Charcoal lumps and a scattering of singed feathers.

Someone opened the chair she'd brought. Offered a rug. A tin mug of sweet tea.

For the shock, she heard.

A terrible thing.

Those poor birds.

They rang Jean for her, who came at once. Ran all the way judging by the state of her when she arrived.

And Jean called Harry, whom she knew. But Jean knew everyone.

'*Big girl pants, Mary,*' she whispered to herself. And time passed. The stink of smoke in her clothes. Her hair. Not wanting to leave the place that had been his. And briefly hers. Mourning him again.

A firefighter.

Someone from the council.

Heads shaking. *Small blessings. But no one was hurt at least*, they said. Aside from the birds, of course. And her.

A day out at the races. She pulled the hat from the hatbox

that she kept on top of the closet and put it on. She hadn't had to buy one after all. A lilac affair, big brimmed, a broad satin ribbon. Wear it with attitude, the lady in the shop advised. You're the mother of the bride. Jean understood if no one else, settling it just so over her curls. And the day passed, and the smoke died back, and Harry said, 'I'm never eating barbecue again.' And they laughed. Because what are you to do?

And the pigeons came back, settling in the yard at her call. Come on, come on, the whistle at her lips. First Lord Paul Gazza. And then Sir Kevin Keegan. And Harry checked his watch and said 'They made good time. Your Jackie knew his birds alright.'

And hours later. The night coming on. Her bones cold, and from somewhere, the scent of eucalyptus. At her feet, a tray of chips that Harry had gone for, and in the dusk, the flap and flutter of the third. The one she had been waiting for. Coming home. And standing, jumping, whooping, Mary called and called, and blew the whistle.

ENDNOTE

For anyone interested in a few facts about the short stories, I was delighted this year to be declared the joint winner of the Alpine Fellowship Writing Prize, 2023, with *The Silent Mrs B.*

How to Catch a Bullet won the Crime Writers' Association/ Margery Allingham prize, 2023.

Auld Bride was longlisted for the CWA Short Story Dagger, 2023. It featured in the Gone anthology, 2022, edited by Stephen S Golds. It was also a runner up in the Glencairn Crime Short Story Contest, 2021.

A Face for Murder was shortlisted for the CWA/Margery Allingham, 2022. It featured in An Unnecessary Assassin, 2023, an anthology edited by Lorraine Stevens.

Snow Day was first published in the Everyday Kindness anthology, 2021, edited by L J Ross.

Florrie and the Mysterious Death of a Fat Rascal first appeared on tables at Bettys in Harrogate in 2023, to celebrate cake, crimewriting, and Harrogate.

And So It Begins is a story which features the childhood version of Michael North, the hero of my action thrillers. Anyone who warmed to Michael might like to check out the latest *Sleep When You're Dead*. Or indeed, read all three!

ACKNOWLEDGEMENTS

Martin Fletcher (who edited this anthology), as well as Jon Wood (my lovely agent) and Laura Palmer. Jaycee Delorenzo (cover/artwork/typesetting). Helen Chappell (IT). Kaylea Cross, Geoff Atkinson, Ruth Burke-Kennedy, Helen LeFevre and Michael Lesslie. Thank you all for your expertise and support.

If you've enjoyed these short stories, please sign up for my newsletter to keep in touch with my news and chit chat about crime fiction.

Join Jude's Readers' Club
https://www.judithoreilly.com/readers-club

You can find me at www.judithoreilly.com
Or @judithoreilly on twitter
And @judithoreillywrites on facebook
And @judith_oreilly on instagram

First published in the UK in 2023 by Loughman Press

A catalogue record of this book is available from the British Library

ISBN (E): 978-1-7384221-1-1
ISBN (PB): 978-1-7384221-0-4

www.loughmanpress.com

IN OUR CRIME

AN ANTHOLOGY OF CRIME STORIES IN THE LOOSEST POSSIBLE TERMS

JUDE O'REILLY

LOUGHMAN PRESS

ALSO BY JUDE O'REILLY

The Michael North Thriller Series

Killing State

Curse the Day

Sleep When You're Dead

And writing as Judith O'Reilly

Wife in the North

A Year of Doing Good

REVIEWS FOR THE MICHAEL NORTH THRIL

'A masterful

LJ I

'Starts off like a fired bullet and never lets up. A sheer delight.'

David Baldacci

'Terrific.'

Lee Child

'A rip-roaring road trip into the dark heart of a corrupt British establishment.' A Best Book of 2022.

Financial Times

'High-octane.'

Sunday Times

'Fast, sharply-written, clever and intense.'

Jeremy Vine

'Fast-paced and packed with action.'

Mick Herron

'Gleefully witty...superb.'

M.W. Craven

Evidemment, il est toujours difficile, au XXIe siècle, de se mettre à la place d'un individu du XVe ou du XIXe siècle.

De la même manière la difficulté doit être tout aussi grande en ce qui concerne quelque chose d'aussi mystérieuse et hermétique que la Légion.

Ainsi, avoir à portée d'amitié l'un des rares espagnols toujours en activité, avec suffisamment d'expérience de la chose, et pas si ignorant au point de ne pas savoir aligner les mots pour constituer des phrases, Joaquin ne pouvait pas le manquer.

Soit.

Que signifie donc Camerone pour un légionnaire, ancien ou en activité?

Pour ne pas faire de la théorie, je me limiterai à essayer d'expliquer ce que cela signifie pour moi, en espérant que, peut-être, cette approche sera partagée par d'autres, nombreux, de mes compagnons. Évidemment, avec les différences inévitables dans le ressenti de gens issus de cultures aussi disparates que, par exemple, un Russe et un Brésilien, un Sénégalais et un Suédois, un Chinois et un Iranien.

Quand j'ai rejoint la Légion étrangère au début des années quatre-vingts, peu après la fin de mon service militaire dans l'anachronique, loqueteuse et franquiste armée de Sa Majesté catholique, Camerone ne me disait pas grand-chose, presque rien pour ainsi dire.

Quelques références dans les bandes dessinées de *Blueberry*, quelques lignes au hasard dans les romans de Lartéguy sur la guerre d'Algérie et guère plus.

Il faut cesser de croire que les jeunes légionnaires s'engagent avec, déjà, la foi chevillée au corps. La « legionitis » est une maladie bénigne, qui, faute de guérison, devient chronique.

Dans mes premières années de service, la commémoration du combat et les festivités y associées étaient, souvent, synonyme de beaucoup de travail : d'interminables et jamais parfaits entrainements à défiler, montage de stands, préparation des divers uniformes, désignations pour la prise en charge des invités, des civils qui viennent s'amuser, alors qu'un autre sert de la bière ou transporte des enfants... En français cela s'appelle *la corvée*** qui pourrait être traduit par labeurs ou tâches.

Je me souviens avec horreur de Camerone 1985, peu après mon arrivée dans la petite république africaine de Djibouti pour un séjour de deux ans. Le colonel avait décidé d'organiser une veillée, un spectacle monté pour l'occasion avec décors, son et lumière, figurants, acteurs d'histoires que j'ai déjà oubliées.

Pendant les loisirs (en réalité le temps de la sieste, obligatoire dans ce pays au climat trop chaud), sciant des planches, plantant des clous, peignant et transportant, je me disais, comme tous mes camarades, que c'était un mauvais moment à passer et qu'à partir du 2 mai, nous pourrions retourner à nos activités de patrouille le long de la frontière avec l'Éthiopie, ou palmer dans le Golfe du Goubet, où la légende situe un monstre marin.

En 1987 ce fut pire encore, de passage à la *maison-mère* à Aubagne début avril, en attente d'une nouvelle affectation après les deux années passées dans la corne de l'Afrique, au lieu de partir en congé de fin de campagne (à cette époque, outre-mer, seules deux ou trois semaines de permission annuelle étaient accordées, les reliquats cumulés étaient à prendre au retour en métropole), tous les détachements ont été bloqués pendant près d'un mois, pour défiler, en renfort du 1er régiment étranger le 30 avril.

Quelle torture après deux années passées dans un pays tropical, de devoir toute la sainte journée défiler sous la pluie froide du printemps français.

Et, peu à peu, inconsciemment, au lieu de compter les minutes restantes jusqu'à la fin, le légionnaire que j'étais à l'époque a commencé à écouter les paroles du récit du combat. A les écouter véritablement.

Cela doit être quelque chose comme ça la révélation, quand saint Thomas a vu la lumière divine ; ceux qui affirment que les croyants les plus pratiquants sont les anciens athées, ont sûrement raison.

Lorsque l'on écoute bien le récit (ce qui nécessite un minimum de compréhension des subtilités de la langue française) on se sent un peu parti, le corps est là, au garde-à-vous, mais l'esprit se dissocie comme s'il s'élevait au-dessus des troupes. C'est quasi physique.

Je sais que cela pourra paraître un peu ridicule, mais, à partir d'un certain moment c'est ce que j'ai ressenti, et bien d'autres Camerone sont passés de pareille manière.

A diverses occasions j'ai assisté à des cérémonies ou des fêtes, dans différents lieux de la planète, au cours desquelles la foule, le groupe, entre collectivement en transe. Je pourrais citer les indiens du Haut Maroni, les Malgaches, les Haïtiens…

Toute proportion gardée, la cérémonie de Camerone, et plus précisément le récit du combat, est la transe collective des légionnaires. Rares sont ceux qui ne ressentent pas un frisson devant tant de simplicité dans le sacrifice librement consenti ; peu de légionnaires pourraient affirmer que *jamais* ils n'ont senti un picotement dans les yeux pendant la minute de silence qui suit la sonnerie aux morts.

Le sceptique (je l'ai été) dira que mon récit est très exagéré, que de nos jours ces sentiments n'existent plus.

Je lui répondrais que les légionnaires sont si obstinés (certains diraient inadaptés aux temps modernes) que Camerone est célébré là où nous nous trouvons, au combat comme à l'étape.

Camerone a été célébré dans la cuvette de Dien Bien Phu, quelques jours avant l'hécatombe finale.

Camerone a été célébré sur le bateau qui nous transportait après la première guerre en Irak. Les marins, bien que leurs familles les attendent à Toulon après cette longue campagne, nous ont fait l'amitié de jeter l'ancre au large de la Corse pour nous laisser à notre caprice ancestral.

En 2008 les légionnaires présents en Afghanistan l'ont célébré, souvent après de périlleux déplacements depuis leurs points de stationnement respectifs.

Une chose qui pourrait être relevée c'est que l'esprit particulier de la cérémonie paraît être contagieux envers des unités, autres, qui parfois sont invitées à participer.

J'ai été le témoin du respect et du recueillement qui ont montré des militaires Belges, Mongols, Américains, Marocains, Brésiliens, Tchadiens, Allemands, Danois… soldats qui habituellement se promènent avec les mains dans les poches et qui ne comprennent goutte de français, se muer en statues le temps de la cérémonie. C'est bien la preuve que « notre » jour transmet des valeurs militaires universelles.

Comme je l'ai dit, je suis très heureux, malgré l'intense effort qu'écrire en espagnol exige de mes pauvres neurones, heureux d'ajouter ma modeste contribution à la réédition du livre de Joaquin.

J'espère qu'il aura beaucoup de succès, que ce ne soit que pour rappeler à nos compatriotes du XXIe siècle, que les Espagnols ont écrit beaucoup et de belles pages de l'histoire légendaire de la Légion étrangère française.

Un légionnaire espagnol
Carlos Diez y Acosta
Major (er) du 1er régiment étranger de cavalerie

PREFACE
DE L'ÉDITION FRANÇAISE

Le serment d'un capitaine

1863. La Légion est encore jeune mais elle a déjà connu beaucoup de vicissitudes, parmi lesquelles et non des moindres, la campagne d'Espagne qui a décimé ses effectifs. Reformée, elle est de tous les combats de la France.

L'Empereur Napoléon III engage l'armée française par-delà l'océan, au Mexique. Étrangement, la Légion n'est pas de la partie. Or, une telle aventure ne pouvait qu'exciter l'esprit aventureux qui anime cette troupe. Ses officiers vont forcer son départ en adressant une pétition à l'Empereur. De lourdes sanctions tombent sur les officiers les plus anciens dans les grades les plus élevés, mais au début de l'année 1863 la Légion embarque deux bataillons pour Veracruz.

Sans le savoir, ces hommes commencent à réunir les éléments d'une tragédie. D'une tragédie et d'une légende.

Comme à son habitude, la Légion veut combattre en première ligne mais se voit attribuer une mission d'escorte de convois, de reconnaissance d'itinéraires et d'arrière-garde, dans la zone la plus insalubre du pays. Qu'à cela ne tienne, les légionnaires s'adaptent. Ils s'installent à Chiquihuite, dans les Tierras Calientes - une région infestée par le typhus, le paludisme et la fièvre jaune ou *vomito negro* - aux ordres du colonel Jeanningros ; légionnaire de fraîche date qui n'est sorti d'aucune école, mais il possède une inestimable expérience de la guerre et des hommes.

Apprenant qu'un convoi est en route pour Puebla assiégée par l'armée française, il décide d'envoyer une compagnie de protection à sa rencontre. Cette compagnie est confiée au capitaine Danjou.

Le 30 avril 1863 au matin, le Capitaine Danjou à la tête de la 3e compagnie du Régiment étranger, attaqué par des hordes mexicaines, accepte le combat et se retranche à Camerone, dans une ferme délabrée, pour y établir un point d'appui et attirer sur lui le principal de l'effort de l'adversaire, fort en nombre. Dans la matinée, sentant la situation s'aggraver à chaque instant mais voulant détourner l'ennemi du convoi, il décide de résister à tout prix. Il fait le serment de se défendre jusqu'à la mort face aux vagues de fantassins et de cavaliers mexicains qui l'assaillent...

Le serment d'un capitaine tissait déjà le linceul de ces hommes et allait faire d'un obscur combat dans les ingrates Terres Chaudes du Mexique, une épopée mondialement connue.

Le combat qui oppose une soixantaine de braves légionnaires à deux mille mexicains, entre de plain-pied dans l'Histoire pour devenir l'immortel Camerone.

Élevé à la hauteur d'un mythe, il fut pourtant bien réel ce combat si intimement lié à Légion étrangère et à l'histoire de l'Armée française. Il est devenu l'expression d'un symbole de résistance farouche jusqu'au dernier souffle du dernier homme : *Faire Camerone !*

Mais tout n'a-t-il pas été dit sur ce combat ? Pourtant, hormis les noms des officiers et des cinq derniers rescapés, qui se souvient de ces hommes ? Qui sont ces braves qui ont voulu - en s'engageant dans les rangs de la Légion étrangère - redevenir des hommes parmi les hommes malgré leurs lourds passés ? Qui sont ces soldats qui ne savent pas encore qu'ils vont être de cette phalange qui va repousser la fatigue, la poussière, la chaleur étouffante de la mort sous un ciel de braise et entrer dans l'Histoire?

Alonso, espagnol des Asturies, est de ceux-là. Il a fui la misère de son village natal, a traversé la frontière et après une courte errance en territoire français, il s'engage à Bayonne. Il a acheté son droit de vivre d'une simple signature et nous allons le suivre heure après heure, minute après minute, lui qui s'interdit de courber la tête sous le souffle horrible de la mort, jusqu'à l'instant précis de son sacrifice, jusqu'au bord de sa mort, jusqu'au bord du néant de sa nuit.

C'est ce que nous raconte "Camerone – Une histoire de la Légion étrangère" qui exalte cette troupe tant enviée et jamais égalée, dans laquelle toutes les nationalités, toutes les classes sociales, toutes les religions se mélangent et tous les espoirs se confondent. « Camerone – Une histoire de la Légion étrangère » nous redit l'exemple du sacrifice sans espoir, de l'honneur des armes, du respect de la parole donnée par amour du chef et des camarades.

« Camerone – Une histoire de la Légion étrangère » nous redit ce qu'est l'orgueil de servir.

Antoine Marquet
L-Colonel à titre étranger (er),
ancien chef du service historique de la Légion
et rédacteur en chef du magazine *Képi Blanc*.

CHAPITRE I

L'HACIENDA

Hacienda de la Trinidad, à Camarón de Tejada (Camerone) Mexique. Vers 9h00 du matin, le 2 mai 1863.

Aux premières heures de ce 2 mai, les hommes de la colonne de secours française reconnurent à divers signes – et notamment au nombre croissant de coyotes en maraude – que le champ de bataille était proche.

Tout à coup, l'éclaireur de tête de l'escouade de reconnaissance qui cheminait sur le bas côté, aperçut au loin quelque chose qui ressemblait à une forme humaine. Il donna aussitôt l'alerte, et tous se tinrent sur leurs gardes, le regard fixé sur la silhouette qui avançait vers eux en chancelant. Ils avancèrent en tenant en joue l'inconnu qui était véritablement effrayant à voir : pieds nus, sans pantalon, vêtu en tout et pour tout d'une chemise noire de crasse et raidie par du sang séché, il avait le visage émacié et les yeux exorbités, comme hallucinés. Ne sachant pas s'il avait affaire à un européen ou à un autochtone, le caporal, chef de l'escouade l'interpella :

– Qui va là ! Répondez !

Mais l'homme ne répondit pas. Manifestement incapable de parler, sa bouche entre-ouverte laissait voir une langue gonflée et tuméfiée. Le capitaine Saussier, qui venait d'arriver, reconnut la chemise réglementaire de l'armée française et réalisa qu'il avait en face de lui un survivant de la compagnie Danjou.

Au moment où le colonel Jeanningros, commandant le Régiment étranger, les rejoignait, le malheureux parvint enfin à balbutier :

– Camerone – Une histoire de la Légion étrangère Mon colonel, je suis le dernier de la troisième…

Un légionnaire le reconnut alors.
– C'est Laï, le tambour du capitaine Danjou !

Il s'agissait en effet de Casimiro Laï, le tambour de la compagnie, l'ami d'Alonso Bernardo.

Ils n'étaient plus qu'à trois kilomètres de l'hacienda de la Trinidad.

✰

Quand le colonel Jeanningros arriva à Camerone, seuls les murs calcinés et encore fumants du bâtiment principal de l'hacienda témoignaient de l'intensité des combats, mais il n'y avait plus trace de matériel militaire. Ils trouvèrent les cadavres des légionnaires sommairement enterrés – plus exactement entassés – dans une fosse commune derrière le mur sud de l'hacienda de la Trinidad.

Surmontant la nausée provoquée par les corps bleuâtres et boursouflés et par l'odeur douceâtre et écœurante des chairs en décomposition, les légionnaires cherchaient à identifier leurs camarades, mais beaucoup n'étaient plus du tout reconnaissables après le passage des coyotes et des vautours.

Le premier sur lequel on put mettre un nom fut le sergent-major Henri Tonel, puis ce fut Danjou, sans sa main de bois articulée, le caporal Favas, un Suisse de Genève, l'ironique sergent Morzycki… Ce fut un véritable crève-cœur de reconnaître le corps de Catteau, littéralement déchiqueté par les coups de feu. Vingt-deux cadavres de légionnaires furent ainsi dénombrés ; un tiers de l'effectif de la compagnie.

Un légionnaire du capitaine Saussier crut reconnaître l'un des corps :

— J'ai l'impression que là, il s'agit de l'Espagnol… Je le reconnais à sa barbiche. Je l'avais rencontré au cours d'une marche…

Le visage gonflé par la putréfaction, Alonso Bernardo avait pour tout suaire sa chemise noircie par la poudre et le sang. Les yeux grands ouverts, le corps d'une rigidité de statue, dans une posture pas trop indigne, il n'avait pas senti le coup de lance que lui avait porté un Mexicain pour s'assurer de sa mort, avant de traîner son cadavre vers l'ignominieuse fosse commune. Son âme était déjà loin, très loin de là.

L'aristocrate suisse Diesbach de Tornay faisait partie des légionnaires qui atteignirent Camerone ce 2 mai, et qui y découvrirent comment les cadavres de leurs camarades avaient été abandonnés aux charognards « …au point de ne pouvoir reconnaître ces malheureux qui, après de tels actes de bravoure furent laissés, deux jours durant, en pâture à ces ignobles bêtes », écrira-t-il par la suite.

Vers 9h30 du matin, le 30 avril 1863,
dans le village de Camerone, Mexique.

La boule qui lui étreignait la gorge quand, précipitamment, toute la compagnie s'est engouffrée dans l'hacienda, lui paraissait encore plus compacte que celle ressentie pendant les premiers accrochages du petit matin. Cette boule dense qui l'empêche de respirer matérialise sa peur. Sa peur s'est faite matière.

Aux premiers moments de l'aube, après la course en quête de matériel égaré et les premières fusillades contre les troupes mexicaines, son courage était fait de pure et folle exaltation ; son cœur battait la chamade, comme dans ses Asturies natales lorsqu'il gravissait un sommet abrupt. Il était nerveux, mais ne pensait à rien.

Maintenant que la compagnie se déploie dans le corral et prend position le long des murs, les expressions en langue française qu'il entend lui paraissent un langage totalement bizarre et étranger, tout comme la première fois dans le dépôt militaire, près de Bayonne, en France.

– Allez, allez ! Vite !

Il a alors une vision terrifiante : un nuage sombre et poudreux se déplaçant au ras du sol. De cette nuée qui s'approche émergent des sons gutturaux... Alonso a la bouche pâteuse, et dans sa gorge semble se solidifier cette espèce de boule amère. Lorsqu'il a l'impression de pouvoir la mâcher, un sentiment de panique le submerge, se traduisant par un désir irrépressible de redevenir un enfant, et un enfant ne devait pas se trouver en ce lieu, si loin de sa maison – en un lieu où, paradoxalement, il comprenait la langue de l'ennemi alors qu'il ne parlait même pas couramment la langue de l'armée dont il portait l'uniforme !

– Attention ! À vos postes !

C'était le capitaine Danjou, commandant la 3e compagnie du 1er bataillon du Régiment étranger qui criait ses ordres.

Alonso, qui le regardait, laisse alors échapper un soupir de soulagement, au moment même où il commençait à perdre son sang-froid, en voyant son capitaine aussi maître de lui, avec des gestes mesurés et sûrs. Si le capitaine est tranquille, se disait-il, c'est que tout ira bien.

Des pensées tumultueuses assaillent Alonso. Observant le mouvement de la compagnie dans le périmètre de l'hacienda, il s'adosse au mur pour reprendre son calme, et sent une brusque bouffée d'orgueil l'envahir. Et en cet instant fugace, dans cette sorte de schizophrénie qui s'empare des êtres pendant le combat, il se sent soldat, totalement et fièrement légionnaire.

L'hacienda se présente comme un carré d'une cinquantaine de mètres de côté, clos par un mur de trois mètres de haut. Le bâtiment principal se dresse au nord, le long de la route. À l'opposé, près du coin sud-est de l'enceinte, se trouvent un hangar en torchis tombant en ruine, et une brèche par laquelle un cheval pourrait presque passer. Le coin sud-ouest est occupé par un petit hangar en meilleur état, mais ouvert à tous les vents, avec un toit reposant sur trois piliers de bois. Le mur ouest comporte deux larges portes-cochères entre lesquelles se trouve un autre petit hangar sans toiture.

– Alonso, aide-moi ! Vite ! lui ordonne le caporal Berg.

Aidé de plusieurs camarades de sa section, Alonso Bernardo commence à transporter caisses et planches pour obstruer les brèches du côté ouest, par lesquelles il aperçoit – avant que sa vision ne soit obscurcie par le nuage annonciateur de mort – une partie de la route reliant Monteviejo à Palo Verde.

Se dirigeant vers le centre de la cour avec son sac-à-dos encore accroché aux épaules et armé de son fusil modèle 1857 à canon rayé et chargement par la bouche, Alonso est surpris de constater à quel point ses mains tremblent. Voyant Karl Wittgens empoigner un timon de chariot, il se saisit fermement de l'autre timon pour masquer son trouble, et ils unissent leurs forces pour traîner le véhicule jusqu'à la deuxième porte-cochère. Ils s'escriment ainsi pendant une vingtaine de minutes qui parurent à Alonso n'avoir duré qu'un bref instant.

☆

La 3ᵉ compagnie, aux ordres du capitaine Danjou, avait reçu l'ordre d'escorter un convoi militaire qui avait quitté La Soledad pour se diriger vers la ville de Puebla, assiégée par les Français. Outre du matériel de siège, des vivres et des munitions, le convoi, composé de soixante-quatre chariots, transportait trois millions de francs-or destinés à la paye des soldats.

Tout commença quand le colonel Jeanningros, commandant le Régiment étranger, apprit par une femme mexicaine dont le mari était l'un des conducteurs de chariot du convoi, que celui-ci allait être attaqué et se faire massacrer. Cette Mexicaine était aussi la fille d'un sergent de la Guardia Nacional. Elle avait surpris une conversation entre un guérillero et le colonel Milán, gouverneur civil et militaire de l'État de Veracruz, qui dînait ce soir-là chez eux.

Le plan des Mexicains, avait-elle affirmé, prévoyait une attaque à la hauteur de Palo Verde.

Jeanningros considérait cette information comme tout à fait crédible, et il réunit aussitôt ses officiers pour les en informer et décider de la conduite à tenir. Comme il lui semblait impossible de dégarnir la place de Chiquihuite pour aller au secours du convoi, il se proposait d'envoyer un émissaire – en l'occurrence, la même jeune femme - à La Soledad, afin qu'elle remette au lieutenant-colonel Giraud un message l'avertissant du péril.

Ce fut le capitaine Danjou, son adjudant-major, qui lui fit part de sa crainte de voir la jeune Mexicaine tomber aux mains de l'ennemi, réduisant à néant ainsi toute la mission… Il estimait préférable d'envoyer à la rencontre de la colonne une compagnie, qui reconnaîtrait la route en direction de La Soledad et qui pourrait donner l'alerte en cas de danger. Si le convoi était attaqué, argumenta Danjou, cette unité pourrait participer à sa défense de manière non négligeable. Après avoir pesé les avantages et les inconvénients de cette solution, Jeanningros se rangea à l'avis de l'adjudant-major.

La compagnie, basée à Chiquihuite, devait donc marcher à l'encontre de la colonne, en direction de Palo Verde, en lui reconnaissant l'itinéraire pour en revenir avec le convoi. Le 30 avril 1863 à une heure du matin elle quitta son cantonnement.

L'épaisse végétation de part et d'autre de la route, la *mata*, comparable au maquis, obligeait les légionnaires à se frayer difficilement un chemin à coups de machettes et de coutelas. Leur progression était lente et épuisante.

Vers deux heures trente, la compagnie fit halte à Paso del Macho (Pas du Mulet), où un poste militaire français était établi au bord d'un ravin, au fond duquel coulait un torrent sinueux. Là, Danjou prit contact avec la compagnie de grenadiers du capitaine Saussier. Celui-ci lui proposa de renforcer sa compagnie d'une section qu'il mettrait à sa disposition, mais Danjou refusa courtoisement cette offre.

☆

Pendant la pause, Alonso Bernardo rejoint son copain Casimir Laï, le tambour de la compagnie, natif de la ville sarde de Cagliari, un petit bonhomme jovial et sympathique haut d'un mètre soixante, au visage barré d'une énorme moustache. Les deux amis échangent leurs impressions en espagnol et en italien, ce qui est, pour eux, beaucoup moins ardu que de discuter en français. Alonso utilise aussi l'espagnol pour communiquer avec Gustave Bartello, natif de Toulon, mais fréquente moins volontiers ce dernier qui est d'un tempérament plus renfermé et taciturne ; Casimir et Gustave ont tous deux neuf ans de moins qu'Alonso, qui aura bientôt trente-trois ans – dont quatre passées sous l'uniforme légionnaire. Bartello n'avait jamais révélé à l'Espagnol où, ni dans quelles circonstances il avait appris à se débrouiller dans sa langue.

Comme la plupart des étrangers nouvellement engagés, Alonso ne parlait pas du tout français au moment de son engagement. Au cours des premières semaines d'instruction à Sidi Bel Abbès, en Algérie, le langage de base de l'instruction était répété à satiété, accompagné par les exercices de démonstration exécutés par les sous-officiers instructeurs, de manière à être parfaitement assimilé par les hommes du peloton. Parmi les instructeurs, il se trouvait toujours quelques-uns à vocation polyglotte qui réussissaient à se faire comprendre avec quelques mots d'allemand par-ci, quelques mots d'italien par-là… plus des bribes d'espagnol apprises auprès de la colonie hispanique qui constituait, avec une forte communauté juive, l'essentiel de la population européenne de Sidi Bel Abbès qui abritait la maison-mère de la Légion étrangère.

Au sein même des compagnies, les légionnaires communiquaient entre eux comme ils pouvaient, élaborant un vocabulaire élémentaire qui leur était propre, afin de pouvoir se comprendre. Étant donnée la quasi impossibilité de tenir une véritable conversation fluide, l'univers légionnaire apparaissait comme un tissu de silences que venaient tromper les cacophonies lors des soûlographies collectives, où tous parlaient sans que personne soit entendu[1]. En réalité, à l'époque, les principales difficultés d'apprentissage de la langue, conformes au contexte historique, venaient du fait que les légionnaires étaient en grande majorité, comme Alonso Bernardo, analphabètes.

☆

La compagnie reprend sa marche dans la nuit. Vers cinq heures du matin le jour se lève, et il est environ six heures trente quand l'unité traverse le hameau de Camarón de Tejada, qui passera à la postérité sous le nom de Camerone (en espagnol, « Camarón » désigne tantôt la crevette grise, tantôt l'écrevisse).

1 Tel que l'explique Douglas Porch.

Camerone est un minuscule village pouilleux, bâti de part et d'autre du Camino Real, emprunté par la compagnie Danjou, et regroupant d'un côté une dizaine de masures crasseuses et puantes, aux toits de paille et aux murs d'adobe, et plus à l'est, des maisons, à proprement parler ; cet ensemble est connu sous le nom d'hacienda de la Trinidad, une propriété abandonnée ayant appartenu à la famille Alarcón.

Sur la gauche, en direction du nord se dresse le bâtiment principal, maison d'habitation, et au sud la grange et diverses dépendances plus ou moins délabrées. Ce n'est pas la première fois que Alonso voit un tel type de hameau et encore moins, depuis qu'au cours de nombreuses marches il avait découvert les paysages d'Algérie mais, malgré tout, cette vision l'a déprimé.

Le capitaine Danjou ordonne une rapide reconnaissance des lieux, pratiquement déserts à cette heure de la matinée ; quelques rares autochtones observent la compagnie avec un mélange de peur et d'étonnement puisque l'unité, composée majoritairement de personnels d'origine germanique, offre à leurs regards des hommes relativement grands pour l'époque, de peau très claire et qui, après un mois passé sous le soleil des *tierras calientes* mexicaines, arborent des visages rouges et parfois même congestionnés.

La manœuvre ne prend guère de temps, et le village est vite dépassé. Ce n'était pas la première fois qu'Alonso traversait des hameaux aussi misérables – c'était un spectacle coutumier en Algérie –, mais la vue de cette extrême pauvreté lui serre le cœur, surtout quand son regard croise celui d'enfants dont les corps menus et les membres grêles ont pour tout vêtement, quelques haillons sous une couche de poussière.

L'Espagnol se souvient de la sensation de faim permanente de son enfance – sensation qui se traduisait par une sorte de bizarre pincement à l'estomac – et de l'intense délectation qu'il éprouvait à l'occasion de la fête du village, lorsqu'il pouvait se gaver sans frein et qu'il pensait que le bonheur suprême consiste à pouvoir se nourrir à satiété. Il savait à quel point la faim peut annihiler les sentiments et la fierté chez l'homme, capable de tout pour manger…

Lui aussi courait pieds nus, comme ces enfants qu'il regarde en cette matinée du 30 avril. Il se revoyait avec ses lourds sabots en hiver, pieds nus l'été, avec la constante sensation de fraîcheur aux pieds due au climat humide de ses Asturies natales.

Camerone se trouve à quelque 70 kilomètres à l'ouest de Veracruz, sur la côte atlantique. Le Camino Real (ou Nacional) part de Veracruz et traverse les villages de La Soledad, Palo Verde, Camarón de Tejada (Camerone), Paso del Macho, Chiquihuite, Córdoba, Orizaba, Puebla, pour arriver enfin à Mexico, la capitale.

Dépassée l'hacienda, la compagnie se scinde en deux sections pour marcher de part et d'autre de la route afin de reconnaître les sous-bois. À une centaine de mètres en arrière, Danjou suit avec un groupe de voltigeurs et les deux mules qui portent les vivres et les munitions. Ordre avait été donné de se regrouper à Palo Verde. Donnant l'exemple et payant de sa personne, il ne monte pas son cheval de dotation mais ne s'en sépare pas toutefois. Menée aux rênes par le muletier Domínguez, sa monture reste le symbole de son rang et de sa condition d'officier ; sa capote à capuche, réglementaire, trône toujours sur sa selle, roulée en boudin et accrochée au pommeau.

Aux environs de six heures trente-cinq, la compagnie bivouaque près de Palo Verde, après quelque 25 kilomètres de marche au départ de Chiquihuite. Alentour, le terrain est marécageux et comporte de nombreuses mares.

A 7h00 du matin (deux heures et demie plus tôt), le 30 avril 1863

Le capitaine Danjou avait ordonné une halte pour le café du matin. Auparavant, il avait expédié à La Joya une escouade aux ordres du caporal Magnin, un Autrichien, pour reconnaître les environs.

La journée s'annonçait déjà très chaude. La compagnie s'était installée au bord d'un ruisseau, ramassant du bois pour allumer du feu. Le café commençait à chanter dans les cafetières. Alonso en profita pour enlever ses guêtres et inspecter ses chaussures rafistolées avec de la ficelle ; les semelles rendraient bientôt l'âme ! Il se disait que dans son cas, le plus précieux butin de guerre serait une paire de chaussures de rechange…

Claude Billod, de Dijon, un homme qui avait des problèmes avec l'alcool, s'était assis un peu à l'écart. Quand il s'enivrait, il devenait agressif, ce qui lui avait déjà coûté les galons de caporal après une soûlerie mémorable. Alonso se remémorait la scène qui se déroula un peu plus tôt dans la nuit, au moment où la compagnie déjà formée, s'apprêtait à partir. S'adressant sans ménagement au Français, le capitaine lui avait sèchement demandé si c'était de l'eau ou du vin qu'il transportait dans sa gourde…

Une quarantaine de minutes s'étaient écoulés à peine, lorsque l'escouade envoyée en reconnaissance sur la route de La Joya signala quelque chose d'anormal, des nuages de poussière apparemment provoqués par une troupe importante.

Ce fut alors qu'une sentinelle s'écria :

– Alerte !

Danjou s'empara de ses jumelles de campagne. Après avoir observé la route sur toute sa longueur, il cria :

– Aux armes ! Rassemblement !

L'ordre fut exécuté avec tout le professionnalisme propre à une unité militaire de cette classe. Les gestes, tant et tant de fois répétés en Algérie, étaient réglés comme un mouvement d'horlogerie…

En cinq minutes à peine, la compagnie était prête au départ. Les légionnaires n'avaient, pour la plupart, pas eu le temps de boire leur café ni de remplir leurs gourdes au ruisseau tout proche.

Débuta alors le repli vers Paso del Macho, à la rencontre de la compagnie Saussier, mais en suivant la direction nord-ouest à l'abri des fourrés et d'un petit bosquet. La compagnie commença d'être harcelée par la cavalerie mexicaine, et le capitaine Danjou l'emmena en terrain accidenté dans l'espoir de gêner l'avance ennemie. En fait, c'est surtout la progression des légionnaires qui devint plus pénible, car ils devaient se frayer un chemin à travers l'épais maquis.

Danjou ordonna au sergent Morzycki et au caporal Maine d'ouvrir, avec leur groupe, la route au reste de l'unité. Le sergent qui était à la tête du dispositif donna des ordres à voix basse :

– Aucun bruit. Faites passer la consigne.

Conrad et Constantin ouvraient le chemin à l'aide de leurs sabres-baïonnette. Voyant que la progression restait malgré tout trop lente, le capitaine changea d'avis et ordonna que l'on reprenne la route en direction de Camerone.

– Venez sur la route. Vite ! Vilain, faites bouger les hommes.

Soudain un cri se fit entendre : le légionnaire Conrad, un bavarois, venait d'être blessé par balle. Sans stopper leur marche, les légionnaires lui portèrent secours, et l'un d'eux se chargea de son sac à dos. Parvenu sur la route, Danjou donna des ordres pour que deux sections marchent de part et d'autre de l'axe, avec un groupe en ouverture et un en serre-file. Les deux mules qui transportaient les vivres et les munitions furent placées au centre du dispositif, avec le capitaine.

Alors que la compagnie amorça son retour vers Camerone, un coup de feu partit de l'une des maisons, à environ trois cents mètres de l'auberge de la Trinidad. Deux sections, dont l'une directement commandée par le capitaine Danjou, s'avancèrent vers l'endroit d'où le coup de feu fut tiré. Vilain fit signe à Alonso d'aller se placer juste derrière le capitaine, qui pourrait ainsi l'utiliser comme interprète en cas de besoin.

À ce moment précis, alors qu'il se déplaçait de maison en maison, collé aux murs, passant d'un bond devant les ouvertures susceptibles d'abriter des tireurs, toujours derrière le capitaine, Alonso ne ressentait plus aucune peur. Tout son équipement était ballotté contre son corps au rythme de sa course, mais il était habitué aux chocs incessants de la musette et de la gourde sur ses hanches ; ses épaules toujours creusées par les bretelles du sac à dos qui, avec la couverture et la toile de tente roulées au-dessus, lui arrivait à la nuque, tous ses sens en éveil absolu.

Rassuré par la présence du capitaine devant lui, il ajusta machinalement son couvre-nuque blanc, cousu quelques jours auparavant au couvre-képi réglementaire confectionné par le caporal Horstein, tailleur de l'unité. Son attention tendue vers le moindre bruit, l'Espagnol était totalement concentré sur son but. Dans le feu de l'action, il sentait son pouls s'accélérer à un rythme effréné, et le sang lui congestionner les tempes. De la pointe de sa baïonnette, il souleva précautionneusement le poncho qui faisait office de porte à l'entrée d'une maison et il constata que la pièce était vide et révélait la même pauvreté que celle de sa maison natale des Asturies – elle était certes plus sale, mais peut-être moins triste…

Alonso revint vers le capitaine qui lui fit signe de continuer. Il fit le tour de la maison mais n'aperçut âme qui vive. Alors seulement, le capitaine autorisa une escouade à aller chercher de l'eau en contrebas, au creux d'un ravin où habituellement coulait l'eau d'une source. Mais un mur effondré avait tari cette fontaine naturelle.

José Domínguez de nationalité mexicaine et ordonnance de Danjou mit à profit ces moments de confusion pour abandonner la compagnie et disparaître.

☆

La compagnie reprend sa marche vers Chiquihuite d'un pas vif et rapide, presque un pas de course, si bien qu'Alonso sent déjà deux rigoles de sueur lui couler dans le dos. La tête penchée en avant, il regarde ses brodequins noirs en partie couverts par les guêtres jaunies. Il ressent une certaine excitation devant le danger, qu'il pressent déjà comme une menace bien réelle, mais sans avoir véritablement peur. Il pense seulement à la fatigue dont il commence à sentir les effets pesants. Le nuage de poussière qui les suit se rapproche de plus en plus, et l'on commence à distinguer les silhouettes des cavaliers mexicains.

☆

Toutes ces manœuvres contrarient vivement le colonel Francisco de Paula Milán, de la cavalerie mexicaine, qui se tient informé des mouvements des légionnaires et qui voit compromis son projet de tendre une embuscade au convoi qui se dirigeait vers Puebla. Aussi ses instructions sont claires : ne laisser, à aucun prix, échapper le détachement français !

À peine la compagnie Danjou a-t-elle quitté Camerone et parcouru cinq cents mètres sur le Camino Real que la section de tête fait demi-tour et alerte le capitaine : la cavalerie mexicaine chargeait ! Alonso observa ceux qui reviennent en courant, la mine décomposée. Tous les légionnaires de la compagnie sont en mouvement, et dans de tels instants, tout n'est que nerfs à fleur de peau.

Joaquín Jiménez, qui commande l'escadron mexicain des « lanciers d'Orizaba », divise son unité en deux pelotons pour tenter d'encercler les Français. Grâce à la reconnaissance effectuée par le lieutenant Anastasio Jiménez – son frère, qui sert dans sa propre unité –, il connaît la composition des forces françaises.

Le capitaine Danjou eut d'abord l'intention de charger les Mexicains au son redoublé du tambour – le petit Italien avait même déjà reçu l'ordre de battre la charge –, mais devant la tournure alarmante prise par les événements, il change d'avis et fait former le carré, comme la Garde Impériale à Waterloo presque cinquante ans plus tôt. Il en éprouve un sentiment de fierté. Ce n'est pas son premier combat et il n'a pas peur. En ce moment précis, il ne pense pas à la mort comme une issue possible, il commande, tout simplement…

C'est le sous-lieutenant Vilain qui organise le carré. Il réfléchit rapidement et place lui-même les légionnaires : huit par côté, sur deux rangs. Au centre du carré, le capitaine, le sergent-major Tonel, et enfin, les muletiers et leurs animaux.

Alonso, qui fait partie de la formation genou à terre, pousse un soupir de soulagement. Dans cette position, le fusil Minié chargé à la main, baïonnette au canon, il se sent plus en confiance. Le légionnaire Jean Verjus est à côté de lui, et le voisinage de ce parisien le tranquillise. Verjus, qui avait été sergent dans la Légion au cours d'un précédent engagement, avait en outre servi pendant presque quatre ans dans la Marine. Avec de tels antécédents laissant certes entrevoir un passé tumultueux – ce qui expliquerait pourquoi il n'a pas retrouvé son grade –, mais la présence d'un vétéran aux côtés d'Alonso est néanmoins rassurante.

Ainsi, serrés les uns contre les autres, les légionnaires sont gênés dans leurs mouvements par les équipements de leurs voisins, d'où les protestations et les coups de gueule qui dissimulent mal leurs peurs. On distingue déjà parfaitement la tenue des Mexicains : épais gilets de cuir, lourds éperons aux énormes molettes et les larges sombreros traditionnels aux couleurs voyantes.

Danjou jette un coup d'œil aux lieutenants Vilain et Maudet. Ils sont calmes. Puis il observe la charge ; les hurlements de la cavalerie mexicaine chargeant sabre au clair, le bruit du galop, se font assourdissants. Au sein du carré, des frémissements se propagent, trahissant l'inquiétude ; ils ne sont plus qu'à soixante mètres.

– Feu !

La salve mortelle produit son effet. Des corps ensanglantés gisent sur le sol, les chevaux hennissent… La charge est rompue.

Les légionnaires rechargent leurs fusils, s'aidant de la baguette pour pousser au fond du canon la balle introduite par la bouche à feu. Ils se remettent aussitôt en position de tir.

Malheureusement, les deux mules placées au centre du carré sous la responsabilité du sergent-major Henri Tonel, affolées par le vacarme, se mettent à ruer, et partent au galop avec les vivres et les munitions de l'unité. Les légionnaires assistent médusés et impuissants à leur fuite, sans toutefois en saisir immédiatement toutes les conséquences désastreuses qui en découleraient. Après ce premier assaut, aucun blessé n'est à déplorer du côté français.

Le capitaine ordonne alors à la compagnie de se replier vers Camerone au pas redoublé tout en maintenant la formation en carré. À présent, plus personne ne ressent la fatigue. Alonso se sent même étonnamment léger, à ce premier stade de la peur qui confère une certaine apesanteur physique comme mécanisme de diversion.

Clovis Pharaon Vanderbulche, le benjamin de la compagnie qui n'a pas encore 18 ans, dissimule mal l'euphorie qu'il éprouve à ce baptême du feu.

Les légionnaires sont tellement concentrés sur la bonne conduite de leur retraite qu'aucun d'eux – y compris Danjou, pressé d'arriver à Camerone – ne prend vraiment garde aux mouvements de l'ennemi.

Ils sont à environ 400 mètres du village, dont ils aperçoivent déjà les premières masures, lorsque le capitaine remarque, un peu plus à l'ouest, bordant le côté sud de la route, un haut talus couronné d'une épaisse ligne de cactus. Il pense engager ses légionnaires dans cette barrière naturelle susceptible d'entraver la progression de la cavalerie mexicaine.

Les derniers Français viennent tout juste de quitter la route lorsqu'ils voient arriver les premiers chevaux ! Contrairement à ce qu'espérait Danjou, les cavaliers mexicains, pour la plupart, réussissent à engager leurs montures dans ce terrain difficile.

Réalisant que la compagnie ne parviendrait jamais à atteindre le hameau à temps, le capitaine ordonne la formation d'un nouveau carré.

Cette fois, l'Espagnol commence à avoir peur, vraiment peur. À peine met-il le genou à terre que les Mexicains sont déjà sur eux, assez proches pour qu'il distingue parfaitement leurs visages. C'est avec soulagement qu'il entend crier l'ordre :

– Feu !

La décharge les aveugle à nouveau.

– Chargez ! Vite, chargez !

De nouveau en position de tir, Alonso réalise soudain à quel point ils sont seuls, isolés, et la situation lui parait sans issue. C'est presque avec détachement, comme si la scène lui était totalement étrangère, qu'il observe le chaos qui résulte de leur salve : chevaux épouvantés, cavaliers s'enfuyant à toutes jambes, corps sans vie… Néanmoins, ce spectacle réconforte les légionnaires qui s'efforcent de mieux ajuster leurs tirs. Danjou félicite ceux qui firent mouche, mais ce fut aussi le moment où les premiers membres de la compagnie tombèrent, touchés à mort, et parmi eux le Suisse Dubois. Les deux poméraniens de l'unité, Fritz et Friedrich, furent blessés à l'épaule.

Leur position se trouve alors à quelque 200 mètres de l'hacienda, et Danjou estime que la seule issue possible est de charger jusqu'à elle. Il en donne l'ordre en précisant que la charge devra être massive et débuter au cri de « Vive l'Empereur ! », pour donner l'impression qu'ils étaient bien plus nombreux qu'ils ne l'étaient en réalité et intimider l'ennemi par leurs hurlements.

– Laï, bats la charge !

Quand il entend ce commandement, Alonso se sent défaillir, comprenant la portée de ce que cela supposait ; impressionné par la détermination avec laquelle Vilain s'élance, suivi avec beaucoup de conviction par le caporal Berg, il crie lui aussi de toutes ses forces : « Vive l'Empereur ! », comme s'il pouvait expulser sa peur en hurlant, et il se lance dans une course éperdue.

Face à la ruée des Français, les Mexicains déconcertés, gênés dans leurs mouvements par l'enchevêtrement de morts, de blessés et de chevaux, battent en retraite.

Alonso retrouve peu à peu son sang-froid en voyant qu'il n'aurait pas à affronter directement un Mexicain. En de tels moments, il appréhende davantage d'avoir à dévisager celui qu'il devra tuer que d'être tué lui-même.

Les blessés, Fritz, Friedrich et Conrad, sont placés au milieu du groupe, soutenus et protégés par leurs camarades.

Le caporal Berg achève un Mexicain, sans se départir de sa belle prestance d'ex-officier de l'armée française, lui, qui fut lieutenant de Zouaves, mais donc la passion pour le jeu, les dettes criantes, et diverses malversations entraînèrent la dégradation, après laquelle il s'engagea discrètement dans la Légion étrangère. Danjou l'apprécie et, encore plus, le blond et juvénile Jean Vilain, âgé de 27 ans, qui considérait un peu le quadragénaire caporal Berg comme un frère aîné.

Le Mexicain abattu par Berg est allongé sur le dos, la bouche béante et la mâchoire déboîtée. Une énorme moustache barre son visage olivâtre. Des deux mains, il se tient le ventre où s'élargi une tache rouge sombre, presque noire. Alonso est surpris par la netteté de la blessure faite par la baïonnette. Mais cette impression fugitive laisse vite place à d'autres pensées, tout aussi fugaces. Tout cela se déroula sous ses yeux quelques quarante secondes avant. En de telles circonstances, il s'agit de se fier à ses réflexes, d'agir sans se laisser troubler par le doute, de repérer le soldat que l'on va attaquer, sans hésitation aucune. C'est seulement ainsi que l'on peut survivre au corps à corps et à la baïonnette. Surtout sans penser ! Il est essentiel de ne pas penser.

Immédiatement après la débandade des Mexicains, les ordres de Danjou, Maudet et Villain se succèdent. Maudet et Vilain à leur tête, les légionnaires se ruent plus ou moins en désordre vers l'hacienda de la Trinidad à environ 200 mètres à l'est de Camerone. Deux cents mètres sont une distance ridiculement courte, mais ici, elle leur paraissait interminable.

Alonso court à toutes jambes, le dos et les flancs meurtris par les heurts de son pesant sac à dos et de sa musette, accablé de fatigue et maudissant son encombrant équipement militaire, la gorge bloquée par l'angoisse, il suit le caporal Berg avec le reste de la compagnie, et tous pénètrent en trombe, par les portes-cochères du mur ouest, dans la cour.

La première chose dont Alonso prend conscience dans la confusion ambiante, ce sont les halètements désordonnés et les clameurs de ses compagnons qui se mêlaient aux cris stridents et quasi hystériques des gradés, pour former une sorte de rugissement planant au-dessus des têtes des légionnaires de la 3e compagnie.

Les premiers légionnaires arrivés affrontent quelques Mexicains qui avaient réussi à pénétrer dans l'enceinte avant l'arrivée de la compagnie de Danjou et s'en débarrassent rapidement.

☆

Il était environ neuf heures. En ce 30 avril 1863, la 3e compagnie du 1er bataillon de la Légion étrangère venait d'entrer dans la légende.

CHAPITRE II

MEXIQUE

Benito Juárez, descendant d'indiens zapotèques, a étudié le Droit et fait une carrière politique comme député local puis national et, plus tard, comme gouverneur d'Oaxaca en 1847 ; il avait quarante et un ans.

Il a dû s'exiler en 1853, au retour du général Santana qu'il avait soutenu dans le passé, mais est revenu dès 1855, lors de la défaite du général à El Alamo, et a alors participé au gouvernement de Comonfort, où il a pris la tête de la réforme libérale qui a conduit à la séparation de l'Eglise et de l'Etat, à la promulgation de la Constitution de 1857 et à l'explosion de la réaction conservatrice qui a mené à la guerre civile.

Dans la période comprise entre 1857 et 1860, le Mexique a vécu une guerre fratricide entre les adeptes du conservateur Félix Zuluoaga et ceux du parti libéral de Benito Juárez.

Juárez a pris le pouvoir, mais la capitale est tombée aux mains des rebelles de Félix Zuluoaga. Après s'être réfugié à Panama, lors de son expulsion de Guadalajara, sa capitale provisoire, il est retourné au Mexique avec l'appui des Etats-Unis. En mai 1858 il a établi le siège de son gouvernement à Veracruz, fait qui a été reconnu officiellement par son voisin du nord le 6 avril 1859, et a poursuivi la guerre jusqu'à la victoire de Capulcapán le 22 décembre 1860.

Cette période conflictuelle a laissé l'Etat mexicain exsangue, ce qui a poussé Benito Juárez à confisquer les biens de l'Eglise et à suspendre le payement de la dette extérieure en 1861 par un moratoire de deux ans. Les trois principales puissances détentrices de la dette mexicaine, mécontentes, ont envoyé un corps expéditionnaire pour appuyer clairement leurs revendications et leur rejet du moratoire. Ainsi, environ sept cents soldats anglais sous les ordres de sir Charles Wicke, six mille soldats espagnols sous le commandement du général Prim et deux mille cinq cents soldats français commandés par le général Dubois de Saligny, ont débarqué à Veracruz le 13 janvier 1862. Peu après le débarquement, le contingent européen a été fortement affecté par la fièvre jaune ou *vomito negro.*

Afin d'éviter la guerre, le président Benito Juárez a ordonné à son armée de ne pas opposer de résistance au débarquement des représentants des puissances européennes, leur proposant d'emblée l'ouverture de négociations, ce que la Triple Alliance a accepté.

L'intervention

Le général Don Juan Prim, à la tête des troupes espagnoles a obtenu, par d'opportunes négociations avec les autorités mexicaines, que ses troupes s'installent dans des lieux ayant de bonnes conditions de salubrité. Peu après, la Convention de la Soledad a légitimé le gouvernement de Benito Juárez. Dans ces négociations le gouvernement mexicain était représenté par son ministre Manuel Doblado, tandis que le général espagnol Juan Prim représentait l'ensemble de la Triple Alliance. Le 19 février 1862 les traités préliminaires de La Soledad ont été signés. Ils précisaient les limites suivantes : le Mexique n'avait besoin d'aucune puissance étrangère pour consolider sa forme de gouvernement ; le Mexique acceptait que les troupes de l'alliance européenne s'installent sur des territoires plus salubres comme Orizaba, Córdoba y Jalapa. Ces troupes seraient placées sous le contrôle des troupes mexicaines de Don Ignacio Zaragoza. En cas d'échec des négociations, les troupes européennes cantonneraient dans le port de Veracruz.

Dès que les accords ont été ratifiés par les représentants de la Grande Bretagne et du Royaume d'Espagne, la Convention de La Soledad a acquis un caractère officiel. En vertu de cette Convention, le Mexique s'engageait à solder sa dette extérieure par l'émission de bons de garantie qui ont été acceptés par Londres et Madrid, mais non par Paris. Du coup, seules la Grande Bretagne et l'Espagne ont décidé de rapatrier leurs soldats en avril 1862.

La France a, délibérément, réclamé des montants exorbitants, de nature à provoquer une réaction de Benito Juárez.

Celui qui présidait alors aux destinées de la France, empereur des Français sous le nom de Napoléon III, neveu de Napoléon 1er, a voulu profiter du fait que les Etats-Unis se trouvaient impliqués dans une terrible guerre civile, pour placer la République Mexicaine sous la dépendance française. Des exilés mexicains de tendance conservatrice fraichement arrivés et qui avaient accès à la très pieuse impératrice Marie Eugénie de Montijo, l'ont incitée à convaincre son époux de l'exécrable persécution dont souffrait l'Eglise catholique mexicaine du fait de Benito Juárez et des libéraux, poussant l'empereur, en lui donnant une vision trompeuse de la situation, à intervenir militairement. Quatre mille soldats français en provenance de l'Empire, arriveront en renfort au Mexique sous les ordres du général Lorencez, qui emmenait avec lui un Mexicain réfugié à la cour de Napoléon III. Celui-ci a réclamé le gouvernement du Mexique.

Le 25 avril 1862, le général comte Charles Ferdinand de Lorencez a écrit au maréchal Randon, ministre de la Guerre à Paris, une lettre lamentable de suffisance, qui a fini par lui coûter cher :

« Nous sommes si supérieurs aux Mexicains par la race, l'organisation, la discipline, la morale et l'élévation des sentiments que je prie votre Excellence d'avoir la bonté d'informer l'Empereur que, à la tête de six mille soldats, je suis déjà le maître du Mexique ».

☆

L'armée française s'est installée sur les hauteurs de Veracruz.

Le 5 mai 1862 les troupes françaises se sont lancées à l'assaut de Puebla, première étape pour atteindre la capitale, Mexico.

Benito Juárez a désigné le général Ignacio Zaragoza comme chef suprême des forces de défense de la ville, qui disposait pour sa protection de quelque douze mille hommes, force plus nombreuse que celle des attaquants.

Les fortes et puissantes murailles qui défendaient la ville empêchaient un assaut définitif des Français. Devant l'échec de l'artillerie des assaillants, les assiégés ont lancé une contre-attaque provoquant d'innombrables pertes, dont celle de deux colonels, parmi les Français. Ceux-ci amorceront le retrait sous la pression des attaques de la cavalerie mexicaine, qui est sortie de la ville pour rompre le siège, évitant, grâce à un déluge salvateur, le total anéantissement, tout en laissant plus de cinq cents pertes sur le champ de bataille.

Le général Ignacio Zaragoza a envoyé le message suivant au président de la nation : « Aujourd'hui les armes nationales se sont couvertes de gloire ».

Ce désastre militaire a provoqué un énorme choc en France. Pour laver l'affront, la France met sur pied un corps expéditionnaire de trente mille soldats sous le commandement du général Elie Frédéric Forey.

Au début de 1863, le nouveau général en chef du corps expéditionnaire, a décidé d'attaquer de nouveau Puebla, avec dix-huit mille fantassins, mille quatre cents cavaliers, deux mille cent cinquante artilleurs, quatre cent cinquante sapeurs, un corps auxiliaire de deux mille trois cents hommes et deux mille combattants mexicains du général conservateur mexicain Márquez. Cette force était dotée de cinquante-six canons et de deux millions quatre cent mille projectiles.

L'armée française a pris la capitale, Mexico, en juin 1863. Une assemblée de notables favorables à la France avec une majorité de conservateurs, a décidé de restaurer l'Empire mexicain, offrant la couronne au prince Maximilien, frère du kaiser autrichien François Joseph, le 10 juillet 1863.

La proposition faite à Maximilien a été rejetée unanimement par sa famille et par la Maison impériale autrichienne qui considéraient l'acceptation de cette proposition comme une aventure hautement risquée, car il ne serait jamais accepté au Mexique, ni lui ni Charlotte, son épouse, de par leur condition d'étrangers. La famille royale belge ne s'est pas montrée plus favorable à ce que le couple accepte la couronne impériale mexicaine, mais Maximilien a manifesté son enthousiasme pour le projet.

Après une réunion avec Napoléon III, Maximilien a accepté la couronne de l'Empire mexicain, renonçant à tous ses droits sur le trône autrichien. Le Traité de Miramar du 10 avril 1864, a scellé toute la négociation : deux mois plus tard, en juin 1864, après une traversée à bord de la frégate française *Novara,* Maximilien I du Mexique ceignait la couronne dans la capitale de son nouvel Empire.

L'approbation de son mandat a été plébiscitée. Cependant, étant donné ses principes, Maximilien oubliant que c'étaient les conservateurs qui l'avaient mis sur le trône, a dirigé son nouvel Empire selon des principes libéraux.

Benito Juárez a pris les armes contre l'Empire ; en constant mouvement, il a installé sa capitale provisoire à Paso del Norte, cela jusqu'à la fin de la guerre en 1867.

En 1866, déjà conscient de son échec et constamment sous la pression des Etats-Unis, Napoléon III a annoncé, en milieu d'année, le retrait de ses troupes (quarante-trois mille hommes dont trois mille Belges, cinq mille Autrichiens et un détachement égyptien).

Le rapatriement des troupes qui devait s'échelonner jusqu'en décembre 1867, s'est terminé neuf mois plus tôt, en mars de la même année. Le retrait s'est effectué avec l'occupation simultanée des lieux par les troupes républicaines de Juárez.

Sans aucune forme d'appui, l'empire de Maximilien se trouvait au bord de l'effondrement. Après le retrait des Français, Maximilien a pensé à abdiquer, mais son épouse, l'impératrice Charlotte Marie, l'a fait changer d'avis. Alors, décidé à continuer la guerre bien que Juárez occupe déjà grande partie du territoire mexicain, il est arrivé même à rétablir l'esclavage, dépassant son propre dogmatisme libéral, uniquement dans le but de gagner l'appui des sudistes américains, récemment défaits pendant la guerre civile nord-américaine et qui émigraient vers le Mexique avec leurs esclaves noirs.

Maximilien a pensé à diverses formules lui permettant de concilier ses principes et ses nécessités politiques, dont l'une a été de donner aux noirs l'état-civil de mineurs ; une autre de les ramener d'Abyssinie (l'actuelle Ethiopie), contractés comme travailleurs. Cependant tout cela a été réduit à néant avec l'assassinat de Lincoln et la succession de son vice-président Johnson, car il semblait plus sage de ne pas irriter les nord-américains avec une question très sensible à leurs yeux au vu de l'horrible guerre civile qu'ils avaient connue.

D'autre part, cet esprit libéral avait fait que Charlotte était intervenue dans le gouvernement, prenant des mesures sociales en faveur des indiens, mais la réalité sociale et le propre système de classes ont fini par s'imposer, ce qui lui a enlevé toute autorité avec la révocation des mesures prises par elle et l'éloignement définitif de l'impératrice du gouvernement par instruction expresse de Maximilien.

Le seul appui qui restait à l'empereur se trouvait dans le secteur le plus extrémiste du conservatisme, qu'il avait trahi, malgré tout, avec ses principes libéraux, tout comme l'Eglise catholique, en admettant la liberté de culte et le régime civil tout en s'opposant à l'annulation de la loi de désamortissement, et ce, malgré les énormes pressions reçues de Rome, au travers de son envoyé spécial, pour restituer le patrimoine confisqué à l'Eglise et pour que l'empire redevienne confessionnel.

Les généraux Miramón et Márquez, qui venaient d'arriver d'Europe, ont été chargés de réorganiser l'armée impériale. Le général Miramón a réussi, lui-même, à se saisir de Zacatecas (et n'a pas réussi à appréhender Benito Juárez de très peu). Mais quelques jours plus tard le général Miramón a été vaincu par le général Escobedo à San Jacinto et Maximilien a décidé que l'empire devait livrer la bataille décisive à Querétaro. Le siège de la ville a duré deux mois mais elle est tombée et a fini par se rendre aux troupes de Benito Juárez.

Maximilien Ier a été fait prisonnier le 15 mai 1867, après la chute de Querétaro. Il a été fusillé au cerro de las Campanas (colline des Cloches, NdT), avec les généraux rebelles Miguel Miramón et Tomás Mejía, sur ordre du président Benito Juárez, le 19 juin 1867.

Sa condamnation à mort a soulevé un élan de solidarité en Europe. Victor Hugo, Garibaldi, des représentants de l'Italie, de la Belgique et de la Prusse, intercéderont en sa faveur auprès de Benito Juárez, mais celui-ci s'est montré inflexible.

L'empereur, âgé de trente-six ans, a fait montre d'une dignité admirable avant de mourir.

Le jour de son exécution, levé à trois heures et demie du matin, il s'est habillé de noir et paré de sa Toison d'or ; pendant ses ultimes heures de vie il s'est fait accompagner par l'abbé Soria. Le prêtre, très nerveux, a dû être tranquillisé par Maximilien lui-même.

Ses deux valets de chambre et servants, Blasio, Mexicain et Grill, Autrichien, étaient anéantis. Il leur remit sa montre pour qu'ils la fassent parvenir à Charlotte qui se trouvait en Europe. A six heures trente du matin, l'Empereur est arrivé sur les lieux de son exécution, remettant à chaque soldat du peloton d'exécution une pièce de monnaie en or. Ceux-ci étaient impressionnés par le port et la sérénité de l'empereur qui a déclaré devant le peloton :

« Je pardonne à tous et je demande à tous de me pardonner. Que mon sang, qui est près d'être versé, le soit pour le bien du pays. Vive le Mexique, vive l'indépendance ! »

Juste avant la fusillade il s'est exclamé : « Charlotte, ma pauvre Charlotte ! »

La résistance offerte en Querétaro a été symbolique et une erreur du propre Maximilien.

Après l'exécution de l'empereur, Benito Juárez est entré triomphalement dans la capitale du Mexique, le 15 juillet 1867. Dans son discours au peuple mexicain, il a déclaré qu'une deuxième indépendance avait été acquise.

Lors des élections du 25 décembre de la même année, il a été réélu sans opposition, président de la République Mexicaine, fédérale et laïque.

Son mandat fut véritablement difficile et compliqué, puisque le pays était sorti déchiré de la guerre. Pour lutter contre les bandits, séquelle du conflit, il a réorganisé l'armée et réformé les pouvoirs de l'Etat Fédéral.

Benito Juárez est mort soudainement le 18 juillet 1872.

L'impératrice Charlotte Marie, après l'exécution de son mari, a vu s'aggraver son état de démence, dont elle avait déjà accusé des signes clairs et annonciateurs. Elle qui avait insisté pour que son mari n'abdique pas, a parcouru l'Europe en quête d'appuis, rencontrant en premier lieu Napoléon III, mais celui-ci avait déjà décidé de rapatrier son armée, pour de puissantes raisons : la pression nord-américaine et la menace grandissante de la Prusse. L'impératrice a cherché aussi l'appui ecclésiastique mais le Pape lui a refusé son aide. Désespérée, elle est tombée malade et n'est pas retournée au Mexique. Montrant de graves symptômes de folie, elle s'est réfugiée dans le palais de Miramar, en Autriche. Plus tard elle sera transférée en Belgique ; dans ce pays elle a eu connaissance de l'exécution de Maximilien et y est morte en 1927, survivant à son mari pendant soixante ans et ayant perdu complètement la raison.

Tant Maximilien que Charlotte constituent un cas complètement paradoxal. Ils s'aimaient, c'était au moins ce qui semblait établi. Cependant, dès la première époque, avant d'embarquer sur le *Novara* à destination du Mexique, ils n'avaient plus de vie maritale ni cohabitaient. On raconte que d'innombrables écarts amoureux ont ponctué tout le séjour de l'empereur au Mexique, mais aucune de ces aventures amoureuses n'a eu de conséquences dans une cour impériale qui, comme toutes, vivait entre pudeurs et potins.

C'est de cette forme tragique que s'est terminé le rêve de Napoléon III d'étendre l'influence française en Amérique pour limiter la force anglo-saxonne dans cette partie du monde. Mais Napoléon a commis de graves erreurs à caractère politique : il a parié en une victoire des confédérés dans la guerre de sécession nord-américaine et a placé un étranger sur le trône du Mexique. L'empereur des Français n'a pas réalisé suffisamment que les Américains du nord n'allaient pas renoncer, en aucun cas, à l'application de la doctrine Monroe, établie par le président qui lui a donné son nom en 1823, proclamant que le continent américain n'était plus un territoire destiné à la colonisation européenne, « L'Amérique aux Américains ». La doctrine en question, proclamait de manière retentissante, que toute velléité, de la part d'un pays européen, d'étendre son influence au continent américain, serait considérée par les Etats-Unis comme une agression à sa propre sécurité nationale.

De cette manière et dans ce contexte international, Benito Juárez a pu arborer l'étendard du patriotisme face aux envahisseurs étrangers.

Pour Napoléon III le retrait du Mexique a été le début de la fin. Le prestige du Second Empire a décliné après le désastre de l'aventure mexicaine, sombrant avec la guerre Franco-prussienne de 1870. En cette même année, le 4 septembre, Napoléon III a capitulé devant les prussiens à Sedan.

Pendant qu'il était entouré par les respectueux mais néanmoins froids officiers du haut état-major des forces ennemies, il s'est souvenu un moment de l'empereur Maximilien - de l'archiduc Max – et a pensé, avec une énorme mélancolie et tristesse, comme il s'était senti là, à Querétaro, trois ans avant, vaincu et prisonnier comme lui. Quelques jours après, Gambetta proclamait l'instauration de la République Française.

La fièvre jaune (vomito negro)

Pour les forces expéditionnaires, la véritable malédiction, de dimensions bibliques, a été, sans aucun doute, la fièvre jaune ou *vomito negro*.

Le *vomito negro* est une maladie infectieuse due au virus jaune, que l'on rencontre essentiellement sous les climats tropicaux tels ceux des Antilles et du Golfe du Mexique, et dont le vecteur est un moustique. La maladie se caractérise par une hémorragie du foie et des reins. Son incubation dure entre trois et six jours et ses premiers symptômes sont une fièvre forte et soudaine, céphalées, nausées, agitation, accélération du pouls, saignements du nez et soif intense. Dans sa phase d'intoxication apparaissent des vomissements de matières noires, d'où son nom (vomi noir) .

Les symptômes peuvent diminuer, mais la mort peut survenir au quinzième jour, précédée de coma lié à des lésions hépatiques et hémorragies importantes.

Les malades sont traités avec de l'huile d'olive et cataplasmes de boue, qu'on leur applique sur les jambes. Un traitement vraiment peu efficace.

La mortalité atteint les environs de 50% parmi les infectés pendant une épidémie. Les cas isolés subissent une mortalité de l'ordre de 5 à 7%.

Ce qui explique que l'épidémie de fièvre jaune, qui décimait des unités complètes, était la première cause de mortalité parmi les troupes du corps expéditionnaire français. La deuxième étaient les désertions et la troisième les morts à l'ennemi. Il transparaît dans le livre de Douglas Porch, par la bouche du légionnaire Charles Zédé, qu'en 1863, un tiers des effectifs de la Légion disparaît pour cette raison. Encore pire, l'officier Diesbach de Tornay avance des pertes encore plus élevées : sa compagnie forte de cent vingt-quatre hommes se voit réduite à vingt-cinq légionnaires.

CHAPITRE III

LE SIEGE

A environ 9h40 du matin, le 30 avril 1863.

La compagnie s'organise à l'intérieur de l'enceinte, regroupant le gros de l'unité dans la masure à moitié ruinée, située contre le mur sud. A quelques mètres de l'angle sud-est une brèche est gardée par une escouade. Soudain, ils sont surpris par des coups de feu venus de la bâtisse principale accolée au mur nord. Sa façade donne sur le sud du Camino Real et, dans l'aile ouest de l'édifice, se trouve une vaste salle qui malheureusement ne comporte pas de porte de communication avec la cour, seulement une fenêtre qu'une escouade se charge de couvrir.

Subrepticement, quelques soldats mexicains ont réussi à s'introduire dans la bâtisse et là, depuis l'étage supérieur, ils harcèlent les hommes de Danjou. Celui-ci commande immédiatement un assaut, mais, en voyant le rideau de feu produit par les troupes mexicaines équipées de fusils Spencer et Sharp, d'origine nord-américaine, qui se chargent par la culasse avec un chargeur de trois cartouches, il reconsidère la situation et envoie dix légionnaires commandés par le sergent-major Henri Tonel, occuper une salle située au nord-est, au rez-de-chaussée du bâtiment, la seule qui possède une fenêtre ouvrant sur la cour.

Etant donnée la hauteur des murs d'enceinte, trois mètres, exception faite des légionnaires postés aux portes-cochères, la compagnie ne dispose pas de vues directes sur l'encerclement mis en place par les forces mexicaines.

Pour l'heure, le capitaine organise fébrilement sa défense et répartit son maigre effectif aux points névralgiques. Le premier portail est confié au groupe du sergent Germeys et du caporal Maine, le second est dévolu au caporal Berg (Alonso Bernardo fait partie de ce groupe), tandis que la surveillance de la brèche sud-est est confiée au sergent suisse Schaffner et au caporal Magnin, l'autrichien. Enfin, le hangar de l'angle sud-ouest est tenu par le sergent Palmaert, un Belge.

Après la course de retour de Palo Verde, Alonso a repris son souffle et son cœur retrouve un rythme normal. Il se sent physiquement mieux maintenant. Il se souvient des terribles marches effectuées en Algérie, des élancements et des courbatures qui lui raidissaient les jambes, de la sensation d'asphyxie qui étreignait sa poitrine. Chaque pas lui semblait devoir être le dernier et, au début, il prenait toujours du retard. Il savait pourtant que l'unité n'attendait pas et qu'en campagne celui qui restait en arrière se condamnait à une mort certaine sous les assauts des arabes… Entre eux, les légionnaires ne s'aidaient pas, et les vétérans eux-mêmes devaient économiser leurs forces s'ils voulaient aller jusqu'au bout. Et quand, n'en pouvant plus, la compagnie faisait halte, les légionnaires s'affalaient sur le sol sans même enlever leur musette car la remettre représentait une véritable torture pour leurs épaules meurtries.

Peu à peu, cependant, l'appréhension d'échouer avait fait place au désir de se surpasser, à la fierté d'être capable de marcher encore et encore en gardant intactes ses forces, de se sentir bien dans son corps toujours svelte, façonné par l'exercice physique.

☆

Le capitaine Danjou se trouvait à la tête de la 3e compagnie, appelé par son destin.

Les sachant atteints de fièvre jaune, tant le commandant d'unité en titre, le capitaine Cazès, que son adjoint, le lieutenant Guérin de Tourville, Jean Danjou, adjoint au commandant du bataillon, s'est porté volontaire pour partir depuis Chiquihuite, à la rencontre du convoi qui, provenant de La Soledad, se dirigeait vers la ville assiégée de Puebla.

Il avait alors 35 ans. Né le 15 avril 1828, il était le quatrième des huit enfants d'un petit commerçant du village de Chalabre, dans l'Aude. L'aîné, Philippe, était prêtre, le second, Jean-Baptiste, agriculteur et Lazare, le troisième, était ingénieur. Jean Danjou a commencé à travailler dans la bonneterie familiale. Mais un beau jour, son père a invité à déjeuner un de ses anciens employés qui rentrait d'Afrique, le sous-lieutenant Canut, qui servait dans les rangs de la toute nouvelle Légion étrangère. Cette rencontre sera décisive car sa vocation s'éveille ce jour-là. Jean Danjou a pris alors la décision qui allait engager son avenir et, en 1847 il réussissait à intégrer l'Ecole Spéciale Militaire de Saint Cyr. Affecté au 51e régiment d'infanterie de ligne, il y restera trois ans et, en 1852, rejoignait le 2e régiment de la Légion étrangère. C'est en 1853, qu'il perdait sa main gauche, en Algérie, pendant des travaux topographiques qu'il effectuait avec le capitaine Rousseau.

Il a participé à la guerre de Crimée et au siège de Sébastopol. Avec le grade de capitaine, en 1856, près de quitter l'armée, il s'est vu affecté au 26e régiment d'infanterie. En février 1857 retourné au 2e régiment étranger il a pris part à la campagne d'Italie.

En 1863, Jean Danjou est entré de plain-pied dans la légende de la Légion étrangère et de l'armée française.

Le sous-lieutenant Clément Maudet, compromis dans la révolution de 1848 s'est engagé à la Légion étrangère pour y trouver une sorte d'asile ; il n'était officier que depuis trois mois, mais il n'en était pas moins pour autant, à 34 ans, le plus décoré du bataillon, notamment décoré de la Médaille militaire brillamment gagnée en Crimée, et il était, pour cette raison, le porte-drapeau du bataillon.

Le sous-lieutenant Jean Vilain, ancien élève du Prytanée militaire de La Flèche s'est engagé dans les rangs de la Légion étrangère à dix-huit ans. Officier depuis quatre mois, il était lui-même fils d'officier. Lors de la campagne d'Italie, sa brillante conduite à Magenta lui a valu d'être fait chevalier de la Légion d'honneur à vingt-six ans. Il était, provisoirement, l'officier payeur du bataillon.

☆

Alonso observe de loin le sergent Morzycki. Un vrai colosse que ce parisien d'origine polonaise, fils d'un ancien officier de l'armée polonaise et vétéran des campagnes d'Italie et de Crimée. Le sergent semble sûr de lui et arbore même un petit air de défi. Alonso, bien qu'assez tranquille, note avec une rapidité assez nerveuse que la plupart des légionnaires de la compagnie, la moitié au moins, sont des soldats aguerris dans les campagnes d'Italie et de Crimée. Il croit que le fait que la compagnie ait pu se réfugier dans l'hacienda, est comme le signe, sans équivoque, que tout se terminera bien, accordant un plus grand intérêt esthétique et une moindre appréhension au nuage de poussière visible à l'horizon. Son heure, se dit-il, n'est pas encore arrivée.

☆

Chacun sait que l'Allemand Ulrich Conrad, ordonnance du capitaine Danjou, garde jalousement dans sa musette, une bouteille de vin en réserve. Le capitaine lui ordonne d'en offrir une gorgée à chaque légionnaire.

Un cavalier mexicain brandissant une énorme étoffe blanche, arrive au galop à l'hacienda. C'est un officier du colonel Milán, le lieutenant Ramón Laisné, de père français, et élève au Collège Militaire de Chapultepec. Il a vingt-deux ans.

Se sentant plus relaxé, Alonso glisse dans une sorte de demi-inconscience qui lui fait perdre tout intérêt pour le cavalier mexicain, d'autant que la nuit précédente, ils n'ont pas dormi plus de trois heures, ils ont marché trente kilomètres, ils ont tenu en respect, en formation au carré et par deux fois, les troupes mexicaines, et ils ont le ventre vide… C'est la voix tonitruante du sergent Morzycki qui le tire de sa torpeur. Entretemps, le Mexicain s'est arrêté à une dizaine de mètres de l'enceinte. Il s'exprime en français :

– Nous sommes plus de deux mille et vous êtes une soixantaine tout au plus. Vous allez mourir inutilement ! Rendez-vous !

Monté sur le toit, au coin nord-ouest du bâtiment principal, le sergent Morzycki transmet cette offre au capitaine Danjou, qui le charge de répondre :

– Dites-lui que nous avons des cartouches et que nous ne nous rendrons pas !

La main gauche du capitaine, en bois poli, miroite sous le soleil déjà brûlant.

Après avoir entendu la réponse transmise par le sergent de la part de son capitaine, il hausse les épaules et, faisant demi-tour, repart au galop.

☆

Les pantalons et les guêtres de toile blanc-cassé, trempés de sueur, virent au beige. Discrètement, pour ne pas encourir de remarques de la part des gradés, les vareuses bleues sont déboutonnées. Seuls les képis avec leurs couvre-nuques restent vissés sur les têtes.

La chaleur devient accablante et Morzycki, sur son toit, est l'un des premiers à en souffrir. Mais le spectacle qu'il a soudain sous les yeux et qui le laisse pantelant n'est pas un mirage : ce sont plus de huit cents cavaliers mexicains qui s'approchent de l'hacienda, auréolés de poussière…

Danjou commence à donner ses ordres, non sans une certaine surexcitation qui ne passe pas inaperçue à l'Espagnol qui, pour chasser son trouble et se donner une contenance, vérifie en professionnel le chargement de son fusil Minié et l'énorme cartouchière qui lui barre le ventre.

Il se met en position et évalue la distance qui le sépare du nuage de poussière qui s'approche. Le roulement sourd des sabots s'accroît jusqu'à emplir l'air d'un vacarme retentissant. L'Espagnol sursaute. Il a l'impression que cette masse énorme va les hacher menu, littéralement ; tout à coup, il peut distinguer parfaitement les silhouettes des cavaliers mexicains et, sans même avoir le temps de ressentir une quelconque sensation de frayeur provoquée par cette onde tonitruante de mort, il entend des ordres en français qui se transmettent par cris successifs.

– En joue !
– Feu !

Assourdis par les déflagrations de leurs propres armes, les légionnaires sont aussi aveuglés pendant quelques instants par la poussière. Quand le nuage commence à se dissiper, ils voient les premiers corps gisant sur le sol et les mouvements désordonnés des chevaux qui galopent sans cavaliers. Certains tournent en rond avec leurs montures afin d'éviter qu'elles ne s'emballent ; d'autres encore, se relèvent et trébuchent maladroitement, encore tout étourdis par leur chute de cheval.

Les notes cuivrées du clairon s'assourdissent, moins distinctes, indiquant aux Français que l'ennemi s'éloigne vers l'ouest du côté des deux portes-cochères. Mais au sud, un petit groupe d'assaillants a réussi à escalader le mur et à grimper sur le toit des hangars. Arrachant la toiture de paille, ils font feu sur les défenseurs et le combat tourne rapidement au corps à corps.

– Chargez !

Les cris tumultueux reprennent de plus belle ; Alonso se sent comme tiré d'un rêve très léger. Pendant ce temps le capitaine fait le tour des légionnaires, les dévisage un à un, sans leur parler.

☆

La compagnie est déployée en divers points de l'hacienda. Au rez-de-chaussée du bâtiment principal les dix légionnaires sous les ordres du sergent-major Henri Tonel tentent toujours de contenir l'ennemi infiltré à l'étage supérieur. Entre les deux portes-cochères du mur ouest se dresse un hangar à moitié détruit occupé par un autre détachement duquel l'Espagnol fait partie. Enfin, le contingent principal occupe la remise découverte de l'angle sud-ouest et l'écurie en ruines du mur sud.

La cavalerie mexicaine se retire au galop. Les cavaliers démontés courent à l'arrière de leur dispositif et les blessés se démènent avec des mouvements saccadés de pantins disloqués, offrant un spectacle pathétique. C'est ce que voit Alonso, bien que dans les deux hangars du mur sud, quelques attaquants ont réussi à escalader le mur et, tirent sur les défenseurs par les ouvertures pratiquées dans les toits dont ils se sont rendus maîtres.

Alonso a l'impression que des milliers de fines aiguilles lui piquent les bras : c'est la conséquence des gestes mécaniques, rapides et répétés, nécessaires au rechargement de son fusil Minié. Il est environ dix heures quarante. Il tente de desserrer sa ceinture bleue, par dessus laquelle est bouclé le large ceinturon de cuir dont la partie centrale est recouverte par la grosse cartouchière qui lui protège le ventre. Il se sent mieux quand il fait glisser la large bande bleu clair qui contraste avec le bleu sombre de sa vareuse sur laquelle il porte des épaulettes vertes. Son képi recouvert de toile blanche comporte un couvre-nuque cousu de fraîche date (c'est ultérieurement que les troupes françaises – y compris la

Légion – seront dotées de sombreros de paille, plus frais que les képis en feutre).

L´Espagnol est étonné qu'en ces instants, après la première charge, aucune pensée transcendante ne lui effleure l'esprit. Il savoure simplement le fait d'être vivant alors que la nuit précédente lui semble dater d'une éternité…

Vers 10h50 du matin

Ils ont résisté à l'assaut. Le poste d'Alonso, entre les deux portails du mur ouest, est la partie la plus dégarnie du dispositif de défense du capitaine Danjou. Mais c'est aussi le seul endroit d'où l'on a une vision plus ou moins claire de ce qui se passe alentour.

Les légionnaires des autres postes, plus vigilants en ce qui concerne les Mexicains installés dans la maison du mur nord, n'ont aucune idée de la marée humaine des assaillants, réalité méconnue dans sa véritable dimension. Alonso est sous les ordres du caporal Évariste Berg, le chef de son escouade, lui-même sous les ordres du sous-lieutenant Vilain. Le capitaine Danjou, qui s'entretient avec Vilain, balaie du regard les différents groupes de légionnaires et soudain s'écrie :

– Non, je ne me rendrai pas !

Jean Vilain lui répond sur le même ton :

– Monsieur, nous ne nous rendrons pas. Je le jure !

Le caporal Berg crie à son tour :

– Je le jure ! Nous le jurons !

Et, à la suite les uns des autres, comme un chapelet qui s'égrène, les légionnaires jurent de ne pas se rendre. Sans même en avoir clairement une notion de ce qu'il dit, inconsciemment, Alonso crie :

– Oui, je le jure !

Alonso, après la tension suscitée par le serment collectif, s'appuie contre le mur et sans qu'il sache pourquoi, le souvenir de Don Pedro ou Don Pedrito, lui revient ; un « fils à papa » de son village pour lequel il se sent tout à coup pris d'une haine féroce. Et il se lance dans un long soliloque d'insultes :

– Putain de ta mère, Pedrito, quel salaud et quel misérable tu fais, et que la vie est injuste. Tu profites de la vie, et moi je vais la perdre sans avoir pu profiter de la moindre des choses que tu as eues et déjà oubliées !

– On va me tuer si loin de mon village vert, de mes prés verts … Et toi, salaud, avec tes beaux habits, ta maison, tes conquêtes, tu te la coules douce ! Ce que j'aimerais être dans les bras d'une femme ! Je vais mourir, mais je ne veux pas l'accepter, Pedrito, parce que personne ne veut voir quand son heure est arrivée. Et moi, un miséreux du village, je vais mourir si loin de la maison, Pedrito, si loin de ma maison !

C'est à ce moment que les légionnaires de la compagnie Danjou commencent à réaliser l'énorme tragédie que représente la fuite des mules avec vivres et munitions. La dotation en munitions est de soixante cartouches par homme, ce qui suppose un total disponible de trois mille sept cent vingt cartouches. Plus de la moitié de leurs gourdes sont vides, et pas de munitions de réserve.

Se sentant mieux – et en tout cas plus décontracté – après cet accès de défoulement et de rage intime, l'Espagnol regarde pensivement les cadavres des Mexicains tombés devant la porte-cochère. Ils sont figés dans des postures qui prêteraient à rire si ce n'était l'expression de leurs visages qui parle à Alonso du tragique de la mort. L'un d'eux est couché sur le dos, les jambes repliées, comme tombé agenouillé, la mâchoire déboîtée, les yeux grands ouverts et vitreux. Sur son ventre, une grande tache noirâtre de sang séché dont les bords laissent voir la peau brûlée. Il porte un pantalon évasé garni de rivets métalliques et il est chaussé de bottes avec de longs éperons qui, étant donné sa posture, sont bizarrement dressés vers le ciel. Toutefois, de nombreux cavaliers mexicains gardent les éperons suspendus aux pommeaux de leurs selles. Alonso a du mal à réaliser que ce corps, qu'en son immobilité il voit comme un simple objet, a été un être vivant, éprouvant les mêmes émotions et les mêmes angoisses qui, maintenant même, l'accompagnent ; anxiété croisée avec d'autres pensées qui en ce moment précis lui donnent l'impression de n'être, dans cette bataille, qu'un simple observateur invité.

La puanteur des cadavres n'est pas encore insupportable.

Vers 11h00 du matin

Les légionnaires ont complètement perdu la notion du temps. Certains d'entre eux pensent qu'il ne s'est écoulé qu'une trentaine de minutes depuis leur entrée dans l'hacienda.

Le capitaine Danjou, pistolet dans la main droite, le bras gauche rigide, traverse la cour. À ce moment il croit encore que le capitaine Saussier aura entendu le fracas de la bataille et qu'il ne tardera pas à se porter à leur secours. En gérant bien son stock de munitions, il pense pouvoir résister encore deux ou trois heures mais ce sera probablement difficile sans eau et sans vivres. Il se dit, en son *for* intérieur, que les Mexicains ne sont pas de mauvais soldats, mais ils ne sont pas meilleurs que les Russes de Sébastopol ou les Autrichiens de Magenta… Son assurance et sa confiance communicative se transmettent à ses soldats. Comme d'habitude, il n'a pas enlevé son képi qui dissimule sa calvitie naissante. Sa fine moustache, soulignée par un petit bouc, accentue le sérieux de son visage, un peu congestionné par la tension nerveuse continue. Le capitaine porte une longue vareuse bleu sombre, boutonnée seulement au col, sur lequel brillait la grenade à sept flammes, symbole de la Légion, laissant voir son gilet à boutons dorés et son sabre accroché au ceinturon. Le pantalon bouffant, couleur garance[2].

La capitaine maniait le pistolet de la main droite. La gauche, en bois, restait à la vue de la troupe quand il levait le bras pour appuyer ses commandements ou lorsqu'il accompagnait par le geste les cris d'encouragement ou les menaces.

Danjou se dit que tant que les attaques seront menées par la cavalerie ils auront des chances de résister, et cette pensée lui apporte quelque réconfort, malgré la fatigue accumulée. Pour rassurer ses hommes et exorciser leur peur, il se déplace constamment au centre de la cour, allant d'un poste à l'autre.

☆

Alonso Bernardo est réveillé par une détonation, une seule, sèche. Il se tourne du côté où a claqué le coup de feu, et la première chose qu'il voit c'est son capitaine écroulé sur le dos. Le tir a été précis, en pleine poitrine. Alonso voit ses yeux grands ouverts, le regard surpris, la bouche entrouverte. Le képi a roulé quelques mètres plus loin, sur la droite du corps.

Il est 11 heures, et le capitaine Danjou vient de mourir en ce 30 avril 1863. Le tir est probablement l'œuvre de l'un des francs-tireurs embusqués au premier étage du bâtiment principal.

Jean Vilain, âgé de seulement 27 ans mais ayant un mois d'ancienneté de plus en grade que Clément Maudet, prend le commandement en criant, de manière quasi hystérique, qu'à partir de ce moment il est le chef de l'unité…

[2] La couleur garance des pantalons sera réglementaire dans l'armée française jusqu'au début de la première guerre mondiale. La grenade à sept flammes, provient, comme un symbole et un distinctif, des régiments suisses au service de la France en 1855, mais c'est en 1874 qu'elle est devenue le symbole officiel de la Légion étrangère. Actuellement elle est représentée avec ses sept flammes dont deux en retour et la bombe évidée.

Les deux flammes en retour sont la création du peintre Andréas Rosenberg, aujourd'hui disparu, et alors caporal-chef de la Légion, en Algérie (NdT).

Alonso reste absorbé par ses pensées en contemplant le capitaine ; deux larmes glissent sur ses joues, et le caporal Berg qui l'observe lui lance un regard affectueux, mais l'Espagnol ne pleure pas sur le sort de son capitaine mais sur lui-même, car dans le visage de Danjou figé par la mort dans une expression d'étonnement, il voit sa propre mort, si proche. Et il n'a pas honte des deux sillons noirs que les larmes ont creusés sur son visage sale et en sueur.

☆

Le colonel Francisco de Paula Milán pense lui aussi qu'il lui sera pratiquement impossible de venir à bout des défenses françaises avec les seules charges de cavalerie, et il décide de faire appel aux fantassins. Le colonel, alors âgé de 41 ans, qui est aussi le gouverneur civil et militaire de l'État de Veracruz, a pour mission de s'emparer du convoi français. Milán est parti le 12 avril de la localité de Jalapa pour couper le Camino Real reliant la ville de Veracruz à Orizaba. Dans la nuit du 29 au 30 avril, il bivouaque avec le gros de ses troupes à La Joya, dans une plaine entourée de collines boisées au nord du Camino Real, et envoie une unité de cavalerie commandée par Jiménez pour reconnaitre les environs.

Danjou n'est pas le seul à être mis hors de combat. Alonso regarde les corps de ses premiers compagnons tombés. Les blessés sont soignés par leurs camarades, qui récupèrent leurs cartouches tout comme celles des cartouchières des morts. Spontanément, sans attendre les ordres de leurs supérieurs, les légionnaires se partagent le peu d'eau qui reste aux rares chanceux qui ont eu le temps de remplir leurs gourdes à l'heure du café à Palo Verde.

Tous les sacs à dos sont posés à terre mais la tenue commence à se relaxer. L'Espagnol se défait de la ceinture bleue, accessoire qui sert à préserver le ventre du froid, tout comme l'utilisaient les paysans de l'époque, froid qui, en zones tropicales, provoquait la dysenterie. En déboutonnant sa vareuse qui se décolle de la chemise, il perçoit une bienfaisante fraîcheur sur le corps et constate qu'il baigne littéralement dans sa sueur.

L'ardeur du soleil ne donne envie à aucun des combattants d'enlever le képi. Les visages tannés par le soleil sont noircis par un mélange de poudre noire et de sueur.

Vers 11h40 du matin

Francisco de Paula Milán rassemble ses troupes. Aux bataillons réguliers se sont jointes les milices de Corcomatopec, composées d'irréguliers, de simples paysans qui flairent une possibilité de pillage. Comme tels, ils sont vêtus de ponchos, larges sombreros de paille et d'amples et longues chemises qui furent jadis blanches, mais qui ont pris avec le temps une couleur beige. La plupart sont chaussés de sandales, mais certains sont pieds nus. En dépit de leur aspect misérable, ces fantassins sont mieux armés que leurs adversaires, car ils sont équipées du fusil nord-américain Sharp, à chargement par la culasse et avec un chargeur à trois cartouches.

Plus de deux mille hommes face à un peu moins de soixante, soit un légionnaire pour trente-quatre Mexicains.

Le colonel Milán pense que le combat qu'il va livrer sera définitif. Pour cette raison, il ordonne de nouveau à Ramón Laisné de se rendre auprès des Français assiégés, pour leur proposer, pour la deuxième fois, la reddition.

Les Mexicains postés au premier étage du bâtiment principal, celui du mur nord, et qui sont heureusement en petit nombre, continuent de harceler les Français sur toutes les positions entre les deux portes-cochères du côté ouest, positions où les légionnaires sont le plus exposés. C'est là que se trouve l'Espagnol.

Si le souvenir de sa diatribe contre le gosse de riches de son village lui paraît maintenant ridicule, une autre image s'impose à lui au fur et à mesure que la tension nerveuse s'accroît, c'est celle de López.

Juan López, un petit Andalou fluet, originaire de la région montagneuse qui s'étend entre les provinces de Cádiz et de Málaga, avait atterri on ne sait comment à Oran, où il s'est engagé dans la Légion étrangère. Forgeron de métier, ou tout au moins sachant ferrer les animaux, il parle peu de sa vie antérieure mais est néanmoins de caractère aimable et ouvert. Cavalier accompli, il sait même débourrer les chevaux. Il se trouve actuellement à Chiquihuite et Alonso l'envie pour cela. Plus tard, López sera intégré à l'escadron de Légion qui sera formé sur le territoire mexicain.

Cependant, les souvenirs de sa maison, de son pays, de son village, du richard haïssable et haï, de la fille qui lui plaisait, tout cela perd de sa réalité, de sa force émotionnelle et s'estompe… Son subconscient lui souffle de se cramponner avec force à la vie. L'important – la seule chose importante en vérité – c'est son potentiel de survie dans ce monde auquel appartient López – et c'est pourquoi le souvenir de ce dernier prend le dessus sur tous les autres qui perdaient de leur importance.

☆

C'est la deuxième fois que Ramón Laisné s'avance au galop vers l'hacienda. Il porte le même drap blanc accroché au même bâton, et en son *for* intérieur il conçoit une certaine affection envers les assiégés.

Il arrête son cheval à la même distance que la première fois, à une dizaine de mètres du mur d'enceinte, met pied à terre, se dirige vers le coin nord-ouest et, toujours dans un français parfait, au nom du colonel Milán, il attire l'attention des légionnaires :

– Bonjour les Français !

Morzycki sort la tête. Le Mexicain continue :

– Dites à votre officier de réfléchir. Si vous vous rendez, le colonel Milán vous promet la vie sauve.

Ramón Laisné souhaite de toutes ses forces qu'ils se rendent ; le sang français qui coule dans ses veines l'y pousse, puis, au fond, il se sent un peu honteux, même s'il ne veut pas l'admettre, d'appartenir à l'autre camp.

Le sergent Morzycki, toujours en vigie sur le toit à moitié écroulé lui répond du tac au tac, sans réfléchir :

— Allez au diable ! vous, vos Mexicains et votre colonel !

Laisné qui a identifié le sergent, attend quelques minutes qu'un officier fasse son apparition. Entre-temps, Morzycki qui guette l'approbation de sa fanfaronnade, réalise qu'il a commis une faute très grave et il s'adresse au sous-lieutenant Vilain :

— Mon lieutenant, je me suis permis…

— D'accord Morzycki, d'accord !

Au fond, Vilain préfère que cela se passe ainsi, car s'il avait répondu lui-même, les Mexicains auraient pu se douter de la mort de Danjou. D'autre part, la légèreté du sergent lui a évité de leur mettre la puce à l'oreille.

Morzycki saute hardiment dans la cour et rejoint le sous-lieutenant.

Ramón Laisné fait faire demi-tour à son cheval et il s'éloigne de l'hacienda, cette fois au pas. À ce moment précis, il se sent triste, car il est sûr que les Français vont mourir. Sur le chemin du retour, il laisse traîner derrière lui le tissu blanc. Il n'y aura plus aucun répit pour les Français.

CHAPITRE IV

LA LÉGION ÉTRANGÈRE

La Légion étrangère fut créée en France par la Loi du 9 mars 1831, promulguée le 10 mars par le décret de Louis Philippe, roi des Français.

Paris, le 10 mars 1831

Louis Philippe, roi des Français,

A tous présents et à venir, salut.

Vu la loi du 9 mars 1831,

sur le rapport de notre ministre, secrétaire d'Etat

au Département de la Guerre,

avons ordonné et ordonnons ce qui suit :

il sera formé une légion composée d'étrangers, cette légion prendra la dénomination de « Légion étrangère »

La tradition d'emploi de troupes étrangères remonte à la guerre de Cent Ans, quand les premières unités de « mercenaires » sous contrat se sont engagées.

L'historien André Corvesier, estime qu'avant la création de la Légion étrangère, il y eut plus de deux cents mille étrangers au service de la France pendant la période comprise entre 1635 et 1792 (Suisses, Allemands, Irlandais, Ecossais, Belges, Italiens, Corses). Louis XIII, pendant son règne, possédait soixante-deux régiments de huit nationalités différentes.

Après la révolution de 1789, les régiments étrangers furent dissous à cause de leur fidélité à la couronne. Au tout début du siècle pendant lequel la Légion étrangère fut créé, les révolutionnaires durent compter avec les étrangers exerçant le métier des armes, face au manque de préparation ou au peu d'ardeur guerrière de l'armée de conscription.

Napoléon sera celui qui recrutera sans pudeur des étrangers de manière massive ; la Grande Armée qui envahit la Russie comprenait presque un tiers de troupes étrangères, parmi lesquelles se trouvait, notamment, une unité espagnole, formée en grande partie d'hommes faits prisonniers pendant la campagne du Danemark.

Pendant la Restauration, le 16 décembre 1814, le roi Louis XVIII promulgua une ordonnance, en son palais des Tuileries, pour la constitution d'un régiment colonial étranger, dans lequel étaient regroupés espagnols et portugais qu'à ce moment-là se trouvaient au service de la France. Ce régiment aurait été composé d'un état-major et trois bataillons.

Postérieurement, Louis XVIII créa une légion royale étrangère à laquelle adhérèrent les Suisses de la Garde, appelée, en 1816, « Régiment d'Hohenlohe » nom de son colonel. Ce régiment, après sa dissolution, constituera l'embryon de base de la toute récente *Légion étrangère.*

La loi et son décret d'application s'appuyaient sur les bases toujours d'actualité qui constituent l'essence même de la Légion étrangère : l'engagement sous identité déclarée par les candidats, et la possibilité pour tout étranger de s'engager.

En cette période, la seconde moitié du XIXe siècle, la France était devenue une terre d'asile pour Allemands, Italiens, Polonais, impliqués dans les révolutions de leurs pays respectifs ; ainsi que d'Espagnols opposés au roi Fernand VII et de soldats Suisses qui avaient été licenciés après la Seconde Restauration. Comme le précisa le Maréchal Soult au commandant en chef en Algérie en 1834 : « …ce corps est simplement un asile pour le malheur ».

Au début de sa première époque, la Légion était composée de sept bataillons dont les membres étaient regroupés par nationalités : trois bataillons allemands et suisses, un bataillon belge, un bataillon polonais, un bataillon italien et un bataillon espagnol (4e bataillon dans l'ordre de bataille). Cette division par nationalités provoqua des frictions entre les différentes unités, et fut supprimée avec l'arrivée du colonel Bernelle, en 1835, quand il décida l'amalgame des nationalités et l'usage du français comme seule langue de service.

La Légion participa à la conquête de l'Algérie en 1832, en luttant contre Abd el-Kader. Ainsi, le 4e bataillon affronta, le 11 novembre 1832, à Sidi Chabal, aux portes d'Oran, les troupes d'Abd el-Kader, fortes de mille fantassins et trois mille cavaliers. Dans cette première période, les Espagnols qui formaient le 4e bataillon, étaient en grande partie d'anciens guérilleros et réfugiés politiques libéraux opposés à Fernand VII.

Ils étaient considérés, grâce à leur dureté et à leur sobriété, comme d'excellents soldats, surtout dans les missions de reconnaissance et d'exploration. Dans la bataille de Sidi Chabal, les légionnaires du 4e bataillon, aux côtés des Zouaves et des Chasseurs à cheval, défirent les troupes de l'émir.

Dès ses débuts, la Légion étrangère s'imposa une discipline de fer pour couper court à toutes les tentatives d'insubordination et de désertion, discipline grandement aidée par l'effet psychologique d'exécutions très sommaires.

Durand la première guerre carliste, la Légion fut cédée à la reine Isabel II d'Espagne (1835-1839). Cette première Légion fut abandonnée à son sort et, le 16 décembre 1835 une ordonnance royale créa la deuxième Légion, qui s'installa aussi en Algérie sous Bugeaud, se nourrissant à nouveau de l'importante immigration européenne qui affectait la France, y compris l'immigration espagnole, partie de la diaspora provoquée par la guerre carliste[3].

En 1837 elle participait à la prise de Constantine, en Algérie. Le 13 octobre, le lieutenant Achille de Saint Arnaud, à un signal, avec son petit détachement, chargeait à la baïonnette et entrait victorieux dans la ville que les chroniqueurs de l'époque considéraient comme imprenable.

Lors de cette prise on tua, pilla et pas fait de prisonniers. Le lieutenant de Saint Arnaud terminera comme maréchal de camp de Napoléon III.

[3] cf. dans la bibliographie, la référence au livre *La intervención francesa en España (1835-1839)* par Emilio Condado Madera, publié en 2002 par Fundamentos Ediciones.

En 1855, la Légion étrangère intervient, de manière héroïque, dans la guerre de Crimée. C'était sa première expérience hors du contexte algérien – hors la parenthèse espagnole – et sa consécration comme troupe d'élite.

En 1840 un bataillon fut formé avec les réfugiés carlistes, exclusivement, après leur défaite de 1839. Gardant le chiffre 4 dans son appellation et atteignant un effectif supérieur à 600 hommes, la création de ce bataillon rompait le principe de l'amalgame des nationalités dans les unités. Cependant, l'existence de cette unité s'avéra un échec au plan militaire, échec dû aux nombreuses désertions et aux mouvements de rébellion[4].

L'oasis de Zaatcha se trouve à quarante kilomètres de Biskra et constituait, en 1849, le point le plus méridional de la pénétration française en Algérie. Le bataillon envoyé à la conquête de cette localité se trouvait sous les ordres d'une autre figure légendaire de la Légion, le colonel Carbuccia qui, après la découverte de vestiges romains à Làmbeze (actuel Tazoult), ancienne capitale militaire de Numidie, où était, autrefois, installée la légion romaine Augusta Vengerese, y faisait inscrire ces mots : « Le colonel Carbuccia de la IIe Légion étrangère à son collègue de la IIIe légion romaine ».

La bataille d'Ischeriden, constitua un autre exploit porté à la connaissance du public français, par la revue L'Illustration qui rapporta la conquête de cette localité algérienne le 24 juin 1857.

Ischeriden est située sur l'un des sommets de Djurdjura, à quelque mille mètres d'altitude. La localité fut d'abord bombardée par les zouaves du 54e régiment de ligne. Mais l'assaut des troupes françaises échoua de telle sorte, que les pertes sont très nombreuses et les régiments restèrent cloués sur place. Alors la décision fut prise d'envoyer le 2e bataillon du 2e régiment étranger.

[4] *La Légion étrangère (1831-1962)*, de Douglas Porch.

Alors les sacs ont été posés à terre et les positions Kabyles ont été contournées par la droite. Nous avons gravi la montagne, accroupis, en silence, sans tirer. Devant nous, le commandant Mangin avançait sur son cheval, il ne mettait pas pied à terre, c'était incroyable ; nous nous demandions comment un cheval pouvait gravir une telle pente, parfois il semblait sur le point de tomber en arrière mais il progressait. Les kabyles tirent sur le commandant, parfois des balles faisaient gicler les pierres devant la monture, ou cassaient une branche, mais le commandant avançait sur son cheval et nous avancions derrière lui... ».

Sans tirer un seul coup de feu, les légionnaires montèrent sur les tranchées, malgré un feu intense et menèrent l'assaut à la baïonnette. La position kabyle tomba.

En 1859 la Légion intervint dans la guerre d'Italie, et notamment à Magenta où le 2e bataillon était aux ordres du lieutenant-colonel Martínez, ancien officier carliste qui atteignit le généralat dans l'armée française.

Le colonel Martínez

Antonio Críspulo Martínez naît à Madrid le 10 juin 1806. Il commence sa carrière comme simple soldat en 1824. Nommé sous-lieutenant en 1838, il combat sous les ordres du général carliste Cabrera. Exilé en France après la défaite des troupes carlistes il est admis comme lieutenant dans la Légion étrangère et nommé capitaine le 10 septembre 1840. Martínez est blessé plusieurs fois au cours de divers accrochages pendant la campagne de Kabylie. Il est fait chevalier de la Légion d'honneur en 1847. En juin 1854 il débarque en Crimée où il se distingue, et est promu officier dans l'Ordre. Le 1er juin 1855 il est promu lieutenant-colonel au 1er régiment de la Légion étrangère.

Il participe, comme colonel, à la campagne d'Italie. Naturalisé français le 24 mars 1851 il reçoit les étoiles de général de brigade et commande la 2e brigade du XVe corps d'armée en 1870. L'année suivante il se retire à Toulouse où il décède le 21 décembre 1877[5].

La seule rencontre entre le colonel et Bernardo Alonso eut lieu au cours d'une revue de la garde descendante, peu avant le départ du régiment pour le Mexique.

Alonso connaissait l'existence du colonel et son aura légendaire, considéré qu'il était par tous, comme un modèle de courage et d'intégration à sa patrie d'accueil.

Dans la Légion étrangère il est de tradition que lors de la revue de la garde ou d'une section, un quelconque légionnaire puisse s'adresser à l'officier qui passe la revue, sans observer la voie hiérarchique ; c'est une manière d'avoir accès à l'officier de grade le plus élevé, pour lui faire part d'un quelconque problème. C'est une particularité qui n'est guère pratiquée dans les autres unités militaires. Les légionnaires s'expriment à grand peine en français, alors que l'officier les écoute patiemment, car c'est une forme d'intégration et d'apprentissage de la langue pour les hommes, et de connaissance des problèmes réels par les autorités.

De la même manière, chaque légionnaire passé en revue se présente à l'officier avec son nom, sa nationalité et son ancienneté de grade et de service.

Quand le colonel Martínez arriva devant Bernardo, un sous-officier lui murmura qu'il se trouvait devant un compatriote. Le colonel s'adressa en français à l'Asturien qui lui déclina son nom, son ancienneté et son origine. L'officier supérieur le regarda fixement et lui sourit, lui disant en espagnol, en guise d'adieu :

– Bonne chance, légionnaire.

[5] Cf. référence bibliographique plus complète en *Españoles en la Legión Extranjera Francesa,* œuvre du même auteur éditée en septembre 2009.

A cet instant, Alonso Bernardo se sentit comblé, fier de connaître personnellement un homme comme le colonel Martínez, devant lequel il se sentait impressionné et face à l'assurance duquel il trembla d'émotion.

La Légion étrangère au Mexique

En 1862, avec à peine plus de trente années d'histoire à son actif, la Légion souhaitait participer à la campagne du Mexique ; alors, une délégation d'officiers s'affranchissant allègrement de la voie hiérarchique, s'adressa directement à l'Empereur, pour solliciter ce départ. Napoléon III accéda à cette demande, après consultation de son ministre de la Guerre, le maréchal Vaillant ; ainsi, deux bataillons furent formés comptant un total de sept compagnies dont une compagnie d'appui. Une Musique militaire complétait le dispositif. Néanmoins, discipline obligeant, l'officier le plus ancien dans chaque grade fut mis aux arrêts pour non-respect de la voie hiérarchique.

La campagne du Mexique allait assurer la survie de la Légion. Le 1er régiment étranger fut dissous et seul le 2e perdura pour devenir le Régiment étranger, seul régiment de Légion. Le 16 décembre, les engagements au titre du régiment étranger (ex 2e) étaient suspendus et, à la fin du même mois, une note ministérielle autorisait les étrangers ayant accompli une année de service au titre du contrat souscrit pour deux ans, à quitter le service actif et rejoindre la vie civile s'ils le désiraient. Mais dès le 22 mars 1864 les engagements reprenaient.

Les deux bataillons quittèrent Sidi Bel Abbès les 27 et 28 janvier 1863, pour Mers el-Kébir pour y terminer leur préparation.

Le 7 février, le général Deligny passait en revue les deux bataillons au cours d'une prise d'armes, et rappelait au régiment ses gloires passées en exhortant les légionnaires à y rester fidèles en ayant un comportement tout fait de courage et d'honneur.

Alonso Bernardo était sur les rangs et plus qu'au garde-à-vous, il était figé. Dans ce contexte et malgré ses connaissances élémentaires de la langue, il comprenait ce que le général leur disait. Il transpirait et avait l'estomac noué ; cela il le devait à la tension nerveuse dans la perspective du voyage qui les attendait et qui les conduisait à la guerre. Sur le moment il se surprit à penser que jamais il n'envisagea que son destin le conduirait un jour vers le continent américain.

L'Espagnol mesurait un mètre soixante-huit, pesait soixante kilos, portait une fine moustache et une barbiche au menton. Il se souvenait, avec une certaine nostalgie, de ses premiers temps de service, des longues périodes de travail à l'air libre, ouvrant des pistes, réparant des routes, en uniforme de toile, sans buffleterie et sans armes, participant même à la réparation de maisons de familles civiles, chose courante à cette époque où l'armée participait à l'œuvre de colonisation de l'Algérie.

Il était apprenti maçon, lui qui n'était, dans son pays, qu'un simple vacher, docker occasionnel dans le port de San Sébastian ou garçon à tout faire dans les bouges de Bayonne. Il pensait qu'à l'époque il eut quelques opportunités, alors que maintenant, dans sa condition de soldat professionnel, il devait partir à la guerre.

Tout en écoutant la harangue du général Deligny, il regardait ses camarades de dos et se demandait combien d'entre eux tomberaient au Mexique, combien en reviendraient et s'il serait l'un d'eux. Il essayait d'imaginer - tendu en ces instants par quelque chose qu'il identifiera plus tard comme de la peur - comment se déroulerait un combat, que pourrait-il ressentir lors de son baptême du feu, serait-il à la hauteur, serait-il courageux ? conscient qu'il était que son unité, le Régiment étranger, serait engagée dans les combats les plus durs, les accrochages les plus violents, les missions les plus ardues. Ses doutes ne concernaient pas son régiment, mais seulement lui, car il ne doutait que de lui-même.

Le 1er bataillon prit la mer le 7 février, suivi le 9 par le 2e bataillon au départ de Mers el-Kébir, pour accoster à Veracruz le

28 mars 1863. L'effectif du 1er bataillon était composé de 21 officiers, 761 hommes et 3 cantinières ; celui du 2e s'élevait à 27 officiers, 671 hommes et 3 cantinières. Le commandement du régiment fut confié au colonel Jeanningros, qui sera promu général au cours de la campagne. Pierre Jeanningros enfant de troupe, s'était engagé en 1831 comme deuxième classe au titre du 66e régiment de ligne alors qu'il n'était âgé que de 15 ans. Nommé caporal deux ans plus tard, en 1833[6], il participa à la guerre de Crimée où il montra d'excellente qualités militaires. Ayant accédé à l'épaulette, ce fut pendant la campagne d'Italie qu'il était promu colonel.

Promu général de brigade le 1er août 1865 il décéda en 1902.

Les deux bataillons étaient commandés par les chefs de bataillon Regnault et Mounier. Le premier effectua la traversé à bord du « Saint Louis » tandis que le deuxième embarquait sur le « Wagram », navire mis en service en 1833[7].

Chaque homme partait avec paquetage, équipement et armement complets et pour la campagne, un complément de trois chemises, trois paires de bottes, trois paires de guêtres, une tente et un bidon à eau de grande dimension. Tous ces équipements devaient être conditionnés pour pouvoir être transportés à dos de mulet.

Les deux bataillons étaient dotés de 37 mulets de combat ; 4 destinés à l'état-major, 28 pour les quatorze compagnies, 4 pour les services administratifs et l'infirmerie et 1 pour la caisse de matériel de l'armurier.

[6] En 1766, une ordonnance de Louis XV, réglemente l'engagement d'un adolescent dans chaque compagnie des différents régiments d'alors, en France, comme apprenti. En conséquence, comme évoqué dans le n° 721 du magazine *Képi blanc* de mai 2010, et selon la réglementation, les enfants de troupe ont été, régulièrement, incorporés dans les régiments de la Légion étrangère depuis sa création, bien qu'il y ait peu de références à ce sujet.

[7] Le *Saint Louis* et le *Wagram* étaient des navires à trois ponts, armés de cent canons, pouvant après quelques aménagements servir au transport de troupes.

La traversée s'effectua sans problèmes. Au large de Gibraltar on apprit à Alonso que la côte en vue était celle du sud de son pays. Il éprouva un désir quasi irrésistible de se jeter à la mer, de gagner la côte et de marcher, marcher jusque chez lui... il dut y renoncer, il ne savait pas nager !

Si la traversée se déroula sans histoires, l'embarquement ne fut pas de même pour le légionnaire Charles Zédé[8]. Le commandant d'un des navires, son frère, lui fit part de ses craintes d'avoir à faire une longue traversée ayant à son bord un ramassis de bandits tels que les légionnaires et de son étonnement de découvrir son propre frère parmi eux.

Les navires accostèrent, pour une courte escale, à île portugaise de Madère avant d'atteindre la Martinique où ils furent groupés, sous escorte, dans un fort, tant les autorités locales craignaient leurs éventuels débordements ! Arrivés à Fort de France le cinq mars, on leur accorda quelques jours de repos et ils reprirent la mer le onze.

Les premières vues des côtes mexicaines ne laissaient augurer rien de bon ; Charles Zédé décrivit ainsi ses premières impressions : « Une côte fangeuse, sans végétation, balisée par les épaves des navires coulés. A notre droite un îlot sur lequel le fort de San Juan de Ulúa tombe en ruines. A notre gauche, l'île « des Sacrifices », aride et couverte d'une multitude de croix qui montrent les sépultures de nos marins morts victimes de l'insalubrité de la région ».

Veracruz offrait un aspect déprimant, clairement renforcé par un accueil sec et hargneux, voire hostile, de la population.

D'autre part les légionnaires voyaient avec étonnement que c'étaient les vautours qui se chargeaient du nettoyage des immondices jonchant les rues. Mais pire que Veracruz étaient les terres basses tropicales qui allaient être le théâtre des opérations légionnaires.

[8] *La Légion étrangère* de Douglas Porch.

Ainsi, dans le livre de l'américain Douglas Porch, déjà cité, il est dit « que l'on confiait à la Légion la mission d'escorter les convois de ravitaillement le longs des très mauvaises routes, jusqu'aux plus hauts massifs, à travers de lugubres sous-bois ».

Le colonel Jeanningros aurait souhaité voir son régiment participer à l'assaut final qui devait mettre fin au siège de la ville de Puebla, mais l'état-major français décida de confier au Régiment étranger la mission d'assurer la sécurité de l'itinéraire entre La Soledad et Chiquihuite.

Le légionnaire Diesbach de Tornay consignait dans son journal : « C'est exténuant, nous manquons de nourriture et de vêtements. Nous dormons au pied des arbres, dans l'eau. Sous une pluie torrentielle permanente nous n'avons rien pour nous sécher et nous changer. Il n'est pas possible d'allumer du feu, nous dormons dans nos vêtements mouillés et au jour il nous faut nous remettre en marche dans les mêmes habits trempés. C'est un vrai supplice que peu de gens connaissent[9] ».

Le 1er avril le régiment prenait le train en gare de Veracruz, mais devait le quitter après huit kilomètres car les rails s'arrêtaient là... La Légion s'installa à Chiquihuite dont le fleuve marque la frontière naturelle avec les terres tropicales.

Vers le nord on trouvait un premier plateau dans une région au climat plus tempéré et dont la capital est Cordóba, située à environ neuf cents mètres d'altitude. Cette zone était occupée par des plantations de cannes à sucre, de caféiers et de bananiers ; sur un autre plateau, plus élevé, on cultivait le blé et le maïs à une altitude de quelque deux mille deux cents mètres.

Au cours des journées des 19 et 20 avril, le maire de Jalapa, Antonio Díaz, attaqua les troupes françaises et sortit victorieux de cet affrontement avec les légionnaires.

[9] *La Légion étrangère*, de Douglas Porch.

Mis en confiance par ce succès il provoqua un deuxième accrochage, mais cette fois les Mexicains furent battus par la compagnie du capitaine Duboscq, du 2e bataillon. Au cours de ce combat, le lieutenant Milson tua lui-même Antonio Díaz. Ce même officier d'origine prussienne participera, sous Bismarck, à la guerre franco-prussienne au cours de laquelle il combattit ses anciens camarades.[10]

Au début, on assigna des missions mineures aux deux bataillons de Légion, consistant surtout à escorter des convois dans la région la plus insalubre du Mexique, la zone tropicale qui s'étend de Veracruz à Cordóba.

En ces premières journées au Mexique, à mesure qu'il entendait parler des accrochages et du harcèlement dont étaient victimes les unités du 2e bataillon, Alonso ressentait, de manière latente, l'angoisse de se savoir en guerre ce qui dépassait sa fatigue de la vie en campagne. Jusqu'à ce que sa compagnie se soit installée à Chiquihuite, la tension due à l'idée d'un combat imminent ou inespéré, l'avait distrait de ses misères de soldat, telles l'humidité permanente de sa tenue, supportée des jours entiers.

Dans les derniers jours d'avril, le 1er bataillon à trois compagnies, installé à Chiquihuite, voyait ses effectifs très diminués par l'épidémie de fièvre jaune (*vomito negro*).

A cette date, le commandement ayant su qu'une embuscade se préparait contre un convoi qui était en route depuis Veracruz à destination de Puebla, emportant, entre autres, trois millions en or destinés à la solde des troupes qui assiégeaient cette ville, désigna la 3e compagnie pour reconnaitre la route et escorter le convoi.

[10] *La Légion*, de Erwan Bergot.

Les officiers de la compagnie étant affectés par la fièvre jaune, Jean Danjou, officier adjoint au commandant du bataillon se porta volontaire pour prendre le commandement de l'unité. Jean Vilain et Clément Maudet se joignirent à lui complétant ainsi l'effectif d'officiers de la 3e compagnie.

L'effectif théorique de cette unité était de 105 hommes, mais le 29 avril 1863, seuls 62 étaient disponibles, auxquels venaient s'ajouter les trois officiers.

☆

Les sous-officiers étaient au nombre de cinq. Le sergent-major Henri Tonel venait de Soissons dans l'Aisne où il naquit le 15 mars 1831 ; c'était un lignard, c'est-à-dire un sous-officier venant de la *régulière*, très compétent, reconnu en outre pour ses qualités de comédien qui divertirent la troupe pendant la traversée de l'Atlantique sur le *Saint Louis,* en créant une pièce de théâtre de boulevard : *Une chambre à deux lits.*

Le sergent Louis Morzycki, français d'origine polonaise, naissait le 5 janvier 1840, et venait de Clayette en Saône-et-Loire.

Le sergent Charles Shaffner, suisse de Berne, naissait le 26 novembre 1831, se fit une réputation de bravoure pendant la campagne d'Italie.

Le sergent Alfred Palmaert venait, lui, d'Anvers, en Belgique où il naquit le 3 mars 1842 et enfin un autre Belge, Jean Germeys, né à Saint Trond le 11 mars 1832, grand gaillard d'un mètre quatre-vingts, doué pour l'effort physique, qui se distingua en Crimée où il fut décoré, puis en Italie où il reçut une blessure.

Les caporaux étaient six.

Le caporal Louis Maine avait trente ans. Engagé à dix-huit ans au 1er régiment de zouaves, il obtint ses galons en Crimée, puis ceux de sergent durant la même campagne. Il était l'un des légionnaires qui plantèrent le drapeau vert sur la tour de Malakoff, ce qui lui valut d'être fait chevalier de la Légion d'honneur. Ensuite il devenait Chasseur, mais, en 1863 il s'engageait à la

Légion étrangère pour pouvoir partir au Mexique renonçant à son grade de sergent et partant comme simple légionnaire avec ses insignes de la Légion d'honneur.

Le caporal Évariste Berg naquit au sein d'une famille militaire. Son père était officier de Marine et sa mère était Elissa Rollan. Il était le neveu de deux oncles maternels issus de l'Ecole militaire de Saint Cyr, l'un artilleur, l'autre fantassin. Garçon intelligent il était titulaire du baccalauréat de Lettres et Sciences. Il s'engagea dans la Marine en 1853 où il fut nommé quartier-maitre puis second-maître en 1854, avant de demander son transfert vers un régiment de zouaves. En 1855 il combattit en Crimée ; devenu sous-lieutenant en Syrie, une obscure affaire de dettes liée à sa passion pour le jeu, le fit se présenter un beau jour à Sidi Bel-Abbès pour s'engager dans la Légion étrangère comme simple légionnaire.

Le caporal André Pinzinger naissait à Landau en Allemagne, le 17 avril 1831. Comptant neuf ans de service il reçut, en Crimée, la médaille de la Reine d'Angleterre et en Italie celle du Corps expéditionnaire.

Le caporal Adolphe del Caretto naissait en Algérie, à Oran, le 26 décembre 1835. C'était un *pied noir* - nom donné par les algériens aux colons à cause des bottines noires que beaucoup portaient. Certains lui attribuent la nationalité espagnole, bien que son patronyme soit italien, faisant de lui le deuxième membre de cette nationalité à l'effectif de la compagnie Danjou. Il déclara, en s'engageant, être comptable de profession, ce qui laissait supposer, à cette époque, quelqu'un de formation supérieure, ce qui expliquait sa rapide nomination au grade de caporal, sans avoir effectué aucune campagne.

Le caporal Charles Magnin, très blond naquit à Gerics en Autriche le 4 mars 1843.

Enfin le caporal Ame Favas de Genève, en Suisse, naquit le 20 septembre 1837.

Les métiers que les légionnaires exercèrent dans la vie civile étaient des plus variés : ferronnier, employé de banque, doreur, relieur, sellier, valet de chambre, tisserand ou carreleur, boulanger ou, simplement, soldat… Il semblerait qu'il n'y eut que huit légionnaires dans la compagnie Danjou qui possédaient des antécédents militaires au moment de leur engagement. Parmi les membres de l'unité on ne trouve aucun légionnaire ayant exercé une profession rurale, telle que bûcheron, jardinier, agriculteur… signe que dans le monde rural européen de la moitié du 19e siècle il n'y avait pas de problèmes de subsistance ou de déracinement, qu'inciteraient les individus à quitter leur terre.

Parmi les sous-officiers il y avait ceux qui étaient étudiants (Morzycki et Palmaërt). Le Belge Germeys se déclara ferronnier et le caporal autrichien Magnin, employé. Huit des légionnaires se déclarèrent ancien militaires.

Du total des soixante-deux légionnaires du rang et sous-officiers seules sont connues les origines et les dates de naissance de cinquante-sept. De ceux-ci, seize étaient d'origine Allemande, des Länder de Wutemberg, Francfort, Berlin et Baden ; quinze Français, treize d'origine Belge, huit Suisses, un Autrichien, un Danois, un Hollandais, un Italien et un Espagnol. Des cinq légionnaires restants les patronymes laissent supposer qu'ils étaient Français et Allemands.

Dans le nº 253 du magazine *Képi Blanc, la vie de la Légion étrangère*, de mai 1968, un article affirme qu'il y avait cinquante-trois sous-officiers et légionnaires d'origine connue : huit officiellement Français et quinze déclarés Belges ; treize Allemands auxquels il conviendrait d'ajouter un Autrichien et huit autres de nationalité Suisse. En plus l'article mentionne deux de nationalité Espagnole, Bernardo et le caporal del Caretto, né à Oran, deux Italiens, le tambour Laï et Bartello (ou Bartelotto), né à Toulon, un Danois et un Hollandais.

Selon les âges, le centre de la pyramide se situe entre 23 et 30 ans, les extrêmes allant des quadragénaires à ceux auxquels il manquait quelques jours ou quelques mois pour atteindre 18 ans.

Presque tous portaient des moustaches, observant ainsi la mode d'alors, et les visages tannés, leur donnaient l'air d'être plus vieux qu'ils ne l'étaient réellement. La moyenne d'âge des légionnaires de la 3e compagnie était de 26 ans et de presque 27 en incluant les officiers. Chez les sous-officiers la moyenne était inférieure à 24 ans ; les caporaux, 28 ans en moyenne et enfin les officiers 32 ans.

Grâce à la connaissance des dates de naissance nous pouvons constater que le 30 avril, trois légionnaires n'avaient pas encore atteint leurs 18 ans :

Louis Lernoud né le 6 juin 1845 à Francfort (Grand Duché).

Jean Louis Timermmans, né le 2 août de la même année à Bilan, en Belgique, lequel, malgré son extrême jeunesse, déclara une expérience militaire à l'engagement.

Pharaon Van der Bulche, né le 22 décembre 1845 à Lille dans le Nord.

Sur la liste publiée par *Képi Blanc* en mai 1968 il est fait mention du légionnaire Reuss, né le 28 mai 1845, engagé à Strasbourg et tombé aux premiers moments du combat, qui, bien qu'ayant dix-huit ans révolus est l'un des benjamins de l'unité. Probablement le dernier incorporé au printemps à Oran. Sur la liste, le légionnaire belge Louis Stoller, né à Bruxelles le 29 septembre 1834, n'apparait pas.

Seuls deux quadragénaires figuraient à l'effectif de la compagnie :

Frederic Fritz, né le 23 novembre 1822 à Kemm dans le Wutemberg et Geoffrey Wensel, né le 4 novembre 1822 à Nettrich en Prusse.

Au total, cinquante légionnaires n'avaient pas encore atteint cinq ans de service et vingt-quatre d'entre eux comptaient moins d'un an dans les rangs de la Légion.

☆

Les personnels étaient de taille moyenne voire petite. Dix-huit légionnaires mesuraient un mètre soixante, minimum exigé pour être grenadier dans l'armée française. Les sous-officiers étaient les plus grands, ce qui pourrait laisser à penser que cela contribuait à l'avancement dans les grades ; parmi les sous-officiers et autres gradés, les Français étaient les plus petits ; ainsi le caporal Berg mesurait un mètre soixante-sept, le sergent-major Tonnel, un mètre soixante-quatre et le caporal Maine, un mètre soixante. Les plus grands de la compagnie étaient les Belges, un Wallon et un Flamand, mesurant tous deux un mètre soixante-dix-neuf. La taille moyenne des Français du 19e siècle était d'un mètre soixante-six et correspondait à l'effectif de la compagnie Danjou.

A la 3e compagnie il y avait quatre roux, alors qu'habituellement on ne rencontrait que huit ou neuf roux par bataillon. Quinze des soixante-cinq hommes étaient blonds et parmi eux, se détachait le Danois qui, cependant, avait des yeux marron. Avec des cheveux noirs on trouvait deux Allemands, deux Français, un Belge et l'Espagnol Bernardo ; les autres légionnaires de l'unité avaient des cheveux bruns[11].

Les descriptions réalisées sur les registres d'incorporation manquent de précision pour pouvoir établir des portraits de ces légionnaires, sauf en ce qui concerne deux d'entre eux qui se décrivirent eux-mêmes très bien. L'un déclara un visage rond, et des traits grossiers ; l'autre, un visage très allongé similaire aux figures des tableaux du Greco. Quinze sont décrits ayant un front normal, un nez ordinaire, le visage ovale et le menton rond, tous ont la tête d'honnêtes artisans.

[11] Képi blanc n° 289, mai 1971.

CHAPITRE V

LE COMBAT

A environ 12h10, le 30 avril 1863.

Après le départ de Laisné, les légionnaires restent en alerte sur leurs positions. La puanteur dégagée par les cadavres devient pénible avec la chaleur de la mi-journée et Alonso Bernardo remarque, déjà fatigué, que les corps gonflent déjà. Les relents putrides lui donnent des nausées, mais il ne vomit pas. Il n'a rien à vomir.

À cet instant, tous ses souvenirs se sont évanouis, aussi bien la rancœur des vieilles humiliations – quand il pensait aux richards de son village – que la nostalgie bucolique, telle l'image de la verte campagne devant sa maison. Plus rien. Le fait de se sentir vivant est quelque chose de si intense que sa perception l'emporte sur ses sentiments. Il ne pense plus, mais il emmagasine avidement tout ce qu'il voit, tout ce qu'il entend et comprend autour de lui. Il est vivant.

Au loin, mais de plus en plus nettement, le son d'un clairon se fait entendre. Quelqu'un s'écrie précipitamment :

– Le capitaine Saussier !

Mais les autres gardent le silence. Aux accents du clairon de plus en plus clairs se sont superposés des roulements de tambour. Casimir Laï a reconnu la sonnerie :

– Ils sonnent le degüello !

Le degüello (l'égorgement) avait retenti vingt-sept ans auparavant au Texas, le 6 mars 1836, lorsque les soldats mexicains de Santa Anna avaient donné l'assaut définitif au fort d'El Alamo, défendu par le colonel Travis et 136 volontaires texans. Sonner le degüello, c'est annoncer à l'ennemi qu'on ne fera pas de quartier !

Les bataillons de la Garde Nationale – celui de Veracruz aux ordres du colonel Rafael Estrada avec les capitaines Sámano, Migoni et Frías, et le bataillon de Jalapa sous le commandement du colonel Téran – sont arrivés. Le bataillon de Córdoba commandé par le colonel médecin Francisco Talavera se joint à eux. L'appellation des bataillons correspond aux villes où ils ont été créés. Au total, quelque 1200 hommes, renforcés par les irréguliers.

Le bataillon de Veracruz porte un uniforme gris à liserés bleus, le bataillon de Córdoba un uniforme bleu. Le bataillon de Jalapa est le mieux habillé, avec une vareuse bleue et un pantalon gris, un képi de coupe européenne avec une cocarde et un couvre-nuque arrivant aux épaules. Les officiers portent presque le même uniforme que la troupe, mais coupé dans un tissu de meilleure qualité, avec un liséré rouge ou bleu sur les côtés du pantalon, des manches de vareuse soutachées à la hongroise, des boutons dorés, des bottes de fine peau et un pistolet au ceinturon.

L'état-major de Francisco de Paula Milán regroupait toujours de nombreux officiers. Ce 30 avril, le colonel est entouré des lieutenants-colonels Francisco et Manuel Marredo, de Huausco, et des colonels José Alaya et Mariano Camacho.

☆

Peu à peu, un nuage de poussière annonciateur de mort s'élève du sol. Les troupes mexicaines s'approchent.

En premier échelon arrivent les bataillons d'infanterie Córdoba, Veracruz et Jalapa, plus les irréguliers de Corcomatopec. Derrière, la cavalerie mexicaine espère achever le travail qui incombe maintenant aux fantassins.

Au sud-est se trouvent placés les groupes Osorio et Escobar, au nord-est, les groupes Canseco et Jiménez ont pris position avec leurs bataillons d'infanterie.

Alonso est posté à un angle, genou à terre, pour voir parfaitement l'horizon par l'ouverture de la porte-cochère. La crosse de son fusil Minié est appuyée au sol et la baïonnette est engagée. Tendu comme un arc, la bouche sèche, les lèvres craquelées par la chaleur, il réalise qu'il n'a plus de salive. Il entend distinctement la respiration lourde et angoissée du camarade placé juste derrière lui, mais il ignore de qu'il s'agit : il ne l'a pas regardé au moment où ils prenaient leurs positions. Le silence règne maintenant à l'intérieur de l'hacienda, seulement rompu, à intervalles réguliers, par les plaintes des blessés, en français et en allemand. L'Espagnol regarde la folle course des irréguliers, leurs larges chemises, jadis blanches et maintenant presque beiges comme les pantalons des légionnaires.

S'ils sont équipés de fusils plus perfectionnés que ceux des Français, des Sharp & Spencer à répétition, beaucoup vont pieds nus, coiffés d'énormes sombreros de paille. Pendant quelques instants, ce spectacle pittoresque distrait même l'Espagnol, lui faisant perdre le sens des réalités qui l'entourent. Les milices sont toutes proches maintenant. Derrière elles, on aperçoit parfaitement les unités régulières…

– En joue !

À l'unisson et comme mécaniquement, toutes les armes sont mises en position de tir.

– Feu !

La salve est forte et sèche. Immédiatement les légionnaires rechargent leurs fusils par la bouche, avant que ne retentisse de nouveau l'ordre :

– Chargez !

– En joue !

Alonso effectue tous ces mouvements automatiquement, bien qu'à ce moment précis son courage soit émoussé. Toute sa vie défile rapidement dans sa mémoire en un soudain accès de tristesse qu'il voudrait surmonter, car il n'arrive plus à se concentrer suffisamment sur ce qui se passe devant lui. Mais ses gestes restent plus rapides que le cheminement de son esprit, car de la rapidité de chargement de son fusil dépend sa survie – et ce qu'il désire par-dessus tout, c'est se sentir intensément vivant.

– Feu !

Le nuage de poudre de cette deuxième salve se superpose pratiquement au premier.

– Chargez !

Les mêmes mouvements sont répétés sans être suivis, maintenant, de l'ordre de tir. Les officiers et les sous-officiers attendent que le nuage de fumée se dissipe pour évaluer les dégâts que la salve a causés chez l'ennemi et avoir une vision précise de la situation. Des Mexicains gisent au sol en très grand nombre, morts ou grièvement blessés. Le bruit de la fusillade est remplacé par les cris déchirants des blessés des deux camps. Sur le moment, Alonso Bernardo se dandine d'une jambe sur l'autre, étourdi par l'épouvantable vacarme des coups de feu et des hurlements qui fusent de toutes parts. L'un de ses camarades posté derrière lui est blessé à l'épaule. C'est l'un des benjamins de la compagnie. Avec une assurance qui le surprend lui-même, Alonso cherche dans sa musette une chemise et la déchire en bandelettes. Pendant qu'il lui applique le pansement improvisé après lui avoir ôté la vareuse, le visage du jeune légionnaire se couvre d'une sueur abondante. Il délire à moitié, balbutiant quelques mots en allemand. Alonso se demande s'il se souvient tout à coup de sa mère, de sa fiancée, de ses amis? Ou bien tout simplement a-t-il peur, une peur qui l'empêche de penser, précisément ?

N'est-il pas étrange que les deux légionnaires, si différents physiquement, d'origines si dissemblables, se retrouvent là, sur un autre continent, combattant sous un autre drapeau que le leur. Le légionnaire Léonhard perd connaissance et l'Espagnol l'adosse au mur se servant d'un sac comme coussin, puis il ramasse toutes ses cartouches et son fusil.

La soif est une torture et Alonso ne pense qu'à l'eau, seulement à l'eau, ce qui le distrait de sa peur. La seule chose qui lui importe est boire, boire de l'eau à en éclater. Il sent bien sa langue enfler ; il la passe sur ses lèvres desséchées et fendues, mais ne parvient pas à les mouiller. Il se souvient alors des cuites de Sidi Bel-Abbès, quand il était ivre à tomber par terre. Il se souvient de la rage de boire qui le saisissait, boire encore et encore les jours où il n'était pas de service, prêt à tout pour pouvoir continuer à boire. Maintenant ce souvenir lui fait un peu honte.

Les samedis où il n'était pas de service, il parcourait les rues de Sidi Bel-Abbès en se délectant par avance à l'idée de s'attabler dans une taverne. Dès les premiers verres il commencerait à ressentir une euphorie débordante, il perdrait sa timidité et ses inhibitions. Il parlerait espagnol avec le tenancier, natif d'Alicante, sachant déjà que tout se terminerait par une bagarre. On verrait quelques légionnaires vendre une pièce de leur uniforme, sans en mesurer les conséquences, pour boire encore un coup, peut-être celui qui les ferait s'écrouler.

Présentement, la seule idée de l'alcool le dégoûte. Il donnerait tout pour de l'eau, seulement de l'eau.

Et les femmes… Pour le moment il n'éprouve aucune émotion au souvenir des femmes. À Sidi bel-Abbès il n'avait aucun préjugé vis-à-vis des bordels arabes, il les appréciait au contraire. Mais les Allemands eux, montraient beaucoup de réticences à coucher avec des arabes ; ils essayaient toujours de trouver des européennes à de rares occasions où il y en avait en tournée dans la zone. Cependant, la modeste solde des légionnaires ne leur permettait guère de se livrer à des orgies, et les réduisait à un monde essentiellement onaniste, les cas d'homosexualité restant très rares. Approcher les villageoises se révélait impossible – et en manifester simplement l'intention pouvait être une source de graves problèmes. Dans les familles, les hommes « veillaient au grain » pour éloigner de leurs femmes, des individus au passé inconnu et peut-être abominable.

Alonso se dit qu'il aurait bien mieux valu qu'il tombe amoureux, qu'il ressente ce frisson intérieur qu'il éprouvait déjà au village, malgré son jeune âge, en présence de Maria. Il se dit qu'il aurait toujours mieux fait de penser à elle, une personne chère, plutôt que de s'encombrer l'esprit avec les détails mesquins et la routine de la caserne. Puis, il s'interroge au sujet de Maria. Pouvait-elle imaginer que ce paltoquet tristounet se trouve sur un autre continent et sur le point de mourir?

Il range les cartouches d'un camarade tué dans sa propre cartouchière de cuir noir, décorée de la grenade à sept flammes et que la boucle empêche de placer au centre du ceinturon. L'une de ses épaulettes vertes est presque décrochée de la vareuse.

☆

Le caporal Berg passe la section en revue car il faut mettre à profit cette trêve d'une vingtaine de minutes pour réorganiser l'unité. En passant, il touche d'une tape amicale l'épaule d'Alonso qui a l'impression que l'ex-officier n'a pas peur, et jusqu'à un certain point c'est vrai. Berg pense que cette douloureuse mais providentielle épreuve lui permettra de se racheter. Lui qui a perdu son grade de lieutenant au moment où il pouvait attendre une promotion, se retrouve comme presque simple soldat dans une armée étrangère livrant une très dure bataille. Il voit là comme un signe, une opportunité qu'il doit saisir. Il se dit dans son for intérieur qu'il doit constituer une pièce vitale de la résistance à l'ennemi, il le pense avec insistance et détermination ce qui lui évite de penser à la mort.

– Bernardo – il l'appelle par son nom – , charge le fusil de Léonhard pour l'utiliser après le tien.

Alonso regarde alors le jeune Allemand, qui fixe le ciel de ses yeux grand ouverts, sous la couverture protectrice dont il l'avait couvert, ce corps est sans vie. Il s'approche et, respectueusement, lui ferme les yeux.

De nouveau les gestes réflexes, automatiques, la balle introduite dans le canon et la cartouche glissée dans la culasse ; il est capable, pense-t-il, de les répéter mille fois, et mille fois encore puisque sa vie en dépend.

– Viens Bernardo, ne t'endors pas !

☆

Le colonel Milán est devenu hystérique. Il frappe tout ce qui se trouve à sa portée, y compris les hommes. Il lui paraît inconcevable que soixante hommes aient pu résister à l'assaut de deux mille de ses soldats ; il se couvre de ridicule en criant, sans réfléchir, qu'il veut voir tous ses hommes dans l'hacienda.

Vers 13h55

Le sergent-major Henri Tonnel sait que c'est une question de minutes avant que les Mexicains postés au premier étage réussissent à percer le plafond pour massacrer ces Français qu'ils savent à l'étage inférieur. Lorsqu'il estime que le moment est venu d'abandonner sa position, il organise la retraite en établissant un véritable mur de feu avec quatre légionnaires : Catteau, Furbaz, Merlet et Haller. Deux autres sont chargés, pendant ce temps, d'évacuer les blessés par la fenêtre ouvrant sur la cour. Au moment où le plafond s'écroule sur eux, ils tirent une salve qui croise les tirs des Mexicains, lesquels, et c'est surprenant, n'ont blessé aucun légionnaire.

C'est le moment que choisit Tonnel, qui voit distinctement les Mexicains dégringoler par l'ouverture béante du plafond, pour crier de toutes ses forces :

– Dehors ! Dehors !

Les légionnaires, sac à l'épaule, se ruent dehors sans abandonner leurs équipements. Ils courent en zigzag, traînant les blessés comme ils peuvent, poursuivis par les tirs des Mexicains qui occupent maintenant tout le rez-de-chaussée. Guidés par le sous-lieutenant Vilain, ils parviennent jusqu'au hangar situé entre les deux portes-cochères, après une course d'une vingtaine de mètres, et là, ils s'affalent, épuisés. Outre les affrontements, ils ont subi le harcèlement continu de l'ennemi qui occupait le premier étage, tentant sans arrêt de percer une ouverture pour pénétrer dans le rez-de-chaussée. Fritz et Rerbers, grièvement blessés, sont restés là-bas, se sacrifiant pour protéger le repli de leurs camarades. Presque cinq heures de tension permanente.

Alonso contemple la scène, muet devant la vertigineuse rapidité avec laquelle les légionnaires ont quitté l'abri, courant et bondissant dans les postures les plus insolites. Il a du mal à croire qu'une telle action ait été possible sous ce soleil de plomb qui les fait fondre littéralement. L'intensité de ces moments a fait perdre à Henri Tonnel toute notion de temps.

L'Espagnol remarque comment le caporal Berg félicite les légionnaires, mais déjà les troupes mexicaines lancent une nouvelle attaque. Elles se trouvent à quelque quarante mètres d'eux.

Le tremblement des jambes et des mains, la nervosité déjà ressentis ce matin, à l'arrivée dans l'hacienda, lui revienne. Cependant Alonso sent son esprit calme et serein. Il réfléchit de façon ordonnée et les idées ne s'entrechoquent pas dans sa tête, néanmoins son tremblement ne cesse pas. En fait, ce qui suscite chez lui cette forme de panique, c'est la peur du néant. Il préfère mille souffrances, se dit-il en son for intérieur, à cette peur de l'obscurité du néant.

Il maintient son fusil Minié en joue et ne cesse de viser, mais l'arme ne tient pas en place parce que ses mains tremblent de façon incontrôlée. Alors, il baisse son fusil. Ce geste paraît signifier qu'il n'a pas peur et même qu'il défie la mort, mais en fait il éprouve le besoin de cacher ce qui met en évidence sa panique : ses mains.

– En joue !

Alonso vise de nouveau, cette fois-ci sans trembler, tendu.

– Feu !

La première ligne de Mexicains s'effondre, mais une deuxième vague les remplace. La deuxième décharge des légionnaires se fait entendre. Ils utilisent, après les leurs, les fusils des morts et des blessés, augmentant ainsi la cadence de tir.

– Ils ont eu le sous-lieutenant ! Ils l'ont eu !

Le tir a touché le sous-lieutenant Vilain en plein front. Il s'est écroulé brutalement, sans même quelques secondes de répit avant de passer de vie à trépas.

Il est environ 14 heures 10, et le sous-lieutenant Vilain est mort. Les Mexicains refluent, impressionnés par le nombre de leurs pertes. Incrédules ils voient leurs morts entassés devant les entrées de l'enceinte.

Les sergents font passer :

– Le sous-lieutenant Maudet prend le commandement !

– Le chef c'est Maudet !

Clément Maudet, le publiciste parisien qui a participé à la révolution de 1848, se trouve à la tête de ce qui reste de la 3e compagnie du 1er bataillon du Régiment étranger au Mexique. Le sous-lieutenant, debout, regarde les foyers de résistance : le hangar du mur ouest entre les deux portes-cochères, le hangar en ruines du coin sud-ouest et le hangar ouvert contre le mur sud. La brèche proche de l'angle sud-est est elle aussi défendue par les légionnaires. Maudet, le visage fermé, se sent un peu abattu intérieurement. La mort à 27 ans, de Vilain, si précise, soudaine, rapide comme le coup de feu qui lui a ôté la vie, l'impressionne. Il pense à présent que Saussier n'arrivera pas, pour une raison qu'il ignore. Les Mexicains, qui avaient sonné pour une charge sans quartier, ne sauraient leur offrir d'autres possibilités de reddition sans faillir à leur honneur. Le sous-lieutenant pense que la situation est désespérée.

☆

Les Mexicains harcèlent maintenant les Français à distance respectable par de continuelles décharges de fusils. Ils espèrent ainsi remporter la victoire en accentuant la pression – l'épuisement de l'adversaire et le manque de munitions faisant le reste. Pourtant les pertes subies leur paraissent véritablement incroyables : une soixantaine d'hommes a réussi à clouer au sol depuis des heures une force de deux mille combattants dont huit cents cavaliers.

La fusillade est continue, et le colonel Milán ressent comme un affront personnel le fait que l'hacienda de la Trinidad soit toujours aux mains des Français. Il ne veut pas attendre l'épuisement de l'ennemi. Ce qu'il veut, c'est en finir rapidement et une bonne fois pour toutes.

Vers 14h50

Maudet essaye d'évaluer la situation et de voir de combien d'hommes il dispose encore. Il y a trente-huit légionnaires plus ou moins sur le pied de guerre. Tous les bidons sont vides et ils n'ont rien mangé.

Le nouveau commandant de compagnie ordonne à ses hommes de récupérer toutes les munitions qu'ils pourront trouver sur les morts et sur les blessés qui sont incapables de combattre. L'officier renonce à unifier tous les points de lutte. Chaque noyau de résistance devra combattre et se défendre comme un élément isolé.

Le sous-lieutenant Maudet s'interdit de penser. Le soleil est, à cette heure, tellement brûlant qu'il accélère considérablement la décomposition des cadavres, et une puanteur quasi insupportable se répand dans l'air tout autour de l'hacienda. Du fait du manque d'eau et de l'excès de transpiration, les légionnaires ont les lèvres desséchées et fendues, ils sentent leur corps tout poisseux de sel.

Beaucoup de légionnaires enlèvent leur vareuse sans que cela change grand-chose. Maudet, d'ailleurs, les laisse faire, réprimander des hommes confrontés à la mort au sujet de leur tenue est non seulement téméraire mais absurde !

Après un comptage précis, il s'avère qu'il leur reste à peine plus d'un tiers de la dotation initiale de trois mille sept cent vingt cartouches de la marque Wessler, celles utilisées avec le fusil Minié.

Alonso se débarrasse de sa veste et constate que sa chemise blanche est devenue grise par la transpiration et par la poudre brûlée qui s'infiltre partout. Jusqu'à maintenant il ne se rendait pas compte de tout ce qu'il avait transpiré. Il s'assied en croisant les jambes en tailleur, conservant son képi, sa chemise, son pantalon et ses guêtres, jadis blanches. Il garde aussi son ceinturon avec l'énorme cartouchière centrale. Il a placé son fusil en travers de ses jambes. À ses côtés, deux autres fusils chargés. Son regard se perd vers le second portail, celui qui est le plus proche du hangar sud-ouest.

Sur le moment, Alonso se sent étranger à tout ce tohu-bohu de cris de douleur, d'ordres lancés et de conversations presque hystériques. Il ne cesse de s'interroger : comment sera son trépas ? Que ressentira-t-il à ce moment de transition où la vie bascule dans la mort ? Quelle absurdité que sa vie… Naître en Asturies pour venir mourir au Mexique.

Soudain le cours de ses pensées change, et il se rappelle la froide humidité de l'église de son village, il se remémore le claquement de ses sabots sur les dalles de l'église ; il se souvient du curé grognon et antipathique. Il se souvient aussi de sa mère, très nettement mais sans émotion. Il se souvient d'elle reprochant à son petit de ne jamais se tenir tranquille.

Lui revient aussi en mémoire leur lugubre maison de pierre, toujours obscure, la cuisine éclairée seulement par la maigre lumière de l'âtre... et la tristesse... il se souvient de beaucoup de tristesse. Mais ces souvenirs ne lui disent rien. Ils apparaissent, tout simplement, comme des images intemporelles – tout comme l'image de ses deux vaches broutant placidement sur les pentes de la vallée. Il se demande comment certains pouvaient jouir d'une telle tranquillité alors qu'il était, lui, soumis à ce rythme démentiel de combat et de mort.

☆

Un beau jour, sans motif, sans aucune raison, il a préparé son petit baluchon. Déterminé à ne pas regarder en arrière, il a quitté son village et s'est mis en chemin. Il a dormi sous les porches, dans les encoignures, sur les seuils de portes, faisant des petits travaux ici et là dans les villages qu'il traversait, pour une miche de pain, parfois pour un verre de vin.

A San Sebastian, il a réussi à trouver du travail sur le port, aidant au chargement et au déchargement des bateaux de pêche. C'est en travaillant ainsi sur le port qu'il a appris qu'il existait d'autres pays avec leurs propres rois, leurs propres armées, des pays où les populations vivaient mieux que lui. Alors, un autre beau jour il a repris son baluchon et a traversé la frontière.

Arrivé à Bayonne, s'exprimant par gestes quand c'était nécessaire, il a trouvé du travail dans une auberge comme homme à tout faire. Parmi les habitués de la taverne il a rencontré des militaires, et c'est par eux qu'il a appris qu'il pouvait être lui-même soldat même sans parler français.

La nuit dans sa « chambre », un simple auvent au sol couvert de paille, garni de deux couvertures déchirées, avec un clou servant de portemanteau pour y accrocher ses deux chemises sales et son veston asturien, il se rappelait avec quelle envie il regardait les gardes civils en uniforme rencontrés sur les routes, leurs visages épanouis de gens qui mangent à leur faim, alors qu'il s'attirait leurs regards suspicieux. Il s'amusait à penser que, lorsqu'il serait soldat, il pourrait se payer tous les jours le luxe de manger à sa faim – et il serait probablement plus respecté. À l'armée personne ne lui demanderait de faire les choses sous les coups ou les insultes. Il se sentait ravi.

À Bayonne il y avait un Dépôt militaire qui servait aussi de bureau de recrutement de la Légion étrangère. Le sous-officier qui l'a reçu se débrouillait un peu en espagnol. Il a regardé Alonso de haut en bas, et son aspect, mince, sec mais musclé l'a décidé à lui faire signe d'entrer. Le bateau qui l'a mené de Marseille à Oran, la peur de la mer, l'impression si lumineuse de la cité oranaise lui ont laissé des images fortes et muettes qui se succèdent rapidement dans sa tête. Elles se superposent à la vision qu'il a des Mexicains et il vit cela comme un sentiment diffus, un état d'étonnement émerveillé presque permanent. Bien plus intensément qu'au moment du débarquement en terre algérienne, il éprouve comme l'impression de découvrir enfin la vie.

☆

Une fois encore, les troupes mexicaines montent à l'assaut, mais avec moins d'entrain, échaudées qu'elles sont par la résistance des Français. Alonso tire sans arrêt. Il distingue parfaitement les soldats ennemis mais cela ne l'impressionne plus. Il tire avec son fusil, puis tire à nouveau avec un deuxième et un troisième fusil chargés à l'avance. La proximité des Mexicains les force à agir rapidement.

Sans trop réfléchir, l'Espagnol et quatre autres légionnaires, le visage décomposé par la rage, se ruent en criant sur l'ennemi, à la baïonnette. Le milicien qui le voit arriver ne s'y attend pas ou bien n'en croit pas ses yeux : un européen fonçant sur lui à la baïonnette! Avec une moue de surprise plus que de terreur, il tombe embroché par l'arme d'Alonso.

Face à cette petite contre-attaque française, les Mexicains battent en retraite. Certains, notamment des miliciens, s'enfuient mais tombent sous le feu des fusils. Les légionnaires regagnent leurs positions derrière les barricades. L'Espagnol voudrait analyser ce qu'il vient de faire, mais son cerveau s'y refuse, il se trouve comme devant un blocage mental. Cependant, il ressent une sorte de fierté, il s'est montré courageux et ce sentiment le rend, au moins pour quelques éphémères instants, véritablement heureux. Lui qui s'interrogeait, il y a peu, sur la mort, il l'a vue de près sur le visage du mexicain qu'il a tué. Il veut vivre, il lui faut vivre, et pour chasser les idées qui tourbillonnent dans sa tête, il recharge frénétiquement les trois fusils qu'il a en compte.

En se démenant il constate alors que son pantalon flotte autour de sa taille et se dit qu'il a dû perdre pas mal de poids. Il resserre son ceinturon d'un cran.

Vers 16h45

La fusillade continue, mais la coordination ne se fait plus entre les différents points de résistance, cependant le hangar entre les portails, le hangar sud-ouest, le hangar sud et le devant de la brèche restent opérationnels.

Le colonel Milán est furieux. Les Français résistent depuis huit heures, jetant la honte et l'opprobre sur lui et ses hommes. Les Mexicains tentent d'ouvrir une brèche dans la partie centrale du mur est. Dans le même temps, voyant qu'un vent fort souffle de nord-est, ils décident de mettre le feu aux toits de paille.

Parmi les miliciens, Ramón Laisné découvre trois hommes qui savent tirer à l'arc : ils lancent des flèches enflammées sur les toits. Il recrute aussi quelques vaillants gaillards, tel le tambour Pablo Ochoa, qui accumulent paille et bouts de bois contre le mur est pour y mettre le feu. Mais Pablo Ochoa a tout juste eu le temps de voir s'élever les premières flammes qu'une balle le frappe à la poitrine, l'emportant dans l'obscurité de la mort.

Les toitures commencent à brûler avec de hautes flammes, dont le crépitement fait penser à des salves de fusil. Les légionnaires sont stupéfaits. Les voici en proie à une nouvelle difficulté à laquelle ils ne s'attendaient pas. La cour est envahie par une fumée noire et suffocante.

Mais ce feu est trop intense pour brûler bien longtemps, d'autant que les ruines donnent peu de prise aux flammes. L'incendie dure moins d'une heure, sans donner aux Mexicains le moyen de terminer rapidement le combat. Néanmoins, le feu leur a permis de renforcer certaines de leurs positions à l'intérieur de l'hacienda. Deux foyers menacent encore les assiégés, et il y a un réel risque que les bâtisses s'écroulent. Vues à travers la fumée asphyxiante, les silhouettes déformées évoquent quelque scène fantastique.

☆

Les Mexicains préparent un nouvel assaut. Alonso tousse à cause de la fumée, ses yeux pleurent, mais peu à peu il retrouve la vue. Les fétus de paille consumés voltigent en l'air, tels de sombres papillons noirs. Il est distrait par ces points noirs qui tombent lentement sur fond de ciel embrasé par le soleil, et il contemple la scène comme il assisterait à un spectacle. Il ne ressent plus la peur de tuer qu'il a éprouvé ce matin – il lui semble d'ailleurs que cela s'est passé il y a une éternité. Maintenant qu'il a tué un homme dans une lutte au corps à corps, il ne ressent rien. Il découvre seulement que la peur de mourir est plus forte que la peur de tuer. Il lui faut acquérir de l'assurance, il pense que les soldats expérimentés comme lui doivent survivre pour mener encore cent batailles, mais il ne parvient pas à oublier son angoisse du matin – et il sent de nouveau cette boule dans sa gorge.

Maudet est stupéfait. Comment ses hommes ont pu tenir près de neuf heures contre un adversaire aussi supérieur en nombre. Comment, à mi-chemin entre Puebla et La Soledad, peuvent-ils être seuls depuis neuf heures de combat, sans que personne ne vienne à leur secours. Avec de la peine plus encore que de la peur, il réalise que c'est fini pour lui, l'officier le plus décoré de tout le bataillon. Tout va se terminer dans ce petit hameau mexicain.

L'air chaud et suffocant qui vient des toitures fumantes est irrespirable. Il ne reste plus qu'une trentaine de légionnaires en état de combattre. À la faveur de la fumée, les Mexicains ont pénétré dans l'enceinte et ils occupent tout le coin nord-est. Ils sont à moins de trente mètres.

Vers 17h30

Tout à coup, comme s'ils sortaient d'un rêve éveillé dans lequel les auraient plongés la soif, la faim et la chaleur, les légionnaires du poste d'Alonso, sont secoués par un tremblement terrible : c'est tout le mur est qui vient de s'effondrer. Les légionnaires distinguent nettement les visages des premiers Mexicains qui apparaissent dans la poussière au-dessus des gravats qui continuent à tomber sur les défenseurs de la brèche sud-est, tenue par Pinzinger, Sergers et Gaetners. Ils chargent à la baïonnette, en essayant de rejoindre Palmaert, mais ils sont submergés par les fantassins du bataillon de Córdoba et faits prisonniers.

Le caporal Berg, posté au portail le plus proche du hangar sud-ouest résiste encore avec les légionnaires Zey, Brunswick et Conrad.

Dans la confusion de l'attaque frontale venant du côté est, Alonso Bernardo réussit, en trois enjambées, à se réfugier dans ce qui sera la dernière position légionnaire. Il se sent tellement vivant que cette sensation intense devient presque euphorisante. Il s'en réjouit, et pourtant il lui vient subitement en mémoire quelque chose qu'il ne comprend plus : un an plus tôt il aurait voulu mourir… Et maintenant, dans ce patelin perdu du Mexique, l'idée lui paraît complètement absurde.

Le légionnaire Brzynski s'était pendu à une poutre à une extrémité du dortoir. Inerte, la tête penchée, le cou empreint de la marque violette laissée par la corde, il ressemblait à un pantin. Alonso refusa de s'en approcher pendant que d'autres légionnaires s'affairaient à le dépendre. Toute cette semaine-là, la vie dure et routinière de la caserne lui devint insupportable. Il était triste, et l'alcool ne lui remontait pas le moral, le rendant au contraire agressif. Il était tenté lui aussi par la solution de Brzynski, dans toute cette absurdité où rien n'avait de sens, ni la misère de son enfance en Asturies, ni cette souffrance dans une armée étrangère, où sa vie s'était résumée à tout subir en silence. Désormais, sa seule idée était de trouver le moyen le plus efficace et le moins douloureux de quitter la vie. D'autres légionnaires l'avaient fait avant lui et d'autres le feraient encore. Cette idée le confortait dans une sorte de langueur. Son travail s'en ressentait et il fut puni de quelques jours d'arrêts.

Et puis après Brzynski un autre suicide eut lieu. Comme souvent dans pareil cas, il se déclenche comme une épidémie, par mimétisme. D'autres légionnaires, aussi abattus moralement que le Polonais, suivirent son exemple. Il y a rarement chez le légionnaire des états d'âme préoccupants : il essaie de s'accommoder d'une vie de garnison sédentaire et abrutissante et d'y trouver son compte. Mais un beau jour il voit comment un de ses camarades a décidé de quitter la vie et il l'imite, sans débat intime, sans aucune déchirure personnelle. Le plus facile s'est de se pendre.

Un matin comme tous les autres matins, alors que l'unité d'Alonso partait pour une marche, laissant Sidi bel-Abbès en arrière, le paysage algérien joliment éclairé par les rayons du soleil lui parut vraiment beau. Il termina bien sa marche, sans problème, et sentit que c'était cela sa vie, la vie de soldat. Il n'y avait pas d'erreur, mais peut-être seulement le désarroi intime d'être né si loin d'un tel environnement guerrier. Tout, dans sa vie lui a alors paru suivre l'ordre naturel et la logique des choses. Il s'est senti content. Il avait surmonté l'accès de nostalgie, le cafard.

CHAPITRE VI

L'ASSAUT FINAL

A environ 17h35, le 30 avril 1863

Alonso est posté, genou à terre, sous l'auvent du hangar sud-ouest de l'auberge, aux ordres du sous-lieutenant Maudet. Plongeant la main dans sa cartouchière, il constate que tout ce qu'il lui reste de munitions peut tenir dans sa main, poing fermé. Il refrène une envie irrésistible de se ruer hors de la cour, puis courir, courir… Son cœur fait un bond dans sa poitrine et son regard s'assombrit lorsqu'il regarde autour de lui. Il voit des silhouettes qui lui paraissent trop minces, des visages crasseux, laqués de sueur, des vêtements imprégnés de poussière et de poudre…

Et au-dessus apparaissent les Mexicains, maintenant parfaitement visibles. L'angoisse l'étreint, il a l'impression que tout est irréel – un bal grotesque, macabre et sans musique. Il pense que c'est ridicule, ridicule de mourir comme ça, à cet endroit.

Dans l'anxiété que provoque la certitude de la mort, il croit voir le visage de Maria. L'image ne lui dit d'abord rien, jusqu'à ce que ce visage frais de jeune paysanne lui sourie. Alors il ressent un bref frisson.

– Eh l'Espagnol ! Réveille-toi !

Il se tourne et constate que c'est la voix du caporal Maine qui lui adresse un sourire d'encouragement. Un sourire qui lui rappelle de nouveau sa mère. Après tant d'années, c'est la peur qui la lui ramenait, celle dont il ne savait rien depuis quatre ans, c'était la mère de son enfance, un visage jeune, maigre et indulgent.

Il commence à réciter le Notre-Père. Il se rend compte qu'il a pratiquement oublié cette prière. Il ne se souvient pas davantage de l'Ave Maria alors il répète comme une litanie : « Ave Maria, mère de Dieu… Ave Maria, mère de Dieu… » plusieurs fois de suite puis change pour « Notre Père, le Fils et le Saint-esprit… », qu'il répète inlassablement.

C'est tout ce qui lui reste.

Cette répétition le détend, l'endort, et il se reproche maintenant son manque d'attention et d'assiduité aux deux séances quotidiennes de prières qui avaient eu lieu sur le bateau pendant la traversée vers le Mexique.

☆

Un dernier foyer de résistance subsiste encore dans le hangar sud-ouest sous les ordres du sous-lieutenant Maudet, qui a rassemblé les légionnaires encore en état de se battre, ou tout du moins capables de tenir un fusil, y compris certains blessés.

Il n'est évidemment pas possible de soigner les plus grièvement atteints, ils sont simplement retirés de la ligne de contact et installés au fond du hangar. Si bien que dans tout le périmètre de l'hacienda, un bruit obsédant et monocorde se superpose aux cris et imprécations des légionnaires et aux insultes que se jettent les belligérants : les lamentations et les gémissements des blessés dont personne ne peut s'occuper. Certains regardent avec une fascination morbide leurs plaies béantes, évaluant le temps qui leur reste à vivre. Ceux qui sont encore indemnes les ignorent pour ne pas avoir à souffrir avec eux.

Les légionnaires ne disposent plus d'eau ni de nourriture depuis de longues heures. Leurs visages noirs de poudre contrastent avec les avant-bras et les cous restés très blancs, ce qui produit un effet irréel.

Alonso se surprend à regarder un blessé qui gît à terre, sans réussir à l'identifier. L'homme cherche à se lever sans y parvenir. Ce faisant, il appuie sur son aine, et sa vessie laisse échapper quelques gouttes qu'il réussit à lécher sur sa main humide. Alonso ressent une grande tristesse et détourne le regard.

Lorsqu'il était enfant, il aimait regarder, depuis une colline proche, l'église de son village, comme incrustée dans sa verte vallée, au pied d'un mont abrupt. Les maisons étaient disséminées tout autour. Il dévalait en courant la pente menant à la maison du Seigneur, qui lui apparaissait comme une forteresse de pierre. L'obscurité et le silence régnant dans la nef lui plaisaient, et il aimait la sensation de protection que ce lieu lui procurait. Sur l'autel, un crucifix. Quelques bancs en bois. Le fond de l'abside était en pierre nue, sans aucun retable.

Cette image lui revient fugitivement, bientôt éclipsée par d'autres, mais elle se maintient quelque temps dans son esprit, et il reste convaincu que c'est le souvenir de quelque chose qu'il ne verra plus jamais.

☆

Alonso, les manches retroussées, palpe de nouveau sa cartouchière avant de charger son fusil Minié. Il lui reste cinq cartouches. Il combat maintenant depuis presque dix heures. Les ennemis dont il voit les visages impavides surgir entre les nuages de poudre et les volutes de fumé sortant encore de la paille brûlée, lui semblent des êtres d'un autre monde. À côté de lui un camarade sérieusement blessé s'épuise en tentant d'arrêter le sang qui jaillit de sa cuisse droite. Mais ses tentatives demeurent vaines et il gémit atrocement.

L'Espagnol est si épuisé que de son cerveau ne jaillit plus aucune pensée et les images produites par son imagination se tarissent. Mais il se sent toujours intensément vivant, comme si toute la lumière et tout le mouvement de cette folle lutte meurtrière le pénétraient par tous les pores de sa peau.

Surgissant comme des diables d'un épais nuage de poudre, de poussière et de fumée, les Mexicains se ruent au corps à corps. La première vague est fauchée par la mitraille ; la seconde déferle sur la position des légionnaires. Alonso fixe son regard sur un Mexicain et pointe sa baïonnette sur lui Il s'arc-boute sur sa jambe arrière en prévision du choc. Mais il a senti comme le coup d'un caillou, sec, sur la poitrine. L'impact a été fort, mais pas douloureux ce qui l'a surpris. Il a le temps de voir le sang jaillir de sa poitrine, mais déjà ses jambes se dérobent sous lui, le noir se fait et il s'écroule sans même entendre le hurlement qu'il lance pour rappeler cette vie qui lui échappe si brutalement. Le Mexicain qui a tué l'Espagnol tombe lui aussi, l'accompagnant dans ce voyage sans retour.

☆

Il est 17 heures 40, et il ne reste qu'une quinzaine de légionnaires en état de combattre sous les ordres du sous-lieutenant Maudet. La cadence des tirs s'espace puis s'éteint. Le silence inquiétant qui s'installe dans l'hacienda rend les légionnaires perplexes. Maudet, Morzycki, Berg, Kunnaceck, Maine, Catteau, Wensel, Gorski, Constantin, Leonhard, Bertollo, Magnin sont encore debout…

Les Mexicains ont pris position dans la cour. Ils savent qu'ils n'ont maintenant plus grand-chose à craindre car les légionnaires sont à court de munitions. Ils sont si près que les assiégés entendent tout ce qu'ils disent.

Une voix tonne, qui fait taire toutes les autres. C'est le colonel Milán :

– Honte à nous. Comment une poignée d'hommes a pu résister à toute une armée ?

Il parle en espagnol, et le caporal Berg cherche instinctivement Alonso du regard. Il le voit alors couché sur le dos, les yeux ouverts et voilés, une énorme tache sombre sur la poitrine. C'est Bertollo qui traduit. Maudet est surpris par les qualités de polyglotte de Gustave, qui a appris l'espagnol sur le port de Toulon et qui, comme son père, est capable de se débrouiller dans toutes les langues parlées dans le pourtour de la Méditerranée.

Milán continue sa harangue :

– Les Français sont à peine une poignée, morts de soif et de fatigue. Nous devons en finir avec eux. Maintenant. Les tuer ou les faire prisonniers. S'ils s'échappent, vos femmes vous cracheront à la figure… Votre honte sera éternelle. Pensez au Mexique, à la patrie, à la gloire de nos armes. Anéantissez cette résistance, et le pays saura vous récompenser !

Plus de place pour l'espoir. Ils ne représentent plus qu'un sixième de la compagnie qui est entrée en courant, il y a une dizaine d'heures, dans la cour de l'hacienda de la Trinidad.

Les assiégés voient parfaitement les assaillants qui se déplacent autour d'eux avec une certaine décontraction. À l'intérieur du hangar on entend toujours les râles et les plaintes des blessés abandonnés à leur sort. Les légionnaires encore debout sont l'image même de l'abattement ; rompus de fatigue, visages noircis, yeux vides et orbites creusées par l'épuisement, chemises en lambeaux. Il ne leur reste rien à boire ni à manger. Dans l'esprit de certains, commence à se faire jour l'idée de la mort comme une libération.

Maudet regarde ses hommes et ses pensées le ramènent quinze ans en arrière. Il se souvient de l'époque où, vêtu de la redingote râpée, propre aux journalistes impécunieux, sa cravate noire à moitié dénouée, il courait plein d'enthousiasme dans les rues de Paris où résonnaient aussi des tirs. Mais au lieu de lui faire peur, ces tirs-là le stimulaient, de même que le rendaient euphorique les gorgées de vin partagées sur les barricades. À moitié ivre, il lançait en riant des slogans exaltés qui lui valaient l'admiration des parisiennes révolutionnaires.

Maintenant il sait qu'il va mourir.

Les corps de Danjou et de Vilain ont été portés dans un coin abrité et pieusement recouverts. Chez les Mexicains, les préparatifs de l'attaque deviennent frénétiques après la harangue de Milán.

Vers 17h55

Le détachement français n'a pas la capacité de tir suffisante pour établir un rideau de feu qui contiendrait les assaillants. Du reste, les légionnaires n'ont presque plus de munitions. Les Mexicains entrent maintenant sans risque dans la cour, pénétrant à la fois par la brèche sud-est, par le coin nord-ouest, qui n'est plus que ruines fumantes et par le portail auparavant tenu par le caporal Maine… Ils crient pour s'enhardir bien qu'ils croient les Français morts. Les Mexicains sentent la victoire à portée de main. Peu glorieuse certes, mais ils entendent bien en profiter, encore faut-il ne pas laisser sa peau dans le dernier assaut. Ils ont besoin de se stimuler et ils le font à force de cris et de tequila, de celle que le commandement fait distribuer de bonne grâce à ce moment de la bataille.

Les premiers coups de feu des assaillants retentissent. Les Français ripostent, mais le bruit de leur salve est dérisoire… Les légionnaires Magnin, Seffrin et Kunnaceg sont submergés par la masse des Mexicains. Gorski attaque à la baïonnette mais est mis hors de combat d'un coup de crosse en pleine face. A demi-morts d'épuisement, Berg, Zey, Brunswick et Conrad devinent plus qu'ils ne voient arriver les silhouettes d'abord floues, puis qui se précisent de leurs vainqueurs : grands sombreros, teint sombre, regards farouches… À la vue de cette masse compacte qui les encercle, les légionnaires épuisés, se savent perdus. Les cavaliers les tirent hors du hangar pour être à l'abri des tirs qui continuent du côté du sous-lieutenant Maudet et de son groupe. Saisi par les bras et les jambes, le caporal Berg est emmené sans ménagement par les fantassins mexicains, tandis que les cavaliers s'emparent des autres survivants qu'ils trainent derrière eux.

Impuissant à secourir ses hommes qui sont déjà hors de vue, Maudet ordonne aux quelques braves qui lui restent de tirer dans le tas.

Les assaillants ripostent, et Gustave Bertollo est touché. Le toulonnais est atteint en plein cœur. Le Suisse Groux tombe aussi, éclaboussant de son sang le vieux Wensel.

Au fond du hangar restent, acculés, le sous-lieutenant Maudet, le sergent Morzycki, le caporal Maine, les légionnaires, Wensel, Catteau, Constantin, Léonhard. Une décharge tirée presque à bout portant atteint Morzycki. Le sous-lieutenant se penche sur lui. Il le retourne et constate qu'il est mort. Fouillant sa cartouchière il trouve seulement deux cartouches.

Vers 18h00

Maudet donne l'ordre de charger à la baïonnette. Les fusils tenus à hauteur de la hanche sont braqués à l'horizontale sur l'ennemi qui n'est plus qu'à cinq mètres. Le sous-lieutenant se tient à l'avant les yeux rivés sur un horizon mexicain mais il ne pense qu'à Paris, la seule chose dont il se souvient, c'est Paris.

Les Mexicains font feu. La décharge est brutale. Le légionnaire Catteau se jette devant son chef pour le couvrir au moment où la décharge les assourdit et les aveugle.

Le sous-lieutenant tombe, la hanche ouverte et le haut de la cuisse droite fracassée. Il essaie de se lever, sent sa vie qui s'échappe et pense alors aux barricades, à la Révolution, aux parisiennes. Mais l'effort est au-dessus de ses forces, et il s'affaisse.

Dix-neuf impacts. Le corps du légionnaire Catteau a littéralement éclaté sous les balles.

Le caporal Maine reste debout, comme cloué sur place après la décharge, abasourdi et aveuglé. Il se sent déjà mort et se demande si la mort, c'est seulement ça : la peur et la cécité. Mais quand le nuage de fumée et de poudre se dissipe, il voit face à lui les mêmes Mexicains.

Se plaçant devant ses hommes, un officier mexicain du bataillon de Jalapa leur ordonne de cesser le feu. S'adressant ensuite, sans hostilité, aux légionnaires, il leur crie :

– Rendez-vous, enfin !

Derrière le caporal Maine, qui est Français, se trouvent Constantin, un Belge et Wensel, un Prussien qui laisse errer son regard absent, égaré. Il semble retrouver un peu ses esprits en fixant le cadavre d'Alonso, étendu sur le dos, le visage cireux sous les plaques de suie, le thorax couvert de sang.

Pour Wensel plus rien n'a d'importance désormais, tout lui est égal. Maine ne réfléchit pas, mais répond :

– Nous nous rendrons si vous nous laissez nos armes et si vous promettez de soigner nos blessés !

À ce moment surgit le colonel Combas qui déclare à voix haute, comme pour se justifier devant ses hommes :

– On ne refuse rien à des hommes comme vous !

Il fait alors signe au colonel Francisco Talavera, chef du bataillon de Córdoba et médecin des troupes mexicaines qui se dirige immédiatement avec ses brancardiers vers les blessés pour lesquels on peut encore tenter quelque chose. Se méfiant de ses brancardiers, qui tendent à se montrer négligents quand il s'agit de s'occuper des vaincus, le docteur Talavera s'occupe personnellement des Français et veille à ce qu'ils soient secourus.

Un poste de secours a été installé hors de l'hacienda, et le spectacle a de quoi faire dresser les cheveux sur la tête. Le sol est entièrement couvert de sang. Les cadavres empilés sont saisis par la rigidité cadavérique dans les postures les plus invraisemblables.

Des viscères, échappés des plaies béantes ou libérés par la putréfaction, s'épandent sur le sol, attirant des vautours qui décrivent des cercles dans le ciel au-dessus de ce lieu sinistre où règne un silence lugubre.

Le colonel Milán pénètre à cheval dans l'enceinte de l'hacienda. Il est stupéfait par l'abondance des flaques de sang sur le sol, par le nombre impressionnant de cadavres qui gisent encore un peu partout, parmi les havresacs éventrés, les armes brisées et les équipements dispersés dans un chaos indescriptible. Il ne parvient pas à s'expliquer les raisons d'une résistance aussi acharnée.

- *¡Pero no son hombres, son demonios!* (Ce ne sont pas des hommes, mais des démons !)

Il a parlé à haute voix sans s'en rendre compte. Le colonel observe maintenant les légionnaires qui se sont rendus et qui restent dans la même position menaçante. Maine est debout, le regard perdu, à peine conscient de ce qui se passe autour de lui. Constantin est debout, lui aussi, mais quelque peu en retrait, les bras ballants, plus épuisé qu'abattu. Un genou à terre, Wensel observe encore Bernardo, comme si ce corps inerte qu'il a connu si énergique allait lui livrer la clé des mystères de la mort.

Un bruit de galop, et tout l'état-major mexicain se fige. Un milicien entre à cheval dans la cour et décharge ses deux pistolets Sharp sur les Français qu'il rate. La monture se cabre et le milicien ivre a beaucoup de mal à se maintenir en selle. Le colonel Angel Lucio Combas, d'origine française comme Laisné, indigné par la conduite de ce soldat, l'œil chargé de haine, dégaine son épée et, menant son cheval au trot, tourne autour du Mexicain jusqu'à trouver le bon angle, puis l'embroche sans pitié. Le colonel Milán assiste imperturbable à la scène. Quand tout est terminé, d'un signe il donne l'ordre de quitter l'hacienda.

Wensel se relève, chancelle et hébété embrasse du regard le champ de bataille. Dans cette cour à peine grande comme une place de village presque une soixantaine de légionnaires et au moins le double de Mexicains aux corps entremêlés ont rendu l'âme. Le Prussien est abasourdi, il ne comprend pas comment tant de corps habités par cette frénésie de combattre sont tombés, les membres raidis, mêlés à ceux de leurs ennemis. Il avance lentement, à petits pas précautionneux comme ceux d'un vieillard, car son organisme lui dit qu'il est épuisé. Il est resté sans manger ni boire pendant plus de onze heures de lutte épuisante, de tension constante. Escorté par deux soldats du bataillon de Jalapa, il s'efforce de ne pas buter sur les objets brisés, dispersés partout.

Parvenus à une centaine de mètres de l'hacienda, les Mexicains font asseoir les trois survivants par terre sous le regard attentif du colonel Combas qui leur fait donner à boire. S'adressant à eux en français, il leur conseille de faire attention, de boire lentement.

☆

Bien qu'il soigne les rescapés de l'un et l'autre camp avec une rigoureuse impartialité, le colonel Talavera est néanmoins sensible au panache dont ont fait preuve les Français et il s'intéresse à la Légion à cause de son recrutement cosmopolite. Il s'est même demandé s'il n'y avait pas un espagnol parmi les survivants, mais, débordé par sa tâche, il n'a pas poussé son enquête plus loin, et n'y a plus pensé. Sur les trente Français blessés, quatre sont moribonds, et plus rien ne peut être fait pour eux. L'artillerie n'est pas intervenue dans la bataille, et le colonel ne se trouve donc pas confronté aux terribles mutilations provoquées par les obus. Balles et armes blanches ont fait des blessures nettes, mais beaucoup de blessés se sont vidés de leur sang et présentent des plaies béantes.

Le colonel Milán est effaré, tout d'abord, par le nombre des pertes mexicaines : près de trois cents. Puis il s'est ressaisi, et c'est désormais sans la moindre émotion qu'il évoque ce carnage. Il a toutefois fait le calcul suivant : étant donné que chacun des soixante-cinq soldats français a reçu une dotation de soixante cartouches, cela fait un total de trois mille neuf cents cartouches, ce qui signifie un homme tué pour treize tirs sans tenir compte des blessés par balle. Un score tout à fait remarquable.

Il remonte à cheval et passe entre les cadavres, qu'il scrute avec un œil de professionnel. Les morts Mexicains ont été pour la plupart atteints à la poitrine ou à la tête. Extraordinaire précision !

☆

Le caporal Maine voit arriver le caporal Berg et le reste des prisonniers sous escorte. Sans pouvoir se contenir il embrasse l'ex-lieutenant des zouaves.

☆

Les dernières heures du 30 avril 1863

La journée du 30 avril 1863 touche à sa fin. Les troupes mexicaines creusent d'énormes fosses communes pour leurs soldats et pour les soldats français. Auparavant, ils les ont dépouillés de leurs vêtements, de leurs objets personnels et de tout leur matériel. Les brodequins sont spécialement recherchés par une troupe habituée à marcher en sandales, voire pieds nus.

Un milicien s'affaire sur les chaussures d'Alonso. L'Espagnol avait dû attendre d'être à la Légion pour posséder sa première vraie paire de chaussures... En Espagne, toute sa jeunesse s'était partagée entre des étés passés pieds nus et des hivers en sabots. Aussi quand pour la première fois il avait chaussé ses souliers de légionnaire il s'était senti fier et heureux, car cela faisait de lui l'égal de Pedro, le richard de son misérable village.

Le Mexicain s'acharne sur ce corps rigide et glacé jusqu'à le laisser seulement en sous-vêtements.

Le tambour Laï est inconscient. Son corps qui a reçu sept coups de lance et deux balles semble presque entièrement badigeonné de rouge sombre. Il n'est plus qu'une chose inerte entre les mains des miliciens qui le dépouillent de ses habits. Ils ne lui laissent, à lui aussi, que sa chemise… Il a eu certes de la chance de ne pas succomber, mais plus encore d'avoir été l'un des derniers à être traîné dans la fosse commune, sur laquelle les Mexicains n'ont jeté que quelques poignées de terre, pressés qu'ils étaient de quitter les lieux.

☆

Cette nuit-là, Laï, qui se réveille enterré vivant, peut se convaincre que la mort est silence et froid. Froid de la nuit et des corps sans vie, rigides et pétrifiés, mais surtout gelés. Maintenant pleinement conscient et en éveil, malgré la faim et la soif, malgré les onze heures de combat ininterrompues, il ressent, abord, une intense panique à l'idée de se trouver au milieu des morts. Il gesticule frénétiquement, fait des pieds et des mains pour échapper à la mort, à ces cadavres. Il était heureusement tombé latéralement dans la fosse, ce qui va lui permettre de ne pas être étouffé par son propre sang ni écrasé par le poids des corps jetés sur lui. Un de ses camarades repose sur lui transversalement, à la hauteur de ses épaules, ce qui lui permet de continuer à respirer pendant qu'il est inconscient. Il réussit ensuite à s'extirper de ces corps sans vie, à rejeter le peu de terre qui le recouvre. Une fois à l'air libre, il essaye de se mettre debout mais n'y parvient pas, et il tombe exténué sur le sol, contemplant les étoiles. Il se sent heureux pendant quelques instants, avant de sombrer dans une demi-inconscience. Plusieurs heures s'écoulent, et la rosée matinale le fait revenir à lui. Il reste encore longtemps immobile. Puis, ayant réussi à se lever il commence à marcher et, retrouvant la route, il prend la direction de Chiquihuite.

Le corps jeté en travers de celui de Casimir Laï, ce corps qui l'a protégé, ménageant une poche d'air qui lui a permis de respirer, c'est – mais il l'ignore – celui de son ami Alonso. Le tambour n'a pas cherché à reconnaître qui que ce fût. Pour lui il s'agit de repousser l'étreinte de la mort qui veut le garder prisonnier. Et il y puise la force suffisante dans les réserves que seule la panique libère.

D'instinct, Laï suit le milieu de la route qui est suffisamment large pour sa démarche zigzagante et chancelante. Il marche sans se rendre compte qu'il est escorté par les coyotes qui voient en lui une proie facile et prochaine. Il n'en a pas conscience mais le saurait-il que cela n'aurait rien changé. Et il marche avec ses sept blessures par lance et deux par balle. Il avait sommeillé quelques heures dans les buissons, malgré la présence des coyotes à l'affût. Cette présence lui donne force et courage pour poursuivre sa marche.

La notion de temps lui échappe complètement, il marche, marche toujours… jusqu'à ce qu'il distingue au loin des silhouettes bleues. Mais cela ne l'impressionne pas. Cela lui est égal.

Plus tard, Casimir Laï, le tambour italien originaire de Sardaigne, de la 3e compagnie du 1er bataillon du Régiment étranger, est fait chevalier de la Légion d'honneur.

☆

Le 2 mai 1863

La nouvelle des tristes événements de Camerone est parvenue au colonel Jeanningros par l'intermédiaire d'un groupe de Mexicains anti-juaristes. Il s'est immédiatement mis en route dans la matinée du vendredi 1er mai 1863, avec les personnels de la 1re compagnie. Après environ une demi-journée de marche, il recueille la compagnie de grenadiers du capitaine Saussier, douloureusement impressionné par ce qu'il vient d'apprendre. Il se rappelle fort bien le capitaine Danjou, et il lui paraît incroyable qu'il ait connu un sort aussi tragique à peine quelques heures après leur rencontre.

Ce même 1er mai, à l'autre extrémité du parcours, le capitaine Cabossel est parti de La Soledad avec sa colonne, il se dirige lui aussi vers Palo Verde. Avec Cabossel, marche l'élément de tête du colonel Dupin et la 5e compagnie du capitaine Ballue.

Comme Jeanningros est arrivé le premier à Palo Verde, après être passé par Camerone, il a informé les officiers arrivant de La Soledad des malheureux événements qui s'étaient déroulés dans l'hacienda de la Trinidad. Ils s'y sont alors rendus ensemble pour rendre les honneurs militaires à la 3e compagnie dont les morts ont été enterrés dans une nouvelle fosse commune, près de l'angle sud-est de l'auberge.

Le mythe de Camerone, comme suprême exemple d'héroïsme et de respect de la parole donnée est né.

Un matin, environ un mois après le combat de Camerone, une femme d'une soixantaine d'années, décharnée, menant une vache au bout d'une corde vers sa maison de pierres sombres, a ressenti comme un coup à l'estomac. Elle s'est assise sur une pierre, passant son foulard noir sur son visage pour sécher ses sueurs froides. À cet instant elle a su que son fils était mort. Celui qui était parti, il était mort. Elle l'a senti dans son ventre et dans son âme qui se déchirait. Elle l'a senti avec une absolue certitude. Cette pauvre femme s'est mise à pleurer. Dans cette vallée asturienne, elle pleurait, affligée par un grand chagrin. Elle avait perdu Alonso, son Alonso.

La peine l'a jetée à terre, la transformant en un corps noir et convulsé sur le sol verdoyant de ce val asturien.

Il lui semble surtout insupportable de ne pouvoir se recueillir sur la tombe de son fils. Son souvenir errerait toujours dans son esprit, sans qu'elle puisse l'associer à un cimetière, sans qu'elle puisse toucher la pierre qui recouvrirait ses os.

Pour cette raison elle pleure avec une infinie tristesse, couchée sur le vert manteau de sa vallée.

Quand elle pense qu'elle ne saura même jamais où se trouvent ses restes, cette ignorance l'abat encore plus dans sa douleur et elle se contorsionne de désespoir par terre, sentant bien qu'aucune consolation n'est désormais possible.

Après tant d'années c'est comme si subitement elle se découvrait mère de Alonso Bernardo, âgé de trente-deux ans et mort.

CHAPITRE VII

LA GUERRE CONTINUE

Après le combat de Camerone, la guerre s'est poursuivie avec intensité, les forces françaises participant à de nombreux combats. En 1864, le régiment est monté sur les hauts plateaux pour prendre part au siège d'Oaxaca. Après, il a continué sa marche vers le nord.

Déjà en 1865, avec la victoire des troupes nordistes dans la guerre de sécession nord-américaine, Napoléon III avait pris conscience que cette guerre ne pouvait être gagnée.

Beaucoup de nord-américains traverseront la frontière pour venir prêter main forte aux troupes juaristes cependant que le niveau de préparation et l'esprit combatif des soldats de l'empereur Français avaient beaucoup décliné.

Pourtant, le combat de Santa Isabel mérite d'être souligné. Le 1er mars 1866 une formation française aux ordres du chef de bataillon Brian et composée de trois compagnies de Légion et des unités locales, cent quatre-vingt-cinq légionnaires et quatre cents Mexicains se préparent à donner l'assaut à une hacienda, mais l'effet de surprise est tombé alors même que la victoire leur était assurée.

Dans ce combat, les compagnies se sont déployées à la sonnerie de la charge. Les légionnaires devaient parcourir quelque sept cents mètres avant d'atteindre les murs d'une hacienda. Une compagnie de voltige a vu sa route coupée par un profond ravin, ce qui l'a obligée à progresser au centre du dispositif. Les compagnies sont arrivées à bout de souffle au hasard, dans le désordre au pied des murs de la ferme.

Le jour commençait à poindre quand les légionnaires ont réalisé qu'un éperon rocheux, à leur gauche, était occupé par l'ennemi. Certains, malgré leur épuisement, essayeront de le gravir, mais ont été atteints par les tirs adverses, qui ont mortellement blessé le chef de bataillon Brian.

Le lieutenant Royaux était tombé, tout comme le lieutenant Smidt mortellement blessé. Le capitaine Moulinier, le lieutenant Ravix et l'adjudant Graveriaux incitaient vainement leurs hommes à poursuivre.

L'adjudant-major Cazès, avec une cinquantaine de légionnaires, a essayé de déborder les mexicains par la droite, mais une voix venant de l'intérieur du bâtiment, probablement un déserteur, a crié en français : « reculez ! ».

Le sergent Racle, de la 3e compagnie, soutenait le chef de bataillon Brian, grièvement blessé, jusqu'à ce qu'une dizaine de cavaliers mexicains les ont achevés. Le premier tombé a été le sergent.

La mort de Brian et la voix qui criait : « reculez » au dernier moment ont déconcerté les Français après que la colonne soit tombée dans l'embuscade. Les légionnaires restés seuls, abandonnés par les troupes locales alliées, ont été complètement encerclés par la cavalerie mexicaine. Malgré tout ces légionnaires « feront Camerone » et un seul a échappé au massacre dont le bilan s'élève à 102 morts et 82 prisonniers dont 40 blessés. Le sergent Fiala dont nous avons déjà conté l'épopée, figurait parmi les prisonniers.

Enhardis par l'enthousiasme de cette victoire, les Mexicains vont attaquer la ville de Parras, défendue par le lieutenant Bastidon qui s'est retranché dans l'église, résistant héroïquement pendant trois jours jusqu'à l'arrivée de renforts aux ordres du chef de bataillon Saussier, le 5 mars 1866.

En 1866 les quatre ans de guerre avaient mis en évidence la misère de ce conflit, comme pour en faire une destination pour les légionnaires. Une part importante de ceux qui se sont engagés, l'ont fait pour pouvoir traverser l'océan grâce à l'armée et pouvoir déserter après, dans l'espoir de pouvoir faire leur vie aux États-Unis. Néanmoins, la Légion s'était forgé sa légende au Mexique grâce à un encadrement extraordinaire, à son audace et à sa témérité. Le légionnaire Charles Zédé, dans ses notes, avait consigné le nom de personnalités déjà légendaires à la Légion, tels le lieutenant-colonel Martínez, espagnol de Madrid qui parlait un français parfait (détail démenti par d'autres sources), le lieutenant Milson, prussien exemple même des vertus guerrières des Allemands, le chef de bataillon Brian, dont l'audace et la valeur ont conduit à la mort à Santa Isabel, l'officier Diesbach de Tornay, Suisse d'ascendance aristocratique. Tous ont contribué à faire de la Légion une force d'élite.

Au Mexique la Légion a montré aussi sa capacité à former des compagnies mobiles où étaient regroupés les meilleurs de chaque bataillon qui développaient des capacités physiques qui, malgré la chaleur écrasante, leur permettaient d'effectuer des marches d'un peu moins de neuf kilomètres à l'heure. Ainsi, en octobre 1863, une compagnie de marche a été créée. Elle comptait les meilleurs cent marcheurs du régiment.

A partir de 1865, avec la victoire des troupes nordistes américaines, Napoléon III a acquis la certitude que la guerre, tôt ou tard, allait être perdue. Beaucoup de nord-américains traverseront la frontière pour épauler, ouvertement, les troupes juaristes. De surcroît, les qualités intrinsèques des nouveaux légionnaires qui s'engageaient à Aix-en-Provence ne valaient pas celles des engagés des premiers bataillons qui avaient débarqué en 1863. En ce temps-là, les nouvelles font état de désertions et de défections de légionnaires qui apprennent leur prochain départ vers le Mexique.

En réalité, pendant la campagne du Mexique, aucune bataille n'a été déterminante, décisive pour l'un ou l'autre des deux camps, pour finir victorieusement cette guerre. La tactique des forces mexicaines durant ces quatre années, a consisté essentiellement en un combat de harcèlement des troupes de l'empereur Maximilien. Le temps, la distance - avec ses bases arrière - la désaffection totale des populations civiles et la fièvre jaune ont fait le reste. A toutes ces contraintes est venue s'ajouter l'impopularité grandissante, en France, de cette guerre et l'aggravation des tensions diplomatiques en Europe, qui ont décidé, finalement, l'empereur des Français à rapatrier ses troupes à la fin de 1866.

Le 18 février 1867, le 1er bataillon de la Légion a quitté le Mexique à bord du *Pomone*. Deux jours plus tard ce sera le tour des 5e et 6e bataillons qui embarqueront sur l'*Aveyron*. Le lendemain, le 2e partira sur le *Var*. Les 3e et 4e bataillons clôtureront définitivement la campagne du Mexique lors de leur départ le 22 mars sur le *Tarn*[12]. Pour échapper aux effets de la fièvre jaune, les bataillons ne bivouaqueront plus d'une nuit sur le port de Veracruz avant l'embarquement.

Le Corps expéditionnaire français a quitté le Mexique en y laissant mille neuf cent dix-huit morts, officiers et légionnaires, dont mille six cents par maladie, surtout liée à la fièvre jaune. Pratiquement 83% des pertes légionnaires sont dues au *vomito negro* et non aux actions de combat. Les légionnaires sont allés au Mexique mourir de souffrances causées par des maladies et seulement une minorité a péri au combat, parmi lesquels, ceux de la 3e compagnie qui, par leur valeur et leur héroïsme ont forgé le mythe fondateur de la geste légionnaire. Le mythe de Camerone.

Juan López

Juan Lopéz attend, sur un quai du port de Veracruz l'ordre d'embarquer. Pendant ces quatre années il s'est intégré à son petit monde mexicain. Il vivait avec une famille mexicaine qui lavait et reprisait son linge, et dans l'humble maison dans laquelle il s'était habitué à manger le guacamole (une préparation à base d'avocat,

[12] *La Légion*, de Erwan Bergot.

tomate, oignon, épices), les haricots noirs et divers plats mexicains très épicés et piquants. Là, il pouvait cuver tranquillement ses cuites à la téquila, prises en dehors du service, et tous partageaient une part de sa miséreuse solde. Il sait qu'il doit les quitter bientôt et il pense alors à sa misère andalouse, sa campagne dans les parages de Cádiz et Málaga.

Quatre ans c'est long ; cependant, en ce lieu, dans ce port, il se souvient de son débarquement sur ces mêmes quais, ses premiers pas chancelants, sur la terre ferme après un mois de traversée et l'odeur de sel qu'exhalaient son corps et ses vêtements. Les heures interminables dans la cale à jouer aux cartes, les promenades organisées sur le pont, craintif devant l'immensité océane. Et la nourriture, il revoit la tambouille pendant ces journées de mer, bien meilleure que tout ce qu'il a pu manger durant ces quatre ans. Au moment de la « soupe » ils étaient servis par plats de dix hommes, une nourriture consistante, généralement composée de soupe, viande, lard, haricots, riz puis café et cognac, qu'ils avalaient sur le pont. Grâce au bétail embarqué, vivant, de la viande fraiche remplaçait les conserves deux fois par semaine. Il se souvient aussi avec nostalgie de la fête organisée au franchissement du tropique du Cancer comme un « passage de la ligne équatoriale », et les crépuscules au son de chansons italiennes et allemandes.

Tout se répète dans sa tête comme si ces derniers quatre ans n'existaient pas, pas du tout. En ce moment il se sent bien dans son uniforme, dans ses belles bottes noires de cavalier, son pantalon rouge aux cuisses renforcées de cuir, et sa vareuse bleu marine, dont beaucoup d'ornements manquent par la rudesse de l'usage en campagne. Et son képi déformé, récupéré après avoir vécu toute la campagne équipé d'un chapeau de paille à larges bords, identique à celui des troupes mexicaines. Mais cet uniforme devient collant à son corps constamment trempé de sueur.

Antonio, Maria et ses trois enfants mâles, sous une voûte, observent l'Espagnol et se sentent captivés. Ils ne disent rien. Ils considèrent presque comme un miracle qu'un soldat français puisse être espagnol, et ait frappé à leur porte et leur ait fait quitter le seuil de la misère absolue pour devenir seulement des pauvres. Ils l'observent et ne disent rien.

Juan attend les ordres. Il sait qu'à l'arrivée en Algérie, son escadron sera dissous et qu'il lui faudra rechausser des brodequins pour parcourir de nouveau le bled algérien.

L'escadron de cavalerie

En avril 1864 un escadron, plutôt une « compagnie montée », a été créé au sein du Régiment étranger. La candidature des légionnaires sachant monter à cheval a été sollicitée. Beaucoup d'Allemands ont répondu à l'appel mais la réalité n'a pas tardé à démentir leurs aptitudes pour l'art équestre. Juan López n'a pas eu de difficultés pour être accepté : il montait, savait ferrer et, espagnol, il parlait la langue de l'ennemi.

L'avantage de cette unité, était, comme le rapporte Douglas Porch dans son livre, se faisant l'écho de commentaires des légionnaires de l'époque, qu'ils n'avaient pas faim, et quand la cavalerie légionnaire s'approchait d'une localité, les Mexicains se débandaient, laissant derrière eux des provisions de toute sorte. Cependant il y avait un très gros inconvénient dans le fait que le commandement français voulant tirer le meilleur parti de l'extrême mobilité de cette unité, lui faisait vivre des journées épuisantes.

Juan López se rappelait bien de ces périodes de plus d'une semaine sans quitter ses bottes et l'effort douloureux qui supposait le moment de se déchausser, quand, couché sur le sol sablonneux du nord du Mexique, les pieds posés en hauteur pour faire désenfler ses chevilles, il regardait le ciel étoilé. Ses souvenirs lui revenaient alors qu'il regardait distrait, cette famille d'adoption.

Les chevaux en provenance d'Europe avaient les pieds fragiles et les fracturaient facilement et devaient être sacrifiés. Moyennant réquisition, l'escadron s'équipait en chevaux autochtones, qui, bien que moins hauts au garrot étaient plus résistants dans cet environnement. Après la prise de Oaxaca, en 1866, les français se sont appropriée une quantité considérable de chevaux mexicains, ce qui leur a permis d'augmenter l'effectif initial de l'unité.

En 1866, l'escadron avait un effectif de 240 hommes, ce qui était clairement insuffisant pour accomplir les missions qui lui étaient assignées.

Juan chevauchait toujours à proximité des officiers pour exercer ses talents de traducteur quand nécessaire. Juan López parlait français avec une certaine aisance, certes avec de grandes difficultés de syntaxe, mais comprenant tout, en plus de posséder un vocabulaire considérable d'allemand, comme Alonso, à force de répéter des mots et de courtes phrases, selon le contexte et des situations déterminées.

L'Espagnol se souvient de l'authentique boucherie faite près de Monterrey quand, en combat, ils ont tué plus de cent douze hommes. Avant le combat ils essayaient maladroitement de nettoyer les uniformes ou cacher leur saleté en faisant reluire les boutons dorés ou les parements des vareuses et cette coquetterie devenait parfois pathétique.

En janvier 1866, il s'est trouvé aussi près de Saltillo, pour finir avec la vie de quarante ennemis, tout comme le 2 mars de la même année quand il a chevauché avec son unité pendant treize heures pour couvrir les cent kilomètres qui les séparaient de Monterrey pour y attaquer par surprise une bande de trente adversaires. Le lendemain du combat il ne pouvait même pas marcher à cause des crampes provoquées par une si longue chevauchée et le dégoût presque physique que la vue des chevaux provoquaient en lui, les pieds enflés et les souffrances endurées en déchaussant ses bottes.

Pour le moment il regarde distraitement la mer, ennuyé de tant regarder sa famille adoptée ; quand il se souvient d'Alonso, enterré dans une fosse commune à cent mètres de l'hacienda de La Trinidad, à Camerone. C'est déjà un vague souvenir, et sa mémoire arrive à peine à distinguer les traits de son visage. Il aimerait bien l'avoir à ses côtés pour pouvoir lui parler de Ludwig.

Les conditions de vie de l'unité étaient réellement dures, sauf dans le domaine de la nourriture, puisqu'ils ne connaissaient pas la faim, ce qui n'était pas le cas des unités d'infanterie. Le succès de son unité était dû au fait que ses membres agissaient comme des pompiers, allant d'un foyer de lutte à un autre, bien que ces combats fussent moins fréquents que les interventions, car la seule arrivée des légionnaires mettait en fuite l'ennemi, cependant ces interventions impliquaient des journées de dix heures ou plus à cheval – journées épuisantes pour les animaux aussi -, bivouaquant sous l'appréhension de possibles attaques et en déplacement, d'éventuelles embuscades, raisons pour lesquelles l'ambiance entre légionnaires était souvent tendue, voire violente et propice aux phobies.

Ludwig (Luis pour Juan López) aimait taquiner l'Espagnol, qui, pour éviter l'affrontement, le supportait comme il pouvait. Néanmoins, peu à peu le ton a changé et de manière obsessionnelle le natif de Baden Baden a fait de l'Espagnol son souffre-douleur lui rendant la vie impossible. Une nuit, en bivouac, Ludwig lui a jeté directement un verre de vin au visage, sans rimes ni raisons. L'Espagnol savait que s'il laissait passer cet affront il serait un homme mort. Il a attendu quelques instants que l'Allemand se relâche, pensant qu'il n'allait rien faire, se moquant de lui en riant. Quand l'hilarité a gagné les légionnaires spectateurs de la scène au tour de Ludwig, Juan a sorti son couteau et lui a fait une balafre au bras. Le sang a giclé à gros bouillons et Juan s'est jeté sur l'Allemand qui, trop préoccupé par sa blessure, ne l'a pas vu venir. Tombés au sol, Juan a pris le dessus et fou de rage, a saisi la tête de l'Allemand et la cognait sur le sol ; il ne se rendait plus compte de rien et bien que la tête blonde commence à se teinter de rouge, Juan López n'arrêtait pas jusqu'à ce que, épuisé, il lâche la tête de son antagoniste. Il l'avait tué.

Deux légionnaires de la compagnie ont saisi le cadavre, sans rien dire et l'ont enterré. Le lendemain personne n'en a parlé et Ludwig a été considéré comme déserteur.

Juan López a passé plusieurs nuits sans dormir jusqu'à ce qu'il ait appris à vivre avec ce souvenir, toujours douloureux, et a assumé la dureté de la vie en campagne comme une sorte de mortification expiatoire, sa pénitence intime. Et là, au port, sur le point d'embarquer, il lui vient à l'esprit l'instant qui a précédé sa rage meurtrière, comme si ce souvenir récurrent pouvait changer quelque chose. Une autre fois il s'est dit que, bien qu'il ait tué beaucoup d'ennemis, surtout à Monterrey, ce n'était pas comme avoir tué Ludwig, et quand lui revenait en mémoire l'Allemand ensanglanté, il fermait les yeux, comme s'il pouvait par-là, effacer son souvenir.

Après cela et après tout, les bataillons successifs qui se formaient à Aix-en-Provence comptaient des espagnols bien qu'en nombre réduit. Juan n'a rien fait pour nouer des relations ou simplement connaître d'autres compatriotes ; il s'est bien intégré au groupe de cavaliers Allemands qui avaient participé avec lui à la création de l'escadron.

L'heure de partir est arrivée. Les troupes françaises ont été cantonnées une seule nuit à Veracruz, pour éviter tout risque de contagion par la fièvre jaune.

La « famille » de Juan López avait pris le train, du lieu où était cantonné l'escadron, simplement pour lui dire adieu, par le regard, pendant quelques brèves heures.

Deux ans plus tard, en Algérie, Juan López a pris congé de la Légion étrangère et s'est installé dans la ville de Mostaganem, où il a créé un atelier de ferrage et entretien de chevaux, se consacrant aussi au commerce de ces animaux.

Avec le temps, ses descendants ont été l'une des nombreuses et prospères familles européennes d'Algérie française, qui bien que Français jusqu'à la moelle, se nommaient Martínez, García, González… ou López.

La Légion n'a plus créé d'unités de cavalerie jusqu'en 1921, année qui a vu la création du 1er Régiment étranger de cavalerie lequel se composait alors surtout de cosaques et russes blancs, émigrés après la révolution bolchévique de 1917.

CHAPITRE VIII

IN MEMORIAM

Le 3 mai 1863, le colonel Jeanningros a fait ériger une croix en bois avec l'inscription « Ici demeure la 3e compagnie du 1er bataillon de la Légion étrangère ».

Ce monument a été remplacé par une colonne avant la fin de la campagne du Mexique.

En 1892, une souscription populaire lancée à l'initiative de Edouard Sempé, consul de France à Veracruz, a permis l'édification d'un monument.

Son état d'abandon absolu a fait qu'en 1948 le colonel Penette, ancien officier de Légion, a construit un nouveau monument, dont l'inauguration a eu lieu en 1963, à l'occasion du centenaire du combat. Mais son inauguration définitive s'est déroulée le 15 décembre 1965. Il porte l'inscription :

Ils furent ici moins de soixante
Opposés à toute une armée, sa masse les écrasa.
La vie plutôt que le courage abandonna ces soldats Français
Le 30 avril 1863.
A leur mémoire, la patrie éleva ce monument.

Chaque année l'armée mexicaine rend hommage devant le monument aux morts français et à leurs propres compatriotes.

Les héros mexicains

Même si ces faits ne sont racontés que par l'une des parties belligérantes, nous ne devons pas oublier que les assaillants ont, eux aussi, combattu avec beaucoup de courage et d'ardeur.

Le lieutenant-colonel José Ayala, chef d'état-major de Francisco de Paula Milán, le capitaine Joaquin Guido, du bataillon Jalapa, le lieutenant Vicente Guido, commandant en second le bataillon Veracruz, les aspirants Rafael Redondo de la cavalerie de Jiménez et Juan Canseco, chef de groupe de cavalerie, sont tombés à l'ennemi en héros.

Le tambour Pablo Ochoa a combattu et est mort vaillamment au moment où il mettait le feu au toit de l'auberge.

Le soldat Barrientos a été le premier à pénétrer dans la cour de l'auberge vers les 17 heures 35 de ce funeste 30 avril : il ne l'a pas pensé, il a avancé à l'intérieur de l'enceinte sans regarder derrière. Enhardi, il voyait parfaitement les portes depuis lesquelles ne partait plus aucun coup de feu. Il a pensé soudain que tout était terminé, et a couru impétueusement, sautant par-dessus les cadavres auxquels ils n'a même pas jeté un regard de commisération.

Quand il est entre dans l'hacienda, la première chose qui l'a surpris a été le sol, tout le sol était d'une couleur foncée ; le tapis de sang par terre était presque noir. Et en entrant par la première des portes-cochères, vue du sud, il s'est tourné vers la droite, et là, il a vu les légionnaires postés dans le hangar situé au sud-ouest, l'ultime bastion de la 3e compagnie, distinguant parfaitement l'un d'eux : celui-ci était mince, mesurait environ un mètre soixante-huit, cheveux noirs, une fine moustache et une barbichette « don quichotesque », le visage noirci et les avant-bras très blancs, dans un uniforme gris… Barrientos lui a tiré dessus. Alors, Alonso a ressenti comme le coup sec d'un caillou sur sa poitrine, un impact fort mais non douloureux. Dans l'action, le soldat Barrientos est tombé atteint par trois balles ; sa dernière vision a été celle d'une poignée de légionnaires, aux visages presque noirs de fumée, de poudre et de saleté, leurs maigres corps flottant dans les uniformes et il a cru voir des démons… en un bref instant, pendant que son corps s'écroulait sur le sol.

Et le soldat Barrientos est mort, seul, face aux assiégés.

EPILOGUE

Les forces du colonel Jeanningros pénétreront dans le village de Camerone dans la nuit du 2 mai 1863. Quelques Mexicains maraudant alentour se volatiliseront immédiatement à l'arrivée des troupes françaises.

Beaucoup de cadavres étaient déjà méconnaissables après le passage des chacals et des vautours. La différence entre les morts Mexicains et Français était facile à voir. Ceux de Danjou étaient dévêtus, alors qu'on avait laissé leurs effets aux hommes de Milán. Le pillage des biens français avait été total.

Une fosse commune avait été creusée à une centaine de mètres de l'auberge de La Trinidad ; ne s'y trouvaient qu'une cinquantaine de corps. Vingt-deux corps de légionnaires et quatre-vingt-seize de Mexicains gisaient à proximité sans sépulture.

Les pertes françaises pendant le siège de Camerone se sont élevées à trente et un morts. Neuf autres sont morts en captivité. Les survivants ont été remis trois mois plus tard à l'armée française.

De tous les prisonniers, quatre ne sont jamais revenus et d'autres ont été rendus à différentes dates. Merlet a été libéré presque une année après, le 16 mars 1864, et Stoller le 2 mars 1865.

Aucun des survivants n'est resté dans les rangs de la troisième compagnie.

Par décision du 4 octobre 1863, le ministre de la Guerre a voulu que le nom de Camerone soit inscrit sur le drapeau du Régiment étranger.

Les noms de Danjou, Maudet et Vilain ont été gravés, par ordre de l'empereur, sur un mur des Invalides à Paris.

Cinq des survivants ont été reçus dans l'ordre de la Légion d'honneur et six autres ont reçu d'autres décorations.

Les caporaux Maine et Évariste Berg ont été nommés sous-officiers et plus tard ils sont devenus officiers. Le premier était déjà titulaire de la Légion d'honneur depuis la campagne de Crimée lorsqu'il a repris le drapeau de son régiment de zouaves à Malakoff, aux portes de Sébastopol.

Le caporal Maine a relaté le premier, en personne, les derniers instants du combat : « Il n'y avait plus d'espoir, cependant, personne ne parlait de se rendre, nous n'étions plus que six, le sous-lieutenant Maudet, un prussien nommé Wensel, Catteau, Constantin, Leonhard et moi. Il était environ dix-huit heures et nous combattions depuis le matin. Le lieutenant a crié « Feu ! », nous avons tiré et, lui en tête nous avons foncé baïonnette au canon. Une formidable décharge nous a accueillis. Catteau s'est jeté devant le lieutenant pour faire rempart de son corps, mais, malgré ce geste, le lieutenant a été touché par deux balles. Wensel a été touché aussi, à l'épaule, mais n'a pas été mis hors de combat.

Nous restions trois, debout, Wensel, Constantin et moi. Pendant un instant nous avons perdu le lieutenant de vue, nous nous préparions à enjamber son corps et à charger de nouveau, mais déjà les Mexicains nous entouraient de toutes parts et la pointe de leurs baïonnettes était pointée sur nos poitrines, mais à ce moment, un officier supérieur au premier rang les a fait s'arrêter, et avec un mouvement de sabre il a soulevé les baïonnettes.

- Rendez-vous !
- Nous nous rendrons – ai-je répondu – si vous nous laissez nos armes et si vous promettez de soigner notre lieutenant qui est blessé.

L'officier a donné son accord. Il m'a offert un bras, pendant qu'il soutenait Wensel, blessé, et ils ont emporté le lieutenant sur un brancard. Nous avons gravi un monticule sur lequel se trouvait le colonel Milán :

- C'est tout ce qui reste ? – a-t-il demandé en nous voyant -. La réponse affirmative le fit s'exclamer :
- ¡Pero no son hombres, son demonios! (Ce ne sont pas des hommes, ce sont des démons !) ».

Le caporal Maine a combattu pendant la guerre franco-prussienne, en 1870, dans une unité de volontaires territoriaux, avec le grade de capitaine.

Les duels

Berg allait mourir au cours d'un duel pour une obscure affaire de jeu et de dettes. Le même motif qui l'avait amené à la Légion où, cherchant une sorte de rédemption il était devenu un héros. En ce temps-là les duels étaient très fréquents et répondaient au haut degré d'agressivité et de violence qui sévissaient dans les quartiers militaires, et sûrement plus encore dans une institution comme la Légion étrangère. Les duellistes incorrigibles, connus comme des « buveurs de sang », constituaient un phénomène social pendant le Second Empire.

Le duel était magnifié parmi le corps des officiers du Second Empire, comme l'exercice suprême de la défense de l'honneur, qui constitue la plus haute valeur de tout bon soldat. Mais en réalité, cela représentait une échappatoire, couverte par la légalité et la dignité, pour laisser la bride sur le cou à une agressivité constante et un degré de violence habituels dans l'armée.

Du point de vue social, les duels, qui étaient encouragés comme un symbole de bravoure et d'affirmation du sens de l'honneur, étaient institutionnellement tolérés. En 1849 il y a eu une tentative pour réglementer le duel, moyennant l'imposition de normes quant à son déroulement et à son exécution. Néanmoins, certaines règles tacites, déjà établies, étaient respectées, comme par l'exemple dans l'armée, seules les personnes de même grade pouvaient se battre en duel. Parmi les civils il fallait appartenir au même rang social. Egalement, était communément acceptée la présence d'un maître d'armes et d'un médecin. Dans certains cas, un petit comité exerçait une sorte de tribunal d'honneur, qui statuait si l'offense infligée était de nature à être réglée en duel ou par un autre type de satisfaction.

Ce qui est certain, c'est que pendant une période, le fait de se battre en duel s'était répandu comme une épidémie, dans laquelle les hommes valorisaient leur degré de bravoure et révélait une attitude morale de la société de l'époque car, avec un taux de mortalité élevé, encore à la moitié du 19e siècle, à cause des guerres constantes, des épidémies et des maladies, elle se rebellait contre ces désastres et entendaient disposer de leur propre destin par duel interposé, arguant de principes aussi élevés que l'honneur.

Cette ardeur pour l'affrontement en duel enserrait en elle, également dans l'environnement militaire, tout un esprit agressif conditionné par la dureté de la vie et qui se justifiait, socialement, par les appels constant à l'honneur et la démonstration, dans ce cas stupide, de la bravoure personnelle.

Les désertions

Une autre conséquence logique de l'extrême dureté de vie du légionnaire et de l'environnement de violence et d'agressivité dans les unités légionnaires, c'était la désertion. Déjà en 1863, l'inspecteur du Régiment étranger constatait que les désertions, depuis le retour du régiment, malgré le bon moral des troupes, avaient été très nombreuses[13]. Cependant, la vision du commandement à cette époque-là, était très positive, puisqu'on prétendait se débarrasser ainsi de soldats dépourvus de l'ardeur et du courage nécessaires pour aller au combat.

[13] Douglas Porch

En 1864, le général Brincourt rapportait quatre cents désertions sur un effectif de trois mille quatre cent soixante-et-un hommes (environ 11,6%), c'est-à-dire, le même nombre que durant l'année 1832, année suivant celle de la création de la Légion. Ce taux chute pendant les années suivantes, jusqu'à 5,8% pendant l'année 1866. Les désertions vont se multiplier lors des expéditions dans le nord du Mexique, quand les unités se trouvaient proches du rio Grande, qui marque la frontière avec les Etats-Unis. Ainsi, en juin 1866, le consul de France à Galveston, se plaignait de la quantité de déserteurs européens qui entraient au Texas.

L'une des explications de ce phénomène c'est que certains de ceux qui s'engageaient en Europe pour aller combattre au Mexique, le faisaient dans l'espoir d'obtenir un voyage gratuit qui leur permettrait d'émigrer vers le Nouveau Monde. Mais ce motif n'explique pas tout car, une bonne partie des désertions avaient lieu sur le territoire français et même, *a contrario,* d'aucuns désertaient dès qu'ils apprenaient que leur destination était le Mexique.

Ainsi, on peut affirmer que tous ne désertaient pas pour émigrer vers les Etats-Unis, en revanche certains passaient à l'ennemi, de telle sorte que le chef rebelle Porfirio Díaz a créé un corps autonome de trois cents transfuges, à majorité ex-légionnaires, comme jadis ce fut le cas en Espagne pendant la guerre carliste de 1835-1839, puisque les troupes de don Carlos avaient réussi à former le « bataillon algérien » d'environ huit cents hommes avec les déserteurs de la Légion étrangère.

Mais au sein de la Légion étrangère, et cela constitue la base même de sa légende, naît toujours l'exemple suprême de l'héroïsme et de la fidélité, comme c'est le cas du sergent Fiala. Les Français faits prisonniers par les Mexicains après la chute de Santa Isabel, en mars 1866, ont été confinés non loin de rio Grande, à la frontière nord-américaine. Sous le commandement du sergent Fiala, de nationalité allemande, ils ont réussi à échapper et à traverser la frontière. Sur le territoire américain, ils se sont dirigés vers La Nouvelle Orléans, d'où ils ont réussi à embarquer à destination de Veracruz et, arrivés à bon port, ils se sont présentés aux autorités militaires françaises.

Le sergent Fiala a été décoré par le maréchal Bazaine, et, à la fin de son contrat, nommé concierge du château de Pau.

Mais habituellement le chemin était inverse, et c'est ainsi que le général Daudignac racontait que, en croyant que les Etats-Unis étaient à deux ou trois jours de marche, des sections entières de légionnaires désertaient avec leurs équipements au complet de Veracruz.

Le problème des désertions n'était pas une exclusivité de la Légion. Il se posait aussi dans les autres unités régulières françaises tout comme il affectait les contingents autrichien et belge.

Le colonel Dupin

Le colonel Dupin a pris connaissance du désastre de Camerone le 2 mai.

Ancien officier de la Légion, Dupin assurait à l'époque, le commandement d'une force de contre-guérilla (précurseur de ce que sont aujourd'hui les forces spéciales des armées modernes). Cette unité militaire avait été mise sur pied par la volonté expresse du commandant en chef des troupes françaises.

Le colonel Dupin était un mélange de *condottieri* de la Renaissance et d'un clairvoyant prédécesseur du combat de guérilla qui mesurait nettement l'importance de la contre-insurrection. Dupin avait participé à toutes les campagnes extérieures : Afrique, Crimée, Italie, Chine, Japon et Mexique. D'une grande intelligence, il avait pour faiblesse, le jeu. Sa carrière avait connu un gros travers quand, pour payer ses dettes, il avait vendu aux enchères publiques, de nombreux trésors du Palais Impérial de Pékin. C'était un joueur invétéré, d'une éducation exquise et dont les actions n'ont pas été ce que de nos jours se qualifierait de « politiquement correct ».

Dupin a reconnu, dans ses écrits, avoir infligé à l'ennemi moins de pertes que celles qui réellement lui étaient imputées. En avance sur son temps, il savait l'importante place qu'occupait la propagande dans les forces irrégulières dans le combat de guérilla. Il confessait à sa petite-fille dans une lettre datée de 1864 :

« J'ai envoyé à peine une douzaine de bandits dans l'au-delà, faisant ainsi du bon travail, car ces criminels avaient tué plus de trente personnes honnêtes. Si tu savais comme j'ai vieilli depuis que je suis arrivé dans cet horrible pays. On me croirait âgé de soixante ans alors que je n'en ai que quarante-neuf ».

Cependant, l'empereur Maximilian et le général Bazaine rejetteront les méthodes de Dupin et il a reçu l'ordre de rentrer en France ; mais une fois arrivé, il a réussi à convaincre Napoléon III de le laisser repartir vers le Mexique, où il a séjourné jusqu'au rapatriement final des troupes françaises en 1867. Dupin avait rejoint alors l'armée française mais était mort un an plus tard ; la rumeur de son empoisonnement avait circulé alors.

Sa troupe était hétéroclite et dangereuse : renégats, propriétaires ruinés, marins, déserteurs et beaucoup d'anciens légionnaires, libérés par fin de contrat qui avaient contracté le mal du pays. L'unité était montée et d'une très grande mobilité et souplesse. Au début il a été rejoint par les compagnies créoles de la Martinique et de la Guadeloupe tout comme par un officier et dix hommes du Régiment étranger. Il avait, comme lieutenant-colonel adjoint, Ney d'Elchingen, petit-fils du maréchal Ney, maréchal de camp de Napoléon Ier. La tenue de la troupe était, elle aussi hétéroclite et certains officiers étalaient volontiers une certaine originalité vestimentaire où prédominaient les énormes sombreros mexicains, vestes écarlates, pantalons blancs, et bottes d'équitation noires.

Le colonel Dupin s'est consacré à pourchasser les troupes mexicaines jusqu'à ce que, le 13 juin 1863 il entre en Cueva Pentada, où il a libéré le légionnaire Vries - le Hollandais de la compagnie Danjou - qui, en raison de ses blessures avait été abandonné là, séparé de ses compagnons prisonniers. Le colonel a réussi a récupérer la majeure partie de l'équipement de la 3e compagnie.

Les guérilleros de Dupin continueront le harcèlement des troupes mexicaines pendant tout le mois de juin jusqu'à l'affrontement de Huatusco, le 28 juin 1863.

Les cent cinquante cavaliers de Dupin, appuyés par deux compagnies de marche de la Légion étrangère, envoyées par Sudrie y Prêt, par un surprenant mouvement d'une grande vitesse, entreront devant les troupes mexicaines dans la ville de Huatusco, repoussant les Mexicains jusqu'au ravin du Diable. Leur fuite est si précipitée et désordonnée que dans la confusion les mexicains s'entre-tueront sous le regard médusé et amusé des cavaliers de Dupin et des légionnaires.

Juan López est l'un de ceux qui regarde le massacre fratricide des Mexicains. Il s'est souvenu de son compatriote Bernardo, l'asturien, et comme le destin l'avait conduit à être un héros anonyme dans un pays si distant du sien. Il voulait imaginer comment le bon Alonso, renfermé et timide, s'était comporté pendant le combat ; il pensait à son ami, celui qu'il avait connu si plein de vitalité et de force dans une unité comme celle-là, qui l'exigeait, qui n'était plus qu'un simple souvenir qui s'estompait dans l'oubli. Il s'est dit qu'il devrait écrire une lettre à sa famille ou à son village en Espagne ; Juan López faisait partie des maigres vingt-cinq pour cent de légionnaires non analphabètes. Il connaissait les coordonnées de Bernardo parce que celui-ci, lors d'une de leurs rencontres, lui avait demandé d'écrire à sa mère une lettre qui lui serait lue par le curé de la paroisse.

Les prisonniers et les blessés de Camerone

Les Français ont été emmenés à La Joya où cinq d'entre eux sont morts. Le lendemain, 2 mai, d'autres prisonniers grièvement blessés sont décédés et enterrés sur les rives du Chiquito.

De cette localité, les forces du colonel Francisco de Paula Milán ont fait mouvement, avec leurs prisonniers, vers Huatusco.

Le transport des blessés a été un véritable calvaire. Deux par mule, leurs souffrances augmentées encore par l'inconfort du voyage et les sursauts des animaux constamment sollicités par les Mexicains qui savaient les Français à leurs trousses, ils gémissaient et se plaignaient continuellement dans une monotone litanie. Les arrêts ne duraient que le temps nécessaire à la sépulture des morts. Ainsi ont péri, Maudet, le sergent belge Germeys, la tête bandée, le silencieux Rohr, qui s'était bandé le visage pour que l'une de ses orbites oculaires, vide, n'attire pas les mouches tel un aimant la limaille, le caporal del Caretto, le légionnaire Constant Dael, bruxellois né le 2 décembre 1842, le légionnaire Jean Kurtz, de Kallemberg dans le land allemand de Wutemberg, né le 2 mars 1844, le Belge Jean Louis Timmermans, de Bilan, né le 2 août 1845 et Claude Billod, dijonnais né le 10 novembre 1832, lequel, blessé par balle, avait un trou béant dans la poitrine causant d'énormes douleurs stoïquement supportées par lui.

Les prisonniers pouvant marcher suivaient derrière les blessés. Ainsi, Gorski, la mâchoire déformée et un œil presque fermé, aidait le sergent Schaeffner ; le caporal de nationalité autrichienne Magnin soutenait son homologue le caporal Pinzinger qui se plaignait d'un début de gangrène dans sa jambe blessée. Wensel avait une épaule bandée. Le benjamin, Pharaon Vanderbulcke, marchait toujours en silence ; Konrad aidait Joseph Schreiblich et Constantin, le prussien Antoine Bogucki, âgé de vingt-neuf ans. Le sergent Palmaert fermait la marche. Il ne souffrait que d'une contusion à une épaule.

Le docteur Talavera a eu l'intention de faire admettre les blessés à l'hôpital de Huatusco, fondé par les *Filles de Saint Vincent de Paul*, subventionné par les dames de la haute société de la région et dirigé par madame Juana Marredo de Gómez, veuve d'un riche commerçant, qu'après la disparition de son mari s'est consacrée aux œuvres de charité, ce qui lui a fait gagner le nom de « Maman Juana » ; cependant, devant la précarité des moyens hospitaliers, elle a accueilli le sous-lieutenant Maudet dans sa propre maison, située juste en face du quartier militaire, à un angle de la place Principal.

Malgré toute sorte de soins et d'attentions, le blessé agonisait après quelques jours et décédait le 8 mai. Avant son agonie, prostré sur son lit, il avait réussi à écrire sur une feuille : « J'ai laissé une mère en France et j'ai rencontré une autre au Mexique ».

Il a été enterré avec les honneurs militaires, rendus par les troupes mexicaines, dans la paroisse de Huatusco ce jour-là à quinze heures. Les frères Marredo ont ordonné que l'on habille le mort avec sa vareuse nettoyée, arborant ses médailles de Sébastopol et Solférino, son képi et son épée. On a placé sur la poitrine du mort une bande tricolore avec l'inscription : « Gloire aux armes de la France » et à côté du gisant un flacon scellé a été placé, contenant un papier sur lequel était inscrit « Clément Maudet est mort le 8 mai 1863. France ».

Le sergent Germeys, le caporal del Caretto, Timmermans, Dael, le taciturne bavarois Louis Rohr, de Niererverbach né le 1er octobre 1832, Jean Kurtz et enfin Claude Billod qui a mérité la récupération de ses galons de caporal, sont morts en captivité aussi. Le légionnaire belge Jean Bass, né le 26 décembre 1842 à Mouscron, a été évacué vers l'hôpital de Jalapa et n'a jamais plus donné signe de vie.

A sa mort en 1864, Manuel Marredo a été transféré jusqu'à Jalapa et lors de ses obsèques les troupes françaises lui ont rendu des honneurs militaires.

Les prisonniers ont été autorisés à écrire une lettre, par la main d'Evariste Berg, bachelier. Celui-ci, pendant sa captivité avait écrit une lettre au colonel Jeanningros datée du 10 mai 1863. Dans celle-ci il rapportait la mort du capitaine Danjou, récit qui s'éloigne du récit classique de sa mort au combat :

« Le capitaine Danjou était splendide par son ardeur et son courage sans que rien ne le distraie. Il y avait seulement trois ou quatre blessés quand le capitaine Danjou a été blessé par une balle qui l'a frappé au milieu du dos et est ressortie sous le sein gauche. Notre pauvre capitaine a souffert encore une heure avant d'expirer dans les bras des sous-lieutenants Vilain et Maudet ».

Sur la fin de Maudet il a écrit :

« Il était magnifique de voir le sous-lieutenant Maudet, seul, à la tête de quelques hommes, tirer au fusil comme un quelconque soldat. Il ne voulait pas se rendre, et au moment de tomber il venait de faire feu ».

Le caporal Berg termine ainsi sa missive :

« La 3e compagnie du 1er bataillon est morte, mon colonel, mais elle en a assez fait pour qu'on puisse dire d'elle qu'elle avait de bons soldats ».

Selon des sources françaises, cette lettre – écrite par le caporal Berg au colonel Jeanningros – sera utilisée par les Mexicains comme instrument de propagande dans la revue *Heraldo* publiée à Mexico le 16 mai 1863. Il convient alors d'observer toute la réserve que ce fait impose.

Le 13 juin, le colonel juariste Antonio Gamacho a proposé à Dupin de libérer les légionnaires capturés à Camerone en échange du colonel Alba. Le lendemain, les prisonniers épuisés, ont été conduits par Luis Alba, frère du captif, vers six heures à Cosmatopec et de là, déjà libérés, par les troupes de Dupin, jusqu'à Orizaba à dos de mulet.

La raison du grand nombre de légionnaires faits prisonniers est due, principalement, à la pénurie de munitions dans leurs rangs, ce qui a permis aux Mexicains de s'approcher à les écraser. C'est pourquoi les légionnaires ont subi de graves blessures y compris les survivants remis à Dupin, entre lesquels les caporaux Maine et Berg et auxquels il faudrait ajouter le légionnaire italien Casimiro

Laï et le Hollandais Vries, celui qui a été libéré par les hommes de Dupin à Cueva Pentada.

Les survivants

Les survivants comme le quadragénaire prussien Wensel, le sergent Suisse Schaeffner, le légionnaire, quadragénaire lui aussi, Frédéric Fritz, de Kemm dans le Wutemberg, le caporal bavarois Pinzinger, qui a réussi à sauver, à l'hôpital de Saint Vincent, sa jambe gangrénée, et le légionnaire Félix Brunswick, né le 24 septembre 1832 à Bruxelles, ont tous été faits chevaliers de la Légion d'honneur. Brunswick resté dans la Légion où il a accompli vingt-cinq ans de service, s'est ensuite installé à Saïda en Algérie où il mourait le 15 septembre 1882.

Magnin, l'Autrichien, le Belge Palmaert, le Français Kunasseg, l'Allemand Joseph Rerbers, né le 15 décembre 1837 à Odirkichen, le jeune Joseph Schreiblich, Prussien de Gruben où il a vu le jour le 25 août 1843, le Français Léon Gorski, nîmois fils de polonais, ont eux, été décorés de la Médaille militaire.

Le légionnaire Fritz, qui avait perdu un bras, a été admis au bénéfice de la pension de retraite en 1867.

En 1902, le tout dernier survivant de Camerone était Hippolyte Adolphe Kunasseg, né le 22 juillet 1843 ; il était natif de Villeneuve-Saint Georges en Seine-et-Oise (aujourd'hui Yvelines), fils de Charles Joseph et de Marie Victoire, née Le Brun. Il s'était engagé dans la Légion étrangère le 18 novembre 1861, pour deux ans, au titre du 2e Etranger. Il a été fait prisonnier à Camerone, puis libéré le 14 juillet 1863. Le 6 du mois suivant il a été nommé caporal. En novembre il a terminé son contrat et s'est installé à Paris. Mais en juillet de l'année suivante il s'est rengagé, cette fois-ci pour sept ans au 57e Régiment de ligne. Sergent en 1867 il a participé à la guerre de 1870, contre la Prusse. Fait prisonnier il a réussi à s'évader. Il était titulaire de la Médaille militaire et de la médaille commémorative de la campagne du Mexique.

En 1902, alors âgé de cinquante-neuf ans, et profitant de l'anniversaire du combat, il a écrit une lettre au colonel Bruneau de la Légion. Cette lettre a été publiée dans *Le Petit Journal* le 19 mai, la même année.

L'horreur, l'angoisse et la peur de mourir dans l'après-midi de ce funeste 30 avril 1863, restaient gravées dans sa mémoire, tout comme le souvenir de la saleté durant les trois mois de captivité, et curieusement, ce dont il se souvenait le plus c'était de ses mains et ses ongles continuellement noirs de crasse ; pieds nus, miséreux, son esprit obsessionnellement tourné vers le souvenir de sa maison, essayant d'échapper par la pensée au monde réel de captif dans lequel il vivait… comment exprimer tout cela ? Cela lui semblait impossible, cependant, il a pu écrire dans sa lettre :

« Parmi les hauts faits d'armes de votre héroïque régiment, le 30 avril est un magnifique anniversaire, notamment pour la 3e compagnie du 1er bataillon. Je veux parler du combat de Camerone qui est inscrit dans les plis de son glorieux drapeau. Cette vaillante compagnie, commandée par les valeureux officiers Danjou, Maudet et Villain a été décimée à Camerone le 30 avril 1863. Je viens dire à la Légion qu'il reste un combattant vieux et malade, mais alors le plus jeune de la compagnie (?). Le 30 avril je lèverai mon verre à la santé de l'héroïque Légion et de son colonel ».

Des soixante-cinq combattants de la 3e compagnie du capitaine Danjou, seulement vingt-six noms paraissent régulièrement dans différents comptes rendus et rapports. C'est vraiment peu.

La résistance de la 3e compagnie a réussi à sauver le convoi qui se dirigeait vers Puebla. La perte de l'effet de surprise et d'un nombre important de ses effectifs, a obligé le colonel Milán à renoncer à l'attaque de la colonne. Son arrivée a permis à l'artillerie d'abréger le siège et Puebla est tombée le 19 mai 1863.

A la suite de cette défaite, Benito Juárez a dû annoncer au Congrès, le 31 mai de la même année, le transfert du gouvernement à San Luís de Potosí, à 320 kilomètres au nord de la ville de Mexico, accompagné de diverses légations étrangères, mais pas celles des Etats-Unis d'Amérique, de l'Equateur, du Pérou et du Venezuela.

Les mois suivants, la route de Puebla est restée ouverte sans menaces d'embuscades.

L'évaluation initiale que, suppose-t-on, Danjou a faite, et correcte par ailleurs, est que la cavalerie seule, ne réussirait pas à prendre l'hacienda. Ce qui ne semble pas avoir été prévu c'est l'intervention de l'infanterie qui, finalement, a réussi à atteindre l'objectif militaire.

La résistance héroïque a procédé de la conviction qu'à eu l'unité, après les deux refus de l'offre de reddition et la certitude que le capitaine Saussier n'arriverait pas à temps, qu'aucune échappatoire n'était possible et son désir alors de mourir dignement suivant l'exemple de ses cadres.

Le colonel Milán, dans une lettre envoyée au général Ignacio de Comofort datée du 30 avril à La Joya, pour lui rendre compte du combat, dit que peut-être la tenace résistance des Français était due à leur conviction d'avoir affaire à de simples guérilleros et que de toute façon ils ne sortiraient pas vivants de l'affrontement.

Plus de onze heures de combat sans eau et sans vivres, sans avoir même dormi la nuit précédente et après avoir subi deux assauts en terrain libre. Tout ce faisceau de circonstances a fait entrer la 3e compagnie du 1er bataillon de la Légion étrangère dans la légende.

☆

Jusqu'à la fin de 1863, les effectifs du Régiment étranger allaient être considérablement réduits par les pertes dues aux travaux, aux marches, aux combats et à la fièvre jaune. Le 1er bataillon s'était installé à Córdoba ; deux compagnies de cent hommes du 2e bataillon avaient établi leur cantonnement à La Soledad et le reliquat de l'unité s'était installé à Chiquihuite.

À la fin de décembre de cette année-là, le Régiment étranger avait poursuivi ses missions d'escorte et de protection des convois dans les *terres chaudes*. Depuis son arrivée, la même année, il avait perdu, au combat ou par maladie, onze officiers et huit cents hommes sur un effectif total de mille quatre cents légionnaires.

En 1864, le régiment étranger avait compté jusqu'à cinq bataillons, un escadron et une compagnie autonomes. Plus tard, un 6e bataillon avait été constitué à Aix-en-Provence.

Juan López avait été affecté à l'escadron de cavalerie qui avait été créé en avril 1864, où il vivait entouré d'Allemands, Polonais, Français et quelques Russes.

Une batterie d'artillerie avait été mise sur pied dans l'intention de créer une subdivision, une grande unité constituée de toutes les armes, et la céder à l'empereur Maximilien, comme quand la Légion étrangère avait été cédée en 1835 à Isabel II, reine d'Espagne.

Heureusement pour la Légion, ce projet n'a jamais abouti et, en 1867 elle a été rapatriée avec l'ensemble des forces françaises.

DIVERS

Legio Patria Nostra

La devise de la Légion est *Legio Patria Nostra, " La Légion est notre Patrie"*, et, curieusement formulée en latin, la langue dans laquelle s'exprimaient ces autres légions qui, il y a plus de deux mille ans marchaient depuis Carthage jusqu'aux confins de l'Asie Mineure, passant par la Grande Bretagne et qui étaient composées de germains, d'ibères, de gaulois, de daces, et bien entendu de romains.

Le caractère essentiellement européen de la Légion – bien qu'aujourd'hui, grâce à la globalisation il est de plus en plus fréquent de voir des candidats à l'engagement d'origines asiatique, arabe y américaine – a amené le Centre d'Etudes Européennes au début des années soixante du dernier siècle, à envisager la possibilité que la Légion étrangère devienne une unité militaire placée directement au service de la Communauté Européenne, dans une approche similaire à celle de l'emploi du corps des marines aux Etats-Unis. Cette réflexion a été publiée par Erwan Bergot dans son livre *La Légion.*

Cette possibilité envisagée il y a presque cinquante ans, pourrait redevenir à l'ordre du jour, bien que comme simple hypothèse, devant le manque d'homogénéité et coordination des différentes armées européennes chargées d'intervenir selon divers scenarii sur la scène internationale.

La langue de commandement et de service est le français et la Légion étrangère fait partie intégrante de l'armée française et se place dans la tradition européenne de celle-ci.

Et ainsi, il y a cent cinquante ans, la 3e compagnie du 1er bataillon du régiment de la Légion étrangère détachée au Mexique qui a succombé héroïquement devant une masse d'assaillants, était composée d'Allemands de divers *Länder*, Français, Belges, Suisses, un Autrichien, un Hollandais, un Italien et un Espagnol…

Camerone 2002 et l'auteur

Mon intérêt et mon énorme curiosité pour tout ce qui se rapporte à la Légion étrangère a débuté, de manière étrange et paradoxale, avec la guerre civile espagnole.

A l'âge précoce, et impropre quant à ces questions, de douze ans j'ai commencé à « dévorer » tout ce qui – évidemment toujours du point de vue du vainqueur – se publiait sur ce conflit fratricide. Le soulèvement du 18 juillet, le siège de l'Alcazar de Tolède, les différents combats, jusqu'à la défaite des républicains, m'ont amené, dans mes lectures, à l'exil des républicains et par là, à la seconde guerre mondiale.

Il me paraissait incroyable la manière dont mes compatriotes avaient lutté pendant neuf ans pour leur cause et leurs principes ; et beaucoup d'entre eux, à la Légion étrangère, qui ont passé de la bataille de l'Ebre à Sidi Bel Abbès, tout comme, juste un siècle avant, l'avaient fait les carlistes qui, défaits, avaient traversé la frontière française.

Ils y ont commencé leur odyssée personnelle à Narvik en Norvège, pour lutter ensuite en Erythrée, en Syrie, en Lybie, pour revenir en Europe lors de la campagne d'Italie puis à la France libérée et à l'Allemagne vaincue.

Grâce à *Flon-Flon*, de Serapio Iniesta, passionnant pour moi, et au livre d'Edouard Pons Prades, *Républicains espagnols dans la Seconde guerre mondiale*, qui lui a valu le prix « Miroir d'Espagne » en 1974 j'ai acquis la connaissance de diverses aventures d'espagnols dans ce conflit mondial.

Flon-Flon (sorte d'onomatopée rappelant la fanfare des marches militaires françaises) c'est une nouvelle presque autobiographique du protagoniste dans laquelle sont narrées ses péripéties en terres norvégiennes, à Narvik, puis en Algérie, au Sénégal, et à Tunis pendant la campagne de 1943 qui se termine par la reddition de l'Afrika Corps et des forces italiennes, et avec la reconquête de la Corse. Le récit est écrit avec du rythme, d'une tonalité ironique sur l'environnement légionnaire de l'époque et d'une manière dure et sarcastique sur la France et son armée d'alors. C'est le premier livre d'un triptyque qui continue avec *Paris cet été-là*, qui traite des problèmes des espagnols dans la Résistance française et ceux qui interviendront dans la libération de Paris par la 2e division blindée de Leclerc. Le dernier s'intitule *Pied noir*, qui est le nom dont les arabes d'Algérie affublaient les européens installés dans le pays, à cause des bottines noires qu'ils portaient aux premiers temps de la colonisation. La colonie européenne, avec une importante proportion d'espagnols (dont certains descendants de Juan López) s'est opposée, y compris par des actions terroristes*, à l'indépendance accordée par la France à son ex-colonie. C'est dans ce contexte, romancé, qui se situe le dernier exemplaire de la trilogie.

Certains espagnols sont restés dans la Légion étrangère, voyant en celle-ci *Legio Patria Nostra* y iront en Indochine pour lutter contre le Vietminh ; c'est ainsi, en lisant, qui m'est venu l'intérêt pour la Légion étrangère en tant qu'institution militaire, me paraissant réellement surprenante la capacité de diriger ce mélange de nationalités, de races et origines sociales, pour atteindre un degré de cohésion militaire tel que, sans conteste, elle soit reconnue comme l'une des plus fameuses troupes d'élite, pour ne pas dire la plus fameuse, au moins dans la littérature. Derrière chaque légionnaire il y a une vie qui constitue à elle seule un sujet de roman ou un exemple de survie : ils se donnent une opportunité à eux-mêmes, acceptant le défi de s'intégrer à ce corps militaire unique, et ce encore aujourd'hui dans un monde qui, bien que nos vies soient constamment sous une pression stressante, tout est ou peut être prévisible.

La Légion, son histoire, ses batailles et l'ensemble de ceux qui la composent, constituent une véritable force d'attraction littéraire.

* Perpétrées par l'Organisation de l'Armée Secrète (NdT)

Algérie, 1960

Dans l'entreprise dans laquelle je travaillais, il y a quelque temps, au cours d'une conversation informelle, un de mes interlocuteurs évoquait la mort d'une personne et les tourments par lesquels celle-ci était passée, lorsque son fils, dans une entreprise de fret, avait mal géré l'établissement et avait dû le quitter ; son père avait dû l'aider, y compris financièrement. Le fils avait trouvé la solution dans l'éloignement, et s'était engagé à la Légion en 1959, pendant la guerre d'Algérie.

Le hasard a fait que j'ai connu l'ancien légionnaire en question lorsqu'il était gérant d'un bar. Après que je me sois identifié il a raconté une anecdote qui a éveillé mon attention. Brièvement il m'a dit qu'affecté au *1er Régiment étranger de parachutistes*, jusqu'à sa dissolution, après la participation de cette unité à la tentative de coup d'état contre de Gaulle, événement connu sous le nom de « *putsch d'Alger* » ou « *putsch des généraux* (NdT) », un beau matin alors qu'il se dirigeait vers l'ordinaire pour la *« soupe »*, son attention a été attirée par la démarche et le physique familiers, bien que vus de dos, d'un légionnaire qui le précédait. Arrivé à sa hauteur, il a pu constater qu'il s'agissait d'un ami d'enfance, ami de ses étés sur les plages de Cádix, en Andalousie.

La célébration de Camerone

Tous les ans, le 30 avril, a lieu au quartier Viénot à Aubagne, siège du 1er Régiment étranger, à quelque quinze kilomètres de Marseille, la célébration du combat de Camerone. L'aigle des armes du Mexique, figure, comme un permanent souvenir, sur l'insigne de ce régiment. (Ce quartier est aussi le siège de la maison-mère de la Légion étrangère).

La main en bois du capitaine Danjou est portée sur la voie sacrée, long couloir entre deux parterres fleuris sur l'immense place d'armes, qui se termine devant le monument aux morts de la Légion, érigé grâce à une souscription populaire en 1931, pour commémorer le centenaire de la Légion étrangère. Cette main avait été localisée par le lieutenant Grüber, le 17 juillet 1865, alors qu'il effectuait une patrouille avec son unité appartenant au corps expéditionnaire autrichien. La prothèse se trouvait en possession d'un agriculteur mexicain d'origine française, monsieur L'Anglais, propriétaire d'une ferme près de Teziutlán. Grüber a réussi à convaincre le propriétaire de la lui vendre, arguant du grand intérêt de la famille Danjou, et a ainsi réussi l'achat pour cinquante piastres.

Plus tard, le lieutenant a remis la prothèse au général comte Le Thun qui l'a fait parvenir à Bazaine, commandant en chef du corps expéditionnaire français, qui a remis cinquante piastres au général autrichien, par billet à l'ordre du commandant supérieur de Puebla, afin de faire rembourser le lieutenant Grüber qui les avait déjà réclamées prétextant des difficultés financières.

Lors du rapatriement des troupes françaises en 1867, le colonel Guilhem a emporté la main à Sidi Bel-Abbès où elle a été installée dans la salle d'honneur du 1er régiment étranger, pour arriver ensuite à Aubagne.

Le monument consiste en un tronc de pyramide en marbre surmonté d'un globe terrestre en bronze portant en doré les territoires où la Légion a combattu ; la sphère qui repose sur des palmes est entourée de guirlandes de laurier et feuilles de chêne est gardée aux coins de la pyramide par des statues de quatre légionnaires en bronze représentant, par leurs uniformes, les époques les plus significatives du premier siècle de l'existence de la Légion*. La main, qui se trouve exposée dans un coffret en bois et en verre dans la crypte du musée de la Légion, est portée chaque année par un ancien de la Légion ayant à son actif de nombreux mérites militaires et une vie civile irréprochable. Il est flanqué par deux autres légionnaires également méritants**.

L'une des principales séquences de la cérémonie est le récit du texte officiel du combat de Camerone fait par un officier de la Légion en activité de service, (qui se place au centre de la voie sacrée, face au monument et au porteur de la main. NdT)

Au cours des trois commémorations auxquelles il m'a été donné d'assister, en 2000, 2002 et 2017, accompagné de Mercedes, mon épouse, assis sur les tribunes réservées aux invités, j'ai pu apprécier le festif mélange de groupes de vétérans qui parlaient en italien, d'autres en allemand, nombreux anglophones et différentes délégations militaires des pays européens, avec une présence majoritaire d'Italiens, suivis, la dernière fois, d'espagnols de la Légion espagnole et de représentants de l'infanterie espagnole.

* A l'origine, le socle du monument avait été taillé dans de l'onyx, extrait par les légionnaires d'une carrière ouverte expressément dans ce but. Une route a dû être construite par eux pour en permettre l'accès. Malgré les soins, le démontage et le transport ont provoqué beaucoup de dégâts et c'est finalement en marbre de Provence qu'il a été reconstruit. Côté place d'armes il porte l'inscription « La Légion à ses morts », côté musée « Honneur et Fidélité ». Dans le monument original cette face recevait, dans une niche dissimulée, le registre des morts de la Légion. Quelques importantes réductions du monumet avaient été réalisées. L'une d'elles se trouve au Musée, d'autres dans les Salle d'honneur de quelques régiments : 1er REC, 2°REI, 1er REG…(NdT)

** Il n'en a pas toujours été ainsi. Parfois cet accompagnement a été fait par des légionnaires en activité, sans mérites particuliers, uniquement pour pouvoir aider, si besoin, un porteur de la main au physique défaillant (NdT).

Les compagnies du 1er Régiment étranger*** marchent à quatre-vingt-huit pas à la minute, au son de la Musique de la Légion, dont les tambours (dits « caisses-claires » NdT) sont portés à hauteur des genoux et dont le roulement est souligné par le son aigu (« contre-ut » NdT) des fifres.

Après la cérémonie militaire, un apéritif à base de vin blanc, produit par les anciens de la Légion, non loin de là, dans le vignoble de Puyloubier, près d'Aix-en-Provence, un coin magnifique de la région provençale, est servi.

La tradition de la célébration de Camerone tient son origine dans un poste de Tu Lung, aux marches du Tonkin, dans ce qui était une partie de l'Indochine, aujourd'hui Vietnam, en 1906, quand, le 30 avril, le lieutenant François a fait la lecture du récit du combat devant ses légionnaires.

La cérémonie a été institutionnalisée avec la solennité et le lustre actuels en 1931, à l'occasion de la célébration du centenaire de la Légion étrangère. Dans un rituel déjà établi, la main de Danjou a été portée sur la voie sacrée pour la première fois en 1936****.

Quand mon épouse et moi nous dirigions vers la kermesse, lors de Camerone 2002 à Aubagne, après le vin d'honneur, j'ai entendu un légionnaire qui s'adressait à un autre qui l'écoutait attentivement, en espagnol. Je me suis identifié auprès d'eux comme espagnol et celui qui parlait m'a dit être originaire de Jaén, ce qui a fait que nous nous sommes salués comme andalous aussi. J'ai questionné l'autre légionnaire mais c'est mon compatriote qui a répondu à sa place, car il s'agissait d'un Portugais.

*** Comme toutes les unités de Légion. La cadence réglementaire, donc obligatoire, est de 88 pas/minute, depuis de très nombreuses années. Jadis, parfois, les unités avaient tendance à adopter une cadence frôlant la soixantaine de pas (NdT).

**** La place d'armes du Quartier Viénot à Sidi Bel-Abbès comportait une voie sacrée, définie par un axe allant du centre de l'entrée du quartier au bâtiment central, passant par le monument aux morts. C'est le modèle qui a été adopté, lors de la construction de l'actuel siège de la maison-mère de la Légion, le bâtiment principal étant, dans ce cas-ci, le musée de la Légion étrangère (NdT).

Et je me suis alors rappelé Alonso Bernardo parlant, dans cette nuit du 30 avril 1863 avec Casimir Laï, l'Italien.

L'adjudant Emilio Condado Madera, espagnol originaire de Cantabrie, était alors le conservateur du musée de la Légion étrangère à Aubagne. J'ai eu avec lui un aimable entretien – qui a constitué comme une curiosité pour moi – dans son bureau militaire ; nous avons parlé du recrutement ; des chinois plus ou moins prédestinés à exercer les métiers de bouche, ou bien des slaves qui intègrent la Musique de la Légion étrangère de par leur condition de virtuose dans les formations musicales de leurs pays d'origine, ou des volontaires espagnols pendant la première guerre mondiale. Le recrutement légionnaire est bien le reflet constant des vicissitudes historiques, sociales, personnelles des légionnaires du monde entier, puisque plus de cent trente nationalités se côtoient dans les rangs de la Légion actuelle.

L'évolution même du recrutement et du personnel engagé constituent la représentation des convulsions politiques et sociales de l'Europe du siècle dernier et du monde dans le siècle actuel. Après la chute du Mur de Berlin le recrutement de la Légion est devenu majoritairement slave, comme il a été espagnol après la guerre civile en 1939 et à une majorité écrasante allemand, à la fin de la seconde guerre mondiale, en 1945.

Dans les années quatre-vingts, après la guerre des Malouines, la Légion a connu une grande affluence anglo-saxonne. A partir de 1989, lors de la chute du rideau de fer, le recrutement était majoritairement slave et ce phénomène a continué de progresser. Ainsi durant l'année 2000, le pourcentage de volontaires en provenance des pays de l'est recrutés, était de presque 55% et en 2002 de presque 39%. L'effectif total de la Légion est de huit mille quatre cents soixante-et-un hommes, alors qu'il a atteint, dans les années cinquante du siècle dernier, autour de trente-six mille légionnaires, à l'époque de la guerre d'Indochine, période où se sont écrites quelques-unes des plus belles pages d'héroïsme et de don de soi de ce corps, au service de la France, les événements de la guerre d'Algérie étant, finalement, l'étape la plus traumatisante pour la Légion qui a dû renaître et redevenir le fer de lance, dans le domaine militaire, de la politique extérieure de la France.

La Légion demeure un authentique mythe devenu réalité, dont l'essence, comme force militaire, a consisté à savoir s'adapter aux différentes missions qui lui ont été et lui sont confiées ; sa participation à tous les grands événements guerriers pendant les deux derniers siècles, en atteste. Mais c'est un mythe bien réel sous l'aspect sociologique, dès lors qu'elle offre une seconde opportunité à chaque engagé et un défi personnel à sa capacité d'adaptation ; ceux qui se sont vus déracinés de leur environnement par des guerres, le chômage ou simplement inadaptation sociale, trouvent dans la Légion étrangère une nouvelle opportunité, une nouvelle famille, sans que rien leur soit demandé en échange, leur disant simplement que cet engagement peut éventuellement les conduire au sacrifice suprême, et les oblige à vivre au quotidien une vie de soldat dont la routine et la dureté peuvent parfois paraître insupportables et, en échange, pour ceux qui ne sont plus rien, la fierté d'appartenir à un corps différent, se sentir différents du commun. Alonso Bernardo a dû ressentir cela, même si son instinct de survie refusait de l'admettre, il savait qu'il allait mourir, lui, le pauvre villageois, triste et mourant de faim, avait trouvé là, sa place dans l'Histoire.

Dans le monde où nous vivons, tout est prévisible ; peu de choses échappent à notre volonté, au moins dans le domaine matériel, le niveau de confort est tel qui nous place très loin de la grandeur qui présuppose être la victime de sa propre vie et de ce que celle-ci peut infliger sans ménagements ni miséricorde.

Beaucoup des problèmes de santé physique et psychique rencontrés actuellement sont le résultat de cette constante abondance alors qu'il n'y a pas si longtemps, dans beaucoup de nos pays, la seule sensation ressentie était la faim constante ; porter des chaussures constituait un authentique luxe. Les cuites colossales étaient l'unique diversion et la seule échappatoire et les sensations fortes étaient procurées par les duels voulus ou acceptés. Les conditions de vie des soldats n'avaient pas beaucoup changé par rapport à celles des soldats romains d'il y a deux mille ans. Et cette dureté – pas toujours, il est vrai – leur conférait de la dignité, dignité pour mourir.

Aujourd'hui où nous avons de tout en excès, il nous manque peut-être quelque chose du sens de l'épique pour croire que l'esprit domine le corps, qu'il s'élève et s'impose à la mort et à la peur que nous en avons et ainsi nous grandit et nous immortalise dans la mémoire des autres. C'est la raison pour laquelle je me rappelle Alonso, son ignorance, sa faim, son déracinement… et sa valeur.

J'ai vibré en écoutant le récit du combat de Camerone au Quartier Viénot, le 30 avril, et écoutant respectueusement La Marseillaise, entouré de Français, Italiens, Allemands, Portugais, tous ensemble sur les gradins, debout ; et c'est dans ces moments que je ressens l'Europe comme une réalité, une réalité vivante là, à Aubagne, et je suis ému.

La Palma del Condado, février 2004.
Pour la deuxième édition, La Palma del Condado, nov. 2011.
Pour la troisième édition, La Palma del Condado, jan. 2022.

ANNEXES

Récit officiel du Combat de Camerone

(Récité chaque année, le 30 avril, devant les troupes de la Légion étrangère* partout où elles sont cantonnées dans le monde).

L'Armée française assiégeait Puebla.

La Légion avait pour mission d'assurer, sur 120 kilomètres, la circulation et la sécurité des convois.

Le colonel Jeanningros, qui commandait, apprend, le 29 avril 1863, qu'un gros convoi emportant trois millions en numéraire, du matériel de siège et des munitions, était en route pour Puebla. Le capitaine Danjou, son adjudant-major, le décide à envoyer au-devant du convoi une compagnie. La 3e compagnie du régiment étranger fut désignée, mais elle n'avait pas d'officiers disponibles. Le capitaine Danjou en prend lui-même le commandement et les sous-lieutenants Maudet, porte-drapeau et Vilain, payeur, se joignent à lui volontairement.

Le 30 avril à une heure du matin, la 3e compagnie, forte de trois officiers et soixante-deux hommes se met en route. Elle avait parcouru environ vingt kilomètres quand, à sept heures du matin elle s'arrête à Palo Verde pour faire le café. A ce moment l'ennemi se dévoile et le combat s'engage aussitôt. Le capitaine Danjou fait former le carré et, tout en battant en retraite, repousse plusieurs charges de cavalerie, en infligeant à l'ennemi des premières pertes sévères.

Arrivé à hauteur de l'auberge de Camerone, vaste bâtisse comportant une cour entourée d'un mur de trois mètres de haut, il décide de s'y retrancher pour fixer l'ennemi et retarder le plus possible le moment où celui-ci pourra attaquer le convoi.

Pendant que les hommes organisent à la hâte la défense de cette auberge, un officier mexicain, faisant valoir la grosse supériorité du nombre, somme le capitaine Danjou de se rendre. Celui-ci fait répondre : « Nous avons des cartouches et ne nous rendrons pas. », puis, levant la main il jura de se défendre jusqu'à la mort et fit prêter à ses hommes le même serment. Il était dix heures. Jusqu'à six heures du soir, ces soixante hommes qui n'avaient pas mangé ni bu depuis la veille, malgré la chaleur, la faim et la soif, résistent à deux mille Mexicains, huit cents cavaliers, mille deux cents fantassins.

A midi, le capitaine Danjou est tué d'une balle en pleine poitrine. A deux heures, le sous-lieutenant Vilain tombe, frappé d'une balle au front. A ce moment, le colonel mexicain réussit à mettre le feu à l'auberge.

Malgré la chaleur et la fumée qui viennent augmenter leurs souffrances, les légionnaires tiennent bon, mais beaucoup d'entre eux sont frappés. A cinq heures, au tour du sous-lieutenant Maudet il ne reste que douze hommes en état de combattre.

A ce moment, le colonel mexicain rassemble ses hommes et leur dit de quelle honte ils vont se couvrir s'ils n'arrivent pas à abattre cette poignée de braves (un légionnaire qui comprend l'espagnol, traduit au fur et à mesure ses paroles).

Les Mexicains vont donner l'assaut général par les brèches qu'ils ont réussi à ouvrir, mais auparavant, le colonel Milán adresse une dernière sommation au sous-lieutenant Maudet ; celui-ci la repousse avec mépris.

L'assaut final est donné. Bientôt il ne reste au tour de Maudet que cinq hommes : le caporal Maine, les légionnaires Catteau, Wensel, Constantin, Leonhard. Chacun garde encore une cartouche ; ils ont la baïonnette au canon et, réfugiés dans un coin de la cour, le dos au mur, ils font face. A un signal ils déchargent leurs fusils à bout portant sur l'ennemi et se précipitent sur lui à la baïonnette. Le sous-lieutenant Maudet et deux légionnaires tombent frappés à mort. Maine et ses deux camarades vont être massacrés quand un officier mexicain se précipite sur eux et les sauve. Il leur crie : « Rendez-vous !».

« Nous nous rendrons si vous nous promettez de relever et de soigner nos blessés et si vous nous laissez nos armes ». Leurs baïonnettes restent menaçantes.

« On ne refuse rien à des hommes comme vous !», répond l'officier.

Les soixante hommes du capitaine Danjou ont tenu jusqu'au bout leur serment. Pendant onze heures ils ont résisté à deux mille ennemis, en ont tué trois cents et blessé autant. Ils ont par leur sacrifice, en sauvant le convoi, rempli la mission qui leur avait été confiée.

L'empereur Napoléon III décida que le nom de Camerone serait inscrit sur le drapeau du Régiment étranger et que de plus les noms de Danjou, Vilain et Maudet seraient gravés en lettres d'or sur les murs des Invalides à Paris.

*En outre, un monument fut érigé en 1892 sur les lieux du combat. Il porte l'inscription**:*

Ils furent ici moins de soixante opposés à toute une armée.
Sa masse les écrasa, la vie plutôt que le courage,
abandonna ces soldats français le 30 avril 1863.
A leur mémoire la patrie éleva ce monument.***

Depuis, lorsque les troupes mexicaines passent devant le monument, elles présentent les armes ».

* Les amicales d'anciens légionnaires, commémorent de par le monde, le combat de Camerone et en font également le récit (NdT).

** A ce moment, le récitant arrête le récit, le commandant des troupes commande « Présentez armes », seulement alors le récitant reprend la parole (NdT).

*** En réalité, la pierre tombale initiale portait une inscription en latin :

QVOS HIC NON PLVS LX
ADVERSI TOTIVS AGMINIS
MOLES CONSTRAVIT
VITA PRIAM QUAM VIRTVS
MILITES DESERVIT GALLICOS
DIE XXX MENSI APR. ANNI MDCCCLXIII
IN MEMORIAM HOC MONUMENTUM SUIS PATRIA PONEBAT
ANNO MDCCCXCII

Lorsque le monument définitif fut érigé, à l'occasion du centenaire du combat, l'inscription a été remplacée par celle, connue, en français. (NdT).

Narration partielle du combat par deux de ses protagonistes

Dans le récit du combat figurent aussi les témoignages de certains protagonistes tels les caporaux Evariste Berg et Louis Maine ; ce dernier a fait sa propre narration des derniers moments du combat avec toute l'intensité dramatique du déroulement d'une telle journée vécue par l'unité légionnaire et dont la fin approchait :

« Je me trouvais entre le sergent Morzicki, placé à ma gauche et le sous-lieutenant Maudet à ma droite. Tout à coup Morzicki reçut à la tempe une balle venant d'un coin de la brèche ; son corps s'inclina et sa tête inerte vint s'appuyer sur mon épaule, je me retournai et le vis face à face, la bouche et les yeux grand ouverts.- Morzicki est mort ! dis-je au lieutenant qui me répondit froidement que notre tour s'annonçait. Il continue à tirer. Nous n'étions plus que cinq, Maudet, un Prussien de nom Wenzel, Catteau, Constantin et moi. Pourtant nous tenions toujours l'ennemi en respect, mais notre résistance tirait à sa fin, les cartouches allaient en s'épuisant. Bientôt il nous restât qu'une à chacun. Il était 6 heures environ et nous combattions depuis le matin. ».

Dans les instants précédant la fin, seuls trois légionnaires tenaient encore debout, l'un d'eux, le caporal Maine qui a maintenu le dialogue en espagnol avec l'officier supérieur mexicain jusqu'à la reddition des trois derniers légionnaires le décrit ainsi :

« ...mais déjà les Mexicains nous entouraient de toutes partes et la pointe de leurs baïonnettes effleuraient nos poitrines. C'en était fait de nous quand un homme de haute taille aux traits distingués, qui se trouvait au premier rang parmi les assaillants, reconnaissable à son képi et sa petite tunique galonnée qui laissait deviner un officier supérieur, leur ordonna de s'arrêter et, d'un brusque mouvement de son sabre, releva les baïonnettes qui nous menaçaient. – Rendez-vous, nous dit-il. – Nous nous rendrons,

répondis-je, si vous nous laissez nos armes et notre fourniment, et si vous vous engagez à faire relever et soigner notre lieutenant que voici, blessé ! L'officier consentit à tout puis, comme ces premiers mots avaient été échangés en espagnol : - Parlez-moi en français, me dit-il, cela vaudra mieux, sans quoi ces hommes vont vous prendre pour un espagnol, ils voudront vous massacrer et peut-être je ne pourrai pas me faire obéir… ».

Ce récit révèle le fait qu'au moins trois des membres de la compagnie Danjou parlaient l'espagnol : les légionnaires Bernardo, Gustave Bertollo et le caporal Louis Maine.

Après la reddition des trois survivants, commandés par le caporal Maine, celui-ci continuait son récit :

« …le colonel Gambas avait été élevé en France et parlait notre langue admirablement (…) Nous étions arrivés ainsi dans un petit pli de terrain à quelque distance de l'hacienda où se tenait le colonel Milán et son état-major. – C'est tout ce qu'il en reste, demanda-t-il en nous apercevant. On lui répondit que oui et, ne pouvant contenir sa surprise – Mais ce ne sont pas des hommes, s'exclama-t-il, ce sont des démons ! ».

Le magazine *Képi Blanc* n° 841 d'avril 2021 a publié un assez long et très complet article du major Frédéric Ambrosino, sur l'évolution des différentes narrations du combat de Camerone, jusqu'à ce qu'elles s'articulent, se construisent et se fondent en un seul récit officiel de l'événement selon les trois principales sources : le commandant Regnault et les déjà cités Évariste Berg et Louis Maine.

En terminant son article le major Ambrosino écrivait : « …et c'est une évidence, chaque légionnaire, d'active ou ancien, où qu'il se trouve, en métropole, outre-mer, à l'étranger, au sein d'une amicale, chez lui en famille, entre amis, au Mali, sur l'Oyapock, à la garde, en stage, à l'hôpital, à Puyloubier, partout dans le monde, s'arrêtera quelques instants pour se souvenir du sacrifice des soixante-quatre braves du capitaine Danjou qui sont allés jusqu'au bout de la parole donnée .».

Et c'est là l'essentiel.

Equipements et uniformes

Une plus grande sobriété dans les uniformes militaires est une tendance bien marquée dans la seconde moitié du 19e siècle. Si, pendant sa première moitié les couleurs vives et les parements servaient à distinguer les belligérants sur les champs de bataille, toujours ouverts sur de grands espaces, nécessitant une grande lisibilité des positions des troupes grâce aux couleurs, un changement s'amorce quand l'artillerie moderne prend une part prépondérante dans la bataille, la guerre de mouvement cède sa place à la guerre de positions, dans les tranchées, puis les guerres coloniales.

L'équipement du légionnaire de la campagne du Mexique était composé du képi avec couvre-nuque en tissu blanc, coiffure qui allait immortaliser l'image du légionnaire, après la première guerre mondiale du 20e siècle.

La vareuse était bleu marine avec des boutons dorés. Les troupes légionnaires ont débarqué avec un pantalon blanc écru, déjà utilisé en Algérie, tout comme les guêtres de même couleur. La vareuse ou manteau des officiers comprenait neuf boutons dorés portant l'inscription Légion étrangère au tour d'une grenade flamboyante ; de ces boutons, seul le premier en haut, se boutonnait, celui du col, sur lequel ils portaient une lavallière de soie noire. Ils étaient armés du sabre modèle 1845, modifié en 1855 et du pistolet à barillet modèle 1833, de tous les types et catégories, modifié en 1853.

Les galons d'officier étaient cousus sur les manches des vareuses, aux avant-bras, entrelacés et formant des *hongroises*, terminés en pointe de lance, haut sur les manches. Les manchettes, ou revers de manche, étaient ornées de petits boutons en cuir doré. Les bottes étaient noires.

Seule la troupe portait sur les épaules des épaulettes à franges, de couleur verte, propres à l'infanterie de ligne. Sur la veste, à hauteur de la taille, ils portaient une ceinture de flanelle rouge, beige ou bleue - cette dernière étant toujours d'actualité sur la tenue de parade des légionnaires – sa finalité était de protéger le ventre des coups de froid. Le ceinturon était large, en cuir noir, avec une énorme boucle en métal doré de forme rectangulaire, et portait une grande cartouchière placée presque en position ventrale, ornée elle aussi de la grenade flamboyante, mais d'un dessin différent de l'actuel et une longue baïonnette. Un sac souple en toile blanche barrait leur poitrine en diagonale.

A dos, un havresac sur lequel une couverture et une toile de tente étaient assujetties au moins de courroies et sur les côtés les piquets et mât de la tente.

Selon un témoignage recueilli, le légionnaire de 1840 emportait « sur son dos une cartouchière de quarante cartouches, un sac à dos rectangulaire en cuir rigide, des rations pour huit jours, chaussures de rechange, chemises, sous-vêtements, chaussettes, un nécessaire à couture et un autre pour l'entretien du fusil, une fourche, plusieurs couteaux, au moins deux cuillères, une bougie, savon et des condiments alimentaires ; accrochés à l'extérieur du sac, un tapis de sol, une peau de mouton, une moitié de tente, un bidon d'un litre et un gobelet en étain. A tout cet équipement il était nécessaire d'ajouter le fusil, la baïonnette, un fagot de bois récupéré en chemin pour le feu du soir qui était porté au sommet du sac ». La majeure partie des légionnaires portaient un bâton à la main qui, selon l'historien Douglas Porch « présente trois avantages : ils s'en aident pour gravir des pentes escarpées, placé sous le sac à dos il permet d'alléger la charge pendant les haltes de courte durée (seuls les novices enlèvent les sacs pour soulager les épaules) et enfin leur sert de mât de tente ».

En 1863, le bidon métallique était de forme rectangulaire, comparable à celui de l'armée britannique pendant la seconde guerre mondiale. Comme bidon supplémentaire ils utilisaient une gourde faite d'une calebasse évidée, dont l'image est liée à celle du pèlerin avec son bâton et sa calebasse pour porter l'eau*.

* Equipement des anciens pèlerins sur le chemin de Saint Jacques de Compostelle (NdT).

Le pantalon garance – comme celui avec lequel les troupes ont débarqué au Mexique - était porté par toute l'armée française en métropole. L'ensemble vareuse bleu marine et pantalon garance est resté en usage dans l'armée française, jusqu'au début de la première guerre mondiale.

Les troupes montées garderont la culotte rouge jusqu'à la fin de la campagne.

Peu après le débarquement au Mexique, des sombreros de paille ornés d'un ruban noir et à large bord ont été distribués aux soldats qui en ont apprécié l'usage. Cependant, les légionnaires de Camerone portaient encore le képi, puisque le combat a eu lieu à peine un mois après leur débarquement, avant la distribution des chapeaux de paille.

En saison froide, sur la vareuse, le légionnaire portait une redingote d'un bleu plus clair qui correspond à l'image littéraire de la Légion dans le désert, au début du 20e siècle.

La cavalerie, après la création d'un escadron en 1864 - dissous à la fin de la campagne – portait la culotte garance avec une bande verticale, de chaque côté, d'une couleur foncée ; les faces internes de la culotte, à hauteur des cuisses étaient renforcées en cuir, pour mieux résister à l'usure provoquée par le frottement sur la selle. La tenue des cavaliers se détachait aussi par l'emploi généralisé du sombrero civil mexicain où même le sombrero indigène, recouvert d'une housse blanche.

Bibliographie, données et références historiques

– *La Légion*, de Erwan Bergot. Editions Balland, 1972 Fr. Asesoria Tecnica de Ediciones, 1976 Es.

– *La intervención francesa en España (1835-1839)*, de Emilio Condado Madera, Fundamentos Ediciones, 2002 Es.

L'auteur y justifie l'engagement d'étrangers, comme explication originelle de création de la Légion étrangère dans les convulsions de la première moitié du 19e siècle, par la nécessité de regrouper les nombreux exilés et réfugiés européens qui essaimaient la France à cette époque, et de les éloigner de la métropole, alors même qu'il était difficilement envisageable d'obtenir des documents d'identité du flot continu d'exilés et d'immigrants qui envahissaient la France.

En 1834, le 4e bataillon composé exclusivement d'espagnols est dissous ; le récit de son rapatriement d'Espagne est recueilli ainsi dans *Intervencion francesa en España (1835-1839)* :

« En 1834, les centaines d'espagnols qui formaient le 4e bataillon et dont le contrat de trois ans touchait à sa fin, libérés de leurs obligations militaires de la Légion, devaient être conduits jusqu'à Toulon. Par l'entremise du chargé d'affaires à Paris il a été sollicité du gouvernement français qu'ils soient acheminés directement d'Oran à Carthagène, pour éviter ainsi que certains succombent aux mains des ennemis déclarés de Sa Majesté, en entrant par la province du nord. Comme indiqué dans le précédent rapport de l'arrêté royal du 29 juin 1834, non seulement la proposition a été acceptée, comme il a été donné dispense à tous les espagnols, du temps de service leur restant à accomplir, comme récompense de l'estime et de l'amitié qu'ils portaient au gouvernement espagnol ».

« Le 18 avril 1834, la frégate espagnole *Victoria* est arrivée au port de Carthagène avec un contingent de quatre cent soixante-douze hommes, trois officiers et un chirurgien, aux ordres du capitaine Antonio Buil. Des ordres ont été immédiatement donnés au gouverneur de la place pour le transfert des anciens soldats à leurs foyers et la question de leur volontariat pour entrer au service de la reine a été posée. Malgré le rapport de Buil, qui reflétait le désir de ces troupes de rejoindre les rangs de la régente Marie Christine, la majorité se sont rétractés et seulement deux cents quarante-quatre individus ont été incorporés au 3e bataillon du régiment d'infanterie de Almansa nº 18 de ligne »

– *La Légion étrangère (1831-1962)*, de Douglas Porch. Fayard, 1994.

Selon Douglas Porch, la piètre opinion du commandement français envers l'unité créée en 1840 et formée exclusivement d'espagnols, une immense majorité de réfugiés carlistes, était basée, à ce moment-là dans la dure réalité des événements, mais a changé par la suite. Ainsi il recueille les différents témoignages suivants, concernant l'année 1844 :

« Les espagnols sont considérés unanimement comme les meilleurs marcheurs, d'apparence chétive, ils ne cèdent dans ce domaine ni aux Belges ni aux Allemands, écrit Randon. Les carlistes semblent avoir fait oublier leur détestable réputation ; en 1844 le général Baril déclare que les espagnols sont en Afrique comme chez eux, pour ainsi dire. Le climat et, jusqu'à un certain point, les habitudes et les manières se ressemblent (je considère l'observation du général quelque peu exagérée). Ces carlistes, habitués aux fatigues et aux dangers de la guerre étaient pour notre Légion étrangère, une source inépuisable de recrutement. Marcheurs infatigables, d'une sobriété absolue, ils étaient de véritables soldats d'élite qui devaient fournir, après leur libération, de solides éléments de colonisation. Mac Mahon louangeait les soldats Allemands sous ses ordres : « La majeure partie ce sont des vétérans énergiques, qui marchent bien, mais comme tireurs ils sont très loin des espagnols. Ces derniers étaient de vrais soldats d'Afrique, intelligents, marcheurs et d'une grande bravoure. Pendant la saison chaude, en rencontrant un cours d'eau, leurs camarades arrêtaient et plongeaient la tête sous l'eau en en buvant d'inimaginables quantités. J'ai vu, dans des cas semblables, succomber plusieurs Allemands sur place, alors que les espagnols et les Turcs ne s'arrêtaient pas et se contentaient d'avaler quelques gorgées puisées au creux de leur main ».

– Revue *L'Histoire,* édition monographique consacrée à la Légion étrangère, année 1996.

– Magazine *Képi Blanc, La vie de la Légion étrangère.* Numéros 241 (mai 1967), 253 (mai 1968),289(mai 1971), 401 (avril 1981), 457 (avril 1986), 584 (décembre 1997), 600 (mai 1999), 610 (avril 2000), 621 (avril 2001), 710 (mai 2009) et 841 (avril 2021).

Un article paru dans le n° 253 du magazine *Képi blanc, la vie de la Légion étrangère* de mai 1968, précise que seuls cinquante-trois des sous-officiers et légionnaires (de la 3e compagnie NdT) sont d'origine connue, dans cet article il est rapporté que huit sont officiellement Français, quinze se déclarent Belges, treize se disent Allemands, auxquels il faudrait ajouter un autrichien et huit de nationalité suisse. Deux Espagnols sont également nommés, Bernardo et le caporal del Caretto, né à Oran ; deux Italiens, le tambour Laï et Bartello ou Bartellotto, né à Toulon, et encore un Hollandais et un Danois.

Dans la compagnie, par les dates de naissance figurent trois légionnaires qui n'avaient pas accompli leur dix-huitième anniversaire le 30 avril 1863 :

- Louis Lernould
- Jean Louis Timmermans
- Pharaon Van der Bulche.

Le sergent Palmaert s'est engagé à dix-sept ans, quatre mois et dix-sept jours, mais s'est déclaré plus âgé d'un an.

Dans le même article de *Képi blanc*, il est fait état du légionnaire Reuss, né le 28 mai 1845, engagé à Strasbourg le 6 janvier 1863 qui est tombé aux premiers moments du combat ; c'était un des benjamins de l'unité. Il a été, probablement, le dernier à rejoindre la compagnie, peut-être même sur le quai du port d'Oran. Il est mort dans les accrochages qui ont précédé l'occupation de l'auberge de la Trinidad ; pourtant son patronyme ne figure pas dans le rapport officiel de la 3e compagnie du 1er bataillon du Régiment étranger. Dans la liste figurant sur l'exemplaire de *Képi blanc* cité, le légionnaire Belge Louis Stoller, bruxellois n'est pas mentionné.

Deux Allemands, Frédéric Fritz et Geoffrey Wensel ont dépassé les quarante ans.

Dans le n° 600 du même magazine, sur la liste de la compagnie Danjou, la localité mentionnée comme lieu de naissance du légionnaire Bernardo, Aloyse (!?), Wilaricho, n'a pas pu être identifiée par l'auteur bien que Emilio Condado Madera, écrivain et sous-officier de la Légion, possède des indices qui indiquent qu'il s'agirait d'une petite bourgade asturienne, ce qui, pour raisons littéraires nous avons tenu pour exact. Mais ce n'est pas un cas unique ; il existe d'autres lieux fictifs donnés comme lieux de naissance de légionnaires de la 3e compagnie, tels que Bilan, lieu ignoré en Belgique, où Timmermans aurait vu le jour (*Képi blanc, la vie de la Légion étrangère*, n° 289, mai 1971) :

Dans le n° 688 du magazine daté de mai 2007, figure la statistique suivante :

- Morts à la suite de blessures : 9
- Prisonniers (dont 17 blessés) : 24
- Cas exceptionnel : 1 légionnaire, le tambour Laï

Dans cet exemplaire Delcaretto est identifié comme un espagnol d'Oran tout comme dans la liste des légionnaires de la 3ème compagnie parue sur le numéro 253 de *Képi blanc*.

En mai 1971, le n° 289 du magazine légionnaire, publie une statistique des combattants par nationalités : vingt Allemands, un Autrichien, seize Belges, un Danois, un Espagnol, un Hollandais, un Italien, huit Suisses et treize Français*, dont six fils de père étranger.

*Beaucoup de légionnaires d'origine française recevaient, au poste de recrutement, un nouveau pays d'origine de langue française : Belgique, Suisse, Principauté de Monaco. Il est donc difficile d'établir, pour certains d'entre eux la nationalité réelle. A un moment, dans le dernier tiers du 20e siècle, la Principauté de Monaco croulant sous les dossiers de désertion à instruire, a demandé à la France de ne plus utiliser la Principauté comme lieu d'origine pour des légionnaires non réellement Monégasques (NdT).

Dans sa livraison de mai 2008, nº 699, *Képi blanc* publiait le texte suivant :

« A Camerone le capitaine Danjou et ses officiers Maudet et Vilain ont « inscrit dans le marbre » ce qui doit être le rôle de tous les officiers, toujours en tête pour donner l'impulsion nécessaire et maintenir l'ardeur de la troupe ».

« A Camerone, le sergent-major Tonel et les sous-officiers Morzycki, Germeys, Palmaert et Schaffner ont été la colonne vertébrale de la défense, depuis la riposte aux premières charges de cavalerie, jusqu'aux instants ultimes, dans le coin de la cour ».

« A Camerone les caporaux Favas et Delcaretto, les légionnaires Bass, Bernardo, Bertollo, Billod, Bogucki, Brugisser, Catteau, Catenhusen, Dael, Daglincks, Dicken, Dubois, Friedrich, Fritz, Furbasz, Groux, Hipp, Konrad, Kurz, Langmeier, Lemmer, Léonhart, Lernould, Rebers, Seiler, Stoller, Timmermans, Van der Meersche, Vandesavel, de Vries et Wittgens ont donné leur vie pour un pays qu'initialement n'était pas le leur, mais qu'ils avaient choisi de servir ».

« A Camerone, les caporaux Berg, Maine et Pinzinger, les légionnaires Gaertner, Gorski, Hiller, Magnin, Merlet, Rohr, Schiffer, Schreiblich, Seffrin, Sergers, van der Bulche, Verjus et Wensel ont souffert dans leur chair les blessures dues au combat, mais qui auront été traités avec respect et ont été échangés par les Mexicains contre certains de leurs officiers prisonniers des Français ».

« A Camerone, les légionnaires Brunswick, Conrad, Constantin, Kunasseg, van Opstal et Zey n'ont pas été touchés pendant dix heures de combat et par le hasard de la mitraille. Combattant debout jusqu'aux derniers instants, ils ont été capturés dans leurs postes de combat encerclés et dont chacun d'eux a été le dernier ; jusqu'à ce Constantin, sorte le dernier de l'hacienda, par ses propres moyens, avec son arme et indemne, soutenant son caporal Maine et son camarade Wensel ».

« A Camerone, le tambour Laï, le plus pittoresque de cet ensemble hétéroclite, presque la mascotte de la compagnie, donné pour mort sur le terrain et qui a été retrouvé le lendemain par la colonne de secours. Il est le seul à être sorti libre de ce combat d'anthologie ».

Selon un article paru dans le *Képi blanc* n° 710 de mai 2009, Casimiro Laï s'était présenté au dépôt de la Légion à Lyon le 22 septembre 1862 prétendant être né le 27 septembre 1839 à Cagliari en Sardaigne (Italie), et déclarant avoir été soldat. De petite taille mais d'une constitution propre à être accepté, il a débarqué à Alger le 3 octobre de la même année. Affecté au 1er bataillon du Régiment étranger, il a été nommé tambour et comme tel il a embarqué le 8 février 1863 pour le Mexique.

Le magazine cité décrit comme suit, le rôle des tambours militaires de l'époque :

« Marchant en tête de colonne, les tambours marquent la cadence du pas et surtout, avec leur roulement, ils s'entendent de loin et se superposent aux autres bruits du champ de bataille devenant ainsi la « voix du commandement ». Ils transmettent les ordres au moyen d'un répertoire particulier de roulements, ordonnant les mouvements tactiques, ils remplissent un rôle déterminant comme moyen de communication directe entre le chef et la troupe ».

« De surcroît, la fonction de tambour octroie une certaine importance à ceux qui l'assurent, qui se voient investis d'un rôle très particulier au combat, cible sans arme et bien visible, l'ennemi acquiert un avantage clair en l'abattant et la voix du tambour se tait. C'est celle-ci, plus ou moins, l'histoire du tambour Casimiro Laï, de la 3e compagnie du régiment étranger, un jour d'avril 1863… ».

Son témoignage personnel rapporte : « Revenu à moi grâce à la fraîcheur nocturne, je me suis trouvé au milieu de cadavres. Je ne pouvais pas bouger, mais j'ai compris que l'on avait creusé des fosses et on m'y avait trainé vivant… ce qui m'a maintenu éveillé et que maintenant me fait horreur en y pensant, c'était la proximité des coyotes. Certainement ils venaient vérifier s'ils pouvaient me dévorer. Trois ou quatre fois ils se sont approchés à me toucher.

J'ai voulu crier, mais le cri est resté bloqué dans ma gorge ; peut-être ça aura été le plus horrible pour moi. J'ai essayé de bouger et j'ai compris qu'enfin je pouvais me libérer de la masse de cadavres qui m'écrasaient. Seul. Une main pendait, inutile, de mon bras paralysé, mais je pouvais me servir de l'autre encore. Je me suis levé et marchand sur les cadavres de mes pauvres compagnons, je suis entré dans le sous-bois en direction du chemin que nous avions suivi, du moins je le croyais. Je ne pouvais continuer et alors je me suis allongé, attendant la mort, là où vous m'avez trouvé. J'avais commencé à recommander mon âme à Dieu ».

Après le combat, déjà en Chiquihuite il s'est remis rapidement de ses blessures.

Le 14 août 1863, le tambour Laï, âgé de 24 ans et avec un peu moins d'un an de service, a été fait chevalier de la Légion d'honneur par le général Forey qui en lui remettant l'insigne de l'ordre a déclaré : « Une conduite exceptionnelle mérite une récompense exceptionnelle».

Laï a continué la campagne du Mexique au sein du Régiment étranger. Il a participé à plusieurs colonnes et opérations. En mars 1867 il est retourné en Algérie. A la fin de son contrat il a quitté la Légion, aussi discrètement qu'il y était arrivé.

Sa croix de la Légion d'honneur est précieusement conservée et exposée dans la Salle d'honneur du musée de la Légion étrangère.

– *Gazette des Uniformes, hors-série*. La Légion. Volume I. Année 2000.

– *« Camerone. 1863 »* Article-dossier du docteur Jean-Philippe Liardet (history4war.com).

– *Quand la Légion écrivait sa légende*, Alain Gandy. Presses de la Cité, 1995.

Dans le roman d'Alain Gandy, apparaît notre protagoniste Bernardo, qui meurt lors des premiers accrochages dans la cour. (Alain Gandy est un pseudonyme. Cet auteur, saint-cyrien, avait quitté l'Armée française avec le grade de capitaine, titulaire de la Légion d'honneur et de la croix de guerre avant de s'engager comme simple légionnaire. Il a quitté la Légion comme adjudant-chef après avoir ajouté une croix de guerre, la médaille militaire et l'Ordre national du Mérite à sa « panoplie ». Il avait été rédacteur au magazine *Képi Blanc.*(NdT).

L'auteur y raconte que l'Espagnol faisait partie d'une escouade que Danjou avait envoyée en renfort pour défendre la brèche du mur est, défendu par le sergent Schaeffner en narrant, littéralement :

« Bernardo n'y est pas parvenu, frappé d'une balle entre les yeux. Son corps a encore couru, mécaniquement, deux ou trois enjambées avant de s'écrouler vers l'avant, cinq mètres derrière ses compagnons ».

La désignation de quelques légionnaires par leurs patronymes, dans l'hacienda, a été extraite également du livre d'Alain Gandy.

– *La Légion étrangère de 1831 à 1887*, du général Grisot et du lieutenant Coulombon (deux tomes). La première édition date de 1888.

– *La Légion en Algérie*, de Pierre Dufour. Editions Lavauzelle, 2002.

– *Historia Spécial* (n° 414 bis). *« 150e anniversaire : La Légion étrangère »*. Année 1981.

– Texte de Licence, Marco Antonio Menes Couttelec, Maire de Camarón de Tejada, paru sur Internet.

– Revue *Champs de bataille. Histoire militaire stratégie et analyse*, numéro 7, article *« La réalité d'un mythe fondateur, Camerone, la Légion étrangère au Mexique »*, de Jean-Philippe Liardet. Dans cet article en guise de conclusion, l'auteur expose :

« Combats comme celui de Camerone, la Légion a en livré des centaines. Mais ce combat prend une dimension dramatique en raison de la disproportion des forces et de la fin tragique que les défenseurs ont choisie, pour respecter jusqu'au bout le serment fait à leur chef. Camerone a été choisi comme symbole presque par hasard, car il a été institué par le père spirituel de la Légion étrangère, le général Rollet, puisqu'il illustre parfaitement les valeurs militaires transposées, au code d'honneur du légionnaire à la fin des années 70 ».

– Magazine *Képi blanc : la vie de la Légion étrangère* n° 732 de mai 2011. Reproduction d'un texte du Père Michel, déjà publié en son numéro 73 de mai 1953, intitulé *« L'absent »*.

C'est un récit au sujet du légionnaire Klabuzcewski, né en janvier 1829 en Cracovie, Pologne, porté malade par dysenterie et envoyé à l'infirmerie la veille du combat de Camerone. Le polonais Klabuzcewski, trois jours avant, le 27 avril avait fêté en Chiquihuite ses quatre années de service à la Légion, arrosant l'événement avec du vin grâce aux bons offices du sergent-major Tonnel ; à la demande du sergent Morzycki il a dansé le *krakowiak*, Delcaretto a chanté et le caporal Mauquin racontait des histoires…

Klabuzcewski a passé la journée du 30 avril, qui s'est écoulée lentement, dans la tente-infirmerie. Il faisait déjà nuit quand il a entendu les cris de ses camarades qui vociféraient « les gars de la 3e compagnie se sont faits tuer ». Il est parti le lendemain, encore malade, tremblant à chaque pas, pour se trouver finalement devant les ruines de l'hacienda et les restes de son ami Morzycki.

Klabuzcewski a combattu dans la guerre franco-prussienne et s'est retiré en 1874 pour s'installer en France, mais le sentiment de culpabilité qui l'habitait pour son absence à Camerone, ne l'a jamais quitté comme si ses rêves étaient hantés par le même cauchemar que celui provoqué par sa dysenterie à Chiquihuite ce 30 avril là… Il est mort, curieusement le 30 avril 1888.

– *La emperatriz del adiós,* de Miguel de Grecia, Plaza & Janes Editores, 1999. Es.

– *Crónica de la Humanidad,* Plaza & Janes Editores, 1988. Es.

Liste extraite du magazine Képi blanc, la vie de la Légion étrangère, *(n° 600, page 35, mai 1999).*

Composition de la 3e compagnie du 1er bataillon

Officiers	dates et lieux de naissance
capitaine DANJOU Jean	15/04/1828 à Chalabre (Aude)
s/lieutenant MAUDET Clément	08/08/1829 à St-Mars-d'Outille (Sarthe)
s/lieutenant VILAIN Jean	03/08/1836 à Poitiers (Vienne)
Sous-officiers	
sergent-major TONEL Henri	15/04/1831 à Soisson (Aisne)
sergent MORZYCKI Louis	05/01/1840 à Clayette (Saône et Loire)
sergent GERMEYS Jean	11/03/1832 à Saint-Trond (Belgique)
sergent SCHAFFNER Charles	26/10/1831 à Berne (Suisse)
sergent PALMAERT Alfred	03/06/1842 à Anvers (Belgique)
Militaires du rang	
caporal MAINE Louis	04/09/1830 à Mussidan (Dordogne)
caporal DEL CARETTO Adolphe	26/12/1835 à Oran (Algérie)
caporal PINZINGER André	17/04/1831 à Landau (Bavière)
caporal MAGNIN Charles	04/03/1843 à Gerics (Autriche)
caporal BERG Evariste	13/01/1834 à Saint-Benoît (Ile Bourbon)
caporal FAVAS Arne	20/09/1837 à Genève (Suisse)
tambour LAI Casimir	27/11/1839 à Caglieri (Italie)
légionnaire GROUX Louis	21/07/1840 à Payerne (Suisse)
légionnaire BERNARDO Aloyse	20/05/1830 à Willaricho (Espagne)
légionnaire BERTOLLO Gustave	23/12/1839 à Toulon (Var)
légionnaire BRUGISSER Nicolas	en 1833 à Oberlandbrofer (Suisse)
légionnaire CATENHUSEN Georges	23/06/1837 à Lavenurg (Danemark)
légionnaire CATEAU Victor	07/04/1837 à Comines (Belgique)
légionnaire CONRAD Pierre	17/09/1839 à Alsbach (Bavière)
légionnaire KONRAD Ulrich	???
légionnaire DUBOIS Charles	11/04/1843 à Le Locle (Suisse)
légionnaire FRIEDRICH Frédéric	04/05/1832 à Langenbieelan (Prusse)
légionnaire FURBASZ Georges	24/02/1842 à Dingling (Bade)
légionnaire HIPP Emile	18/05/1838 à Paris
légionnaire LANGMEIER Félix	16/03/1842 à Buchs (Suisse)
légionnaire LERNOULD Louis	06/05/1845 à Francfort (Grand-Duché)
légionnaire SEILER Daniel	27/12/1837 à Lensbourg (Argovie)
légionnaire VANDESAVEL Henry	17/05/1832 à Hasselt (Belgique)
légionnaire DICKEN Pierre	29/05/1842 à Erkumer (Prusse)
légionnaire TIMMERMANS Jean-Louis	02/08/1845 à Bilan (Belgique)
légionnaire DAEL Constant	02/12/1842 à Bruxelles (Belgique)
légionnaire ROHR Louis	01/10/1832 à Niedereverbach (Bavière)
légionnaire KURZ Jean	02/03/1844 à Kallenberg (Würtemberg)
légionnaire BILLOD Claude	10/11/1832 à Dijon (Côte d'or)
légionnaire BASS Jean	26/12/1842 à Mouscron (Belgique)
légionnaire FRITZ Frédéric	22/11/1822 à Kemm (Würtemberg)
légionnaire RERBERS Joseph	15/12/1837 à Odinkirchen (Prusse)
légionnaire SCHREIBLICH Joseph	25/08/1843 à Gruben (Prusse)
légionnaire DE VRIES Hartog	13/03/1838 à Amsterdam (Hollande)
légionnaire WENSEL Geoffroy	04/11/1822 à Nettrich (Prusse)
légionnaire BOGUCKI Antoine	11/06/1833 à Posen (Prusse)
légionnaire CONSTANTIN Laurent	06/07/1826 à Bruxelles (Belgique)
légionnaire DAGLINCKS François	31/10/1834 à Anvers (Belgique)
légionnaire VAN DER MEERSCHE Jacques	31/12/1832 à Alost (Belgique)
légionnaire BRUNSWICK Félix	24/09/1832 à Bruxelles (Belgique)
légionnaire GAERTNER Aloïse	17/11/1839 à Bulach (Bade)
légionnaire GORSKI Léon	01/03/1844 à Nîmes (Gard)
légionnaire JEANNIN Adolphe	23/01/1836 à Genève (Suisse)
légionnaire KUNASSEG Hippolyte	22/07/1843 à Villeneuve-St-Georges
légionnaire LEMMER Frédéric	03/03/1836 à Hesselbach
légionnaire LEONHART Baptiste	19/03/1834 à Liège (Belgique)
légionnaire MERLET Edouard	04/04/1836 à Moskirch (Suisse)
légionnaire SCHIFFER Hermann	19/10/1839 à Canstadt (Wurtemberg)
légionnaire SEFFRIN Jean	22/12/1838 à Niersinten (Bavière)
légionnaire VAN DER BULCHE Pharaon	21/12/1845 à Lille (Nord)
légionnaire ZEY Nicolas	17/02/1842 à Beuren
légionnaire VERJUS Jean-Baptiste	12/02/1839 à Paris
légionnaire STOLLER Louis	24/09/1834 à Bruxelles (Belgique)
légionnaire WITTGENS Karl	???
légionnaire VAN OPSTAL Luitpog	???
légionnaire SERGERS Joseph	???
légionnaire HILLER ???	???

Cartes du Mexique (Képi Blanc n°600 mai 1999)

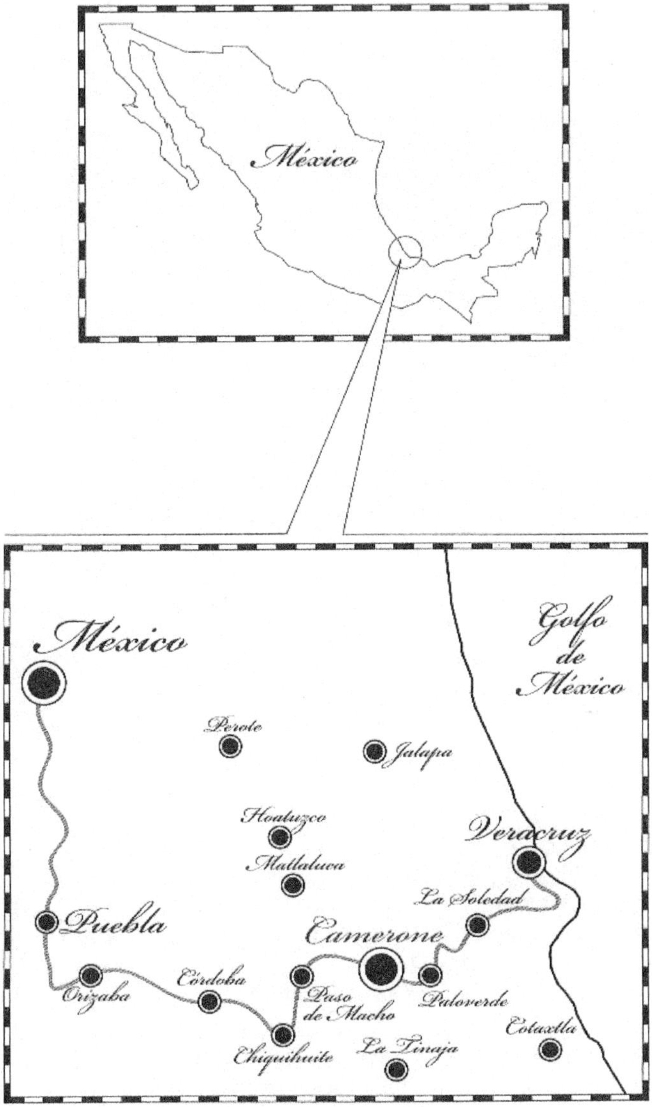

Plan de l'hacienda (Képi Blanc n°600 mai 1999)

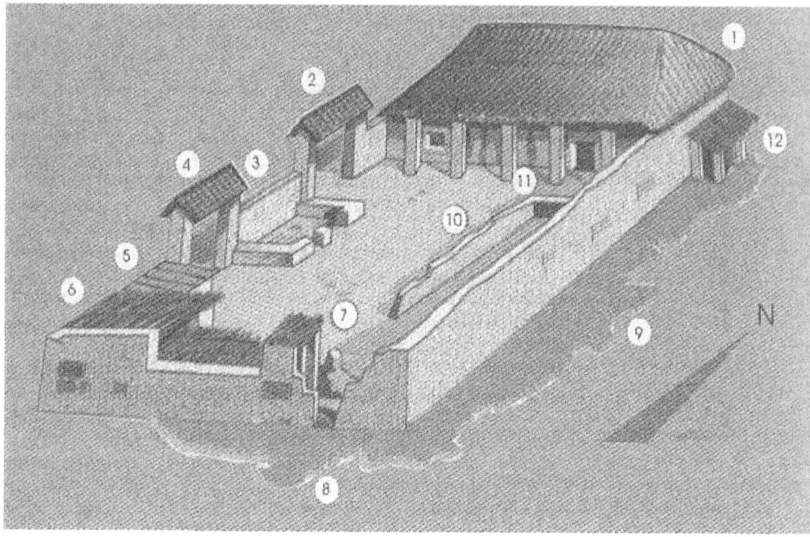

L'hacienda de Camerone telle qu'elle devait se présenter en 1863. D'après une aquarelle originale de Daniel Lordey (légionnaire honoraire de 1ère classe NdT), réalisée selon les indications de Raymond Guyader (officier de pompiers, conservateur du musée de l'uniforme de la Légion étrangère. NdT).

1 – Bâtiment de la grange.
2 – Première porte d'accès à la cour.
3 – Ruines d'un ancien hangar.
4 – Deuxième porte d'accès.
5 – Hangar presque intact.
6 – Hangar ouvert soutenant un toit de chaume. (C'est l'emplacement des légionnaires avant la dernière charge).
7 – Ruine d'un troisième hangar sans armature.
8 – Brèche sud-est.
9 – Emplacement approximatif d'une brèche pratiquée par les Mexicains.
10 – Restes d'un mur de soutènement d'un ancien hangar disparu.
11 – Emplacement approximatif d'une autre brèche.
12 – Petit hangar extérieur.

Plan des mouvements de troupes

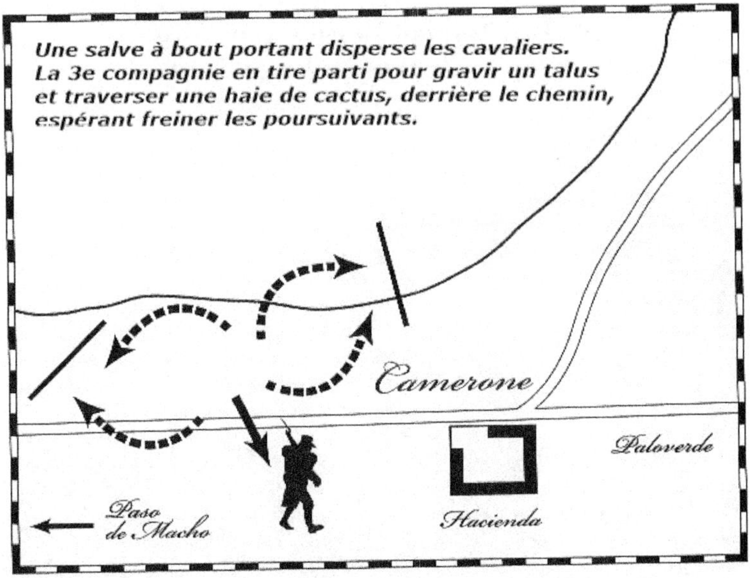

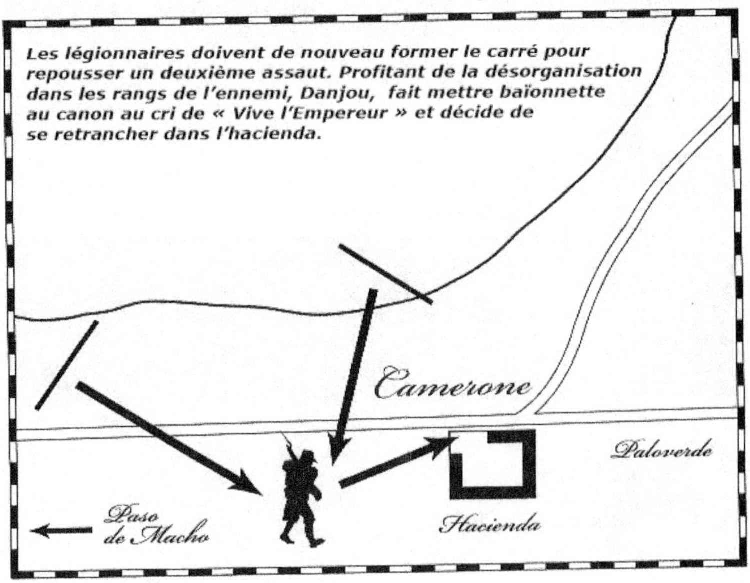

La compagnie de Danjou s'apprête à se réfugier dans l'hacienda de Camerone.
(Revue *« Champs de Bataille » n° 7)*

Légionnaire au Mexique
par l'adjudant-chef Burda, illustrateur à Képi Blanc

(Revue Képi Blanc, n°457, Avril 1986)

Le capitaine Danjou
(Revue « Champs de Bataille » n° 7)

Caporal Maine.
(Magazine Képi blanc n° 253 mai 1968)

Mannequin. Musée de l'uniforme légionnaire. Puyloubier

Mannequin capitaine Danjou.
Musée de l'uniforme légionnaire. Puyloubier

Présentation du livre et contexte historique.

Le mythe est un récit qui transfigure ce qu'est réellement une personne ou une chose et lui donne l'apparence d'être plus importante ou attractive. Personne ou chose entourée d'estime.

L'homme, lorsqu'il surpasse sa propre humanité, c'est-à-dire, quand il surmonte sa peur de la mort, se donne une opportunité d'imposer sa mémoire à la postérité, et peut-être un exemple, épique, pour les autres ; il sera un héros et son souvenir se perpétuera comme un mythe. C'est ce qui est arrivé à Alonso Bernardo, notre protagoniste, ce 30 avril 1863, comme soldat de la 3e compagnie du Régiment étranger de l'Armée française au Mexique.

Chaque 30 avril, la Légion étrangère célèbre en France et partout où elle se trouve dans le monde, le combat de Camerone au cours duquel, soixante-cinq de ses membres, appartenant à cette compagnie, ont été attaqués par plus de deux mille Mexicains dans une bourgade nommée Camarón de Tejada, entre Veracruz et Puebla - Camerone pour les Français - résistant jusqu'à son annihilation militaire, dans la cour d'une hacienda durant toute une journée sans eau et sans nourriture.

Ce n'est pas la seule histoire guerrière et épique, connue, dans l'absolu. Tout au long de l'Histoire beaucoup d'événements militaires analogues se sont produits et chaque pays peut se glorifier d'avoir le sien (c'est le cas de El Alamo, des 55 jours de Pékin, les derniers des Philippines, tous avec la correspondante version cinématographique), mais celui-ci est un fait de valeur héroïque à l'état pur, d'acceptation de la mort devant le sens, exclusivement, du devoir accompli jusqu'au bout.

Tous ces soldats n'étaient pas français (et ceux qui l'étaient devait s'engager sous une identité d'emprunt) ; pour beaucoup, ce n'était pas leur armée, ni leur terre, ils n'étaient pas là pour des causes idéologiques ou religieuses qui pouvaient les rassembler : rien ; ils avaient une mission à accomplir et ils l'ont accomplie. C'est cette différence avec d'autres situations similaires d'héroïsme et de valeur militaire, qui a éveillé mon intérêt et ma curiosité pour ce fait d'armes.

Ce récit est basé sur l'attraction, la force magnétique qu'exercent pour tous les hommes, les narrations d'actes de courage et d'acceptation du destin, la soumission, le domaine de l'angoisse devant l'imminence de la découverte de notre mystère le plus profond, celui de la mort.

Cette acceptation, la domination de la peur, l'histoire, la description, font que le récit épique, reste, à mon humble avis, toujours d'actualité : il cherchera à être toujours un modèle car la peur et l'angoisse accompagnent l'homme, comme un permanent bagage, pour certains une légère charge, pour d'autres un lourd fardeau.

Le récit épique ne passera pas de mode, il existera toujours avec plus ou moins de bonheur, car nous voudrons toujours savoir comment conserver la dignité dans le moment le plus important de notre vie, la rencontre avec la mort, comme l'ont fait ceux dont les existences sont contées, pour comprendre ce mystère ; ainsi nous dévorons les pages de ces récits pour comprendre leurs vies et essayer de dévoiler le secret.

L'éclosion de la narration ou récit historique, contexte dans lequel nous situons notre récit épique, a été énorme ces dernières années. Les changements technologiques, économiques et sociaux ont été si vertigineux ces dernières vingt années, à la vitesse où tout évolue – de véritables transformations sociales ou technologiques se développent et mûrissent sur des périodes d'à peine quatre ou cinq ans – que, à notre avis, nous sentons comme une nécessité de nous arrêter dans le temps, pour ne pas perdre la conscience de notre passé, qui pour revivre le Moyen âge, qui pour se plonger dans les passionnantes convulsions du 19e siècle.

Si l'Espagne a cessé d'avoir une présence comme puissance mondiale à partir du début du 18e siècle, éteignant sa flamme dans le concert des nations les plus puissantes de la Terre, néanmoins l'Espagnol s'est maintenu en tout événement historique par le biais de ses enfants dispersés. Il n'y a pas un événement au monde où l'on ne puisse pas trouver trace de quelque compatriote qui intervienne en tout ce qui mériterait d'être conté (il faut simplement enquêter).

Alonso Bernardo était un jeune espagnol dont la pitoyable existence, pour ne pas dire misérable, l'a mené au combat de sa vie qui allait lui donner la transcendance de la postérité.

Dans la seconde moitié du 19e siècle, des hommes s'engageaient dans la Légion étrangère, comme en tout autre formation militaire, essentiellement poussés par la faim ; Alonso y est allé pour manger. C'était un refuge contre le déracinement, « un asile contre le malheur » comme l'a qualifié un général français, et non un abri pour la délinquance, un monde analphabète dans lequel les engagés étaient de provenance plus urbaine que rurale, puisque la campagne alimentait ses enfants qui n'avaient pas besoin de s'embarquer dans de folles aventures. Cette seconde moitié du siècle voit se dessiner déjà la révolution industrielle, qui cause, dans ses premiers temps, exclusion et pauvreté. Avec la révolution industrielle nous voyons émerger le prolétariat comme classe sociale et dont le seul bien consiste en sa puissance de travail, mais devant l'excès de l'offre sur la demande en matière de travail, soumettait celui-ci à de très dures conditions. Les légionnaires de Camerone exerçaient tous les professions les plus diverses : forgerons, relieurs, selliers, employés de bureau, barmans, doreurs et nombreux autres, mais lors du débarquement au Mexique le seul métier dans lequel ils avaient de l'expérience c'était celui de soldat. Le 19e siècle - puisque notre action se situe en 1863 -, a été un siècle politique prolifique en guerres et révolutions ; de surcroît, avec la conquête de nouvelles colonies, le besoin en soldats était grand. Ce que désire notre protagoniste c'est manger, tout simplement, et peut-être accéder à un traitement plus digne ; ainsi, il plonge dans un monde étranger, dans lequel il réussit à peine à s'exprimer et où les conditions de la vie militaire, en Algérie, sont extrêmement dures.

Dans ce contexte, le 19e siècle et en particulier sa seconde moitié, c'est un siècle de convulsions, paradoxal et contradictoire. Avec un écart de cent cinquante ans depuis lors jusqu'à nos jours, cette période montre de grandes similitudes avec l'époque contemporaine :

Ainsi un choc s'est produit entre le premier monde (France, Royaume-Uni, Espagne) et la République du Mexique représentation du Tiers Monde, asphyxiée par le remboursement de la dette extérieure qu'il était devenu impossible de satisfaire. L'argent, si présent de nos jours dans notre vie, sert parfois de cause et d'excuse pour tout. D'où les opérations conjointes des différentes puissances pour occuper, *manu militari*, un pays lointain, pour l'invasion duquel les problèmes logistiques militaires sont partagés par tous.

La Légion étrangère, ou à cette époque, le Régiment étranger, est constitué en une force multinationale regroupant des individus d'origine exclusivement européenne, qui, nonobstant les différences d'origine et de langue, opère avec une énorme efficacité en campagne. Dans les années soixante au 20e siècle, le Centre d'Etudes Européennes a soulevé l'hypothèse d'utiliser la Légion étrangère comme une unité d'intervention de la Communauté Européenne, puisque la défense européenne est le talon d'Achille de l'Union : le manque d'une défense commune avec des unités multinationales propres et pleinement intégrées.

De plus en plus d'unités complètement professionnalisées sont employées dans le contexte international, alors qu'auparavant les armées se constituaient par des levées massives, un peu à l'aveuglette, de la population civile pour un conflit donné. Également, dans la guerre du Mexique nous voyons apparaître une unité militaire comme celle du colonel Dupin, comme précurseur des opérations de contre-guérilla, dont le degré d'efficacité et les résultats subséquents étaient plutôt d'ordre psychologique, servant à la propagande, que d'ordre purement militaire, ce qui était voulu en réalité.

Ces dernières années nous constatons une situation alarmante causée par l'emploi d'enfants-soldats dans les conflits ouverts en Afrique, aux Amériques et en Asie, mais un mouvement d'éveil de la conscience sociale s'est fait jour contre ce qui peut être considéré comme un fléau. Mais revenons à notre histoire. L'unité militaire à laquelle appartenait notre protagoniste comptait trois benjamins de moins de dix-sept ans dans ses rangs. Le colonel Jeanningros qui commandait le Régiment étranger, s'était engagé dans l'Armée française à l'âge de quinze ans.

Hier comme aujourd'hui les Etats-Unis sont une terre de promesses. Dans le passé, pour les européens et dans le présent pour les hommes du monde entier. Alors que la campagne du Mexique était déjà bien avancée, beaucoup des légionnaires qui s'engageaient en France pour rejoindre le combat au Mexique, le faisaient pour y déserter, traverser la frontière et rejoindre ainsi les Etats-Unis. Il y en avait qui, dans leur ignorance, désertaient à Veracruz, croyant que le Rio Grande, marquant la frontière, se trouvait seulement à deux journées de marche. Cependant, dans le même temps, il y avait des cas exemplaire du sens du devoir. Le sergent Fiala, a été fait prisonnier en 1866 et emprisonné près du Rio Grande ; il a réussi à s'échapper avec plusieurs autres légionnaires, à traverser la frontière et rallier La Nouvelle Orléans. Dans cette ville il s'est mis en contact avec le Consul de France pour embarquer et retourner par voie maritime au Mexique, pour pouvoir continuer la lutte.

Malgré ces signes et ces événements qui lui donnent contemporanéité, le 19e est un siècle qui, sous d'autres aspects, a peu progressé par rapport à l'époque médiévale.

C'est un monde dans lequel surgissent, avec une force apocalyptique, les épidémies meurtrières sans que l'homme puisse faire quelque chose, sauf utiliser des remèdes de grand-mère, qui, tout en les soulageant de leurs souffrances ne font pas guérir les malades. La fièvre jaune a décimé les forces d'invasion et a eu un résultat plus mortifère que la guerre proprement dite, sans même que l'on connaisse des remèdes palliatifs contre la maladie : on leur appliquait de l'huile d'olive et des cataplasmes de boue sur les jambes.

Toujours en vigueur et parfois réglementé, le butin de guerre. L'intendance des armées en campagne laissait beaucoup à désirer et les besoins des armées étaient assurés avec ce que les soldats trouvaient, le pillage.

En ce qui concerne le comportement des belligérants au combat, d'authentiques actes de chevalerie sont relevés sur le champ de bataille, actes qui procèdent du Moyen âge, influencés, pouvons-nous penser, par l'avènement du Romantisme. Ce courant intellectuel et artistique trouve ses fondements essentiellement dans les émotions et les sentiments, dans l'élan patriotique et le goût pour la tradition historique, ce qui amène ses adeptes à adopter les valeurs propres au Moyen Âge ; ainsi, l'influence de ces valeurs sur la guerre du Mexique, permet la reddition des troupes ennemies qui, ayant lutté avec courage, pouvaient garder jusqu'à leurs armes et que les blessés soient soignés au même titre que ses propres troupes. C'est pour cette raison que l'on voit une dame mexicaine soigner un officier de la compagnie d'Alonso blessé, avec la dévotion d'une mère et à sa mort, l'armée mexicaine lui donner une sépulture décente et lui rendre les honneurs militaires. Les Français rendront à cette dame, les corps de ses deux frères tombés au champ d'honneur.

Pour ce qui est des duels, il faut signaler qu'ils sont communs et fréquents dans cette moitié du siècle. Des joutes chevaleresques on est arrivés à défendre l'honneur de manière stupide, mais il en résulte un phénomène si transcendant dans la sphère sociale, que l'on essaye d'en réglementer la pratique. Certains pourraient être qualifiés de viciés aux duels, ceux que l'on appelait alors en France, les « buveurs de sang ». L'un des survivants du combat de Camerone mourra plus tard au cours d'un duel.

En ce contexte, contradictoire et passionnant à la fois, la guerre entre Mexicains et Français augmente en intensité, de 1862 à 1867, parfois avec une dureté inhabituelle.

Seuls les pauvres vont à la guerre. Alonso Bernardo, le protagoniste, se trouve au Mexique, fuyant sa misère et le destin fini par le rattraper lorsqu'il intègre une compagnie du Régiment étranger de France, assiégée dans la cour d'une hacienda mexicaine. Ils auraient pu se rendre, rester en vie sans perdre leur honneur, mais surgit alors un sentiment inexplicable, un mécanisme émotionnel collectif se déclenche, mu par un élan vital qui les a fait lutter jusqu'à la fin ; l'accomplissement du devoir s'impose qui les a fait oser à franchir le seuil du mystère le plus angoissant pour l'homme : son rendez-vous avec la mort. Tous résistent et aucun ne choisit de déserter ou se rendre, récupérant par-là le sens de la dignité que la vie avait ravi à la majorité d'entre eux. C'est ainsi que s'est comporté notre héros, car les légionnaires de Camerone n'occultent pas un passé honteux ni de délinquance, mais un passé de vie rude et dure, de pauvreté, d'amours perdues ou, simplement, d'autres guerres, puisque quand on contraint le corps on élève l'âme.

La suspension du paiement de la dette externe décrétée en 1861 par le président de la République du Mexique, Benito Juárez, a donné à Napoléon III un motif parfait pour occuper militairement ce pays. Les autres nations alliées, le Royaume Uni et l'Espagne, se considèrent satisfaites par les négociations qui aboutissent avec le Traité de La Soledad dont les préliminaires avaient été signés le 19 février 1862, mais le gouvernement français impose des exigences tellement excessives, impossibles à assumer par le gouvernement légitime mexicain, qu'il peut justifier pour cette raison l'occupation militaire du Mexique.

Et c'est ainsi qui a débuté la conquête du territoire mexicain, alors que les membres du parti conservateur mexicain, alliés des Français, proposent à l'archiduc Maximilien Fernand d'Autriche, frère de l'empereur austro-hongrois François Joseph, et marié à la princesse Charlotte, fille du roi des Belges, de ceindre la couronne de ce qui deviendrait le Second Empire du Mexique (le premier a eu une brève, une éphémère existence, pendant l'année 1821 sous Iturbe) et instrument de la politique expansionniste de Napoléon III. C'est dans ce contexte d'occupation par les Français que, le 30 avril 1863, a eu lieu le combat de Camerone.

Un an plus tard, en juin 1864, Maximilien a été couronné empereur des Mexicains dans la capital, Mexico. La guerre – qui se déroule simultanément à la guerre de sécession américaine – ne cesse pas. Quand elle a pris fin, les Etats-Unis ont clairement appuyé Benito Juárez, suivant la maxime de la doctrine de Monroe « L'Amérique aux Américains », et évidemment ni Maximilien ni les Français l'étaient. Maximilien, homme de principes libéraux et progressistes, bien que soutenu exclusivement par le secteur le plus conservateur de son Empire, a envisagé de renouer avec l'esclavagisme afin d'obtenir l'appui et le soutien des confédérés Américains, c'est-à-dire des sudistes Américains (ce fait est bien illustré par le film *Les Géants de l'Ouest* (The Undefeated) interprété par Rock Hudson et John Wayne).

Mais la situation, était considérée par les Français comme intenable militairement et au début de 1867 la France s'est retirée du Mexique en abandonnant Maximilien à son sort, à qui tous conseillaient d'abdiquer et de retourner en Europe. C'est son épouse Charlotte qui l'a convaincu de ne pas le faire : c'est elle qui est revenue pour tenter d'obtenir de l'aide, mais sur le vieux continent, personne n'a voulu l'écouter, ni son pays ni celui de son mari, ni même le Vatican où elle avait rencontré le Pape.

Maximilien a lutté jusqu'à la fin mais a été fait prisonnier à Querétaro. Benito Juárez l'a condamné à mort et, malgré un mouvement international demandant sa clémence, il a été fusillé finalement sur la colline de Las Campanas (Les Cloches), le 17 juin 1867, à l´âge de trente-six ans faisant montre d'un courage et d'une dignité exemplaires.

L'instant de la fusillade est saisi dans un tableau* d'Edouard Manet peintre impressionniste, courant pictural qui s'appuie sur le *plein air*** et par des touches de couleur qui, sous la perspective de la distance, donnent forme à l'ensemble. Le tableau a eu une grande diffusion imprimée dont on trouve des exemplaires dans une pinacothèque allemande.

Son épouse Charlotte est devenue folle et a promené sa démence par les cours d'Autriche et de Belgique, pendant soixante ans encore. Elle est morte en 1927.

Celui-ci est le contexte historique dans lequel évolue notre protagoniste. En fin de compte, tout se résume à l'Homme comme centre et axe de tout. Le reste n'est que simple anecdote. L'essentiel c'est la vie qui transcende la mort, et le véritable mystère réside dans la manière de passer de l'une à l'autre, avec les valeurs qui sont les nôtres, qui correspondent à notre propre nature : courage et dignité. Et tout cela se déroule pendant les onze heures de combat, décrites dans le livre (qu'il faudra lire, bien entendu).

Il y a beaucoup d'action en tout homme rêveur et beaucoup de rêves en tout homme d'action et dans ce mélange le protagoniste et l'auteur se sont croisés. Ce dernier a cherché une explication à un comportement, essayant de transmettre une émotion comme celle d'un témoin. C'est ainsi qu'a surgi « Le mythe de Camerone ».

Connaître le passé c'est comprendre notre présent pour tenter, si possible, d'améliorer le futur, étant donné que certains d'entre nous trouveront toujours passionnant de participer à l'aventure de l'Histoire, l'aventure de l'Homme.

La Palma del Condado, 28 janvier 2005

* Il existe trois versions de ce tableau largement inspiré de celui de Goya, *El tres de Mayo*.
** En français dans le texte.

INDEX

AVANT-PROPOS..9
PREFACE..15

CHAPITRE I. L'HACIENDA.......................................18

- Hacienda de la Trinidad, à Camarón de Tejada (Camerone) Mexique. Vers 9h00 du matin, le 2 mai 1863
- Vers 9h30 du matin, le 30 avril 1863, dans le village de Camerone, Mexique
- 7h00du matin (deux heures et demie plus tôt), le 30 avril 1863

CHAPITRE II. MEXIQUE...37

- L'intervention
- La fièvre jaune « vomito negro »

CHAPITRE III. LE SIEGE...48

- A environ 9h40 du matin, le 30 avril 1863
- Vers 10h50 du matin
- Vers 11h00 du matin
- Vers 11h40 du matin

CHAPITRE IV. LA LÉGION ÉTRANGÈRE...............63

- Le colonel Martinez
- La Légion étrangère au Mexique

CHAPITRE V. LE COMBAT...81

- A environ 12h10 du matin, le 30 avril 1863.
- Vers 13h55
- Vers 14h50
- Vers 16h45
- Vers 17h30

CHAPITRE VI. L'ASSAUT FINAL................................98

- A environ 17h35, le 30 avril 1863
- Vers 17h55
- Vers 18h00
- Les dernières heures du 30 avril 1863
- Le 2 mai 1863

CHAPITRE VII. LA GUERRE CONTINUE...............113

- Juan López
- L'escadron de cavalerie

CHAPITRE VIII. IN MEMORIAM.............................123

- Les héros mexicains

EPILOGUE...126

- Les duels
- Les désertions
- Le colonel Dupin
- Les prisonniers et les blessés de Camerone
- Les survivants

DIVERS..141

- Legio Patria Nostra
- Camerone 2002 et l'auteur
- Algéric, 1960
- La célébration de Camerone

ANNEXES...151

- Récits officiel de Camerone
- Narration partielle du combat par deux de ses protagonistes
- Equipements et uniformes
- Bibliographie, données et références historiques
- Composition de la 3e compagnie du 1er Bataillon.
- Cartes du Mexique
- Plan de l'hacienda
- Plan des mouvements de troupes
- Vue « les moments qui ont précédé l'invasion de l'hacienda »
- Un légionnaire au Mexique en tenue d'époque
- Photo du capitaine Danjou
- Photo du caporal Maine
- Uniforme de légionnaire (musée de Puyloubier)
- Manequin du capitaine Danjou (musée de Puyloubier)

**PRÉSENTATION DU LIVRE
ET CONTEXTE HISTORIQUE...............................178**

Cet ouvrage a été composé par
Philippe Hugounenc Distribution à Paris

Dépôt légal : Janvier 2023

Printed in Great Britain
by Amazon

28444393R00106